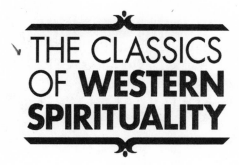

THE CLASSICS OF WESTERN SPIRITUALITY

THE CLASSICS OF WESTERN SPIRITUALITY
A Library of the Great Spiritual Masters

CRUX CHRISTI NOSTRA GLORIA
Symb. 2 Cor. 6 v. 10
Als die Traurigen aber alle Zeit frölich
HENRICUS Müller
Weyland der H. Schrifft DOCTOR
und PROFESSOR der THEOLOGISCHEN
FACULTÆT SENIOR und SUPERINTEN-
DENS in Rostock

Als die Sterbenden und siehe wir leben
Was Satans Reich zerstört, was Gottes Reich vermehret,
Das hat Herr Scriver hier in diesem Buch gelehret.
Wem denn ein rechter Ernst sein Seele zu erlaben,
Les' diesen Seelen-Schatz, so wird er Labung haben.

Seventeenth-Century Lutheran Meditations and Hymns

EDITED AND WITH AN INTRODUCTION
BY ERIC LUND

Paulist Press
New York • Mahwah, NJ

Cover art: The cover shows a hymn of thanksgiving by Martin Luther from Luther's hymnal *Geystliche Lieder*.

The images on page iv are of Heinrich Müller (top) and Christian Scriver (bottom). The image on page xii is of Johann Gerhard.

Cover and caseside design by Cynthia Dunne, www.bluefarmdesign.com
Book design by Lynn Else

Library of Congress Cataloging-in-Publication Data

Seventeenth-century Lutheran meditations and hymns / edited with an introduction by Eric Lund.
p. cm. — (The classics of western spirituality)
Includes bibliographical references and index.
ISBN 978-0-8091-4729-8 (alk. paper) — ISBN 978-0-8091-0600-4 (alk. paper)
1. Meditations. 2. Lutheran Church—Prayers and devotions. 3. Lutheran Church—Hymns. I. Lund, Eric, 1948- II. Title. III. Series.
BV4801.S39 2011
242—dc22
2011004708

Published by Paulist Press
997 Macarthur Boulevard
Mahwah, New Jersey 07430

www.paulistpress.com

Printed and bound in the
United States of America

CONTENTS

LUTHERAN HYMNS

The Editor and Author of This Volume

ERIC LUND is professor of religion at St. Olaf College in Northfield, Minnesota. He earned his bachelor's degree from Brown University, a master's of divinity from Yale Divinity School, and a PhD from the Yale University Graduate School. His primary field of research has been sixteenth- and seventeenth-century religious life in Germany, but he has also done work on the English Reformation, on Scandinavian Lutheranism, and on historical interactions of Judaism, Christianity, and Islam.

Eric Lund published *Documents from the History of Lutheranism 1517–1750* with Fortress Press in 2002 and was coeditor of *Word, Church, and State: Tyndale Quincentenary Essays*, published by the Catholic University of America Press in 1998. His articles in journals and several chapters in books have focused on popular piety and practical religious literature in Germany from the period of the Protestant Reformation to the rise of the Pietist movement.

After teaching for twenty-five years in the Religion Department at St. Olaf College, he became director of International and Off-Campus Studies in 2005. In keeping with his interests in the interplay between religion and culture and experiential education, he has taught courses abroad twenty times for St. Olaf in the Middle East, Italy, Germany, and Africa. In recent years he has been teaching a course on the Renaissance and Reformation in Italy and Germany every other year and, in the alternative years, a course in South Africa on religion and cultural diversity.

Author of the Preface

ROBERT KOLB is professor emeritus of systematic theology at Concordia Seminary in Saint Louis, Missouri; member of the continuation committee of the International Congress for Luther Research; author of *Martin Luther, Confessor of the Faith*, and *Bound Choice, Election, and Wittenberg Theological Method*; coauthor of *The Genius of Luther's Theology*; editor of *Lutheran Ecclesiastical Culture, 1550–1675*; and coeditor of *Hermeneutica Sacra: Festschrift for Bengt Hägglund* and of *The Book of Concord*. He was also associate editor and later coeditor of *The Sixteenth Century Journal*. Dr. Kolb holds a PhD from the University of Wisconsin in Madison.

Preface

Throughout the sixteenth century reformers of all stripes—Catholic, Anabaptist, Anglican, Reformed, and Lutheran—strove for improvements in public morals, in the organization of church government, in public teaching, and also in popular piety. Different accents and emphases distinguished these various movements for reformation. Protestant reformers protested against the ritualistic form of religion they found prevalent in village and town. This system, they asserted, cultivated dependence on the performance of certain sacred tasks to establish or at least maintain a good relationship with God. These reformers repudiated a view of sacramental rites that regarded the rites as effective *ex opere operato*, simply through the human performance of the ritual, whether faith in God was present in the performer or not. Such a dependence on the execution of holy forms cultivated indifference to the living trust in God that the Protestant reformers defined as the heart of Christian living and piety.

For instance, in preparing to lecture on scripture at the University of Wittenberg and in his Augustinian cloister, Martin Luther encountered a God of conversation and community. He found the God who presents himself in the scriptures to be a sovereign Creator whose word of promise given in Jesus Christ changed human identities as it came through external forms of his word in oral, written, and sacramental forms. Luther abandoned his earlier fascination with certain aspects of monastic "mystical" piety, although he never cast aside some of the insights Tauler and Bernard had bequeathed him. He came, however, to insist that inner voices were uncertain pillars for the comfort of the gospel. The consolation of consciences rested upon the external forms of the word.

It can be said that Luther continued the medieval emphasis on *poenitentia*. But he transformed the concept into the rhythm of daily repentance, the repetition of the death to sin and rising again as a child of God definitively effected in God's chosen people through baptism. "The whole life of the Christian is a life of repentance," he wrote in the first of the Ninety-five Theses.[1] In his *Small Catechism* of 1529 he deepened the concept; explaining the ongoing significance of baptism, he wrote that each day "the old creature in us with all sins and evil desires is...drowned and dies through daily contrition and repentance, and on the other hand a new person...comes forth and rises up to live before God in righteousness and purity forever."[2] The life of repentance he envisioned displayed the effect of God's word working as law—what God requires from the human being's performance of his design for human life—and gospel—the promise of new life in Christ. Thus, Luther's piety cultivated a deeply personal relationship of trust and love between the human creature and Jesus Christ.

Luther's training by instructors steeped in the Ockhamist tradition had also brought him to reject aspects of the medieval distinctions of the sacred and profane, believing that this trust in Christ sanctified all actions since Paul had written that everything not done in faith is sin (Rom 14:23). He believed that for the person whom God has justified by his grace through the life of trust in Christ all activities are equally holy, not producing righteousness in God's sight but necessary for being the right kind of human being that God's promise in Christ had re-created. Therefore, he believed that many of the sacred activities of the medieval church had dishonored God, often because they were human commands, not God's, but also because they distracted from the service to God entailed in service to the neighbor within the context of daily life and because they fundamentally served the interest of the person doing them, not God or the neighbor. This spirituality of the everyday embraced both prayer and praise to God and service to his creatures, above all, his human creatures. It was practiced by carrying out his commands in the contexts of the situations of life to which he had called human beings in home, economic activities, society, and church.

Thus, Luther continued to practice and propagate many of the forms of liturgical actions of the congregation and of the faithful living of its people from previous generations. Sometimes he altered them little in context; sometimes he cast them into the context of his new understanding of the conversation and community created by forgiveness of sins and faith in Christ. The same—quite normal human—mixture of continuities and discontinuities appears also in the plans for pious living, the suggestions for spiritual devotion, which Luther's followers cultivated over the century and a half following his death. Luther had adapted a number of the forms of medieval devotional writing, including meditation on Christ's passion, on the various parts of the catechism, and on the consolation of consciences. Luther also renewed the medieval tradition of hymnic praise of God and made the first steps toward cultivating congregational singing in worship. He cultivated the spirituality of the common people through his postils, continuing the tradition of preparing model sermons on the weekly lessons, and through his catechisms. Lutherans have continued to meditate on their catechism and on sermons, to compose music and poetry, and to meditate upon these hymns as an important part of their devotional life.

This volume presents key samples of the spirituality that flowed out of Luther's Reformation and mixed with other streams of older and newer perceptions of God's relationship to his people and theirs to him. Collections of sermons and catechisms also served families and congregations as sources for meditation and praise, but this devotional literature is exemplary of the approaches offered by this varied and rich landscape of aids prepared for popular devotion. As Eric Lund notes in the Foreword to this volume, the seventeenth century was a period of considerable creativity within the Lutheran churches of northern and central Europe. Although most scholarly attention, at least until recently, has focused on the dogmatic works of leading theologians, as Lund notes, the piety of the people and the life of the congregations depended on preaching and regular worship services and also, to an ever increasing extent, on the devotional literature designed to be read by individuals and in the family circle. Devotional literature, hymnic and prose, flourished, flowing from the pens of university professors such as Johann Gerhard and Heinrich Müller, pastors and church leaders such as Christian Scriver and Paul Gerhardt, and lay people, such as the musicians Ahle, father and son, the courtier David Denicke, and Christiana Cunrad, a physician's wife, and Countess Emilie Juliane von

Schwarzburg-Rudolstadt. Johann Sebastian Bach inherited and continued this tradition of meditation and praise.

This volume enables readers to assess how the piety of Luther's followers found form and formulation in the ever-changing world of central Europe over a century and a half. Readers can experience the rhythm of the daily Christian encounter with God which these writers strove to focus and therein perceive how Luther's way of listening to God's word and responding in prayer and praise was adapted to new situations and new sets of problems as the events of early modern European history unfolded in the German lands. As the history of God's Old Testament people teaches and the Book of Acts reveals in the earliest years of the New Testament church, the people of God, products of his concept of time and movement in the human story, continually adjust their hearing of God's word and their responses to it. That, too, is the history of Lutheran piety.

Robert Kolb

Notes to Preface

1. *D. Martin Luthers Werke* (Weimar: Böhlau, 1883–1993), 1:233, 10–11, *Luther's Works* (Saint Louis: Concordia; Philadelphia: Fortress, 1958–86), 31:25.

2. Small Catechism (1529), fourth question on baptism, *Die Bekenntnisschriften der evangelisch-lutherischen Kirche*, 11th ed. (Göttingen: Vandenhoeck and Ruprecht, 1992), 516–17; *The Book of Concord*, ed. Robert Kolb and Timothy J. Wengert (Minneapolis: Fortress, 2000), 360.

FOREWORD

The sixteenth-century Protestant Reformation and the formative stages of the Lutheran movement have been widely studied, and most people with a basic awareness of Christian church history have some familiarity with the innovations introduced in theology, church practice, and social life by Martin Luther and his co-reformers. By comparison, Protestant religious life in seventeenth-century Germany and Scandinavia is under-studied. This has begun to change in recent years as more and more scholars in Europe and North America have become interested in the process of confessionalization going on in Europe after the Reformation and have begun to investigate the long-range impact of that period of dramatic religious change. Nevertheless, most people have a better sense of religious developments associated with the Puritan movement in seventeenth-century England and North America than they do with Protestant religious life in the same period on the European continent. Simplistic stereotypes still prevail, painting a picture of stagnation or even decline in the Lutheran churches of Germany.

This volume attempts to deepen awareness of religious ideas and practices during the second century of the Lutheran movement. It also provides evidence against the widely held impression that the Lutheran theologians of that day devoted their attention to esoteric matters of dogma and concentrated their energies mostly on polemical refutations of the viewpoints of other religious groups. The texts included in this book reveal a less-well-known side of Lutheran religious life. These selections display some of the tensions within Lutheran theology that developed during the seventeenth century, but they also show that many church leaders were deeply concerned with matters of spirituality and with the provision of practical guidance on Christian living that would be accessible to simple lay people. They deal not only with doctrinal concepts (*Lehre*) but also with the shaping of an intentional way of life under the influence of religious beliefs (*Leben*).

The seventeenth century was a period of considerable creativity in the Lutheran Church. Some of the most important books of Lutheran devotional literature come from this century, and many of the tradition's most popular hymns were written during these years. Three pastors stand out as major contributors to practical prose religious literature: Johann Gerhard (1582–1637), Heinrich Müller (1631–75), and Christian Scriver (1629–93). The texts by these authors that have been selected make it possible to trace how religious sentiments evolved under the influence of earlier formative figures such as Martin Luther (1483–1536) and Johann Arndt (1555–1621) and led to subsequent developments such as the Pietist movement. The Lutheran hymns included in this book also draw attention to some of the memorable religious poetry of this era and reveal how hymns became important not only as a way for lay people to be actively involved in communal worship but also to express and shape religious feelings as a part of individual or family devotional life outside of the times of church services.

Some of these writings have been available in English before, but most of the prose texts have been out of circulation for up to a century or more. The early English translations that exist seem very archaic today, so I have prepared fresh translations in a modern idiom. There are also a few texts here that have been well known in Germany or Scandinavia but have never been translated into English. I hope that making these texts available will be beneficial to anyone interested in Christian spirituality, whether that interest is related to academic study or to some other more practical and personal religious aspiration. It is interesting to notice the influences of earlier Classics of Western Spirituality in these works but also the fresh and imaginative ways in which the authors addressed the new religious needs of their day. Even though spiritual needs and religious preoccupations have changed over the years, there is still much to be appreciated in these texts, which are full of interesting metaphors, creative phrasing, and heartfelt appeals for an intense commitment to self-examination and spiritual growth.

Introduction

The texts in this book were written by German pastors from the second century of the Lutheran tradition. These writers manifest the influence of both Martin Luther and Johann Arndt, who preceded them, and they in turn helped shape the perspectives of many people associated with the subsequent Pietist movement and the nineteenth-century German Awakening. There are volumes in the Classics of Western Spirituality series devoted to each of these authors and movements.[1]

Johann Gerhard (1582–1637), the first author included in this volume, was a contemporary of such Catholic spiritual writers as François de Sales, Jeanne de Chantal, Robert Bellarmine, Pierre de Bérulle, Jean-Jacques Olier, Jean Eudes, Vincent de Paul, and Louise de Marillac, as well as Protestant spiritual writers such as Jacob Boehme, George Herbert, John Donne, Lancelot Andrews, Lewis Bayly, Richard Sibbes, and Joseph Hall. The other two Lutheran devotional writers, Heinrich Müller (1631–75) and Christian Scriver (1629–93), from later in the seventeenth century, overlapped the lives of such Catholic authors as Brother Lawrence, Angelus Silesius, Blaise Pascal, Armand-Jean de Rancé, Marguerite Marie Alacoque, Sor Juana Inés de la Cruz, François Fenelon, and Jean Baptiste de La Salle. Protestant writers who were active in the same period include Johann Amos Comenius, Jean de Labadie, George Fox, Jeremy Taylor, Thomas Traherne, Richard Baxter, and John Bunyan. The hymns chosen for inclusion here were published in the first half of the seventeenth century, between 1599 and 1666.

The seventeenth century has often been called the Golden Age of German Lutheran hymn writing. It was also the century in which many of the most enduringly influential Lutheran devotional books were written. The prose works included in this volume were all reprinted frequently over a period of more than two hundred years.

Most of them were translated into the Scandinavian languages and a few texts were also translated into English. Johann Gerhard's *Sacred Meditations*, the one work reproduced here in its entirety, appeared in 115 editions during the seventeenth century, 51 during the eighteenth century, and 31 between 1801 and 1900. Initially written in Latin, it was translated into German within one year of its first publication, into English within ten years, and into twelve additional vernacular languages during the next hundred years.[2]

Most of the hymns included in this volume continue to be used today for worship in Lutheran churches around the world and in some other church traditions, but the once popular books of prose meditations have been largely forgotten now for almost a century. Since they were so historically important, have many interesting literary features, and may still be found by some to have value as resources for spiritual formation, they deserve to be reintroduced to both scholars and general readers. Fresh English translations have been made of all of the texts, and several selections appear here in English for the first time.

The Historical Context

Some historians view the seventeenth century as a period of general crisis in Europe with political, economic, social, and intellectual dimensions.[3] Even if that notion is still much debated, it is clear that the writers profiled in this book lived in troubled times in Germany. They often faced significant personal hardship and, in their pastoral work, dealt with people who had been deeply unsettled, even traumatized, by the changes in society taking place around them. This situation influenced the religious outlook of the authors and the themes about which they wrote.

Although the Peace of Augsburg in 1555 had brought about a degree of peaceful coexistence between Catholics and Protestants in the Holy Roman Empire after the Schmalkaldic War, a growing number of religious and political conflicts in various regions of Germany during the second half of the sixteenth century raised questions about the viability of the terms of agreement. The established religion of each territory was to be determined by its ruler (the *cuius regio, eius religio* or "whose realm, his religion" principle), which became problematic in regions in which Catholics and Protestants stuck to their convictions and still intermingled in daily life. Lutherans feared the resurgence of Catholicism, particularly in the southern regions of Germany, and Calvinists resented the fact that their confession had been excluded as a legal option. The tenuous balance of power was threatened further when a number of territorial rulers switched their confessional allegiances. When requests by the Protestant princes for modifications in the peace treaty were rejected by their Catholic counterparts at an Imperial Diet in 1608, they formed a Protestant Union to protect their interests. This prompted the creation of a rival Catholic League.

War finally broke out in 1618 when Protestant nobles in Bohemia resisted efforts by their king to rescind a local agreement that had tolerated their religious practices. The Protestant Union came to their defense, but because some Lutheran princes refused to cooperate with Calvinists, whom they viewed as rivals, the revolt was crushed by the Catholic League. Catholic forces began a campaign of reconquest in Austria and Germany, which prompted greater solidarity among the Protestants. The Lutheran king of Denmark intervened on their behalf in 1625, but the forces of the Catholic emperor continued to win battles. In 1629 Ferdinand II imposed the Edict of Restitution, which called upon the Protestants to relinquish any territorial gains they had made since 1552. Protestant prospects improved when King Gustavus Adolphus of Sweden marched troops into Germany to defend his Lutheran coreligionists. By then, the war had created great destruction over many regions. Numerous towns were repeatedly besieged, and soldiers, many of whom were mercenaries, plundered widely to make up for their unsatisfactory pay. Famine and plague often took the lives of those who managed to escape a violent death directly connected to the military conflicts. In the final stage of the war France entered on the side of the Protestants, making clear that political motives as well as religious identity influenced the combatants in what had become the first real pan-European war. The troops of the Catholic League now sustained heavier losses, but in the end neither side could prevail over the other. In 1648 the German princes and their foreign allies agreed to a new treaty, the Peace of Westphalia, which reaffirmed the right of princes to determine the religion of their territories. The only notable difference from the Peace of Augsburg was the recognition of Calvinism as a legitimate choice along with Lutheranism or Catholicism.

The effects of the Thirty Years' War were experienced unevenly across the whole of Germany, but the conflict would have been a formative experience for almost any German living in the first half of the seventeenth century. Although no consensus estimate has emerged about the extent of casualties during the war, it is probable that the overall population of the Holy Roman Empire was reduced by at least 15–20 percent.[4] Up to one-third of the population of some cities perished, and as much as two-fifths of the rural population in certain regions were killed between 1618 and 1648. The war also led to a general disintegration of society that lasted for decades after the conclusion of the peace treaty. Although cultural life did not disappear, widespread destruction and instability did not allow Germany to be as culturally productive as Spain, France, England, or the Netherlands were in the same period.

In times of war many people are willing to compromise their moral values in order to increase their chances of survival. Numerous church leaders in the second half of the seventeenth century were convinced that a general coarsening of society had taken place around them. The prospect of death by violence, disease, or starvation had been prominent enough that many were also left with a deep sense of anxiety and insecurity. Years of sporadic devastation enhanced eschatological consciousness and speculations about the imminence of the end of the age and the coming of the Last Judgment. For some, the crisis provoked skepticism about traditional religious interpretations of the world and prompted the first notable manifestations of a trend toward secularization or atheism that would become more prominent in the eighteenth century. Many Lutherans were deprived of adequate pastoral care because of the death of clergy and the disintegration of ecclesiastical institutions. This appears to have weakened the communal aspect of religious life. There are indications that some sought refuge in an introspective, individualistic piety and looked for consolation in the prospect of bliss in the life to come. Others, instead of withdrawing, were stimulated by the crippled state of society to stress the need for individual repentance and spiritual renewal in society as a whole.[5]

The Age of the Baroque/Confessionalization/Orthodoxy

The post-Reformation period, encompassing the years leading up to the Thirty Years' War and the following decades when the impact of the war was most pronounced, has been variously called the Baroque Age, the epoch of Confessionalization, or the period of Lutheran Orthodoxy. Each of these concepts points to a different aspect of life in this era.

The term *Baroque* was first used with reference to stylistic developments in the visual arts and music, especially in Catholic countries after the start of the Catholic Reformation (1575–1770). By extension, it has been applied to sentiments expressed in literature and philosophy. Generalizing broadly about the outlook and mood in Europe during the Baroque era, José Antonio Maravall speaks of a widespread pessimism about human beings and the world due to the series of calamities that disrupted society. For many, the world seemed to be a confused labyrinth, even a mad or diseased place. Distrust and chagrin were widespread.[6] German literature from this period, especially lyric poetry written between 1600 and 1720, is characterized by a consciousness of human suffering and the fragility of earthly existence. This awareness prompted contrary impulses, no doubt aroused by the hardships resulting from the Thirty Years' War. There were many literary comments about the vanity of all worldly endeavors, often accompanied by an advocacy of ascetic self-restraint and interest in mystical religiosity. For other poets and writers the uncertainty of life prompted advice to seize whatever pleasure is immediately available, however transient it may be.

The term *Confessionalization* has been widely used since the 1980s to describe a long process going on throughout Europe after the Reformation to differentiate and stabilize social groupings based on distinctive religious or theological identities. It points especially to the efforts made by political rulers to impose social discipline through control of the policies and practices of church institutions.[7]

In this respect it was the first stage in a trend toward political absolutism in Europe. In the Lutheran regions of Germany there were multiple territorial churches ultimately under the control of noble rulers who appointed clergy to carry out the administration of church affairs. The chief ecclesiastical figure in most territories was called a general superintendent, and urban centers within a territory were administered by superintendents. In addition, most Lutheran territories had a consistory, or church council, to which the superintendents were accountable. The consistories were made up of clerics and prominent lay figures who made recommendations to the secular ruler about appointments to church positions and any policies related to standards of belief and religious practice. A Church Order (*Kirchenordnung*) set forth the doctrines that were to be normative within a territory, guidelines for liturgical practice, and other administrative details related to the functioning of church institutions. These documents also frequently addressed policies related to care for the poor and the education of youth. In the post-Reformation period the clergy were almost all educated at universities, which had theological faculties closely associated with the territorial church. This helped to internalize and consolidate the norms that were established in each confessional state.[8]

The period has also been called the Age of Orthodoxy, a term that draws more attention to the theological characteristics of the era. In the years immediately after Martin Luther's death in 1546, a series of doctrinal disputes arose within the Lutheran churches over issues such as the relation of good works to faith in the process of salvation, the role of the human will in the regeneration of sinful humanity, and the nature of Christ's presence in the Lord's Supper. Some Lutheran theologians suspected others of betraying the reform movement by adapting positions more closely associated with Catholicism or Calvinism than with the perspective of Martin Luther and the first official statement of Lutheran beliefs, the Augsburg Confession. The proliferation of internal disagreement became a matter of concern to the Lutheran princes as well as the theologians and prompted a series of initiatives to promote reconciliation between the major factions. In 1577 two mediating theologians, Martin Chemnitz and Jakob Andreae, managed to persuade most of the Lutheran territorial churches in Germany and

Scandinavia to accept a doctrinal summary known as the Formula of Concord.[9] The restoration of relative unity within the Lutheran movement by this more elaborate confessional agreement has generally been seen as the start of the period known as the Age of Orthodoxy. The period is often subdivided into several stages: Early Orthodoxy, from 1580 up to the career of Johann Gerhard; High Orthodoxy, from the last stage of the Thirty Years' War until 1686; and Late Orthodoxy, which overlapped the rise of the Pietist movement.[10] Some of the most notable theologians, in addition to Johann Gerhard (1582–1637), were Nikolaus Hunnius (1585–1643), Georg Calixtus (1586–1656), Johann Konrad Dannhauer (1603–60), Abraham Calov (1612–86), Johann Andreas Quenstedt (1617–88), and David Hollaz (1648–1713).

Concern about the danger of internal disagreements as well as mistrust generated by the war between parties who were initially differentiated by their confessional identities intensified interest among church leaders in clarifying and defending correct doctrine. Throughout the seventeenth century Lutheran theologians tended to devote themselves to showing continuity between the Bible, the early creeds of the church, the theology of Martin Luther, and articles of belief summarized in the Augsburg Confession and the Formula of Concord. They defined Lutheran identity quite precisely over against other rival religious movements. Theological leadership in the Age of Orthodoxy was exercised by ordained professors who taught at several prominent universities located in Wittenberg, Jena, Tübingen, Straßburg, Leipzig, Rostock, Gießen, and Helmstedt. During this period the Bible continued to be the final measure of all claims to religious truth, but some important innovations took place in how Lutheran theology was clarified and defended. University theologians, such as Johann Gerhard, one of the early innovators, began to make extensive use of philosophical resources, especially Aristotelian metaphysical categories, as an aid for their analysis of articles of faith. This rise of a kind of Protestant scholasticism was a departure from the approach taken by Martin Luther, who had severely criticized the use of philosophy, especially Aristotle, in late medieval Catholic theology.

The Orthodox dogmaticians produced massive, comprehensive systematic theologies that usually followed the *locus* method developed by Luther's coworker, Philip Melanchthon. In this approach theology was treated as a collection of articles of faith that could be separated into discrete units for precise investigation. Over time, more and more subcategories were created to distinguish among different facets of key topics, and these distinctions eventually became standard elements of the next generation's dogmatic compendia. For example, the process of salvation (or *ordo salutis*) came to be divided for analysis into six or seven aspects related to how the grace of God was understood to be received. A typical subdivision would have been vocation, repentance, justification, conversion, renewal, new birth, and mystical union with Christ.[11]

Critical Evaluations of the State of Religious Life

In addition to defending the reliability of the scriptures and showing how the Lutheran confessions were consistent with this sole source of divine revelation, the university-based theologians devoted significant energy to pointing out errors in the viewpoints professed by other religious groups. Many of the treatises published during the Age of Orthodoxy were not only complex and abstractly didactic but also strongly polemical. These characteristics prompted a critical reaction among some Lutheran pastors who began to feel that a divide was developing between the preoccupations of well-educated church leaders and the needs and concerns of simple believers. Some scholars have argued that the Lutheran movement at the end of the sixteenth century experienced a "crisis of piety" with which it struggled throughout the whole period of Orthodoxy. According to this interpretation, there is evidence to suggest that the third generation of Lutheran church leaders was less effective than the original reformers in showing how doctrine related to daily living.[12] The extent and possible causes of this so-called crisis continue to be debated, but there is no doubt that a current of discontent with the state of piety and church life prompted new attention to the production of practical devotional literature that would be easily accessible to the Lutheran laity. One of the leaders in this countermovement was Johann Arndt (1555–1621).

In his influential devotional work *Four Books of True Christianity*, Arndt, a Lutheran pastor in Lower Saxony, proclaimed that there were many in his day who professed to be Christians but manifested few signs of the rebirth or renewal that should result from the effects of grace in their lives. They might be believers and church-goers, but they lacked true sanctifying faith, which purifies the heart, unites the soul with God, frees the heart from interest in earthly things, creates a hunger for righteousness, and makes itself known in acts of love.[13] Arndt was not the first to claim that there were deficiencies in spiritual life within the Lutheran movement, but he differed from other critics in his explanation of the causes of these problems. He suggested that the Lutheran pastors and theologians contributed to a decline in moral and religious life by preaching only "half a Christ." Many, he said, treated theology as if it were mere learning instead of living experience and practice. They were learned but not saintly; adept in the use of words but lacking in spiritual power. Furthermore, he stated,

> It is not enough only to write against sects and heretics, to preach and dispute, to maintain pure doctrine and true religion as the Apostle Paul indicated so that one may dispute with and conquer those who contradict sound doctrine. These activities have fallen into great misuse in our times so that beside the many, heavy disputations, polemical sermons, writings and tracts, Christian life, true repentance, godliness, and Christian love are almost forgotten. It is as if Christianity consisted only in disputations and the production of polemical books, and not far more in seeing to it that the holy gospel and the teaching of Christ is practiced in a holy life.[14]

In *True Christianity*, which was first published in 1606 and expanded several times before its final version in 1610, Arndt devoted minimal attention to the exposition of contested theological issues and focused instead on creating a guide to how to "use the grace of God to lead a holy life." He aroused his readers from spiritual complacency, summoned them to repentance, set forth the life of Christ as a model to be imitated, and described the joy and peace that come when Christ fills the soul that has been emptied of all earthly distractions. Arndt emphasized not only how Christ died *for* humanity on the cross but also how he comes to live *in* the Christian, providing consolation in the face of suffering and new strength to grow in holiness. He envisioned a mode of Lutheran piety that was both active in the world, showing concern for others through works of love, and also deeply personal with an inward-looking contemplative dimension.

Lutheran Devotional Literature

Arndt's *True Christianity* was the single most influential devotional book in Lutheran history, but his efforts to promote spiritual reform inspired many others to create additional resources of practical religious literature for use by individuals and families to supplement communal worship and the pastoral care offered by the clergy. A quarter of all the books printed in Germany between the Reformation and the Enlightenment were devotional works, and the production of this kind of literature reached its qualitative and quantitative apogee for the Lutheran movement during the seventeenth century.[15] Works of all sorts were abundant. Some focused on particular spiritual problems such as the approach of death or addressed specific social groups such as youth, soldiers, women, or the elderly.[16] There were also practical commentaries on biblical books or the catechism and more comprehensive works such as postils (printed collections of sermons on the gospel or epistle texts set out by the lectionary for the whole church year). Sometimes sermons originally addressed to a congregation were reshaped to be particularly appropriate for daily individual devotion. Prayer books had been one of the most frequent kinds of practical religious literature since the 1550s. More than 370 editions of various Lutheran prayer books had already been published by 1600, and more than 200 authors added new options during the seventeenth century.[17] Even more popular were hymn books. Martin Luther had encouraged congregational singing from the very start of his reform movement and, along with many of his associates, produced new vernacular hymns to facilitate lay participation in worship. In the late sixteenth century, Lutherans accounted for 70 to 85 percent of the hymn books printed in Germany. From the start, but even more so during the seventeenth century, parishioners were encouraged to use these hymns for devotions within their homes as well as when assembled for services in a church. More and more hymns were specifically designed for private use instead of public worship. These hymns instructed, offered consolation, or served as prayers for forgiveness and personal renewal.[18]

Johann Arndt was only one in a long line of Lutheran devotional writers, but he made a significant contribution to several of these genres. In additional to his *Four Books of True Christianity* he authored a prayer book called *The Garden of Paradise* and published a postil of sermons. All of these works were repeatedly reissued throughout the seventeenth century. (*Pia Desideria*, the manifesto of Lutheran Pietism written by Philip Jacob Spener, first appeared in 1675 as a preface to a new edition of Arndt's *Postilla.*) His emphasis on repentance, evidence of rebirth, continuous spiritual growth, and mystical union with Christ became commonplace in seventeenth-century devotional literature, and these themes reappear in many of the authors included in this volume. Johann Gerhard had a strong personal connection to Johann Arndt. He grew up in Quedlinburg while Arndt was a pastor there. Arndt provided him with pastoral care when he became seriously ill at the age of fifteen and gave him advice he valued when he embarked on the study of theology. Gerhard had reservations about the way Arndt expressed some of his views in *True Christianity* but endorsed his other writings. Gerhard's *Sacred Meditations* appeared a year after the first edition of *True Christianity.* Heinrich Müller and Christian Scriver have generally been considered "disciples" of Arndt because they clearly integrated many of his concerns and concepts into their writings. Both of them had a connection to the University of Rostock, which became the base for a reform party within Lutheranism that sought to redirect and deepen spiritual life.[19] Among the hymn writers, Paul Gerhardt had an evident connection to Johann Arndt. He turned several prayers from Arndt's *Garden of Paradise* into hymns and is generally seen as fitting into the highly introspective, heartfelt, ethically oriented stream of piety associated with Arndt.[20]

Orthodoxy or Pietism?

Johann Arndt has sometimes been considered the father of Lutheran Pietism, although that movement first gained its name more than fifty years after his death. Müller and Scriver have also been considered Proto-Pietists, Early Pietists, or at least precursors of the Pietism reform movement. To be sure, characteristics of their theology and concern for reform continue to be features of the writings of the "classic" Pietists, Philip Jacob Spener and August Hermann Francke. Such a designation tends to suggest, however, that their practical concerns and mystical inwardness were not part of the perspectives of the contemporaneous theologians most closely identified with Lutheran Orthodoxy. Thinking of this sort has often been influenced by the simplistic stereotype of Orthodoxy that was promulgated by radical Pietists such as Gottfried Arnold (1699). It was reinforced by the clearer lines drawn near the beginning of the eighteenth century between Orthodox and Pietist factions within the Lutheran churches and by later Rationalist negativity toward dogmatics during the Enlightenment. This exaggerated assessment of Orthodoxy was already challenged in an effective way by Hans Leube as far back as the 1920s but still persists today because so many historians have a superficial familiarity with church life in the seventeenth century or tend to view it too monolithically.[21] Theological disputations written in Latin and prepared for a university setting would clearly have been incomprehensible and seemingly worthless to ordinary lay people, just as much scholarly literature today is dismissed as insignificant and unnecessarily pedantic by less-educated people. There is also no doubt that subtle argumentation about matters of doctrine made its way beyond the halls of the universities into many pulpits during the seventeenth century in Germany. It should also be recognized, however, that theology was widely seen as a "practical" discipline, and that theologians generally addressed the practical use or application of the teachings they discussed after meticulously defining concepts and analyzing truth claims.[22] Writers of academic theology were also quite capable of writing practical religious literature for a wider audience and were often interested in doing so. The best example of that is Johann Gerhard, the foremost Lutheran theologian of Arndt's day, who wrote *Sacred Meditations* and *School of Piety*, both of which appear in this volume, as well as very scholarly texts such as his nine-volume *Loci Theologici* (1610–22).[23]

Johann Gerhard was not as explicitly critical of learned scholars as were Arndt and later writers such as Heinrich Müller and Christian Scriver, but he too could lament signs of a disconnection between knowledge and practice in his day. There are also some lines of continuity between the sentiments he expressed in his devotional writings and the perspectives presented by the writers who have sometimes been called Proto-Pietists. It is clear, then, that it would be problematic to dissociate the writers included in this volume entirely from Lutheran Orthodoxy. Some scholars argue that the term *Pietism* should be used more narrowly to describe the movement to institute significant structural innovations such as use of small-group meetings (*collegia pietatis*) to promote spiritual renewal, in addition to the advocacy of a theology of rebirth. The same scholars contend that the devotional writers covered in this book differed from many later Pietists with regard to some other theological issues. For example, they did not share the chiliastic worldview that was an important motivating factor of Spener's reform efforts. Given the overlap of some features of piety between figures associated with both Orthodoxy and Pietism, other terms have also been proposed to point to their distinctive place within seventeenth-century Lutheran religious life. They have been spoken of as part of a special "piety movement" within Orthodoxy that might be called "Reform-Orthodoxy."[24]

Johann Gerhard

Johann Gerhard is generally considered to be one of the three most significant shapers of early Lutheran theology, along with Martin Luther (1483–1546) and Martin Chemnitz (1522–1586). He has also been called the church father of Lutheran Orthodoxy.[25] Gerhard was born on October 17, 1582, in Quedlinburg, where his father served as city counselor and treasurer. At the age of fifteen, while he was attending the city gymnasium, he faced a year-long struggle with dropsy (*Wassersucht*) and consumption (*Schwindsucht*). Johann Arndt, his pastor, was at his side daily and helped him to overcome the severe spiritual anxiety that his sickness had aroused. Gerhard was very grateful to Arndt for this counseling and kept up a correspondence with him for the rest of his life. In 1598 plague hit Quedlinburg and took the life of Gerhard's father. He also caught the plague himself but was fortunate to survive, supposedly because he had been mistakenly given a double dose of medicine.[26] Gerhard moved to Halberstadt to continue his education, since some of his teachers in Quedlinburg had died during the plague. In 1599 he entered the University of Wittenberg to study philosophy and theology. There he was exposed to the writings of Aristotle, which would have a significant influence on his innovative method of writing theology. He also acquired his thorough familiarity with the Bible and the church fathers. In 1601 Gerhard switched to the study of medicine at the insistence of a relative, but after that relative's death he transferred to the University of Jena to resume the study of theology. He graduated first in his class in 1603 and gave his first university lecture three days later on Aristotle's logic. In the winter of 1603 he became sick again. This prompted him to write his will and testament, a document that has survived, in which he gave a detailed testimony of his faith and asked his friends to pardon him if he had engaged in excessive philosophical speculation. When he recovered, he pursued further theological studies in Marburg and accompanied his mentor, Balthasar Mentzer, on a study tour to the universities of Heidelberg, Straßburg, and Tübingen. In 1605, when the Landgrave of Hesse decided to make Calvinism the normative confessional allegiance of the territory, the Lutheran theological faculty of the university moved elsewhere and Gerhard returned to Jena.

In 1606 he was made a doctor of theology and shortly thereafter accepted a call from Duke Johann Casimir of Coburg to become superintendent of the church in Heldburg. He had just turned twenty-four years old. Two years later he married a thirteen-year-old girl. She died in 1610, two months after giving birth to his first son. He would marry once more, in 1614, and father eleven children altogether, five of whom died before he did. One of his sons became an important theologian in his own right in Jena. As superintendent, Gerhard conducted a visitation to evaluate the state of church life in the region around Heldburg. He also preached frequently and participated in Lutheran conferences called to address the disputed theological issues of his day. In 1615 he was elevated to the office of general superintendent for the whole Duchy of Saxe-Coburg. Among his achievements in this role was the preparation of a new Church Order.

Throughout his years as a church administrator Gerhard frequently turned down offers of professorships from Lutheran universities. In 1616, however, he finally accepted a call to be head of the theological faculty at the University of Jena. He would remain there for the rest of his life, serving four times as university rector. During his twenty-one years as an academic theologian, he was a prolific writer. In addition to completing a nine-volume systematic theology, his *Loci Theologici*, he composed a *Harmony of the Gospels* and wrote *Confessio Catholica*, a four-volume work designed to show that Lutheran teachings were not only consistent with the Bible but also with the earlier theologians honored by the Catholic tradition. In this work and in another titled *Bellarminus Orthodoxias Testis*, he offered the most important Lutheran response to the formidable defense of Catholic teachings mounted by the Jesuit theologian Robert Bellarmine. Gerhard lived through four periods of the plague in Jena and managed to survive the plundering of the city by Swedish troops during the Thirty Years' War. He died on August 17, 1637, when he was only fifty-four years old.

One of the remarkable features of Johann Gerhard's life work is the fact that in addition to being one of the most erudite systematizers of Lutheran theology, he was also able to communicate effectively with ordinary lay people through his highly influential works of practical devotional literature. It has been said that he was not only the Thomas Aquinas of seventeenth-century Lutheranism but also its Bernard of Clairvaux.[27] Gerhard was only a twenty-four-year-old student when he published his *Sacred Meditations* in 1606. He was a well-established professor when he issued the five-part *School of Piety* in 1622. In between, he also published a book of meditations on the suffering and death of Christ, a manual to comfort the dying, and a prayer book.[28]

Gerhard's Meditations

Gerhard was a master of the practice of meditation, understood both as deep reflection on a sacred text and going into oneself for an examination of one's relation to God. The roots of this practice go back to the Middle Ages and the fourfold schema of the *lectio divina* (divine reading) practiced by monks. First one read a passage (*lectio*), carefully reflected on its meaning (*meditatio*), prayerfully considered one's personal response to what the Holy Spirit had illuminated (*oratio*), with the hope that by grace one might come into experiential contact with God (*contemplatio*). Martin Luther also made meditation an important part of theological investigation. In a famous comment, written in 1539, about how one should study theology, Luther spoke of the importance of *oratio, meditatio*, and *tentatio*. Theology begins with an encounter with the scriptures (*oratio*), which should then be prayerfully considered until its meaning is held deeply within the heart (*meditatio*). What has been thereby discovered is tested further by the facing of temptation in daily life (*tentatio*).[29]

Gerhard began to write his *Sacred Meditations* around 1603 to console himself during his illness. It has been described as a kind of spiritual therapy. In the preface of the first published edition Gerhard indicated that his goal was not only to state what should be believed and hoped for but also to influence the will so that the reader's whole life might move toward conformity with Christ's life. He likened theology to the discipline of medicine, which has both a theoretical and practical aspect. It has principles that should be studied and defended, but its ultimate purpose is to cure disease. Theology sets forth the true spiritual medicine that cleanses a person from the disease of sin but also brings about a spiritual revitalization. His book, in keeping with this analogy, reflects on both Christian teachings (*Lehre*) and Christian living (*Leben*). Through vivid descriptions of how far humans have fallen and how much Christ suffered to redeem them, Gerhard moves the readers toward repentance and a new way of living prompted by gratitude for divine grace, just as his mentor Johann Arndt did in *True Christianity*. Like Arndt, Gerhard also uses resources from the past as well as his own fresh thoughts about Christian living. He explicitly indicates his debt to Saint Anselm in his meditations on the substitutionary atonement of Christ. He also draws frequently from the writings of Augustine, Bernard of Clairvaux, Thomas à Kempis, and Johannes Tauler. The meditations are relatively free of polemics, except for scattered laments about how few true Christians there are in his day. He even makes use of some Reformation-era Catholic writers such as the Dominican mystic Luis de Granada (1504–88).[30] Gerhard gives expression to his own mystical side, especially when he writes about the spiritual marriage of Christ and the soul. Faith, he says, grafts believers into Christ such that they become one in spirit with him (1 Cor 6:17). However, this mysticism never slips into the spiritualistic individualism that some Lutheran critics claimed to find in his mentor, Johann Arndt. Gerhard bases the possibility of union with Christ on the imputation of Christ's righteousness and emphasizes how Christ's presence is linked to reception of the sacraments of baptism and the Lord's Supper.[31]

Gerhard's later work, *The School of Piety*, is also centered on the practice of meditation. It has been called the first Lutheran devotional book to make meditation a pervasive characteristic of Christian existence.[32] There are some reasons to believe that it was written as a gentle corrective to Arndt's *True Christianity*, which had become a focus of controversy around 1619. Mindful of the criticisms Arndt faced for paraphrasing passages from mystical writers and straying in the direction of Spiritualists such as Valentin Weigel and Kaspar Schwenckfeld, Gerhard seldom makes reference to mystics in this book, though he also rarely cites Martin Luther.[33] The governing theme of the book is inspired by a phrase found in 1 Timothy 4:7: "Train yourself in godliness." The first section of the work lays out the reasons why one should be devoted to the practice of piety. A second section describes the essential components of true piety and the means that contribute to its practice. The third section of the book offers an extensive exposition of the Ten Commandments as an overview of the Christian virtues that a renewed person should practice. The section from this book that has been selected for inclusion in this anthology describes eight recommended forms of meditation.

Heinrich Müller

Born on October 18, 1631, in Lübeck, where his family had temporarily taken refuge during a difficult stage of the Thirty Years'

War, Heinrich Müller returned to Rostock for his schooling. He spent a period of study at the University of Greifswald, but he received his master's degree from Rostock in 1651. Müller was influenced in his studies by Joachim Lütkemann (1608–55), a professor of metaphysics and sometime rector of the University of Rostock, who was an influential transmitter of Arndtian piety through his own devotional writings. After travels to many German cities to meet other notable theologians, at the age of twenty-two Müller became the youngest member of the Rostock clergy when in 1653 he was appointed archdeacon at the church his family attended. Müller was energetic and outspoken throughout his career. He antagonized the city council soon after his ordination by criticizing its treatment of a mentally ill woman. Because of his youthfulness and perhaps also his irksome assertiveness, he was not immediately awarded a doctorate in theology, although he had completed all the requirements. He was also denied an appointment to a professorship for several years. Blocked in Rostock, he turned to the University of Helmstedt to get his doctorate. Eventually, in 1659, he managed to get approval as professor of Greek at the University of Rostock and became a professor of theology in 1662. In addition to his academic work he served as superintendent of the Rostock churches for the final years of his life. He was only forty-three years old when he died in 1675.[34]

Müller wrote many scholarly treatises on topics such as justification, the Calvinist view of reprobation, and the Catholic view of merit, baptism, and the Lord's Supper, but he is especially remembered for his numerous practical religious writings. In *Heavenly Kiss of Love or the Practice of True Christianity*, published in 1659, Müller reiterates many of the themes found in Johann Arndt's *True Christianity*. He reviews how the love of God is present in creation, redemption, and the regeneration of humanity, encouraging his readers to respond to this love by showing love themselves toward other people. In the same year Müller published *Soul Music*, a collection of four hundred hymns with ten meditations on the place of music in worship. Ten of his own hymns were gathered in *Heavenly Flame of Love*, and some of his sermons on the passion of Christ were later versified by Picander and used by Johann Sebastian Bach as texts for his St. Matthew's Passion. In *Spiritual Hours of Refreshment*, issued in 1664–66, Müller reworked material from some of his sermons for home use as devotional readings. Some of the passages offer encouragement to those facing suffering or spiritual trials, but others are bluntly accusatory. Much as Johann Arndt had done before him, Müller presents criticisms of some of his fellow clergy who, he claims, have knowledge (*Wissen*) but little conscience (*Gewissen*). In a passage that stirred up considerable controversy, he described the baptismal font, the pulpit, the confessional bench, and the sacramental altar as four idols worshiped by "Mouth Christians" who think that regular participation in church rituals is sufficient to gain eternal life and show no signs of being transformed by the power of the Spirit. As the passages included in this volume show, Müller writes as if he were carrying on a conversation. He makes extensive use of rhetorical questions and colorful metaphors to touch the hearts of his readers. Twenty-four editions of *Spiritual Hours of Refreshment* were printed before 1700 and twenty-two more by 1750.[35]

Christian Scriver

Christian Scriver was a contemporary of Heinrich Müller who also studied with Joachim Lütkemann at the University of Rostock. He was born on January 2, 1629, in Rendsburg, a town in Schleswig-Holstein, and experienced a number of tragedies during his early years. His well-to-do family lost most of its resources as a result of plundering during the Thirty Years' War. His father and two sisters died of the plague a half year after his birth. Scriver himself almost drowned at the age of five. The pastor whom his mother subsequently married also died when he was six years old. A relative paid for Scriver's schooling in Lübeck, and in 1647 he entered the University of Rostock to study theology. Scriver overlapped some of Heinrich Müller's time at this institution, but it is not known whether they met each other. In 1653 he was appointed archdeacon of the church in Stendal. After fourteen years in that city he took a pastorate in Magdeburg. The composer Georg Philipp Telemann, whose father was pastor at another city church, was born during this period. Later, Telemann would make use of three of Scriver's hymns in his own compositions. In 1679 Scriver became senior of the ministerium in Magdeburg and in 1685 the inspector of churches and schools for forty parishes. Among the challenges he faced during that period was an attack of plague in 1681, which killed one-third of the population. Scriver was offered positions in Halberstadt, Berlin, and Stockholm, which he turned down, but in 1690, after twenty-three years in Magdeburg, he left to become court preacher in Quedlinburg (the town of Johann Gerhard's birth). He made this move based on the advice of Philip Jacob Spener, with whom he carried on a long correspondence. Three years later, in 1693, he died of a stroke at the age of sixty-four. Married four times, Scriver outlived all of his wives and twelve of his fourteen children.[36]

Scriver was a gifted preacher, a hymn writer, and most notably, author of several widely circulated devotional books. The longest excerpt from his writings to be included in this volume is taken from *Gotthold's Occasional Devotions*, because this book is an interesting example of emblem literature, a genre of meditation that was particularly popular in the seventeenth century. Pioneered by an Italian humanist, Andrea Alciato, who published *Emblemata* in 1531, emblem books most commonly centered on a visual image that was meant to convey a moral or spiritual lesson. Sometimes the image was accompanied by a short explanatory text. In the case of Scriver's *Gotthold's Occasional Devotions*, published in expanding versions between 1663 and 1671, a prose description of some object or scene, a "word-emblem," takes the place of the more usual visual image.

Scriver was familiar with a range of English devotional books and was influenced especially by Joseph Hall (1574–1656), an Anglican bishop with Puritan sympathies who published a collection of "occasional" meditations in 1630. These are seemingly random portrayals of outward occurrences rather than formally structured meditations created for a larger program of spiritual formation, such as Ignatius Loyola's *Spiritual Exercises*. Hall's *Occasional Meditations* came to be known by Scriver through German translations by the poet Georg Philip von Harsdörffer or Margaretha Maria von Buwinghausen. Scriver's book contains four hundred emblematic meditations. Like Johann Arndt, who focused on the Book of Nature in the fourth book of *True Christianity*, Scriver uncovers features of God's creation that instruct, console, or motivate those whose eyes have been opened. In addition to features of nature, manmade objects or short depictions of human activities provide the starting points for Scriver's spiritual lessons.[37]

In his most famous work, *The Treasure of the Soul*, which was enlarged in several stages between 1675 and 1692, Scriver reworked seventy lengthy sermons to provide a comprehensive picture of the progress of the soul. The overall theme of this book was built around Matthew 16:26: "What profit is it to gain the whole world, if the soul is thereby forfeited?" In part one, Scriver presents eight meditations contrasting the original excellence of the soul with its degradation under the influence of sin. In a manner reminiscent of Johann Arndt, he describes how the soul was created for God's indwelling but the image of God in humanity was deformed into the image of Satan. The twelve sermons in part two describe how the soul can be converted through the grace of God and prepared for a spiritual marriage with Christ. For this to take place the sinner must truly repent and turn away from sin. Scriver notes in this context how many so-called Christians show no signs of rebirth. Like Arndt and Müller, he sees abundant evidence of hypocrisy and false security in society. He also criticizes the learned who shed light like the moon but give out no heat. They have knowledge but no personal spiritual experience.

The excerpt from *The Treasure of the Soul* that has been included in this volume is taken from part three, where twenty-five meditations describe the necessity of a holy life and the means that contribute to spiritual growth. In this section Scriver recommends not only participation in the sacraments but also daily self-examination and disciplined living. Part four offers advice for dealing with suffering and the trials of life. Part five contrasts the world and its vanity with the joy and peace of the life to come. Scriver lived into the era of Pietism and stressed themes that were common among the Pietists, but he also cited many authors associated with Lutheran Orthodoxy. Scriver quotes Martin Luther more than any other author in this work and also makes frequent references to the devotional writings of Arndt, Gerhard, Lütkemann, and Müller.[38]

Lutheran Hymnwriters

The many troubles besetting German society during the seventeenth century seem to loom in the background of the hymns of this era. Some hymns express longing for relief from earthly suffering.

Others offer consolation by reflecting on the promise of life with God after death or offer assurance that God is present in the time of need. Hymn writers often reminded the faithful that they should recognize the many blessings God has given them and be thankful even in their darkest hour. Most of all, they express appreciation for the saving work of Christ. The hymns, like the prose devotional books, are the product of careful self-examination. The poets point out the extent of human sinfulness and summon believers to repentance. Much attention is devoted to the innocent suffering of Christ for the sake of humanity—often with vivid descriptions of his wounds and unmerited humiliation that are designed to arouse strong feelings of sorrow, wonder, and love. Some hymns articulate the Orthodox Lutheran stress on justification by grace through faith, while others anticipate the preoccupations of the Pietists and ask God for strength to grow in holiness. The poetic texts collected in this volume show the wide range of settings in which hymns were used. Some were written specifically for liturgical festivals such as Advent, Christmas, Lent, or Easter and use the communal "we" to express shared sentiments. Others use the more personal "I" and were intended for use as part of morning and evening devotions by individuals or families.[39]

Philip Nicolai (1568–1608) was both a polemical theologian and a devotional writer. He wrote critical treatises primarily against Calvinism but is most remembered, along with Martin Moller and Johann Arndt, for contributing to the mystical turn in Lutheran piety. Educated at the universities of Erfurt and Wittenberg, he served as a parish pastor and court preacher in several locations. He was ministering in Unna, Westphalia, in 1599 when a plague devastated the town. This event inspired him to write *Mirror of Joy*, a collection of meditations on eternal life. Nicolai urged his parishioners to ignore the troubles of this world and to set their eyes on things above. He described heaven as an eternal wedding in which Christ and the Christian are united in a perfect bond of love, but he also held that union with Christ could be experienced during earthly life. His two most famous hymns first appeared in this book. "Wake, awake," based on the parable of the ten maidens waiting for the coming of the bridegroom (Matt 25:1–13), is usually used during the Advent season or as a morning hymn. "O Morning-Star," inspired by

Psalm 45 and the Song of Songs, also uses the motif of the bride and the bridegroom. It is commonly sung around the time of Epiphany. Johann Sebastian Bach used both of these chorales in his cantatas.

Josua Stegmann (1588–1632) was educated at the University of Leipzig and later received a doctorate in theology from the University of Wittenberg. He served as a parish pastor and church superintendent and in 1621 became a professor of theology at Rinteln. The invasion of troops forced him to flee that city for a while during the Thirty Years' War, and he had difficulty reclaiming his position when he returned because the Edict of Restitution restored Catholic control to some territories. His hymn "Abide with us, O Savior" takes its start from the words spoken by the disciples when they encounter the resurrected Jesus in Emmaus (Lk 24:13–27). It is often sung at evening time or at the conclusion of a church service.

Johann Heermann (1585–1647) also had a difficult life due to the ravages of the Thirty Years' War and ill-health. A Silesian, he served for many years as a pastor in Köben. Four times during his ministry Catholic troops sacked his town. He suffered early on with eye problems and had to give up his preaching prematurely because of an affliction in his throat. Heermann is generally seen as second only to Paul Gerhardt among the Lutheran hymn writers of the seventeenth century. His vivid depiction of the sufferings of Christ in his hymn "Alas, Dear Jesus" (1630) has sometimes been seen as marking the transition from the more objective focus of Reformation-era lyrics to the more subjective focus of many Baroque hymns. Hymns such as "Ah, Lord our God" and "O God, Thou Faithful God" seek God's protection in the midst of danger and ask for strength to endure and remain faithful when "life is dark and cheerless."

Martin Rinckart (1586–1649), from Saxony, studied theology and philosophy at the University of Leipzig and held pastoral positions in Eisleben and Erdenborn before returning to his hometown, Eilenburg, to serve as archdeacon. The town was pillaged and burned several times by Swedish troops and in 1637 was hit by the plague. Rinckart was the only pastor to survive and had to celebrate up to four thousand funerals in one year. His well-known hymn "Now thank we all our God" is a poetic rendering of Sirach 50:22–24. First published in 1636 as a song to be used as a table grace, it was subsequently used in Germany on numerous occasions of national thanksgiving, such as when the Treaty of Westphalia, ending the Thirty Years' War, was signed. Matched with a new tune by Johann Crüger in 1647, it was incorporated later into two Bach cantatas and used by Felix Mendelssohn in his second or "Hymn of Praise" symphony.

Martin Opitz (1597–1639), another Silesian, studied in Heidelberg and several other places but never completed a university degree. In a difficult phase of the Thirty Years' War he wandered through several countries before returning to Silesia to devote himself to poetry. Opitz was a member of the Fruitbearing Society, which sought to standardize German as a vernacular language and promote it as a respectable medium for literature. His 1624 *Book of German Poetry* established the stylistic guidelines by which German baroque poetry would be measured, and a year later he was named imperial poet laureate. Opitz wrote several collections of religious poems. His morning hymn "O Light, who out of Light was born" asks God to unite the church and bring an end to war and persecution.

Paul Fleming (1609–40), like Martin Rinckart, sang in the boys' choir of the St. Thomas School in Leipzig and continued his studies in medicine at the universities of Leipzig and Leiden. A poet who wrote in both Latin and German and viewed Martin Opitz as his main model, he was crowned imperial poet laureate in 1632 at the age of twenty-two. He participated in trade missions to Russia and Persia before settling down in Latvia. He later moved to Hamburg, where he finished work for his doctorate in medicine. Fleming is best known for his sonnets and secular love poetry, but he also wrote hymns. "Where'er I go" makes reference to travels in distant lands and expresses confidence in God's continuous protection and guidance.

Johann von Rist (1607–67), another Baroque poet who wrote both sacred and secular works, studied theology in Rostock and Rinteln. In the latter city he met Josua Stegmann, who first interested him in hymn writing. Rist eventually became a pastor in the town of Wedel, near Hamburg. In 1641 he published the first edition of his *Heavenly Songs*, which were intended primarily for home rather than church use. Two years later Swedish troops invaded Wedel and destroyed much of his collection of literary manuscripts while plundering his home. In 1644 he was named imperial poet laureate and elevated to the ranks of the nobility. Altogether, Rist wrote at least 659 hymns, published in ten separate collections. The hymns included here are mainly ones intended for communal worship, including one for use at the celebration of the Lord's Supper.

Paul Gerhardt (1607–76) produced far fewer hymns than Rist, but more of his have stayed in use for over three hundred years. Born in the small Saxon town of Gräfenhainichen near Wittenberg, he lost his father when he was twelve and his mother when he was fourteen. He attended an elite school in Grimma on scholarship and studied from 1628 until 1642 at the University of Wittenberg, the bastion of Lutheran Orthodoxy. It is not entirely clear why it took him fifteen years to get his theological degree, although it might be relevant that Wittenberg was plundered by Swedish troops, beleaguered by the plague, and heavily damaged by a fire during those years. The Thirty Years' War may also have contributed to his difficulty in finding a position as a pastor. He was forty-four years old when he got his first call to serve a church in Mittenwalde, near Berlin, and he did not marry until he was forty-five. In 1657 he became one of the ministers at the Nicolai church in Berlin, where he worked with two outstanding musicians, Johann Crüger and Johann Georg Ebeling. Eighteen of his hymns appeared in Crüger's influential 1648 hymnal *Praxis Pietatis Melica*, and many more were added in subsequent editions. Later, in 1666, Ebeling would publish a collection devoted entirely to Gerhardt's hymns. When the Elector of Brandenburg, Friedrich Wilhelm, called upon the Lutheran clergy to sign an agreement that they would not criticize his Calvinist faith from the pulpit, Gerhardt refused to do so. Even though some well-placed friends persuaded the elector to grant Gerhardt a personal exemption from this requirement, he felt that his allegiance to the Lutheran Formula of Concord obligated him to reject any compromise. He left Berlin and took a pastorate in the town of Lübben, where he remained until his death in 1676.[40]

Gerhardt wrote many hymns about the passion of Christ. The best known of them, "O sacred Head now wounded," was one of seven hymns based on a medieval hymn cycle by Arnulf von Löwen that focused meditation on parts of Christ's body. This hymn is used in several of Bach's cantatas, and altogether Bach used twenty-two of Gerhardt's hymns in his vocal works. Six other hymns versified prayers from Johann Arndt's *Paradise Garden*, the most notable of which is "Jesus, Thy Boundless Love to Me." The best-known English translation of this hymn was published by the founder of Methodism, John Wesley, in 1739. Many of Gerhardt's hymns are deeply personal and convey a wide range of emotions. Having known hardship and suffering himself, he offered words of consolation and encouragement to those who have known bitter anguish through phrases such as: "Cometh sunshine after rain; After mourning, joy again." Some hymns are very somber, but others are cheerful expressions of great joy for salvation and God's watchful care. Gerhardt also wrote hymns that celebrate the beauty of God's creation, such as his morning and evening hymns "The Golden Morning" and "Now All the Woods Are Sleeping."[41]

Georg Neumark (1621–81) left his native Thuringia to escape the turmoil of the Thirty Years' War but faced a further setback to his plans to enter the University of Königsberg when he was robbed of all his possessions. He had to look for work to replenish his resources, and after great difficulty he found a position as a tutor in Kiel. His best-known hymn, "If thou but suffer God to guide thee," about trusting in God's guidance, is believed to have been written around 1641, when he began to emerge from a period of great difficulty. Neumark eventually reached Königsberg, where he studied law and made the acquaintance of notable poets and musicians. After further travels he returned to Thuringia, where he became court poet, librarian, and secretary of the ducal archives in Weimar. Like other members of the Fruitbearing Society, he wrote both sacred and secular literature.

Johann Franck (1618–77) also studied law at the University of Königsberg. He returned to his hometown of Guben in Brandenburg to serve as councilor and mayor. During his lifetime he wrote around 110 hymns, the best known of which is "Jesus, Priceless Treasure." Bach also used this hymn as the basis for one of his motets and in a cantata. Many of Franck's hymns speak of the vanity of earthly existence, the "gloomy haunts of sadness," where "hidden rocks and shifting wind" always threaten, but he finds gladness in his "dearest friend," Jesus. The trend toward very personal and more individualistic hymn writing is especially evident in his work.

Notes on the Texts

I have translated Johann Gerhard's *Sacred Meditations* from the modern critical edition of this work: Johann Gerhard, *Meditationes Sacrae (1606/7) Lateinisch-deutsch*, edited by Johann Anselm Steiger (Stuttgart-Bad Cannstatt: Frommann-Holzboog, 2000). A second volume in this edition provides the German version of the originally Latin work, which was published in 1607 or 1608. The critical edition contains an extensive critical apparatus with textual variants and references to probable source materials that inspired the writer. The extent of this supplemental material vastly surpasses what is commonly included in this Paulist Press series, so it has been mostly excluded.

An English translation of this book by Ralph Winterton, a fellow of King's College Cambridge, first appeared in 1625 and went through nineteen or more editions. A blank verse version of the book was also produced in English by an Anglican vicar, William Papillon, in 1801. In 1896, C. W. Heisler, a Lutheran pastor in New York, published a new English translation of the work that has been reprinted several times down to the present. These versions, however, no longer read like the English we use today, so I have undertaken a fresh translation from the original Latin version. If I encountered difficulties in interpreting the author's intent, I looked to the earliest German translation for further insights.

My translation of the excerpt from Johann Gerhard's *School of Piety* is taken from the 1736 edition printed in Nuremberg, which I used in the Howard and Edna Hong Kierkegaard Library and Research Center at St. Olaf College. The original German title is *Schola pietatis, oder, Übung der Gottseeligkeit*.

I had access to the 1735 edition of Heinrich Müller's *Spiritual Hours of Refreshment*, published in Berlin by J. A. Rudigern. The original German title is *Geistliche Erquick-Stunden, oder, Dreyhundert Hausz- u. Tisch-Andachten, nebst einigen theologischen Bedencken von der Abgotterey der heutigen Maul-Christen und bruderlicher Bestraffung*. This book has never been translated into English before.

Christian Scriver's *Gottholds zufällige Andachten* appeared in several installments, the first part in 1663 and the full collection of four hundred devotions in 1671. The work was translated into English in 1857 by Robert Menzies, but he took considerable freedom with the text, excluding whole sections he considered less relevant and putting the selections into a different order. I have translated only thirty of the four hundred devotions, but this gives a representative impression of the nature of this appealing emblem book. Each unit is here presented in its entirety and in the original order.

Christian Scriver's *Seelenschatz* was an immensely popular work in Germany and also circulated widely in a Swedish translation. However, it is appearing here for the first time in English.

I have tried to use contemporary English syntax in my translations as much as I could without distorting the original Latin and German texts. I have also tried to make the translations as gender inclusive as possible unless the specific context seemed to intend a male or female reference. This is easier to do with the text of Gerhard's *Sacred Meditations*, since Latin does not usually specify pronouns with third-person verbs. The German texts by the other authors sometimes interchange references to "he" or "you," and in some instances I have therefore felt justified in using the more gender-neutral "you" to translate sentences, as long as it did not produce an awkward reading.

Seventeenth-century German texts do not conform to modern English customs of paragraphing. In order to make the text more readable and easier to search, I have made some of my own additional paragraph breaks in the translations.

The biblical references placed in parentheses in the translation of Gerhard's *Sacred Meditations* originally appeared as marginal notes in the earliest Latin or German editions. Many of those early references were wrongly recorded. These mistakes have been corrected, following the critical edition. Direct and complete biblical quotes are placed within quotation marks, but these markings are not included if the author paraphrases or uses only selected phrases from the text.

I have not attempted new rhyming translations of the hymns in the volume because this task was done better than I can do it during the nineteenth century by several English authors. Most of the translations are those of Catherine Winkworth, who had a special interest in the German chorale. She published editions of her book, *Lyra Germanica*, in 1853 and 1858 and also included German hymns in another collection titled *The Chorale Book for England* in 1863. Another translator, John Kelly, an English Presbyterian, published a collection of Paul Gerhardt's hymns in 1867. Some of Gerhardt's hymns, however, were already available in English in the eighteenth century. John Wesley, the founder of Methodism, was influenced by German Moravians and became widely familiar with German hymnody through that connection. For a few additional hymns I am grateful for contemporary translations by Matthew Carver, who lives in Nashville, Tennessee, and has an extensive project of producing new English versions of German Lutheran hymns.

Acknowledgments

A few of the translated excerpts in this volume appeared previously in a volume I published in 2002 through Fortress Press titled *Documents from the History of Lutheranism 1517–1750* and are copyrighted by the press. I am grateful it has have given me permission to reuse this material in this book. These selections include Chapters 13 and 28 from Johann Gerhard's *Sacred Meditations*, chapters 31 and 152 from Heinrich Müller's *Spiritual Hours of Refreshment*, and five selections from Christian Scriver's *Gotthold's Occasional Devotions* ("The Sailors," "The Rowers," "The Plant in the Cellar," "The Butterfly Catchers," and "The Vine and the Lute").

Two copyrighted hymn translations by Matthew Carver are also used by permission: Johann Heermann's hymn *Hilf mir, mein Gott* (translated here as "Oh, help me, God") and Christian Scriver's hymn *Der lieben Sonne Licht* (translated here as "The lovely Sun hath ushered west").

Notes to the Introduction

1. Philip Krey and Peter Krey, ed., *Luther's Spirituality*, Classics of Western Spirituality (New York/Mahwah, NJ: Paulist Press, 2007); Johann Arndt, *True Christianity*, ed. Peter Erb (1979); Peter Erb, ed., *Pietists: Selected Writings* (1983); David Crowner and Gerald Christianson, ed., *The Spirituality of the German Awakening* (2003).

2. Ernst Koch, "Therapeutische Theologie. Die Meditationes sacrae von Johann Gerhard (1606)," *Pietismus und Neuzeit* 13 (1987): 41–42.

3. From the perspective of political and economic history, see Trevor Aston, ed., *Crisis in Europe 1560–1660* (Garden City, NY: Doubleday Anchor Books, 1967); Geoffrey Parker and Lesley M. Smith, *The General Crisis of the Seventeenth Century*, 2d ed. (London: Routledge, 1997); Geoffrey Parker, *Europe in Crisis 1598–1648*, 2d ed. (Oxford: Blackwell, 2001). Concerning religious life, see Hartmut Lehmann and Anne-Charlotte Trepp, eds., *Im Zeiten der Krise: Religiosität im Europa des 17. Jahrhunderts* (Göttingen: Vandenhoeck and Ruprecht, 1999); Hartmut Lehmann, "Die Krisen des 17. Jahrhundert als Problem der Forschung," in *Transformationen der Religion in der Neuzeit: Beispiele aus der Geschichte des Protestantismus* (Göttingen: Vandenhoeck and Ruprecht, 2007), 11–20.

4. Geoffrey Parker, *The Thirty Years' War*, rev. ed. (New York: Military Heritage Press, 1987), 208–26.

5. Thomas Kaufmann, *Dreißigjähriger Krieg und Westfälischer Friede: Kirchengeschichtliche Studien zur lutherischen Konfessionskultur* (Tübingen: Mohr Siebeck, 1998); Hartmut Lehmann, "Zur Bedeutung von Religion und Religiosität im Barockzeitalter," in *Religion und Religiosität in der Neuzeit* (Göttingen: Vandenhoeck and Ruprecht, 1996), 19–27; Hartmut Lehmann, "Endzeitwartung im Luthertum im späten 16. und im frühen 17. Jahrhundert," in *Die lutherische Konfessionalisierung in Deutschland*, ed. Hans-Christoph Rublack (Gütersloh: Gerd Mohn, 1992), 545–54. One of the earliest influential explorations of this topic is Karl Holl, "Die Bedeutung der großen Kriege für das religiöse und kirchliche Leben innerhalb des deutschen Protestantismus," in *Gesammelte Aufsätze zur Kirchengeschichte III: Der Westen* (Tübingen: JCB Mohr, 1928), 302–84.

6. José Antonio Maravall, *Culture of the Baroque: Analysis of a Historical Structure*, trans. Terry Cochran (Minneapolis: University of Minnesota, 1987), esp. chap. 6: "The Image of the World and Human Being," 149–72.

7. John Headley, Hans Hillerbrand, and Anthony Papalas, eds., *Confessionalization in Europe 1555–1700. Essays in Honor and Memory of Bodo Nischan* (Aldershot, UK: Ashgate, 2004); Johannes Wallmann, "Lutherische Konfessionalisierung—ein Überblick," in Rublack, *Die lutherische Konfessionalisierung* (1992), 33–52. For further discussion of periodization and terms for designating this period, see Robert Kolb, ed., *Lutheran Ecclesiastical Culture, 1550–1675* (Leiden: Brill, 2008), 1–14.

8. Robert Christman, "The Pulpit and the Pew: Shaping Popular Piety in the Late Reformation," in Kolb, *Lutheran Ecclesiastical Culture*, 259–303.

9. Irene Dingel, "The Culture of Conflict in the Controversies Leading to the Formula of Concord (1548–1580)," in Kolb, *Lutheran Ecclesiastical Culture*, 15–64.

10. Johannes Wallmann, "Lutherische Orthodoxie," in *Religion in Geschichte und Gegenwart*, 4th ed., vol. 6 (Tübingen: Mohr Siebeck, 2003), 696–702; Markus Matthias, "Orthodoxie. I. Lutherische Orthodoxie," in *Theologische Realenzyklopedie*, vol. 25 (Berlin: deGruyter, 1995), 464–85; Robert Preus, *The Theology of Post-Reformation Lutheranism*, vol. 1 (St. Louis: Concordia Publishing House, 1970), 27–71; Eric Gritsch, *A History of Lutheranism* (Minneapolis: Fortress, Press, 2002), 109–40; Eric Lund, ed., *Documents from the History of Lutheranism 1517–1750* (Minneapolis: Fortress Press, 2002), 216–44.

11. This, one of the earliest presentations of the *ordo salutis*, was set forth by Nikolaus Hunnius in *Epitome credendorum* (1625); Emil Wacker, *Ordo salutis: die Heilsordnung* (Breklum: Christian Jensen, 1960); Max Koch, *Der Ordo Salutis in der Alt-Lutherische Dogmatik* (Berlin: A. Duncker, 1899).

12. Winfried Zeller, *Der Protestantismus des 17. Jahrhunderts* (Bremen: Carl Schünemann, 1962), xiii–xix. See also Eric Lund, "The Second Age of the Reformation: Lutheran and Reformed Spirituality 1550–1700," in *Christian Spirituality: Post-Reformation and Modern*, ed. Louis Dupré and Don E. Saliers (New York: Crossroad, 1989), 213–23; and Walter Sparn, "Die Krise der Frömmigkeit und ihr theologischer Reflex im nachreformatorischen Luthertum," in Rublack, *Die lutherische Konfessionalisierung*, 54–82.

13. Johann Arndt, *True Christianity*, ed. Peter Erb (Mahwah, NJ: Paulist Press, 1979), Book 1, chapter 5, pp. 45–48.

14. Ibid., Book 1, chapter 39, pp. 173–74.

15. Hartmut Lehmann, "The Cultural Importance of the Pious Middle Classes in Seventeenth-Century Protestant Society," in Hartmut Lehmann, *Religion und Religiosität in der Neuzeit*, ed. Manfred Jakubowski-Tiessen and Otto Ulbricht (Göttingen: Vandenhoeck and Ruprecht, 1996), 53. See also Gottfried Merkel, "Deutsche Erbauungsliteratur," in *Jahrbuch für Internationale Germanistik* 3, no. 1 (1971): 30–41.

16. Cornelia Moore, "Praeparatio ad Mortem: Das Buch bei Vorbereitung und Begleitung des Sterbens im protestantischen Deutschland des 16. und 17. Jahrhunderts," *Pietismus und Neuzeit* 19 (1993): 9–18. Two comprehensive overviews of all genres and important authors were written at the end of the nineteenth century: Hermann Beck, *Die religiöse Volkslitteratur* (Gotha: Friedrich Andreas Perthes, 1891); and Constantin Grosse, *Die alten Tröster* (Hermannsburg: Missionshandlung Hermannsburg, 1900).

17. Bernard Vogler, "Die Gebetbücher in der lutherischen Orthodoxie (1550–1700)," in Rublack, *Die lutherische Konfessionalisierun*, 423–34; and Christopher Brown, "Devotional Life in Hymns, Liturgy, Music and Prayer," in Kolb, *Lutheran Ecclesiastical Culture*, 245–54. For a more extensive older overview of this topic, see Paul Althaus, *Forschungen zur evangelischen Gebetsliteratur* (Gütersloh: C. Bertelsmann, 1927; reprint: Hildesheim: Olms, 1966).

18. Patrice Veit, "Das Gesangbuch als Quelle lutherischer Frömmigkeit," *Archiv für Reformationsgechichte* 79 (1988): 206–29; Patrice Veit, "Das Gesangbuch in der Praxis Pietatis der Lutheraner," in Rublack, *Die lutherische Konfessionalisierung*, 435–54; Christopher Brown, *Singing the Gospel: Lutheran Hymns and the Success of the Reformation* (Cambridge, MA: Harvard University Press, 2005).

19. Beck, *Die religiöse Volkslitteratur*, 130–38; F. Ernest Stoeffler, *The Rise of Evangelical Pietism* (Leiden: Brill, 1971), 217–27; Jonathan Strom, *Orthodoxy and Reform: The Clergy in Seventeenth Century Rostock* (Tübingen: Mohr Siebeck, 1999).

20. Elke Axmacher, *Johann Arndt und Paul Gerhardt* (Tübingen: Francke Verlag, 2001).

21. Hans Leube, "Die Theologen und das Kirchenvolk im Zeitalter der lutherischen Orthodoxie," in *Orthodoxie und Pietismus: Gesammelte Studien*, ed. Dietrich Blaufuss, 19–35 (Bielefeld: Luther Verlag, 1975); Elke Axmacher writes, "Das Bild von der monolithischen Einheit der lutherischen Orthodoxie (gedeutet als Erstarrung in logischem Schematismus und als ängstliche Absicherung der 'reinen Lehre') ist ja wissenschaftlich längst obsolete geworden, wenn es sich auch in populären

Darstellungen hartnäckig hält" (in *Johann Arndt und Paul Gerhardt*, xii); Johann Anselm Steiger writes, "No fundamental revision of the widespread horror story of 'dead' and 'stiff' Orthodoxy has been forthcoming.... This artificial and elaborate picture of 'evil' Orthodoxy is nothing more than a deception and smoke screen.... The accepted legend of the weak spot in Orthodoxy managed to hold the field because of its simplicity and because of the general lack of first-hand acquaintance with original sources even though the legend is false" ("Pastoral Care according to Johann Gerhard," *Lutheran Quarterly* 10, no. 3 [1996]: 320–21).

22. Kenneth Appold, "Academic Life and Teaching in Post-Reformation Lutheranism," in Kolb, *Lutheran Ecclesiastical Culture*, 65–115. The prolegoumena to most Orthodox theological summaries made comments such as the following: "Practical sciences...require knowledge of whatever is to be done, but do not end in this, nor have it as their aim, which is, rather, to lead to practice and action. We think that theology is to be numbered, not with the theoretical, but with the practical sciences" (Johann Quenstedt, *Theologica Didactico-Polemica*, cited in Lund, *Documents from the History of Lutheranism*, 221). See also: "Theologia est habitus intellectus practicus e verbo Dei scripto de vera religion haustus, ut ejus opera homo peccator per fidem ad vitam perducatur" (Johann Friedrich König, *Theologica Positiva* [Rostock, 1699]).

23. In the preface to *Sacred Meditations*, Gerhard writes: "If theology is practical instruction its goal will not be mere *gnosis* (knowledge) or subtle *theoria* (theory) but rather practice." In *Loci Theologici* he writes, "Theology, considered systematically and abstractly, is doctrine drawn from the Word of God by which men are instructed in true faith and pious living to eternal life." See a full discussion of Gerhard's practical orientation in Johann Anselm Steiger, *Johann Gerhard (1582–1637): Studien zu Theologie und Frömmigkeit des Kirchenvater der lutherischen Orthodoxie* (Stuttgart: Friedrich Frommann Verlag, 1997), esp. 17–157. Steiger argues that if Arndt and Scriver are considered Early Pietists, then the term would rightly be applied also to Johann Gerhard, who is usually seen as the foremost representative of Lutheran Orthodoxy.

24. This term was introduced by Arnold Schleiff in 1937 and analyzed more recently by Johannes Wallmann: "Pietismus und Orthodoxie: Überlegungen und Fragen zur Pietismusforschung," in *Pietismus-Studien* (Tübingen: Mohr Siebeck, 2008), 8; Martin Brecht, who favors a broader definition of Pietism, proposes using the term *new piety movement* in Germany ("Das Aufkommen der neuen Frömmigkeitsbewegung in Deutschland," in *Geschichte des Pietismus, Bd. I: Der Pietismus vom siebzehnten bis zum frühen achtzehnten Jahrhundert* [Göttingen:

Vandenhoeck and Ruprecht, 1993]). For further discussion of definitions of Pietism, see Jonathan Strom, "Problems and Promises of Pietism Research," *Church History* 71, no. 3 (September 2002): 536–54; and Harm Klueting, *Johann Jakob Fabricius (1618/20–1673): Ein Beitrag zu Konfessionaliserung und Sozialdiziplinierung im Luthertum des 17. Jahrhunderts* (Münster: Lit Verlag, 2003), 1–22. Johannes Wallmann has argued that *Pietas* was the central concept of Lutheran Orthodoxy—not of Pietism: "Pietas contra Pietismus: Zum Frömmigkeitsvertändnis der lutherischen Orothodoxie" (in *Pietas in der Lutherischen Orthodoxie*, ed. Udo Sträter [Wittenberg: Edition Hans Lufft, 1998], 6–18).

25. Johann Anselm Steiger, "Der Kirchenvater der lutherischen Orthodoxie: Johann Gerhard (1582–1637) und ein Forschungsprojekt," *Kerygma und Dogma* 43 (1997): 58–76. See two additional biographical summaries by Jörg Baur, "Johann Gerhard," in *Orthodoxie und Pietismus*, ed. Martin Greschat (Stuttgart: Kohlhammer, 1982), 99–119; "Die Leuchte Thüringens: Johann Gerhard (1582–1637) Zeitgerechte Rechtgläubigkeit im Schatten des Dreißigjährigen Krieges," in *Luther und seine klassichen Erben* (Tübingen: J.C.B. Mohr/Paul Siebeck, 1993), 335–56.

26. Robert Scharlemann, *Thomas Aquinas and John Gerhard* (New Haven, CT: Yale University Press, 1964), 37–43.

27. Steiger, "Der Kirchenvater der lutherischen Orthodoxie," 61: "Gerhard ist nicht nur der lutherische Thomas von Aquin, sondern auch der lutherische Bernhard des 17. Jahrhunderts. Oder anders: Gerhard vereint die beiden Naturen des Thomas von Aquin und des Thomas von Kempen in einer reformatorischen Person."

28. *Erklärung der Historien des Leidens und Sterbens unsers Herrn Christi Jesu* (1611), *Enchiridion consolatorium morti* (1611), and *Exercitium pietatis quotidianum* (1612). He also published two postils: *Postilla: Außlegung und Erklärung der Evangelien* (1613) on the lectionary gospel readings and *Postilla Salomonea* (1631) on the Song of Solomon. Modern critical editions of these works are being published by Friedrich Frommann Verlag.

29. Bengt Hägglund, "'Meditatio' in der lutherischen Orthodoxie," in Sträter, *Pietas in der Lutherischen Orthodoxie*, 19–31.

30. Johann Anselm Steiger, "Die 'Meditationes Sacrae' im Kontext der Meditationsliteratur des Mittelalters und des 16. Jahrhunderts im Überblick," in *Johann Gerhard: Meditationes Sacrae (1606/7)*, vol. 2 (Stuttgart-Bad Canstatt: Friedrich Frommann Verlag, 2000), 657–75.

31. Martti Vaahtoranta, "Unio und Rechtfertigung bei Johann Gerhard," in *Gott und Mensch in der nachreformatorischen Theologie*, ed.

Matti Repo and Rainar Vinke (Helsinki: Luther-Agricola Gesellschaft, 1996), 200–245; Steiger, *Johann Gerhard: Studien*, 52–123.

32. Udo Sträter, *Meditation und Kirchenreform in der lutherischen Kirche des 17. Jahrhunderts* (Tübingen: J.C.B. Mohr/Paul Siebeck, 1995), 50.

33. Wallmann, "Pietas contra Pietismus," 11–13; Sträter, *Meditation*, 44–52.

34. Strom, *Orthodoxy and Reform*, 222–28.

35. Eric Lund, "The Problem of Complacency in Seventeenth-Century Lutheran Spirituality," in *Modern Christian Spirituality: Methodological and Historical Essays*, ed. Bradley Hanson (Atlanta, GA: Scholars Press, 1990), 151–54; Gary Sattler, "The All-Sufficient Jesus in Heinrich Müller's Geistliche Erquickstunden" in *Perspectives on Christology: Essays in Honor of Paul K. Jewett*, ed. Marguerite Shuster and Richard Muller (Grand Rapids, MI: Zondervan Publishing House, 1991), 127–39.

36. Holger Müller, *Seelsorge und Tröstung: Christian Scriver (1629–1693) Erbauungsschriftsteller und Seelsorger* (Waltrop: Hartmut Spenner Verlag, 2005), 38–133; Fritz Becker, *Christian Scriver und sein literarisches Werk* (Münster: Buchdruckerei Althoff, 1929).

37. Michael Bath, *Speaking Pictures: English Emblem Books and Renaissance Culture* (London: Longman, 1994), 160–98; Peter Daly, *Literature in the Light of the Emblem*, 2d ed. (Toronto: University of Toronto Press, 1979), 73–121; Axel Simonsson, "Christian Scrivers natur-skildring och hans relationer till Joseph Hall," *Svensk teologisk Kvartalskrift* 48, no. 2 (1972): 69–83.

38. Martin Brecht, "Ein 'Gastmahl' an Predigten: Christian Scrivers Seelenschatz (1675–1692)," *Pietismus und Neuzeit* 28 (2002): 72–117; Martin Schmidt, "Christian Scrivers 'Seelenschatz,'" in *Widergeburt und neuer Mensch* (Witten-Ruhr: Luther Verlag, 1969), 112–28.

39. Ingeborg Röbbelen, *Theologie und Frömmigkeit im deutschen-lutherischen Gesangbuch des 17. und frühen 18. Jahrhunderts* (Göttingen: Vandenhoeck and Ruprecht, 1957); Joyce Irwin, *Neither Voice Nor Heart Alone: German Lutheran Theology of Music in the Age of the Baroque* (New York: Peter Lang, 1993).

40. Christian Bunners, *Paul Gerhardt: Weg-Werk-Wirkung*, 4th ed. (Tübingen: Vandenhoeck and Ruprecht, 2006).

41. For in-depth studies of Gerhardt's hymns and theology, see Elke Axmacher, *Johann Arndt und Paul Gerhardt* (Tübingen: Francke Verlag, 2001); Lisbet Foss, *Paul Gerhardt: Eine hymnologisch-komparative Studie* (Copenhagen: University of Copenhagen, 1995).

LUTHERAN DEVOTIONS

Johann Gerhard Sacred Meditations (1606)

Foreword by the Author

There are many who compare theology to the art of medicine, and they seem to be right in doing so. Just as medicine has two goals, the conservation of the health of the human body and the restoration of it if it has been lost, so theology, insofar as it deals with sicknesses of the soul, has in the same way a double purpose, not only to free us from sin but also to sustain us in the state of grace. As Gregory said, since medicine for the body and for the soul comes from God, there is one author of both. Medicine for the body has its incontestable principles, namely *logos* (reason) *kai peiran* (and experience), which are called supporting structures by them. What is harmonious with them is accepted and what is dissonant is rejected. So, theology has indisputable and unchanging principles, namely the word of God, comprised of the writings of prophets and apostles. It too accepts what is in agreement with them and rejects what is not.

Others go further and show that true medicine always springs from a regeneration, because nothing is able to regenerate that has not been regenerated itself. Therefore, the cleansing of vital spirits from the impure taint of disease, which is like a regeneration, requires a regenerated body, in other words, spirits, which are called spiritual bodies on account of their penetrating and tinting powers but are nonetheless also corporeal spirits. So also the true goal of theology is the spiritual rebirth of the inner man, which, as Truth testifies, takes place by water and the Spirit (John 3:5).

Some add a comparison of the philosopher's stone with the blessed cornerstone of the church, but since these things are not familiar to all or accepted by all I do not want to linger on them. It is sufficient to my intention if I can most clearly show by the comparison of theology with medicine that theology is practical instruction and that they perceive less rightly who contend that it is speculative, among whose number are some of the scholastics. Although matters to be believed and hoped for and not only matters of practice are set forth in this heavenly philosophy, it is nevertheless no impediment to considering it practical, for medicine is also concerned with theory but is not, on account of that, considered to be a merely theoretical discipline. *Theoria* (theory) is pursued for a practical reason and in order to support practice. The situation in theology is similar, so it now goes without saying that in believing those very things, or in articles of faith, not only knowledge is required but also assent, in other words, an act of the will by which they confirm that these are appropriate arguments and that this cure pertains to them.

If theology is practical instruction its goal will not be mere *gnosis* (knowledge) or subtle *theoria* (theory) but rather practice. "If you know these things, blessed are you if you do them," our Savior says to his disciples (John 13:17). Justin says: "The substance of our religion consists not in words but in things done." Ignatius says *ou legein monon, alla kai einai poiei christianous*: "To be a Christian is not only to speak but also to do." Augustine says: "The chief content of the Christian religion is to imitate him whom you worship." Basil says *ti esti christianismos; Theou homoiosis kata to endechomenon anthropou phusei*: "What is Christianity: the imitation of God insofar as it is possible by human nature." If the goal or perfection of the Christian religion is not mere *gnosis* (knowledge) but *praxis* (practice), how few true Christians you will find today. There is much knowledge, but little conscience. Indeed, it is most right that *orthodoxia* is defended in books, disputations, preaching, and all manner of ways, but the life of the professing Christian should respond by doing deeds. "If I have knowledge of all mysteries but have not love, I am nothing," the Apostle says (1 Cor 13:2). How then will they respond who do not have all knowledge of mysteries but only a little, have not a perfect grasp but a tenuous one, and nevertheless are proud, condemn others, or look down on them, and have scarcely any disposition toward Christian love?

I will write down this saying from a certain excellent little book. "Whoever wants fully to understand the words of Christ and to relish them should endeavor to make his whole life conform to his life. What use is there in disputing about high matters concerning the Trinity if you lack humility and thereby displease the Trinity? If you knew the whole Bible and sayings of all the philosophers, what good is all that if you are without love of God and grace? Vanity of vanities, all is vanity except to love God and serve only him" (Thomas à Kempis, *Imitation of Christ* 1:1). What value is there in introducing knowledge of God without fear of God? If I know everything in the world and have not love, how will that help me in the presence of God? "The more and the better you know something, the more harshly you will be judged, unless your life has been made more holy. Therefore, do not seek to be lifted up by this or that knowledge but rather fear for the knowledge that has been given to you" (Thomas à Kempis, 1:2). A saying by Erasmus is pertinent here. "What use is there in contending about the way in which sin should be accounted, whether it is merely a privation or a stain inhering in the soul? A theologian should do his best to make all sin hated and shunned. We dispute without end about what distinguishes the Father from the Son and both of them from the Holy Spirit, about the nature of their relationship, how they are said to be three, each not being the other, while they are one essence. How much better it would be if we piously worshiped and adored the Trinity, whose majesty surpasses scrutiny, and, by our own concord, gave expression, as much as is possible, to that ineffable concord into whose fellowship we will be admitted. We debate how it could be that fire by which the souls of the impious are tortured can affect an incorporeal entity when it is material. How much more useful it would be if we were to struggle with all our powers so that this fire might find nothing that is burnable in us" (Erasmus, *Annotationes I Timothy*). However, I repeat again that it is not the thing itself that is to be reproached but the abuse of it. It is proper that there are works and studies laying out accurate knowledge of articles of faith, to defend *orthodoxia* (orthodoxy) against heresies, provided that the whole content or perfection of the Christian religion is not judged to consist in this, and provided that we also have regard for Christian life and love. Life is bad where there is no belief in God, but, on the other hand, belief is useless where life is not lived well. True faith is not present internally where external works are not apparent (Jas 2:17). They who do not walk in the light are not children of the light (Eph 5:6). They are not Christians who do not live a life worthy of a Christian.

Therefore, in this most cold age, when the *hupekkauma* (fuel) of piety is almost extinct, I have written this book of sacred meditations in my spare hours so that I might add a *hormeterion* (starting place) for those who are tardy on the way of the Lord, and remind myself and others of our duty. Following in the footsteps of Augustine, Bernard, Anselm, Tauler, and others, I often sprinkle their words through this handbook, yet to make it easier, I have refrained from adding the names of authors or noting passages from the scriptures, for I was afraid that I might disrupt the meditation of the reader.* I do not think it matters much to know if the words expressed are from one of the fathers or my own words, as long as one zealously pays attention to what is said. If it pleases someone to attribute all that is said aptly and agreeably to the holy fathers and what is expressed less well to me, I will not protest. I only seek that profit might flow freely to the sons of the church. I will indeed believe that I have realized my wish if some pious and holy thought comes forth from reading this book to even one soul for one moment. Should anyone think my words are not Ciceronian enough or less aptly applied, I add also if certain words in accordance with the analogy of faith present themselves as less appropriate (which I hope not), do not immediately reject the whole book or brand me as a heretic, but take into account the style of writing. I am writing homilies, not precise disputations. I want to devote my attention to the substance more than the words. You will not find discussion of thorny questions here but, rather, fervent exhortations to a holy life. You will not find mocking wit but spiritual riches for the inner man. You will not find that it trains you in the subtleties of disputation but instructs you in the way of humility. I make use of allegories sometimes, not because I am of the opinion that everything should be transformed into allegories. This mode of writing is directed toward teaching and admonishing and not toward disputing, which it

*The scriptural references that appear within the following text were added in the margins of the seventh and ninth editions, published in Jena in 1617 and 1622. This translation also notes, in brackets, some of the most important authors that Gerhard quotes or paraphrases within his text. These references are based on the apparatus in the critical Latin edition published by Johann Anselm Steiger in 2000.

should not be seen as rejecting. But, do I need to add more about this or offer more in defense of myself when I have already said enough for the fair-minded reader and will never be able to say enough to satisfy unfair critics?

I address and offer these sacred meditations to you most honorable, thoughtful, and prudent men as a public testimony of my esteem for you. You are known and recognized by all for your constancy in upholding the purity of religion, your singular prudence in governance, and your benevolence toward the learned. For these and similar reasons I could name, I offer, without hesitation, these first fruits of my studies, the product of my winter free time, as a testimony of the high esteem I owe to you, and all the more so because I have the honor, in blessed memory of my grandparents on my father's as well as my mother's sides, to be related to some in your circle of celebrated dignity by virtue of blood-friendship. Receive then, most esteemed men, this simple paper gift with cheerful faces and favorable minds, place me under your patronage, and continue to favor my studies in the future as you have in the past. I offer prayers and supplications to the most high God that he will allow all good things to continue for you and will let the deposit of his holy word, peace and rest, favorable growth of the common good, indeed all good that he has done in your city according to his mild grace, be transmitted to your offspring. Jena, April 1606.

Meditation One

True Recognition of Sin

Acknowledgment of a sickness heals it.

Holy God, Just Judge, my sins are observed by my eyes and by my soul. Every hour I think about death because death is looming every hour. Every day I think of judgment, because an account must be rendered for every day at the Last Judgment (2 Cor 5:10). I examine my life and see that it is totally vain and profane. My actions are vain and useless, many of my words are vain, and many of my thoughts are even vainer. My life is not only vain, but also unholy and impious. I find nothing good in it. Whatever might seem good in my life is still not truly good or perfect because the disease of original sin and my corrupt nature taints it.

Virtuous Job said, "All my works make me afraid" (Job 9:28). If a virtuous person complains in this way, what should an impious one do? "All my righteousness is like a filthy rag" (Isa 64:6). If this is true of our righteousness, then what of our unrighteousness? "When you have done all you were ordered to do," the Savior says, "then declare: we are worthless servants" (Luke 17:10). If we are worthless when we are obedient, then surely we will be detestable when we transgress.

If I owe you my whole self, holy God, and whatever I can do even when I do not sin, what can I offer back to you when I have sinned? Our own righteousness, such as it appears, is nothing but unrighteousness when compared to divine righteousness. A lamp appears to shine in the darkness of night, but placed in the rays of the sun, it is overshadowed. Often a stick is thought to be straight, if it is not brought near to a measuring rod, but when it is placed next to a measuring rod, it is found to be crooked where it has swollen. Often the image on a seal seems perfect when examined by your eyes, but it is seen to be full of imperfections when viewed by the eyes of its maker. Likewise, an act that seems shameful to a discriminating judge seems glorious in the estimation of the doer. For, the judgment of God is one thing and human judgment is another.

Remembrance of my many sins terrifies me, but many more are still unknown to me. Who can recognize his own faults? Cleanse me from my hidden faults (Ps 19:12). I dare not raise my eyes to heaven because I have offended the one who dwells in heaven (Luke 18:13). Nor can I find a refuge on earth, for how can I dare to hope for favor from creatures when I have offended the Lord of all creatures? My adversary, the Devil, accuses me (Rev 12:12). "Most Fair Judge," he says to God, "declare this one to be mine on account of his guilt, because he did not want to be yours through grace." He is yours through nature, but mine because he takes pleasure in sins; he is yours through your passion, but mine through my persuasion; he is disobedient to you, but obedient to me; he accepted the robe of immortality and innocence from you, but accepted the ragged tunic of this evil life from me; he abandoned your garment and came to you with mine. Judge this one to be mine and condemn him along with me."

All the elements accuse me. Heaven says, "I supplied you with light for your comfort." The air says, "I gave you all sorts of birds for your pleasure." The water says, "I gave you different kinds of fish to eat." The earth says, "I gave you bread and wine to nourish you, but nevertheless you have abused all of these in contempt of our creator. Therefore, let all our benefits be transformed to punishments of you." The fire says, "You should be burned up by me." The water says, "You should be drowned by me." The air says, "You should be blown about by me." Earth says, "You should be swallowed up by me." The fire says, "You should be devoured by me."

The holy angels accuse me. God assigned them to me to be my servants and, in the future life, to be my companions, but because of my sins I deprived myself of the ministry of these holy ones in this life and the hope of their company in the life to come. The very voice of God, namely, the divine law, accuses me. It is both impossible for me to fulfill the law and unbearable to perish in eternity. God, the most severe judge and most powerful executor of his eternal law, accuses me. I cannot deceive him for he is wisdom itself, nor can I flee from him for his power reigns everywhere.

To whom, then, should I flee? To you, O holy Christ, our only Redeemer and Savior (Ps 139:7). My sins are great, but your satisfaction is greater; my unrighteousness is great, but your righteousness is greater. I acknowledge my sins; you overlook them. I uncover them; you cover them. I reveal them; you conceal them. There is nothing in me but damnation; there is nothing in you but salvation. I have committed many sins for which I can most justly be condemned, but you have not given up the power by which you can mercifully save me. I hear the voice in the canticle by which he bids me to hide myself in the clefts of the rock (Song 2:14). You are the firmest rock; your wounds are the clefts of the rock in which I may hide myself from all accusations of all creatures (1 Cor 10:4). My sins cry out to heaven, but your blood shed for my sins cries louder (Heb 12:24). My sins powerfully accuse me before God, but your passion is stronger in defending me. My unrighteous life powerfully condemns me, but your righteous life is more powerful for saving me. I appeal from the throne of justice to the throne of mercy, for I do not desire to come to judgment unless your most holy merit is placed between your judgment and me.

Meditation Two

An Exercise of Penitence from Contemplation of Our Lord's Passion

Consider the suffering Christ.

Look, O faithful soul, at the pain of the one suffering on the cross, his wounds as he hangs there, the torment of his dying. That head, before which the angelic spirits tremble, is pierced with many thorns; that face, the beauty of which exceeds that of all the sons of man, is disfigured by the spit of the ungodly; those eyes, brighter than the sun, are darkened in death; those ears, which heard the praise of angels, ring with the insults and scoffing of sinners; that mouth, which uttered divine eloquence and teaches the angels, drinks gall and vinegar; those feet, at whose footstool supplications are made, are fastened with nails; those hands, which stretched out the heavens, are extended on the cross and affixed with nails; that body, holiest seat of the Godhead and most pure of all habitations, is flogged and pierced by a lance (Luke 23:34); nothing remains uninjured except his tongue, so that he might pray for his crucifiers. He who reigns in heaven with the Father is most bitterly afflicted upon the cross by sinners. God dies, God suffers, God pours out his blood. From the magnitude of the ransom price, estimate the greatness of the danger; from the cost of the remedy, estimate the danger of the disease. Your wounds were so great that they could not be healed except by the wounds of his living and life-giving flesh; truly, so great a disease could not be cured except through the death of the physician.

Consider, O faithful soul, the most vehement wrath of God. The eternal, only-begotten, and dearly beloved Son himself became our intercessor after the fall of our first parent, but God's fury was still not averted (Heb 1:2). He through whom the worlds were formed interceded for us and took up the defense of miserable sinners as the highest advocate of our salvation, but God's fury was still not averted (1 John 2:1). The Savior put on our flesh so that the glory of his divinity communicated to our flesh might purify sinful flesh, so that the healing power of his perfect righteousness communicated to our flesh might thoroughly clean away the poisonous quality of sin inhering in our flesh and his grace might lay hold of us, but God's fury was still not averted. He transfers our sins and the punishments for our sins onto himself; his body is bound, beaten, wounded, pierced, crucified, laid in a tomb; blood copiously flows forth like dew from all his suffering limbs; his most holy soul is saddened beyond all measure; he is afflicted even unto death and subjected to the pains of hell (Matt 26:38); the eternal Son of God declares himself to be forsaken by God, such copious bloody sweat pours forth, he begins to feel such anguish that he, who comforts all angels, needs the comfort of angels; he, by whom all the living are given life, dies (Luke 22:43).

What will happen to dry wood if this happens to green wood (Luke 23:31)? What will happen to sinners if this happened to the one who is righteous and holy? How will he punish your own sins if he acted so harshly toward such a one? How will he continually tolerate in a servant what he fiercely punishes in his Son? What will those he rejected suffer if the one he so loves suffers so much? If Christ, who came without sin, could not depart without scourging, how much suffering do they deserve who come into the world with sin, live in sin, and depart with sin? The servant rejoices while the beloved Son suffers so severely for this person's sins. The servant accumulates the wrath of the Lord while the Son labors to alleviate and placate the Father's wrath. O infinite wrath of God, O indescribable fury, O immeasurable rigor of justice! If God is so furious toward his only beloved Son, who shares his divine nature, not because of the Son's own offense but because he is an intercessor for the servant, what will God do to the servant who perseveres complacently in sins and offenses?

The servant should fear and shudder and feel sorrow for his faults when the Son is punished for no fault of his own. The servant who does not cease to sin should fear when the Son is so afflicted for these sins. The creature who crucified his creator should fear; the servant who killed the Lord should fear; the ungodly sinner who so afflicted the righteous and holy one should fear. Let us hear the dearest one crying; let us hear his weeping. He cries from the cross: "See, O man, how I suffer for you; I cry to you because I am dying for you. See the punishments with which I am afflicted, see the nails with which I am pierced. There is no pain to compare to what torments me. Yet while there is such exterior pain, the interior grief is worse when I find out that you are so ungrateful."

Have mercy, have mercy upon us, most merciful God, and convert our stony hearts to you (Ezek 26:36).

Meditation Three

The True and Earnest Fruit of Repentance

Christ proclaims, "Come to your senses."

The foundation and beginning of a holy life is salutary repentance. For, where there is true repentance, there is remission of sins. Where there is remission of sins, there is the grace of God. Where the grace of God is, there is Christ. Where Christ is, there are his merits. Where Christ's merits are, there is satisfaction for sin. Where there is satisfaction for sin, there is justification. Where there is justification, there is a joyful and tranquil conscience. Where there is tranquility of conscience, there is the Holy Spirit. Where the Holy Spirit is, there is the whole blessed Trinity. Where the Holy Trinity is, there is eternal life. Therefore, where there is true repentance, there is eternal life. Where there is no true repentance, there is neither remission of sins, nor the grace of God, nor Christ, nor his merits, nor satisfaction for sins, nor justification, nor a tranquil conscience, nor the Holy Spirit, nor the Holy Trinity, nor eternal life.

Therefore, why do we delay our repentance? Why do we put it off until tomorrow (Sir 5:7)? Neither tomorrow nor true repentance is in our power. We will not only have to render account at the Last Judgment for tomorrow but also for today. Indeed, tomorrow is not certain, but the annihilation of the impenitent is certain. God promises favor toward the penitent, but he does not promise tomorrow. Where is the satisfaction of Christ found except in a truly contrite heart? "Our sins separate God and us from each other," the prophet

Isaiah testifies (Isa 59:2), but through repentance we turn back to him. Recognize and regret the guilt of your sins, and you will see that God is reconciled to you in Christ. "I blot out your iniquities," says the Lord (Isa 43:25), which implies that our sins were recorded in the court of heaven. "Turn your face from my sins," pleads the prophet (Ps 51:9), which implies that God sets our iniquities before his eyes. "Turn toward us, God," Moses pleads (Ps 90:13), which implies that sins separate us from God. "Our sins testify against us," Isaiah complains, which implies that they accuse us before the court of divine justice (Isa 59:12). "Wash me of my sins," David pleads (Ps 51:4), which implies that sin is the most foul abomination before God. "Heal my soul, because I have sinned against you," he says (Ps 51:6), which implies that sin is a sickness of the soul. "Whoever has sinned against me, I will blot out of my book," says the Lord (Exod 32:33), which implies that because of sin we are erased from the book of life. "Cast me not away from your face," pleads the Psalmist (Ps 51:13). Therefore, on account of sin we are rejected by God. "Take not your Holy Spirit from me," which implies that sin ejects the Holy Spirit from the temple of the heart, just as bees are put to flight by smoke and doves by a foul odor. "Restore onto me the joy of your salvation" (Ps 51:10), which implies that sin suffocates the soul and drains off the sap of the heart. "The earth is contaminated by its inhabitants who have transgressed the laws," cries Isaiah (Isa 24:5), which implies that sin is a kind of contagious poison. "Out of the depths I have cried unto you, Lord," says the Psalmist (Ps 130:1), which implies that sin presses us down to hell. "Formerly we were dead in sins," says the Apostle (Eph 2:1), which implies that sin is the spiritual death of the soul.

Through mortal sin a person lets go of God. God is infinite and incomprehensibly good. Therefore, to let go of God is an infinite and incomprehensible evil. Just as God is the greatest good, so sin in the greatest evil. Punishments and calamities are not true evils because many good things are gained from them. Indeed, that they are good is evident because they come from the greatest good, namely God, out of whom nothing except good proceeds. Moreover, they afflicted the greatest good, namely Christ, and the greatest good is not a partaker of true evil. They also lead to the greatest good, namely eternal life, for through suffering Christ entered his glory and through tribulations Christians enter eternal life (Acts 14:22). Truly, the greatest evil is sin, because it draws us away from the greatest good. The more you draw near to God, the more you retreat from sin; the more you draw near to sin, the more you retreat from God. How salutary repentance is, for by it we let go of sin and bring ourselves back to God. As great as sin is, so great is God who is offended by sin. God is truly so great that God cannot be contained by heaven or earth (1 Kgs 8:27). On the other hand, repentance is truly great because, as great as he is, we are led back to God by repentance. The conscience that one has violated, the creator who is offended, the fault by which one has transgressed, the creature who one has misused, and the Devil whose impulse one has followed, each accuse the sinner. How salutary repentance is that it frees us from such accusations!

Let us hasten, therefore, let us hasten to such healing medicine for sin; if you repent at death, you do not relinquish sins but sins relinquish you. You scarcely find anyone who truly repents at death except for that one thief on the cross. "Fourteen years I have served you," Jacob said to Laban (Gen 31:41); "it is time that I look out for my own house." And so, if you have served this world and this life so many years, is it not right that you should begin to look out for your soul? Each day our flesh piles up offenses, so each day the Spirit should cleanse it through repentance. Christ has died so that sin might die in us, and are we willing to let live and reign in our hearts that which took away his life, that for which the Son of God himself died?

Christ does not enter the heart of a person through grace unless John the Baptist prepares the way through repentance. God does not pour out the oil of mercy into any vessel except one that is contrite. The Lord mortifies first through contrition so that afterward he might vivify through the consolation of the Spirit. First he leads the soul to hell through deep sorrow so that he might bring it back from hell through the taste of grace. Elijah first heard a great and powerful wind overthrowing the mountains and grinding the rocks to powder and after the wind an earthquake and after the earthquake a fire. Finally there followed a still small voice to his ear (1 Kgs 19:11–12). So, the taste of divine love is preceded by terror; sadness precedes consolation. God does not bind up your wounds unless you first acknowledge and deplore them. God does not cover them unless you first uncover them; he does not pardon sins unless you first acknowledge them, does not justify you unless you first condemn yourself, does not console you unless you first despair of yourself. God prompts this true repentance in us through his Spirit.

Meditation Four

On the Name of Jesus

What name can be sweeter than "Jesus"?

O good Jesus, be also my Jesus and because of your name, have mercy on me. My life condemns me but the name of Jesus will save me. For the sake of your name, deal with me according to your name. Since you are the truly great Savior, you are mindful also of truly great sinners. Have mercy upon me, good Jesus, in the day of mercy lest you damn me on the Day of Judgment. If you will receive me into the bosom of your mercy, you will not be diminished on account of me. If you will distribute to me a morsel of your goodness, you will not be poorer because of me. You have been born for me (Isa 9:6); you have been circumcised for me; you are also a Jesus for me. How sweet and delectable is this name. For, what is Jesus if not a Savior? What then could happen to harm those who are saved? What else in addition to this salvation could we seek or expect?

Receive me, Lord Jesus, among the number of your children so that, one with them, I might be able to praise your holy and saving name. If I have damaged my purity, I have certainly not taken away your mercy. If I, miserable one that I am, have been able to destroy and damn myself, would you, on account of that, merciful one, not be able still to save me? Do not take notice of my sins such that you forget your mercy. Do not weigh and estimate my faults such that they outweigh your merit. Do not be mindful of my evil such that you forget your goodness. Do not think of your anger toward such things, but remember your mercy toward the wretched. Will you who gave a soul to me so that I might be able to desire you now do away with my desire for you? Will you who showed me my unworthiness and justifiable condemnation now hide your merits and the promise of eternal life from me? My case must be pled before the heavenly tribunal, but it consoles me that the name of Savior is assigned to you in the heavenly court because that name for you was brought from heaven by an angel (Luke 2:21). O most merciful Jesus, to whom will you be a Jesus, if not to miserable sinners seeking grace and salvation? Those who trust in their own righteousness and sanctity seek salvation in themselves, but I, finding nothing worthy of eternal life in myself, flee to you, O Savior. Save the damned, have mercy on the sinner, justify the unrighteous, absolve the accused. You, Lord, are truth; your name is holy and true. Therefore, may your name be true with regard to me; may you be Jesus and Savior for me.

Be my Jesus in this present life; be my Jesus in death; be my Jesus at the Last Judgment; be my Jesus in eternal life. My good Jesus, you will assuredly be so since you are unchanging in essence and unchanging in mercy. Your name will not be changed, Lord Jesus, because of one miserable sinner like me. Nay rather, you will still be my Savior, for you will not cast away anyone who comes to you (John 6:37). You have granted that I should want to come to you, so you will also grant that I am received when I come, for your word is truth and life (John 14:6).

Although the propagation of original sin in me should condemn me, nevertheless you are my Jesus. Although my conception in sin should condemn me, nevertheless you are my Jesus. Although my formation in sin and under a curse should condemn me, nevertheless you are my Savior. Although my corrupt birth should condemn me, nevertheless you are my salvation. Although the sins of my youth should condemn me, nevertheless you are my Jesus. Although my whole life is stained by grave sins, nevertheless you remain my Jesus. Although death should be inflicted upon me for my sins and various faults, nevertheless you are my Savior. Although the most severe sentence of the Last Judgment should condemn me, nevertheless you are my Jesus.

In me there is sin, reprobation, and condemnation; in your name, there is justification, election, and salvation. I was baptized in your name, I believe in your name, I will die in your name, I will rise in your name, I will appear in your name at the judgment. All things are provided for us in this name and stored up like a treasure. I have given up so many of your benefits; I have deprived myself of so much by my mistrust.

I pray, O good Jesus, through your name, that you will remove this mistrust from me lest I, whom you wish to save by your precious merits and salutary name, be condemned by my faults and incredulity.

Meditation Five

Exercise of Faith from Love of Christ in the Agony of His Death

The grace of Jesus is my gain.

See, Lord Jesus, how wrongly I have acted toward your passion. My heart is distressed and my soul is made exceedingly sad because I have no good works nor are any merits present in me. Nevertheless, may your passion be my act; may your works be my merits. I act wrongly toward your passion because although it is all-sufficient, I anxiously seek to supplement it with my own works. If I could find righteousness in me, your righteousness would be of no use to me and I certainly would not desire it so much. If I seek after the works of the law, I will be condemned by the law. Nevertheless, I know that I am no longer under the law but under grace (Rom 6:14).

I have lived shamefully. Holy Father in heaven, I am not worthy to be called your son. Do not refuse to call me your servant (Luke 15:19). I ask that the most holy fruits of your passion not be denied to me. I ask that your blood not be sterile, but that it might be fertile in liberating my soul. My sins have always lived in my flesh, but I ask that they might die with me. My flesh has always, until now, had mastery over me, but I ask that your spirit might triumph. Let the outer man be subjected to decay and worms so that the interior man might emerge in glory.

I have always, until now, submitted to the suggestions of the Devil, but I ask that he might be trampled under my feet. Satan is present and accuses me, but he does not have any power over me. The thought of death terrifies me, but death will be the end of my sins and the beginning of a holy life. Then, at last, I will be able to perfectly please you, my God. Then, at last, I will be confirmed in goodness and virtue. Satan terrifies me by my sins, but let him, instead, call to account the one who took up my infirmities, whom the Lord smote because of my sins (Isa 53:4). My debt is very great, nor will I be able to pay any part of it, but I trust in the riches and kindness of my bondsman. Let him free me by paying my debt for me; let him cover for me who took my debt upon himself. I have sinned, Lord, and my sins are so many and so very great, yet I do not wish to commit that most atrocious sin of accusing you of a lie when you testify by word and deed and by an oath that satisfaction has been made for my sins. I do not fear my sins because you are my righteousness (1 Cor 1:30). I do not fear my ignorance because you are my wisdom. I do not fear my death because you are my life. I do not fear errors because you are my truth. I do not fear the decay of my body because you are my resurrection (John 11:25). I am not afraid of the pains of death because you are my joy. I do not fear severity of judgment because you are my righteousness.

May the dew of your grace and vivifying consolation be instilled into my withering soul. My spirit is drying up, but I will soon spring back to life in you. My flesh is weak and limp, but you will make it sprout very soon. I must perish, but you will free me from decay as you have freed me from all other evils. You created me, so in what way can such a work of your hands be destroyed? You redeemed me from all my enemies, so in what way can death by itself prevail? Your body and blood and all that was yours you gave up for my salvation, so in what way can death keep in its grasp that which you redeemed by such a precious *lutron* (sacrifice)? You are righteous, Lord Jesus, so my sins will not prevail over you. You are life and resurrection, so my death will not prevail over you. You are God, so Satan will not prevail over you.

You have given to me the pledge of your Spirit (2 Cor 1:22), so that in this I glory, in this I triumph, and I firmly believe, never doubting, that it will be granted to me to go to the marriage supper of the Lamb (Rev 19:7). You are my nuptial garment, dearest spouse, which I put on at my baptism (Gal 3:27). You will cover my nakedness, nor will I sew any piece of my own righteousness to your dear and beautiful garment, for what is human righteousness but a filthy rag (Isa 64:6)? Therefore, how could I dare to sew this abominable rag onto the precious garment of your righteousness? I will appear in this garment before your face at your judgment when you will judge the whole world with righteousness and equity (Acts 17:31). I will appear in this garment before your face in the heavenly kingdom. I will cover my confusion and impropriety with this garment so that they will no more be remembered in eternity. There I will appear glorious and holy before your face, and this flesh of mine, this body of mine, will put on the most blessed glory which will be eternal and will never pass away in all eternity.

Come, Lord Jesus, and let whoever loves you say, "Come" (Rev 22:20).

Meditation Six

Consolation for the Penitent from the Passion of Christ Taken Principally from Anselm

The cross of Christ is our crown.

All the glory of the pious is in the humiliation of the Lord's passion (Bernard of Clairvaux, Sermon 4). All the rest of the pious is in the wounds of our Savior. Our life is in his death; our glory in his exaltation. How great is your mercy, heavenly Father, almighty God. I have been able to offend you by myself but have not been able to reconcile myself to you by my own efforts. You, therefore, reconcile me to yourself in Christ (2 Cor 5:18).

See, then, O Holy God, the mystery of his flesh and remit the guilt of my flesh. Consider what your good Son has endured, and ignore the evil that your servant has done. My flesh provoked you to wrath, but I pray that the flesh of Christ might turn you to mercy. What my evil deeds deserve is great, but what the devotion of my Redeemer merited is far greater. My unrighteousness is great, but much greater is the righteousness of my Redeemer. For, as superior as God is to humanity, so inferior is my wickedness to his goodness in quality as well as quantity. All that I am is yours because you made me, but make it all be yours also through love (Anselm, "Meditation on Redemption").

You who made me seek; make me also receive. You bring it about that I seek, so also allow me to find (Matt 7:7). You teach me to knock, so open to me when I knock. From you comes my desire; let me also obtain from you what I desire. From you I have the will; let me also accomplish what I will (Phil 2:13). O Holy God, Just Judge, if my sins are hidden, they are incurable. If they are seen, they are detestable. They burn me with pain, but they terrify me more with fear. I pray that you will not withhold such true mercy where you know there is such true misery. You find here great sins; may your grace be greater and more abundant. O Holy Father, do not seek to pour your wrath over me now that you have struck down your Son on account of my sins.

O Holy Jesus, free me from divine wrath, which you took upon yourself on the cross on account of me. O Holy Spirit, protect me with your consolation against the wrath of God, for it is you who, in the gospel, announced mercy to the penitent and contrite.

O Holy God, Just Judge, I can find no place to which I can flee from the face of your wrath. If I ascend to heaven, you are present there; if I descend to hell, behold you are there. If I take the wings of the morning and dwell in the uttermost parts of the sea, there also your hand will lead me and your right hand will take hold of me (Ps 139:7–10). Therefore, I will flee to Christ and hide myself in his wounds. O merciful God, look at the body of your Son, which is wounded in every part, so that the wounds of my sins will not be seen. May the blood of your Son wash me from the stain of all my sins (1 John 1:7). Hear the most ardent prayers offered to you for the salvation of the elect.

O Holy God, Just Judge, my life terrifies me, for if I ponder diligently, it plainly appears to be totally sinful and unfruitful, and whatever fruit is seen in it is either illusory or imperfect or in some other way so corrupt that it is either unable to please you or is displeasing to your eyes (Anselm, "Meditation to Arouse Fear"). Certainly, my whole life is either sinful and damnable or unfruitful and contemptible, but how can I differentiate between unfruitful and damnable? In any case, if it is unfruitful, it is damnable, for any tree that does not bear good fruit is thrown into the fire (Matt 3:10). Not only the tree that bears bad fruit is thrown into the fire but also the one that bears no fruit. The goats that are placed to the left of the judge terrify me, not because they did something evil but because they did nothing good (Matt 25:33). They did not give food to the hungry or drink to the thirsty.

Therefore, O dry and useless wood (Luke 23:31), worthy of eternal fire, what will you say on that day when it is demanded of you in the twinkling of an eye to give an account of how you spent your whole life? Not a hair of your head will perish nor a moment of time. Oh, what a strait to be in! On this side, accusing sins, on that side, terrifying justice. Beneath is the horrifying open abyss of hell; above is the enraged judge. Within is a burning conscience, without is a burning world. The righteous will scarcely be saved, so which way will a sinner who has been caught turn? It will be impossible to escape notice. It will be intolerable to be seen (Anselm, "Meditation to Arouse Fear").

Whence, then, will my salvation come, O soul? Where do I find counsel? Who is he who is called "mighty counselor" by an angel (Isa 9:5)? It is Jesus himself, the very one who is judge, in the midst of whose hands I tremble. Refresh yourself, O soul, lest you despair. Find hope in him whom you fear. Flee for refuge to him from whom you fled. Jesus Christ, for this your name's sake, deal with me according to your name; be mindful of me as I invoke your name in my misery. If you will admit me into the broad lap of your mercy, it will not be narrowed because of me. It is true, O Lord, that my conscience deserves damnation and my penitence does not suffice as satisfaction, but it is certain that your mercy surpasses all my offenses.

In you, O Lord, I trust. Let me not be confounded for eternity.

Meditation Seven

The Fruit of the Passion of the Lord

My hope is in the passion of Christ.

As often as I reflect upon the passion of the Lord, I picture for myself the greatness of the love of God and his forbearance toward my sins. He inclines his head to kiss me; he extends his arms to embrace me; he opens his hands to give to me; he opens his side to reveal his heart burning with love; he is raised above the earth so that he might draw all people to himself (John 12:32). His wounds are painfully discolored but also glow with love. So it is that through the opening of his wounds we should go into the secret place of his heart. Redemption is truly abundant with him (Ps 130:7), because a bounteous flood of blood, not just a mere drop, flowed from the five parts of his body. Just as a bunch of grapes thrown together in a winepress is crushed by the weight placed upon it and pours out its juice from all sides, so likewise the flesh of Christ, pressed down by the weight of divine wrath and the gravity of our sins, pours forth blood from every side.

When Abraham was willing to offer up his only son, the Lord said, "Now, truly, I know that you love me" (Gen 22:12). You should also acknowledge the great love of the eternal Father, who was willing to deliver up his only-begotten Son to death for us. If we were loved by him when we were still enemies (Rom 5:6), will he be unmindful of us when we are now reconciled through the death of his Son? Could he forget the precious blood of his Son when he counts up the tears and steps of the godly (Ps 56:8)? Could Christ be able to forget in his life those for whom he was willing to endure death or be able to forget in glory those for whom he endured such torment?

Consider, O faithful soul, the many fruits of the passion of the Lord. Christ brought forth bloody sweat for us lest the coldest sweat oppress us in the agony of death. He wanted to fight with death so that we might not grow weak in the agony of death. He wanted to endure the most grave anguish and sadness even onto death so that we might be made partakers of the eternal joy of heaven. By a kiss, which is a sign of friendship and benevolence, he was willing to be betrayed so that the sin by which Satan betrayed our first parents under the semblance of a special benevolence might be extinguished. He was willing to be seized and bound by Jews so that he might release us who have been bound by the chains of sin and should be cast into eternal damnation. He wished for the beginning of his passion to take place in a garden, so that he might expiate the sin that had its beginning in the garden of paradise. He wanted to be comforted by angels so that he might deliver us into the company of angels in heaven. He was deserted by his own disciples so that he might bind to himself us who were torn away from God by our foul defection. He was accused by false witnesses before the council lest we be accused by Satan through the law of God. He was condemned on earth so that we might be absolved in heaven. He who committed no sin was silent before sinners so that we might not be forced to become silent when brought before the judgment of God on account of our sins. He let himself be struck a stinging blow so that we might be freed from the sting of conscience and Satan. He endured ridicule so that we might be able to pour ridicule upon the taunts of Satan. His face was covered so that he might remove the veil of sin that obstructs our view of God and leads to damnable ignorance. He let himself be stripped of his garment so that the garment of innocence that was lost through sin might be restored. He was pricked by thorns so that he might heal the pricks of our hearts. He bore the weight of the cross so that he might remove the burden of eternal punishment from us. He cried out that he was forsaken by God so that he might prepare for us an eternal habitation with God. He suffered thirst on the cross so that the dew of grace might be gained for us and we might not have to perish eternally of thirst. He let himself be burned by the heat of divine wrath so that he might take the fire of hell away from us. He was judged so that he might free us from God's judgment. He was condemned so that we might be freed from condemnation. He was struck by the hands of the godless so that he might deflect the blows of the Devil. He cried out in pain so that he might protect us from eternal weeping. He shed tears so that we might wipe away our tears. He died so that we might live. He deeply felt the pains of hell so that we might never feel them. He was humiliated so that medicine might be procured for our pride. He was crowned with a crown of thorns so that he might gain a celestial crown to us. He endured suffering from all so that he might offer salvation to all. His eyes were darkened in death so that we might live in the light of heavenly glory. He heard jeers and insults so that we might hear the rejoicings of angels in heaven.

Therefore, faithful soul, so that you might not despair because an infinite good was offended by your sins, an infinite price was paid. You ought to be judged because of your sins, but the Son of God has already been judged for the sins of the whole world, which he took upon himself. Your sins should be punished, but God already punished them in his Son. The wounds of your sins are great, but the balm of Christ's blood is most precious. Moses pronounces judgment upon you because you did not do all that was written in the book of the Law (Deut 27:26), but Christ was made accursed for your sake. An accusing document was written against you in the court of heaven, but that was blotted out by the blood of Christ (Col 2:14). Therefore, your passion, O Holy Christ, is my last refuge.

Meditation Eight

The Certainty of Our Salvation

Good hope cannot be confounded.

What troubles you, my soul? Why do you still have doubts about the mercy of God? Think about your creator. Who created you without your help? Who formed your body in secret? When was the frame of your body formed in the lower parts of the earth (Ps 139:15)? Will not he who undertook to care for you when you were nothing continue to care for you after he created you in his image?

I am a creature of God, so I turn myself to my Creator. Even though my nature is infected by the Devil or wounded and injured by the robbers (Luke 10:30), which are my sins, nevertheless my Creator still lives. He who was able to make me is able to remake me. He who created me without any sin at all is able to rid me of all evil that, having entered me by the Devil's suggestion, the transgression of Adam, or my own action, spread through my whole substance. Accordingly, my Creator can remake me if only he so wills. In any case he is willing, for how can he hate his own creation? Are we not before him like clay in the hands of a potter (Jer 18:6)? If he hated me, he would not have created me from nothing. He is the Savior of all, and assuredly, those in particular who believe (1 Tim 4:10). It is marvelous that he created me, and all the more marvelous that he redeemed me. Never was it revealed more clearly that the Lord loves us than in his passion and wounds. Truly we are loved if for our sake the only-begotten Son is sent from the bosom of the Father. If you did not desire my salvation, Lord Jesus, why did you descend from heaven? But, you did descend to earth, to death, and to the cross (Phil 2:8). In order to redeem the servant, God did not spare his Son (Rom 8:32). Truly, therefore, humanity is embraced by a great love if God was willing to surrender his Son to be afflicted, struck down, and crucified for the redemption of humanity. Oh, what a dear and truly great price it was by which we were redeemed (1 Pet 1:18). Precious and great is the mercy of the Redeemer. It could seem that God loves his elect as much as his only-begotten Son, for indeed, that for which we pay something is more dear than that which we pay. So that he might have adopted sons, God did not spare the Son who shared his very own nature. What a great thing it is that he has prepared dwellings for us in a heavenly home at the same time that he was giving up his Son in whom there was the fullness of divinity (John 14:2). Certainly, where there is fullness of divinity there is also fullness of eternal life and glory. If he has given fullness of eternal life in Christ, how could it be that he would deny us a little particle of that? Truly, the heavenly Father must embrace us, his adopted sons, with a great love, because he delivered up his only-begotten Son for our sake. Truly, the Son must enfold us with great love because he surrendered himself for us. In order to make us rich, he endured extreme poverty, for he had nowhere to lay his head (Matt 8:20). In order to make us sons of God, he himself was born as a man, and, once he has accomplished the work of redemption, he does not neglect us afterward, but, seated at the right hand of divine majesty, he still intercedes for us. Will he not obtain whatever is necessary for my salvation, if he has given himself to merit salvation for me? What will the Father deny to the Son, who was obedient to him unto death, even death on a cross? What will the Father deny to the Son if he has already received the *lutron* (sacrifice of atonement) offered by the Son?

My sins may accuse me, but I trust in this intercessor. He who excuses is greater than he who accuses me. My weakness terrifies me, but I glory in his strength. Satan may accuse me, but this mediator excuses me. Heaven and earth may accuse me and my iniquities may accuse me, but it suffices for me that the creator of heaven and earth and righteousness itself defends me. It is sufficient with regard to merit for me to know that my merit does not suffice and to have him be gracious to me, though it is against him alone that I sinned. Whatever he has declined to impute to me shall be as if it has never been. It does not disturb me that my sins are severe and widespread and often repeated, for unless I was burdened with sins I would not have desired his righteousness. Unless I had a disease, I would not have asked for the aid of a doctor. He is the physician (Matt 9:12), he is the Savior, he is righteousness, and it is not possible for him to deny himself (2 Tim 2:13). I am sick, I am condemned, I cannot deny myself.

Have mercy on me, O Physician, O Savior, O Righteousness. Amen.

Meditation Nine

Loving God Alone

May you be bound to God by love.

Arouse yourself, faithful soul, and love the highest good in whom are all good things and without whom nothing else can truly be good. No creature can satisfy our will, because no creature possesses the perfect good but only as much of a share as has been given to it. Certainly, a small stream of good may flow to it from divinity but the source always remains in God. So, why would we want to leave the source to go after the stream? All good in the creature is a mere image of that perfect good that is in God or, rather, is God. So, why would we want to forsake that real thing itself to lay hold of a mere likeness of it? The dove sent out from the ark of Noah was not able to find any place in the whirling waters where it could rest its feet (Gen 8:8–9). So, our soul cannot find anything in the totality of all earthly things that might fully satisfy its desire because of the extreme inconstancy and fragility of all things. On the contrary, one does injury to oneself in loving something beneath one's dignity.

Now our souls are truly nobler than all creatures because they are redeemed by the passion and death of God. So, why would they want to love creatures? Isn't that contrary to the majesty to which God exalted it? We love something because of its power or wisdom or beauty, but what is more powerful than God, wiser than God, more beautiful than God? All the power of earthly kings is from him and under him. All human wisdom is foolishness compared to

God's wisdom. All the beauty of creatures is deformity compared to God's beauty.

If a most powerful king should undertake through messengers to make a marriage with a young woman of poor means and condition, would not that woman be acting stupidly if she wanted to dismiss the most powerful king and cling to the inferior messengers and ministers of the king? Similarly, God wanted to call us to himself through all the beauty of his creatures and to excite love for him. Therefore, why would our soul, which Christ the Bridegroom earnestly seeks, want to cling to creatures or the messengers of this spiritual union? The creatures themselves cry out: "Why do you cling to us? Why do you regard us as the fulfillment of your desires? We cannot satisfy your appetites. Go to the creator of us both." We should not hope for love to be returned by creatures, and, furthermore, no love begins with creatures. But God who is love itself (1 John 4:16) cannot help but love those who love him. Indeed, he anticipates all our desires and all our love by his love, so how much should we love him who first loved us so much? He loved us when we did not yet exist, for it is by divine love that we were born into this world. He loved us when we were still enemies (Rom 5:10), for it was out of divine mercy and love that he sent his Son as Redeemer. He loved us when we had fallen into sin, for it was by divine love that he does not deliver us over to death immediately if we sin, but rather awaits our conversion. It is because of divine love that, beyond what we deserve, even despite what we deserve, he leads us to the celestial palace.

You do not come to saving knowledge of him without the love of God. Without the love of God all knowledge is useless, even harmful. Why does love exceed the knowledge of all mysteries (1 Cor 13:2)? It is because the latter is found in the Devil but the former only in the godly. Why is the Devil the unhappiest of all creatures? It is because he is not able to love the highest good. Why is God, on the other hand, the most happy and blessed? It is because he loves all things and is delighted by all his works (Wis 11:25). Why is the love of God not perfect in this life? It is because we love only as much as we know, and truly in this life we know only in part and enigmatically (1 Cor 13:12). In eternal life we will be perfectly blessed because we will love God perfectly, and we will love perfectly because we know perfectly. No one can have hope in the perfect love of God in the age to come who does not begin to love God in this one. The kingdom of God ought to begin in our hearts in this life, otherwise it will not be brought to perfection in the future. There is no desire for eternal life without the love of God, for how will anyone be a partaker of that greatest good who does not love it, seek it, or desire it? However your love is, so are you, because your love changes you into itself.

Love is the greatest chain because the one loving and whatever is loved become one. What bound together the most righteous God and lost sinners who were so infinitely distant from each other? Infinite love did. So that the righteousness of God might not be overthrown, the infinite price of Christ intervened for us. What can join together God the creator and the faithful created soul since they are so infinitely distant from each other? Love can. How can it be that in eternal life we will be united with God to the highest degree? It is because we will love him to the highest degree. Love unites and transforms. If you love fleshly things, you will be fleshly. If you love the world, you will be made worldly. For truly flesh and blood will not inherit the kingdom of God (1 Cor 15:50). If you love God and divine things, you will be made divine.

Love of God is the chariot of Elijah ascending to heaven (2 Kgs 2:11). Love of God is the delight of the mind, the paradise of the soul. It excludes the world, conquers the Devil, shuts up hell, and opens heaven. The love of God is that seal by which God marks the elect and believers (Rev 7:3). In the Last Judgment, God will not acknowledge as his own those who are not marked with the seal. In fact, faith itself, the only cause of righteousness and our salvation, is not true unless it exhibits itself through love (Gal 5:6). Faith is not true unless it is firm trust, and there is no trust without love of God. A benefit is not acknowledged if we do not give thanks for it, and we do not give thanks to him if we do not love him. Therefore, if your faith is true, it will acknowledge the benefit of Christ, the Redeemer; it will acknowledge and give thanks; it will give thanks and will love him.

Love of God is life and rest to our soul. When the soul withdraws in death, the life of the body perishes. When God withdraws from the soul through sin, the life of the soul perishes. In turn, God dwells through faith in our hearts (Eph 3:17) and dwells in our soul through love, because the love of God is diffused in the hearts of the elect by the Holy Spirit (Rom 5:5). There is no tranquility for the soul apart from the love of God. The world and Satan are a great disturbance for it, but God gives the greatest rest to the soul. There is no peace for the conscience except in those who are justified by faith. There is no true love of God except in those who are endowed with a childlike trust in God. Therefore, love of ourselves, love of the world, love of creatures must die in us so that the love of God, which begins in this age and is perfected in the future, might live in us.

Meditation Ten

Our Reconciliation with God

Christ has paid my debt.

Truly, Christ took up our weaknesses and carried our sorrows (Isa 53:4). O Lord Jesus, the eternal punishment that we deserve you transferred to yourself. The burden that was pressing us down to hell, you took upon yourself. You were wounded for our transgressions and bruised for our evil deeds. Through your blood we were healed. The Lord has laid all our iniquities upon you (Isa 53:6). The exchange is altogether wonderful. You transfer our sins onto yourself and give us your righteousness. The death owed by us you inflict upon yourself, and you give us life. Therefore, I cannot henceforth doubt your grace in any way or despair on account of my sins. The worst that is in us you transferred to yourself.

How could you then despise the best that is in us, your own work, namely, our body and soul? You will not leave my soul in hell nor will you allow your holy one to see corruption (Ps 16:10). Truly, anyone is holy whose sins have been obliterated and taken away. Blessed is the one whose iniquities have been remitted, to whom God does not impute sins (Ps 32:1, 2). How can the Lord impute our sins to us since they were imputed to another? On account of the sins of the people he struck down his beloved Son. Therefore he will justify many by his knowledge and bear their iniquities. How will he justify us?

Hear, O soul, and pay attention to this: he will justify us by his knowledge, by the recognition of saving mercy and divine grace in

Christ, or by a firm apprehension of this through faith. This is eternal life, that they might recognize you as the only true God and the one you have sent, your Son Jesus Christ (John 17:3). Consequently, if you confess with your mouth that Jesus is Lord and believe in your heart that God raised him from the dead, you will be saved (Rom 10:9). Moreover, faith lays hold of the satisfaction of Christ, for he bore your iniquities and the sins of all and made intercession for the transgressors (Isa 53:11, 12). Truly, he would have had few righteous souls if he had not mercifully received sinners. You would have few righteous souls, O Jesus, if you had not remitted the sins of the unrighteous. Therefore, how could Christ judge severely the sins of the penitent whom he received onto himself? How could he condemn the guilt of sinners if he was himself made sin for them (2 Cor 5:21)? Will he judge those whom he calls his friends? Will he judge them for whom he interceded? Will he judge those for whom he died?

Rise up, my soul, and forget your sins, for the Lord has forgotten them (Isa 43:25). Whom do you fear as the punisher of sins if not the Lord, but it is he who made satisfaction for sins. If anyone else had paid the full *lutron* (ransom) for my sins, I could still be in doubt about whether the just judge would accept that satisfaction! If a person or some angel had made satisfaction for me, there would at least be a doubt whether it was a sufficient payment for redemption. But now the ground for doubt is removed. How would he not accept the payment who paid it himself? How could that not be sufficient that is from God himself?

Why are you still confused, my soul? All the paths of the Lord are mercy and truth (Ps 25:10). The Lord is righteous and his judgments are righteous (Ps 119:137). Why are you confused, O soul? Let divine mercy uplift you. Let divine righteousness also uplift you. For, since God is righteous, he will not exact a double satisfaction for the sin of one person. Since he struck down his Son for our sins, how could he strike us, his servants, for the same? Having inflicted punishment on his Son for sins, will he inflict punishment on us, his servants, for the same? The truth of the Lord will not be overthrown in all eternity (Ps 117:2). "I do not wish for the death of the sinner, but rather that the sinner be converted and live," says our Lord (Ezek 33:11). "Come to me, you who labor and are burdened, and I will refresh you," exclaims our Savior (Matt 11:28). Shall we accuse the

Lord of lies and try to repress his mercy by the weight of our sins? To accuse the Lord of lies and to deny his mercy is a greater sin than all the sins of the whole world. Hence also, Judas sinned more in despairing than the Jews in crucifying Christ. Indeed, even more, where sin abounded, there grace also abounded, for it outweighs by an infinite measure the weight of our sins (Rom 5:20). Sins are from human action, but grace is from God. Sins are temporary, but the grace of our Lord is from eternity to eternity. Satisfaction has been rendered for our sins; the grace of God has been recovered by the death of Christ, and it has been established for all eternity. Devoutly and in humble supplication, I flee to it for refuge.

Meditation Eleven

Satisfaction for Our Sins

The death of Christ is the life of the godly.

Come to me, you who labor and are burdened. I will refresh you (Matt 11:28). These are the words of our Savior. Truly, Lord Jesus, I am exceedingly burdened and groan under the weight of my sins, but I hasten to you, the fountain of living water. Come to me, Lord Jesus, so that I can come to you. I come to you, Lord, because you first came to me. I come to you, Lord Jesus, and I long for you anxiously, because I find nothing good in myself. If I should find anything good in myself, I would not long for you so anxiously. Truly, Lord Jesus, I labor and am burdened. I am not able to compare myself to any of your saints or even to any penitent sinner, except perhaps to the thief on the cross. Have mercy on me, Lord, as you were merciful to the thief on the cross. I have lived immoderately, I have lived in sin, but I desire to die in a godly manner and in righteousness.

Now, godliness and righteousness are far from my heart. So, I flee to your godliness and righteousness. Lord Jesus, may your soul, offered as a *lutron* (ransom) for many, come to my aid (Matt 20:28). May your most holy body, which was assaulted for me by whips, spit, blows, and thorns, come to my aid. O Jesus, may your most holy blood, which flowed from your side in your suffering and dying and cleansed us from all sins, come to my aid (1 John 1:7). May your most holy divinity, which supported your human nature in your suffering, come to my aid. Your divinity accomplished the most celebrated acclaimed mystery of my redemption by adding infinite strength and weight to your most holy passion, so that God might procure me, a wretch, for himself by his blood (Acts 20:28). May your wounds, which are my only medicine, come to my aid. May your most holy passion come to my aid. May your merit, which is my final refuge and remedy against sin, come to my aid. What you suffered, you suffered for me. Therefore, what you merited you merited for me in my unworthiness. Therefore, God commended his love toward us and, by a testimony surpassing the understanding of all people and even of all angels, confirms it, that Christ died for us while we were still sinners and enemies of God (Rom 5:8). Who will not marvel at this? Who will not be amazed? Asked by no one, and even though hated by humanity, the most merciful Son of God not only makes supplications for sinners and his enemies but also gives satisfaction to divine justice by his most poor birth, his most holy life, his most bitter passion, and his most cruel death.

O Lord Jesus, you have interceded, suffered, and died for me, before I desired your merit and passion, or moved you by prayers to pay the *lutron* (ransom). How could you fling me away from your face? How will you deny the fruit of your most holy passion when I now cry to you from the depths or earnestly beg for the fruit of your merit by tears and sighs (Ps 130:1)? I was by nature an enemy, but since you died for me, I have been made your friend, brother, and son by grace. You were attentive to me when I was still an enemy who was not yet praying to you, so how can you despise your friend coming to you with tears and prayers? You will not cast me out when I come to you because your word is truth (John 6:37). You have spoken to us in spirit and in truth, and we have received from you the words of eternal life (John 6:68).

Listen and be encouraged, my soul. Formerly we were sinners by nature, but now we are truly justified by grace. Formerly we were enemies, but now we are truly friends and neighbors. Formerly our help was in the death of Christ, but now it is truly in his life. Formerly we were dead in our sins, but now we are truly made alive in Christ (Eph 2:5). Oh, how great is the love of God by which he loved us. Oh, how abundant are the riches of divine grace by which he makes us to sit with him in the heavens. Oh, the heartfelt mercy of our God with which the day dawning from on high visited us (Luke 1:78). If the death of Christ brought righteousness and life to us, what will his life be able to do? If in dying the Savior paid the Father's ransom price, what will he do when alive and interceding for us? For Christ lives and dwells in our heart if only a remembrance of his most holy merit lives and flourishes in us.

Draw me, Lord Jesus, so that I might truly possess in fact what I now firmly long for in hope. I, your servant, seek to be with you, to see the glory that the Father gave you and to inhabit the mansion over yonder that you prepared in the house of your Father (John 14:2). Blessed are they who dwell in your house, Lord. They will praise you forever and ever (Ps 84:4)

Meditation Twelve

The Nature and Characteristics of True Faith

It is living and victorious if it is true faith.

O dear soul, consider the virtues of faith and thank God, the sole giver of faith. Faith alone unites us again with our Savior. Just as, for example, the young branches draw the sap from the vine (John 15:4), so we draw righteousness and salvation from his life. Adam fell from the grace of God and lost the divine image by his unbelief, but we are received back again into grace and the image of God began to be reformed in us by faith. Through faith, Christ is made ours and dwells in us (Eph 3:17). Therefore, where Christ is, there is the grace of God. Where the grace of God is, there is the inheritance of eternal life.

By faith, Abel offered a better sacrifice to God than Cain (Heb 11:4). So, we offer spiritual sacrifices to God through faith, the fruit of our lips. By faith, Enoch was taken up to God (Heb 11:5). So, faith takes us from the human community into a heavenly fellowship, even while we are in this life, because Christ dwells in us now and eternal life is in us now, though hidden (Col 3:3). By faith, Noah made ready the ark (Heb 11:7). So, by faith we enter the church in which souls are preserved, while all who remain in the vast sea of the world perish. By faith, Abraham left the land of idolaters (Heb 11:8). So, by faith we go out of the world, and, leaving parents, brothers, and all our kindred, we cling to the word of Christ who calls us. By faith, he journeyed and looked for the Promised Land. So, by faith we look for the heavenly Jerusalem that God has prepared in heaven (Rev 21:2). We are foreigners and pilgrims in this work, aspiring by faith to reach a heavenly land (Ps 39:12). By faith, Sarah was able to give birth to her son, Isaac, although she was old (Heb 11:11). So, though spiritually dead, we receive power from Christ to conceive spiritually. For, just as Christ was conceived in the womb of the Virgin Mary, so, in faith, the soul that keeps itself pure from worldly company is spiritually born. By faith, Abraham offered up Isaac (Heb 11:17). So, we offer up our own will, the beloved son of the soul. By faith, we spiritually offer and sacrifice ourselves, because those desiring to follow Christ must practice self-denial, renouncing their own wills, their own honor, and their self-love. By faith, Isaac blessed Jacob (Heb 11:20). So, by faith we are made partakers of all divine blessings, for in the seed of Abraham, in other words, in Christ, all people are blessed. By faith, Joseph prophesied about the exodus of the Israelites from Egypt and gave orders concerning the burial of his bones (Heb 11:22). So, by faith we await our exodus from this spiritual Egypt, that is to say, the world, and the blessed resurrection of the body. By faith, the child Moses was protected from death for three months (Heb 11:23). So, faith hides us from the tyranny of Satan until at last we are led into the royal palace of God and received as spiritual kings. By faith, Moses chose to be a participant in the misfortune of his people rather than to live in the glory of Egypt (Heb 11:25). So, faith arouses in us contempt of glory, honor, riches, and the pleasures of this world, and a desire for the heavenly kingdom. By faith, we choose the humiliation of Christ rather than the treasures of this world. By faith, Moses left Egypt and did not fear the wrath of the king (Heb 11:27). So, faith endows us with courage and strengthens us so that, not terrified by the tyrants of this world, we obey the calling of God with a bold and steady soul. By faith, Israel celebrated the Passover (Heb 11:28). So, by faith we celebrate our Passover. Christ, whose flesh is food indeed and whose blood is drink indeed, was sacrificed as our Passover. By faith, Israel crossed the Red Sea (Heb 11:29). So, by faith we pass through the sea of this world. By faith, the walls of Jericho fell down (Heb 11:30). So, by faith we pull down all the fortifications of Satan. By faith, Rahab was saved. So, in the total destruction of this world, we are protected by faith from annihilation. By faith, the fathers vanquished kingdoms, stopped the mouths of lions, extinguished the power of fire (Heb 11:33). So, by faith we destroy the kingdom of Satan, evade the fury and snare of the infernal lion, and are freed from the burning fire of hell.

Therefore, faith is not an empty opinion or profession but a lively and efficacious apprehension of Christ, which is set forth in the gospel. It is the fullest conviction of the grace of God, rest and peace for our trusting heart, relying on the merit of Christ. This faith is born from the seed of the divine word, for faith and spirit are one. Furthermore, the word is the vehicle of the Holy Spirit. Fruit corresponds to the nature of the seed, and faith is the divine fruit. Therefore, it is necessary for the divine seed, namely, the word, to be present. Just as light arose from the word of God in creation, for God spoke and there was light, so the light of faith arises from the light of the divine word. "We will see light in your light," the Psalmist says (Ps 36:9).

Faith conjoins us to Christ, unites us with Christ, and for that reason it is also mother of all virtues in us. Where faith is, there is Christ. Where Christ is, there is a holy life that consists of true humility, true gentleness, and true love. Christ and the Holy Spirit cannot be separated. Where the Holy Spirit is, there is true holiness. Where there is no Spirit, Christ is also not there. Where there is no Christ, there is no true faith. Whatever branch does not draw life and moisture from the vine should not be judged to be conjoined with the vine. So, we are not conjoined to Christ through faith unless we draw life and moisture from him.

Faith is a spiritual light. Our hearts are illumined by faith that scatters forth rays of good works. Indeed, where there are no rays of spiritual life, there is also no true light of faith. Evil deeds are works of darkness. Faith is light, and what company can light keep with darkness (2 Cor 6:14)? Evil deeds are Satan's seed. Faith is Christ's seed, so what company can Christ keep with Satan? Our hearts are purified by faith. Therefore, how can there be inner purity of heart where impure words and impure deeds appear outwardly? Faith is our victory (1 John 5:4). Therefore, how can true faith be where the flesh conquers the spirit and leads it captive? Through faith, we have Christ and in Christ eternal life. No one who is impenitent and perseveres in sin is a partaker of eternal life, so how can that person be in Christ or have faith?

Kindle in us, O blessed Christ, the true light of faith so that we may attain eternal life.

Meditation Thirteen

Spiritual Marriage of Christ and the Soul

Jesus is the bridegroom of the soul.

"I will betroth you unto me forever," Christ says to the faithful soul (Hos 2:19). Christ wanted to take part in the wedding celebration in Cana of Galilee in order to show us that he had come to earth to celebrate a spiritual wedding (John 2:2). Rejoice gladly in the Lord and take delight, O faithful soul, in your God, for he has clothed you with the garments of salvation, he has covered you with the robe of righteousness, as a bride adorns herself with necklaces (Isa 61:10). Rejoice because of the honor of your bridegroom; rejoice because of the comeliness of your bridegroom; rejoice because of the bridegroom's love. His honor is the greatest, for he is true God, blessed forever (Rom 9:50). How great then is the dignity of this creature, this faithful soul, that the Creator himself wishes to take her as a spouse! His beauty is the greatest, for he is more handsome in form than the sons of man (Ps 45:2) since they beheld his glory, the glory as of the only-begotten of the Father (John 1:14). His face shone like the sun (Matt 17:2), and his garments were white as snow (Mark 9:3). Grace is also poured onto his lips (Ps 45:2). He is crowned with glory and honor (Ps 8:6). How great then is his mercy, that, though he is the perfection of beauty, he does not disdain to choose for his bride the soul of the sinner deformed by the stain of sins. How great is the majesty of the bridegroom and the infirmity of the bride; the beauty of the bridegroom and the deformity of the bride; and yet the bridegroom's love toward the bride is greater still than the bride's toward her most esteemed and most beautiful bridegroom.

Consider the immense love of your bridegroom, O faithful soul, a love that drew him down from heaven to earth, that bound him to the pillar to be scourged, that affixed him to the cross, that enclosed him in the sepulcher, that dragged him down to hell. What made him do all this, if not love for his bride? But our hearts must be harder than stone and lead that the bond of such love does not draw us upward to God, from whom it first drew God down to us. The bride was naked (Ezek 16:22), nor could she be brought into the royal palace of the heavenly kingdom; but he clothed her with the garments of salvation and righteousness (Isa 61:10). When she lay wrapped in the dirty tunic of her sins and in the most foul rags of her iniquities, he gave her linen, bright and pure, so that she might cover herself. The linen is the righteous deeds of the saints (Rev 19:8); the garment is the righteousness procured by the death and passion of the bridegroom.

Jacob worked fourteen years in order to get Rachel as his wife (Gen 25:27). For almost thirty-four years Christ endured hunger, thirst, cold, poverty, ignominy, insults, chains, whips, the bitterness of gall, death, the cross so that he might acquire the soul as his bride. Samson went down and sought for a wife among the Philistines, who were thought to be the ruin of his people (Judg 14:3). The Son of God descended and chose his bride from people who were damned and destined for eternal death. The people from whom the bride came were hostile to our heavenly Father, but God reconciled them through the most bitter passion. The bride lay trampled in her blood, cast down upon the face of the earth (Ezek 16:22), but he washed her with the water of baptism and cleansed her in the most holy bath (Eph 5:26). He washed away the blood of the bride with his own blood because the blood of the Son of God cleanses from all sins (1 John 1:7). The bride was filthy and disfigured, but he anointed her with oil, in other words, with mercy and grace. The bride was not honorably dressed, but he gave her bracelets and earrings (Ezek 16:11). He adorned her with virtues and various gifts of the Holy Spirit. She was very poor and did not have a dowry. He gave her a spiritual dowry. He accepted from her the dowry of his flesh and led her into heaven. The bride was hungry but he gave her fine flour, honey, and oil (Ezek 16:19). Giving her his own body to eat, he nourished her to eternal life. She is often disobedient and violates her marriage vow. She fornicates with the world and the Devil, but in his immense love he graciously receives her back again as his bride whenever she returns to him in true conversion.

Acknowledge, O faithful soul, so many and such great signs of his infinite love. Cherish, O faithful soul, the love of him who out of love for you descended into the virgin's womb. We ought to love him as much as and more than we love ourselves, since he who gave himself up for us is greater than we are. All of our life should be given back to him, in conformity to him who out of love for us totally conformed himself to us. Whoever does not return love to Christ, who first loved him, is deservedly considered most ungrateful. Oh, how much we ought to love him who out of love of us disregarded his majesty. Oh, happy the soul that is united to Christ by the bonds of this spiritual marriage: she may securely and confidently apply all the benefits of Christ to herself, just as a wife, in other respects, radiates the reflected honor of her husband.

It is by faith alone that we are made participants in this blessed spiritual union, as it is written, "I will betroth you unto me in faith" (Hos 2:19). Faith grafts us into Christ like branches into a spiritual vine (John 15:2), so that we draw all our life and strength from him; and as those who live together in marriage are no longer two but one flesh (Matt 19:6), so anyone who clings to the Lord through faith is one spirit with him (1 Cor 6:17), because Christ dwells in our hearts through faith (Eph 3:7). Faith, if it is true, is efficacious through love (Gal 5:6). Just as in the Old Testament the high priests were restricted to taking virgins as their wives (Lev 21:7), so this heavenly high priest spiritually unites himself with the virgin soul, which keeps herself whole and unspotted from the embraces of the Devil, the world, and the flesh.

Make us worthy, O Christ, to be admitted someday to the marriage of the Lamb (Rev 19:7). Amen.

Meditation Fourteen

The Mystery of the Incarnation

The cradle of Christ shines.

Let us divert our souls for a while from temporal things and contemplate the mystery of the nativity of the Lord. The Son of God descends to us from heaven so that we might attain the adoption of sons (Gal 4:5). God became human so that humans might become partakers of divine grace and of a divine nature (2 Pet 1:4). Christ wished to be born in the evening period of the world, in order to make known that the benefit of his incarnation does not concern this present life but rather eternal life. He wished to be born at the time of peaceful Augustus because it is he who made peace with God for the human race. He wished to be born at the time of Israel's servitude because it is he who is the true liberator and vindicator of his people. He wished to be born under the rule of an alien lord inasmuch as his reign is not of this world (John 18:36). He is born of a virgin so that he might signify that he is not conceived or born except in the hearts of those who are spiritual virgins (2 Cor 11:2), whose minds do not cling to the world or the Devil but to God by one Spirit. He is born pure and holy so that he might sanctify our impure and contaminated birth. He is born of a virgin betrothed to a man to show the honor of marriage as a divine institution. He is born in the darkness of night because it is he who was the true light of the world, illuminating the darkness. He is placed in a manger because it is he who is the true food of our soul. He is born among oxen and asses so that humans who were reduced to beasts of burden through sin might be led back to pristine dignity. He is born in Bethlehem, which means City of Bread, because it is he who brought with him the richest food of divine benefits. He is the firstborn and only-begotten of his mother on earth, because, according to his divine nature, he is firstborn and only-begotten of his Father in heaven. He is born poor and needy so that he might prepare us for heavenly riches (2 Cor 8:9). He is born in a lowly cattle stall so that he might lead us to the palace of the heavenly court. He is sent from heaven as messenger of so much favor because no one on earth was able to understand the magnitude of this.

One who holds a divine office is also deservedly the messenger of heaven. The angels rejoice that, because of the incarnation of the Son of God, they are able to have us as companions in their happiness. Such a miracle is first announced by shepherds because the true shepherd of souls came to lead the lost sheep back onto the right way. The matter of great joy is announced to those who are despised and lowborn because none can be partakers who are not displeased with themselves in their own eyes. This birth is announced among those who are watching their flocks because those who are partakers of such a gift are not those who snore away in their sins but those whose hearts are attentive to God. The choir of the heavenly hosts, which was made miserably sad by the fault of our first parent, is now jubilant. The clarity of that Lord and King appears in the heavens though in his lowliness he was despised by people on earth. The angel called upon the shepherds to abandon their fear because he who was born was to clear away all causes of fear. Joy is announced from heaven because the author and giver of all joy has been born. They are called upon to rejoice because the enmity between God and humans, which is the cause of all sadness, has been removed. God, whom our first parent sought to violate by an improper transgression of a command, is glorified in the highest. True peace is imparted by this birth because, in the past, humans were enemies of God, were previously at odds with their own conscience and mutually in disagreement with one another. True peace is returned to earth because he who held us as captives has been vanquished.

Let us go with the shepherds to the manger of Christ, in other words, the church, and let us find this little infant wrapped in swaddling clothes, that is to say, enclosed in the Sacred Scriptures. Let us also, with Mary the holy mother of the Lord, ponder the words about such a mystery, and let us continually call them to mind each day (Luke 2:19). Let us join in with the surrounding angel voices and give thanks for such benefits. Let us be jubilant and rejoice with all the host of heaven. For, if the angels rejoice for our sake, how much more will the rejoicing be for us for whom this infant was born and given. If the Israelites lifted up their voices and shouted when the ark of the covenant was brought to them (2 Sam 6:16), for the ark is a figure and foreshadowing of the incarnation of the Lord, how much more ought we to rejoice to whom the Lord himself descended by the assumption of our flesh? If Abraham rejoiced when he saw the day of the Lord, and the Lord appeared to him, having assumed human form for a time, what ought we to do when now he joined our nature to himself by a perpetual and indissoluble bond?

Let us marvel at the immense goodness of God, who, when we were not able to ascend to him, wished to descend to us. Let us marvel at the immense power of God, who was able to make one perfect union from two very different natures, that is to say, one divine and one human, so that he is now, one and the same, God and human. Let us marvel at the immense wisdom of God, who was able to find a way for our redemption when neither angel nor human could see a way. An infinite good was offended; an infinite satisfaction was required. Humanity offended God, so a satisfaction was required of humanity, but such an infinite satisfaction could not be discharged by humanity, nor could divine justice be satisfied without an infinite price. Therefore, God became man so that the one who sinned might offer satisfaction, and the one who was infinite might pay the infinite price. Let us marvel at this stupendous balance of justice and divine mercy, which no creature could find before God was made manifest or fully comprehend after it was made manifest. Let us marvel at this but not probe too curiously. Let us desire to look into this closely even though we cannot totally grasp it. Let us acknowledge our ignorance rather than want to deny the power of God.

Meditation Fifteen

The Salutary Benefits of the Incarnation

Be grateful for redemption through Christ.

"I announce to you a great joy," says the angel at the birth of our Savior (Luke 2:10). Truly, it is great and greater than human intelligence can grasp. It was the greatest evil that we were held as captives under the wrath of God, under the power of the Devil, and subject to eternal damnation. This evil was all the greater because humans were either ignorant of how great the evil was or were untroubled by it. Now, truly, a great joy is announced to us because one who has come into the world has freed us from all these evils. The physician comes to the sick, the redeemer to the captives, the way to those who have strayed, life to the dead, and salvation to the condemned. Just as Moses was sent from the Lord to the people of Israel when they needed to be freed from slavery in Egypt (Exod 3:10), so now Christ has been sent from the Father to rescue the whole human race from captivity by the Devil. Just as a dove brought back a small branch from dry land to the ark of Noah after the flood (Gen 8:11), so Christ came into the world to preach peace and to reconcile the human race with God. Therefore, it is right that we should rejoice when we imagine the great mercy of God. What will he, who loved us so much that while we were still enemies he did not disdain assuming our nature into the closest embrace with his divinity, deny to those when joined to them through participation in their flesh? Whoever has hatred for his own flesh (Eph 5:29)? Therefore, how can he withhold that great and infinite mercy from us when we have now been made partakers of his own nature?

Who can comprehend the greatness of this mystery by thought, still less express it by words? Here is the greatest sublimity and the greatest vileness, the greatest power and the greatest weakness, the greatest majesty and the greatest fragility. What is more sublime than God or viler than humanity? What is more powerful than God or weaker than humanity? What is more glorious than God or more fragile than humanity? But, that utmost power found a way for all these to be conjoined when that utmost justice required such a necessary union. Still, who can comprehend the magnitude of this mystery? An infinite price of equal value was required to pay for human offenses because humanity had turned itself away from the infinite good, which is God. But what can be equal in value to an infinite God? Therefore, infinite justice took from itself, as it were, a price of equal value to itself; furthermore, God the creator suffered in the flesh so the flesh of the creature would not suffer for eternity. The infinite good was dishonored and only a mediator of infinite power could intercede. Yet, what is infinite besides God? Therefore, God himself reconciled the world to himself (2 Cor 5:19), God himself became the mediator. God himself redeemed the human race by his blood (Acts 20:28).

Who can comprehend the magnitude of this mystery? The highest creator was offended, and the creature was not concerned about propitiation or reconciliation. The very one who was offended also became the reconciler by the assumption of the creature's flesh. Humanity abandoned God and, becoming an enemy of God, turned to the Devil, but the very one who was abandoned attentively seeks out the deserter and most generously invites humanity to come back to him again. Humanity had withdrawn from that infinite good and had fallen into infinite evil, but the very one who was the infinite good, having offered the infinite price of redemption, frees the creature from that infinite evil. Does this infinite mercy not surpass the thought and understanding of finite humanity? Our nature has been made more glorious through Christ than it was stained by the sin of Adam. We received more in Christ than we lost in Adam. Sin was abundant, but divine grace was superabundant (Rom 5:20). We lost our innocence in Adam; we received full righteousness in Christ. Some marvel at divine power, but divine generosity is more marvelous, although to God power and mercy are equal in that both are infinite. Some marvel at creation, but it pleases me more to marvel at redemption, although both creation and redemption are actions of infinite power. It is a great thing that God created humans who did not deserve anything because they did not yet exist. Still, for God to redeem humans who deserved punishment and to take upon himself the satisfaction of the debt seems to me to be even greater. It is amazing that God formed our flesh and our bones were formed for us. It is still more amazing that God himself willed to become flesh of our flesh and bone of our bones.

O my soul, be grateful to your God that he created you when you were nothing, redeemed you when you were under condemnation for your sins, and prepared heavenly joy for you if you cling to Christ through faith.

Meditation Sixteen

The Spiritual Refreshment of the Godly

What is God to the soul? Light, medicine, food.

Our most gracious God has prepared a great banquet, but those who come to it must have hungry hearts (Luke 14:16). No one can understand the sweetness of the heavenly banquet who has not tasted it. No one tastes it who does not desire to eat. To believe in Christ is to come to the heavenly banquet, but no one can believe who, having recognized sin, is not truly contrite and repents. Contrition is spiritual hunger of the soul. Faith is spiritual food.

God gave manna, the bread of angels, to the Israelites in the desert (Exod 16:4). In this banquet of the New Testament, God gives heavenly manna to us, in other words, his grace, pardon for sin, and, indeed, also his Son, the Lord of the angels. Christ is the true bread of heaven who descends from heaven so that he might give life to the world (John 6:51). One who is full of the husks that pigs eat (Luke 15:16), that is to say, the delights of this world, does not desire that heavenly sweetness. The outward nature does not perceive what is sweet to the inner nature. In the desert God gave his manna in the place where all earthly food, in other words, where all earthly consolation of the soul, was taken away. [In the parable of the great banquet] those who had wives avoided coming (Luke 14:20), while chaste virgins, that is to say, souls not clinging either to the Devil or the delights of the world, go to this banquet. "I have promised you as a chaste virgin to one man," says the Apostle (2 Cor 11:2). Our soul, then, ought not to indulge in spiritual adultery so that God can contract a spiritual marriage with it. Those who persist with the desire to look after their fields are reluctant to come (Luke 14:18). Those who love the pleasures of the world do not long for that heavenly sweetness. Desire is the food of the soul. Our soul does not approach this mystical banquet unless it has the desire to do so. The soul cannot be full of the consolations of this world and at the same time desire the heavenly sweetness. When the rich young man heard that he had to give up the riches to which his soul clung, on account of Christ, he went away sad (Matt 19:22). Christ, the heavenly Elijah, does not pour in the oil of heavenly sweetness unless the vessel has previously been entirely emptied (2 Kgs 4:3).

Love of God does not enter the soul unless all self-love and love of the world have previously been expelled. Where our treasure is, there is our heart (Matt 6:21). If you have the world for your treasure, your heart is in the world. The power of love unites. If you love the world, you will be worldly. If you love heaven, you will be heavenly. Those who buy and trade oxen do not come to Christ (Luke 14:19).

Those who cling with their hearts to riches do not search for heavenly riches. The riches of this world fulfill the desires of the soul with a certain kind of false satisfaction such that it does not seek in God that true satisfaction that alone assuages its appetite. All the riches of this world consist in created things—silver, gold, buildings, lands, and herds. However, nothing created truly satisfies our soul because it is superior to all created things that have been established for its use. How inadequate created things are in filling and satisfying our desires is made clear at death, when we are separated from all creatures. It is amazing for us to cling so firmly to created things when they cling to us so weakly and precariously. When Adam turned himself from the consolation of God and sought delight in the tree of the knowledge of good and evil, he was expelled from paradise (Gen 3:24). If our soul turns from God to creatures, it is deprived of the consolation of heaven and inwardly kept away from the tree of life.

Truly, what awaits those who neglect this banquet? The world passes away and all who cling to it (1 John 2:17). Created things pass away and all who place their hope on them. The heavenly Father has sworn that they who prefer oxen, fields, wives, in other words, whatever is earthly, to the sweetness of the heavenly banquet will not taste that meal (Luke 14:24). After the meal, no other food is prepared. No other remedy remains for those who neglect Christ. They are punished with eternal hunger and live in eternal darkness. Those who do not want to hear Christ calling, "Come to me all you who labor and are burdened" (Matt 11:28), will sometimes hear him rebuke them, saying, "Go, you cursed ones, into the eternal fire" (Matt 25:41). The people of Sodom were consumed by fire (Gen 19:24). When they were called to this banquet by Lot's address, they refused to come. The fire of divine wrath, which lasts for all eternity, will consume those who, having been called by the gospel, spurn this. The virgins, going out to the bridegroom, whose lamps were devoid of oil, join together in making excuses for their delay (Matt 25:8). Meanwhile, the door is closed. The heart that is not filled with the oil of the Holy Spirit in this world will not be admitted by Christ to his joy, because the door of leniency, the door of mercy, the door of consolation, the door of hope, the door of grace, the door of good works will be closed to it.

Furthermore, there is a certain internal call of Christ. Fortunate is the one who hears it! Christ often knocks on the door of our heart with holy longings, devout sighs, and godly thoughts (Rev 3:20). Fortunate is the one who opens when he knocks. As soon as you feel some desire for heavenly grace in your heart, conclude for certain that Christ knocks on your heart, and let him in so that he does not pass by and afterward close the door of his mercy to you. As soon as you feel some small flame of pious thoughts in your heart, judge that it was lit by the fervor of divine love, which is the Holy Spirit. Keep that flame alive and tend it so that it grows into a fire of love, so that you do not extinguish the Spirit and impede the work of the Lord (1 Thess 5:19). Whoever destroys the temple of the Lord will undergo his most severe judgment. Our heart is the temple of the Lord (1 Cor 3:17). It is destroyed when a person refuses to give a place to the Holy Spirit calling within through the Word. The prophets in the Old Testament were able to hear the Lord speaking within. In the New Testament all of the truly godly feel the inner moving and drawing of that Spirit. Blessed are all who hear and follow.

Meditation Seventeen

The Fruits of Baptism

Baptism is a sacred cleansing.

Be mindful, faithful soul, of the great grace of God offered to you in the salutary washing of baptism. Baptism is the washing of regeneration (Titus 3:5). Therefore, whoever has been made wet by the washing of baptism is no longer fully in the garments of fleshly birth but, having been born from God, in other words, through water and the Spirit (John 3:5), is now also a son of God and, being a son, is also an heir of eternal blessing. As the eternal Father proclaims at the baptism of Christ, "This is my beloved Son" (Matt 3:17), so all who believe and are baptized are adopted as sons (Rom 8:14). Just as at the baptism of Christ the Holy Spirit appeared in the form of a dove, so also the Spirit is present at our baptism and bestows power upon us. Indeed, the Spirit is given to believers and effects a new movement within them such that they are as wise as serpents and as innocent as doves (Matt 10:16). As it was at the time of creation, so it is also in our regeneration. In the first creation of all things, the Spirit of the Lord hovered over the waters and conferred on them a living power (Gen 1:2); so also in the water of baptism the Holy Spirit is present and makes it a salutary means of our regeneration. Our Savior, Christ himself, wished to be baptized in order to testify that we are made members of his body through baptism. Often medicine is applied to the head so that other members of the body might be made well. Christ is our spiritual head and took upon himself the medicine of baptism for the healing of the mystical body. In circumcision God entered into a covenant with his people in the Old Testament (Gen 17:11). So, through baptism, we enter into a covenant with God in the New Testament because baptism has taken the place of circumcision (Col 2:11–12). Whoever is in covenant with God need not fear the accusation of the Devil. In baptism Christ is put on (Gal 3:27). Hence, the saints are said to have whitened their robes in the blood of the Lamb (Rev 7:14). The perfect righteousness of Christ is the most beautiful garment. Whoever, therefore, is covered by this garment need not fear the stain of sins.

There was a pool in Jerusalem near the sheep market into which an angel descended at certain times and stirred up the waters (John 5:2). Whoever descended first after the disturbance was healed from any kind of disease. The water of baptism is such a pool that heals from the disease of all sins when the Holy Spirit descends into it and stirs it by the blood of Christ, who was made a sacrifice for us, just as, in former times, the sacrificial animals were washed in that pool in Jerusalem. Around the baptism of Christ, the heavens were opened (Matt 3:16); so also at our baptism the door of heaven is opened. At the baptism of Christ the whole blessed Trinity was present, as also happens at our baptism. And so, in the word of promise, which is bound to the element of water, faith receives the grace of the Father who adopts us, the merit of the Son who cleanses us, and the efficacious work of the Holy Spirit who regenerates us.

Pharaoh and all of his army were submerged in the Red Sea, but the Israelites crossed over safely and unharmed (Exod 14:28). So, in baptism, all of the army of vices is submerged and the faithful arrive safely at the promised inheritance of the heavenly kingdom. Therefore, baptism is also that sea of glass that John saw (Rev 4:6), for, through it, the splendor of the Son of righteousness enters our minds in the same way as through glass. So it was that this sea was in front of the throne of the Lamb. The throne of the Lamb is the church, through which, alone, the saints have the grace of baptism. The prophet Ezekiel saw waters leading from the temple that vivified and cleansed all things (Ezek 47:1). In the spiritual temple of God, which is the church, the salutary waters of baptism still gush forth, into the depths of which our sins are thrown (Mic 7:19). All who come into that torrent are cleansed and made alive. Baptism is a spiritual flood into which all sinful flesh is plunged. The unclean raven, the Devil, withdraws, and the dove, or Holy Spirit, truly flies down with an olive leaf (Gen 8:7–8); in other words, it breathes peace and tranquility into the mind. Be mindful, therefore, faithful soul, of this great grace offered to you in baptism and give thanks, as you ought, to God.

Moreover, the richer the grace conferred on us through baptism, the more diligently we should guard the gift conferred. We are buried with Christ through baptism into death (Rom 6:4), so that just as Christ was raised from death to the glory of the Father, we also might walk in newness of life. We are made well; therefore, we should sin no more so that nothing worse happens to us (John 5:14). We have put on the righteousness of Christ, that most precious garment by far. Therefore, we should not befoul it with the stain of sins. Our old nature is crucified and put to death in baptism. Therefore, a new nature lives. We are regenerated and our minds are renewed by the Spirit in baptism, so the flesh should not have dominion over the Spirit. The old has passed away; behold all things have become new (2 Cor 5:17). For that reason, do not let the oldness of the flesh prevail over the newness of the Spirit. We have been made sons of God through spiritual regeneration. Therefore, let us live in such a way as is worthy of the Father. We have been made a temple of the Holy Spirit. Consequently, let us prepare a place for such a dear guest. We have been received into the covenant of God. As a result, we should beware lest we serve as a soldier of the Devil and so be cut off from the covenant of grace.

Accomplish all this in us, O blessed Trinity. One God who has given such grace in baptism, give us also perseverance in such grace.

Meditation Eighteen

Salutary Participation in the Body and Blood of Christ

The flesh of Christ is the fountain of life.

"Whoever eats my flesh and drinks my blood will live eternally," Christ says (John 6:54). It is altogether a great benefit of our Savior that he not only assumed our flesh and carried it to the throne of heavenly glory, but also that he nourishes us with his body and blood to eternal life. O what a salutary delight of the soul! O what a desirable feast! O heavenly and angelic food!

Although the angels desire to look into that great mystery (1 Pet 1:12), Christ has taken the seed of Abraham, not angels, unto himself (Heb 2:16). Our Savior is nearer to us than to the angels, for we know his love for us in that he gave his Spirit to us, and not only his Spirit but also his body and blood (1 John 4:13). For, so he says of the bread and wine of the Eucharist: "Truly, this is my body, this is my blood" (Matt 16:26:26). How could the Lord forget those whom he redeemed by his body and blood, whom he nourished with his body and blood! Whoever eats the flesh and drinks the blood of Christ remains in Christ and Christ in that person (John 6:56).

Therefore, I do not marvel so much that the hairs on our heads are numbered (Matt 10:30), our names are written in heaven (Luke 10:20), that we are written in the hand of God (Isa 49:16) and carried in his bosom as in a mother's (Isa 46:3), because we are nourished by the body and blood of Christ. The worth of our souls must be really great if they are nourished by the precious *lutron* (ransom) of their redemption. The worth of our bodies must also be great if they are dwelling places redeemed and fed until satiated by the body of Christ. They are temples of the Holy Spirit and habitations of the most sacred Trinity. It is not possible that they will remain in the grave, since they are nourished by the body and blood of our Lord. Here, in this most grand food, we eat him, but rather than his changing into our body, we are changed into his. We are members of Christ who are made alive by his Spirit and nourished by his body and blood. This is the bread that descends from heaven and gives life to the world (John 6:33). Whoever eats of it will not hunger in eternity. This is the bread of grace and mercy. Whoever eats of it will taste and see how the Lord is good (Ps 34:8) and will receive from his fullness grace for grace (John 1:16). This is the bread of life that is not only living but also life-giving, for whoever eats of it will live eternally. This is the bread that descends from heaven (John 6:58), that is not only heavenly but also makes them become heavenly guests. Those who eat it rightly and in the Spirit will be heavenly guests because they will not die but will be resuscitated in that new day. They will not rise again to judgment, because whoever eats of this bread does not come to judgment. They will not be condemned, because there is no condemnation for those who are in Christ but rather life and salvation (Rom 8:1). Whoever eats the flesh of the Son of man and drinks his blood has life and lives because of Christ (John 6:53, 57). His flesh is true food and his blood is true drink (John 6:55). Therefore, let us not be filled with our own works but with the food of the Lord. Let us not be intoxicated with the rich drink of our houses but with the Lord.

Here is the true fount of life. Whoever drinks this water will have a fount of life that flows within to eternal life (John 4:14). All you who thirst, come to this water, and you who have no money, hasten to buy and eat. Let the thirsty come (Isa 55:1). Come also, my thirsting soul, distressed by the heat of sins. What if you are destitute of any tokens of merit, hasten all the more. Forsaking your merit, hasten more fervently to the merit of Christ. Hasten, therefore, and buy without money. Here is the chamber of Christ and the soul, from which no sins can deter us, and into which none of our merits also enters. What can our merits be? "They expend money for that which is not bread and work for what will not satisfy," the Prophet says (Isa 55:2). Our works do not satisfy, and grace cannot be bought by the tokens of our merits.

Hear, therefore, my soul. Eat what is good and you will take delight in rich food. These words of mine are spirit and truth (John 6:63), and they are words of eternal life. The cup of blessing is the communion of the blood of Christ, and the bread we break is a participation in the body of the Lord (1 Cor 10:16). We cling to the Lord. Therefore, we are one spirit with him (1 Cor 6:17). We are united with him, not only by his sharing in our nature but also through a participation in his body and blood (John 6:53). Thus, I do not say with the Jews, "How can his flesh be given to us to eat?" Rather, I exclaim, "How does the Lord distribute his body to us for eating and his blood for drinking?" I do not pry into the majesty but honor his goodness. I believe in his presence, though I am ignorant about the mode of his presence. With certainty, I know it to be most close and deep.

We are members of his body; flesh of his flesh, bones of his bones (Eph 5:30). He lives in us and we in him. My soul desires to sink into the contemplation of this more profound abyss. It has not yet found out how and with what words to express or explain this goodness, but it is utterly overwhelmed by consideration of the great grace of the Lord and the glory of the blessed.

Meditation Nineteen

The Mystery of the Lord's Supper

To marvel, not to probe, is true wisdom.

In the holy Supper of the Lord, a mystery is placed before us that should astonish us and should be adored by all means. It is a treasure and storehouse of divine grace. We know that a tree of life was planted by God; its fruit might have preserved our first parents and their posterity in the blessedness of the immortality with which they were created (Gen 2:9). For, a tree of the knowledge of good and evil was set in paradise, but that same one, which was given by God for salvation and life and for the exercise of obedience, was also the occasion of their death and condemnation when they pitifully submitted to the incitements of Satan and their desires. Similarly, here again, in the Lord's Supper a true tree of life has been prepared, a sweet wood, the leaves of which are medicine and the fruit of which is for salvation (Ezek 47:12). Its sweetness destroys all evils and also the bitterness of death. Manna was given to the Israelites so that they might be nourished by a food from heaven (Exod 16:15). In the Lord's Supper, though, is that true manna, which descends from heaven so that the world might be given life. Here is the bread of heaven and the food of angels. Whoever eats of it will never hunger

(John 6:35). The Israelites had the ark of the covenant and the mercy seat where they were able to hear the Lord speaking face to face (Exod 25:21, 22). Here, [in the Lord's Supper,] is the true ark of the covenant, the most holy body of Christ in which all the treasures of knowledge, understanding, and wisdom are hidden (Col 2:3). Here is the true mercy seat (Rom 3:25) in the blood of Christ, who brought it about that we might be loved in the Beloved (Eph 1:6).

He not only speaks to us through inner consolation but dwells in us. He does not feed us with the manna of heaven but rather with himself. Here is the true gate of heaven and the ladder of the angels (Gen 28:12), for surely, can it be that heaven is greater than he who is in heaven? Is heaven united more nearly to God than the flesh and human nature that he assumed? Heaven is certainly the throne of God (Isa 66:1), but the Holy Spirit rested in the nature assumed by Christ. God is in heaven, but the fullness of divinity dwells in Christ (Col 2:9). Truly, this is the great and infallible pledge of our salvation. He did not have anything greater that he was able to give. For what could be greater than himself? What is united more closely to him than his human nature, which he assumed into the fellowship of the blessed Trinity and which was made the treasury of heavenly blessings? What is so nearly bound to him as his body and blood? Yet, he truly refreshes us miserable little worms with this celestial food and makes us partakers of his nature. Why not also then of his grace? Who can possibly hate one's own flesh? How then can the Lord possibly despise us who feed on his flesh and his blood? How could he possibly forget those to whom he gave the pledge of his body? How could Satan possibly overthrow us when we feed on this heavenly food so that we might not fail in battle?

Christ cares for us because he purchased us for a dear price. He cares for us because he feeds us with dear and precious [food]. He cares for us because we are of the same flesh and members of his own body. This is the one cure-all for all spiritual diseases, this *tes athanasias pharmakon* (medicine of immortality), for what sin is so great that the holy flesh of God cannot atone for it? What sin is so great that the living flesh of Christ cannot heal it? What sin is so mortal that it cannot be taken away by the death of the Son of God? What arrow of the Devil is so deadly that it cannot be quenched in this fount of divine grace? What stain on the conscience is so great that it cannot be cleansed by his blood? The Lord was present with the Israelites in a cloud and fire (Exod 13:21). Here, however, there is no cloud but rather the sun of righteousness itself (Mal 4:2), the present light of our souls. Instead of the fire of divine wrath, here one feels the heat of love that does not retreat from us but makes its home with us (John 14:23).

Our first parents were introduced to paradise, that most fragrant and pleasant garden that is a prototype of eternal blessedness (Gen 2:8), so that, being mindful of this divine goodness, they might discharge the obedience owed to their creator. Behold how this place is more than paradise, for the creature is filled by the flesh of the creator. The remorseful conscience is cleansed by the blood of the Son of God. The members of Christ, the head, are fed by the body of Christ. The faithful soul is nourished at a divine and heavenly banquet. The holy flesh of Christ, which the angels adore in one person, which the archangels venerate, which makes the principalities tremble, and which the powers admire, is our spiritual food. Let the heavens rejoice and the earth exult (Ps 96:11), but even more so the faithful soul to whom such great gifts have been given.

Meditation Twenty

Serious Preparation before Use of the Holy Supper

Be a prudent guest of Christ.

It is neither a common meal nor the banquet of some king we are dealing with, but rather the most holy mystery of the body and blood of Christ. Therefore, special preparation is required of us, lest we meet with death instead of life and receive judgment instead of mercy.

How that most holy patriarch [Abraham], distinguished for his faith, trembles when the Son of God appears in the form of a man and announces his intention to destroy Sodom (Gen 18:2). Here, the Lamb of God is put forth, not just for viewing but to be tasted and eaten. When Uzziah imprudently approached the ark of the covenant, he was immediately struck with leprosy (2 Chr 16:16).

Therefore, is it amazing that judgment comes upon one who eats this bread and drinks this wine unworthily? For, this is the true ark of the new covenant, which the old one prefigured. Therefore, the Apostle teaches true preparation in one word: "Examine yourself," he says, "and only then eat of this bread" (1 Cor 11:28). Every godly examination should be undertaken according to the norm of divine scripture. This is also the case concerning this, which Paul requires.

Therefore, let us in the first place consider our infirmity. What is a human being? Dust and ashes (Gen 18:27). We are born from the earth, live from the earth, and return to the earth. What is a human being? A stinking seed, a sack of dung, and food for worms. A man is born to work, not to honor. A man is born of a woman and, for this reason, is guilty. He lives for a brief time and is thus fearful (Job 14:1). Life is full of misery and thus with weeping. Truly there are many miseries, because he is both body and soul. A man does not know his origin or his end. We are like plants that live but a short while in the summer. Although this life is brief, its pains and labors are by no means brief.

Let us in the second place consider our unworthiness. Certainly any creature relative to the Creator is a shadow, a dream, a nothing, and so also is a man (Ps 39:6). But, a man is unworthy in more and graver ways: by his sins he has offended his creator. God is naturally and essentially righteous. Therefore, God is naturally and essentially angered by sins. What else are we but stubble for this consuming fire (Deut 4:24)? How can our stinking actions stand up? How can our iniquities endure when you set them before you or our errors when you place them in the light of your face? God is infinite and always the same in his infinite righteousness and infinite wrath. If God is great in all his works, so he is also in his wrath, his righteousness, and his vengeance. Will he who did not act sparingly toward his own Son ever spare a mere creature? Will he who did not act sparingly toward the most Holy ever spare a worthless servant? Sin is so odious before God that he even punishes it in those he loves the most, as is seen in what happened to Lucifer, the foremost of the angels.

Furthermore, let us not only examine ourselves but also this blessed bread, which is the communication of the body of Christ. Then, the fount of grace, the inexhaustible spring of mercy, will appear. God will surely not disregard those who are made partakers of his flesh, for who ever hates his own flesh (Eph 5:29)? Therefore, these holy foods transform our souls. These holy foods make us humans divine, until in the end, as partakers of future blessing, we will be made *Theou holou kai monou choretikoi kai holoi theoeideis* (wholly like God and filled with all the fullness of God) (Gregory Nazianzus, *Oratio* 30). What we have here in faith and mystery, we will have there in actual fact and most openly. Our bodies, also, which are temples of the Holy Spirit and are sanctified and vivified by the indwelling of the body and blood of Christ, have attained this dignity, that they may be able to see God face to face (1 Cor 13:12). This most holy medicine heals all the wounds of sin. This vivifying flesh surpasses all mortal sin. This is the most holy seal of the divine promise, which we are able to show at the divine judgment. We glory in this all-sufficient pledge, given to us for eternal life. If the body and blood of Christ are presented to us, so also are all the benefits provided for us through that holy body and blessed blood. Will he who has given lesser benefits deny us the greater ones? Will he who gave us his Son not give us all things with him?

Therefore, rejoice, you bride, because the time is near when you will be called to the marriage feast of the Lamb (Rev 19:7). Put on the precious robes, receive the nuptial garments, so that you are not found to be naked. That garment is the righteousness of the bridegroom, which we put on in baptism. Our righteousness is as unsuitable to be a nuptial garment as the rag of a menstruating woman would be (Isa 64:60). Therefore, let us fear to wear the most ugly and stinking garments of our works to that solemn marriage feast.

Clothe us, Lord, lest we be found naked (2 Cor 5:30).

Meditation Twenty-One

The Ascension of Christ

It is ours to ascend with Christ.

Ponder, O faithful soul, the ascension of your bridegroom. Christ withdrew his visible presence from his faithful followers so that faith might be exercised; for truly those who believe but do not see are blessed (John 20:29). Where our treasure is, is also where our heart will be (Luke 12:34). Our treasure is Christ in heaven. Therefore, our heart should cling to heavenly things and ponder those things that are above (Col 3:2). With sighs, the bride longs for the return of her bridegroom. So, the faithful soul always longs for that day to come when it will be led to the marriage feast of the Lamb (Rev 19:7). It should trust in the pledge of the Holy Spirit that the Lord left behind at his ascension. It should trust in the body and blood of the Lord, which it receives in the mystery of the Supper, and believe that our body, which is nourished by this incorruptible food, will someday be raised again. What we now believe, we will then see and then our hope will be realized. The Lord is now present to us pilgrims in another form, but we will know and look upon him in a different way in the heavenly fatherland.

Our Savior wished to ascend from the Mount of Olives (Acts 1:12). The olive is a sign of peace and joy. Thus, it was fitting for him to ascend from the Mount of Olives, since he brought tranquility to terrified and troubled consciences by his passion. It was fitting for him to ascend from the Mount of Olives because he was received with great jubilation into the heavenly court. That mountain calls us to heavenly things. We should follow holy desires because we cannot follow him with our bodily feet. Similarly, Moses ascended a mountain to the Lord (Exod 19:3); the holy patriarchs worshiped on a mountain (John 4:20); Abraham chose the mountains when Lot chose a plain (Gen 13:11). The faithful soul should leave behind the plain of this world and struggle by devotion toward the holy mountains of heaven so that it will be able to feel the sweet address of God speaking within, so that it will be able to worship God in spirit in its prayer (John 4:24), so that it will be able to flee with Abraham from the eternal fire prepared for the worldly plain.

Bethany signifies a village of humility and affliction through which it is possible for the approach to the kingdom of heaven to stand open to us, just as Christ made his way to heavenly joy through the village of affliction. Formerly, heaven seemed closed and paradise above seemed guarded by a flaming-red sword (Gen 3:24). Now, Christ the victor opened heaven so that he might show to us the way into the heavenly fatherland, from which we were banished. The disciples stood and, lifting their eyes, gazed toward heaven. So the true disciples of Christ lift the eyes of their heart, contemplating heavenly things.

O Lord Jesus, how glorious is the ending that followed your passion. How happy and sudden is the change. How I saw you suffering then on the Mount of Calvary and how I see you now on the Mount of Olives. There you were alone; here there is a company of many thousands of angels. There you ascended onto the cross; here you are ascending into the clouds to heaven. There you were crucified among thieves; here you are exalted among a choir of angels. There you were affixed by nails to the cross and condemned; here you are free and the liberator of the condemned. There you were dying and suffering; here you are joyful and triumphant.

Christ is our head and we are his members (Eph 5:30). Therefore, be joyful and rejoice, O faithful soul, in the ascension of your head. The glory of the head is also the glory of the members. Where our flesh reigns, there we should believe ourselves to reign.

Meditation Twenty-Two

Homily concerning the Holy Spirit

God seals the elect with the Holy Spirit.

When our Lord ascended to heaven and entered his glory, he sent the Holy Spirit to his disciples on the day of Pentecost (Acts 2:1). Just as in the Old Testament God promulgated his Law by descending to Moses on Mount Sinai (Exod 19:3), so, when the gospel was to be spread throughout the world by the apostles, the Spirit itself descended to the apostles. In the first instance there was thunder and lightning and the most blaring blast of horns because the Law was thundering against our disobedience and declaring us to be answerable to divine wrath. In the second instance there was, however, the more gentle rustling of the wind because the preaching of the gospel cheers the terrified mind. In the first instance there was fear and dread among all the people because the Law brought wrath (Rom 4:5). In the second instance the whole multitude came together and heard of the wonderful works of God because an approach to God was made open through the gospel. In the first instance Jehovah descended in fire, but in a fire of wrath and fury such that the mountain moved violently and smoked (Exod 19:18). In the second instance, however, Jehovah as Holy Spirit descended in fire, but in a fire of love and longing such that the house was not moved by divine wrath but was totally filled with the glory of the Holy Spirit (Acts 2:2). Is it amazing that the Holy Spirit was sent from heaven to bestow sanctification if the Son was sent to liberate the human race? The passion of Christ would have been of little use if the announcement of it were not made through the gospel to the world, for what use is a treasure concealed? Thus, our most merciful Father not only prepared a great benefit through the passion of his Son but also willed to offer it to the whole world through the sending of the Holy Spirit. As a faithful mother offers both breasts to her frail child, so our faithful God sends both his Son and the Holy Spirit to us, miserable sinners.

Therefore, the Holy Spirit came upon the apostles when they were continuing altogether in prayer (Acts 1:14), for it is the Spirit of prayer (Zech 12:10). It is obtained by prayers and impels one to pray. Why? Because it is the bond through which our heart is united with God, just as the Son is united with the Father and the Father with the Son. Love is the shared essence of the Father and the Son. This joining of our spirit with God comes about by faith. Faith, moreover, is the gift of the Spirit. It is obtained by prayer, but true prayer is brought about by the Spirit.

In the temple of Solomon, when incense was burned to the Lord, the glory of the Lord filled the temple (1 Kgs 8:11). So, if you offer the sweet fragrance of prayers to God, he will fill the temple of your heart with the glory of the Holy Spirit. We should marvel here at the mercy and grace of God. The Son intercedes for us (Ps 50:15), and the Holy Spirit prays in us (Gal 4:6). The angels bear our prayers to God, and so all the court of heaven is opened by our prayers (Tobit 12:12). Our merciful God gives the inclination to pray because he gives the Spirit of grace and prayer to us. He also gives the result of prayer because he always clearly hears our prayer, if not according to our will then according to our need.

The Holy Spirit came when they were altogether in one place, for truly it is a Spirit of love and harmony. It joins us to Christ through faith; it joins us to God through love; and it also unites us with our neighbor through loving affection. The Devil, the author of discord and division, separates us from God through sin. Through hate, contention, and strife the Devil separates people from one another. As the Holy Spirit joined a divine and human nature in Christ by his marvelous overshadowing (Luke 1:35), so also it joined humans to God and God to humans by its gifts poured into us. As long as the Holy Spirit remains in a person by its grace and gifts, that person remains united with God. As soon as the first man fell from faith and love through sin and discarded the Holy Spirit with its grace and gifts, he was separated from God and that blessed union destroyed.

Whoever has the Holy Spirit does not hate a brother. Why? Because we are made partakers of the mystical body of Christ through the Spirit. If all the godly are members, who truly can hate a member of his own body (Eph 5:29)? Certainly, whoever is ruled by the Lord's Spirit also loves any enemies. Why? Because whoever clings to God is of one spirit with him (1 Cor 6:17). Truly God lets his sun to rise over both the evil and the good (Matt 5:45) and hates nothing that he has made. Whoever has the Spirit of God is ready to serve all people, do good things for all, and be useful to all because God is also the fount of all mercy and grace toward all people. Now the Holy Spirit truly produces impulses of a particular sort in a person that are of the same quality as itself. Just as the soul animates the body and makes it feel and move, so the Spirit makes a person spiritual. It saturates the mind with sweet and divine delights and directs all members to the following of God and the serving of the neighbor.

A sound was made from heaven that was a sign of the coming of the Holy Spirit because this Holy Spirit is of a heavenly nature, is surely of the same essence as the Father and the Son, and proceeds from the Father and the Son through all eternity. It also makes humans reflect on heavenly things and seek things that are above. Whoever clings to earthly things and is united by love with the world has not yet been made a partaker of this heavenly Spirit. It came under the sign of breath because it supplies living consolation to the afflicted and because we live according to the flesh by the breathing in and out of air. For that reason the Spirit came under the sign of breath, which it bestowed lavishly so that we might live according to our better part. The wind blows where it wishes, and you hear the sound of it but you do not know whence it comes or where it goes (John 3:8). So it is with all who are born of the Spirit. It is also appropriate for that which proceeds by one breath from the Father and the Son from eternity to come by the sign of breath. This breath is forceful because the grace of the Holy Spirit is not feeble but rather a vigorous action. This Holy Spirit moves the godly in which it lives toward all things good (Rom 8:14), and it moves in such a way that they pay no attention to the threats of the tyrant nor to the snares of Satan or the world's hatred. It confers the gift of tongues upon the apostles because their sound was destined to go out into all the earth (Ps 19:4). So then, the confusion of tongues that was the punishment for pride and temerity in building the tower of Babel (Gen 11:7) was lifted and now those nations that were dispersed by diversity of languages are brought together to a unity of faith by the gift of the Holy Spirit. It is appropriate that it came under the sign of tongues because by it the holy people of God were inspired to speak. It spoke in the apostles and placed the word of God in the mouth of the ministers of the church (1 Pet 1:21).

For such gifts the Holy Spirit should be praised and glorified with the Father and the Son forever.

Meditation Twenty-Three

The Dignity of the Church

The church is the bride of Christ.

Consider, O devout soul, what a benefit God offered to you when he called you into the fellowship of the church. "My beloved is the only one," the bridegroom says in the Canticle (Song 6:9). There is truly one because there is only one true and orthodox church, the beloved bride of Christ. Outside of the body of Christ there is no Spirit of Christ (Rom 8:9). Whoever does not have the Spirit of Christ is not one of his. Whoever is not of Christ cannot become a partaker of eternal life. Everyone who was outside the ark of Noah perished in the flood (Gen 7). Everyone who is outside of the spiritual ark of the church is going off to destruction. No one will have God as Father in heaven who does not have the church as mother on this earth. Consider, devout soul, that many thousands of souls descend to hell daily because they are outside the bosom of the church. Your nature has not separated you from them but only the grace of God toward miserable sinners. When palpable darkness enveloped Egypt, there was light only for the Israelites (Exod 10:23). Similarly, the light of divine knowledge is only in the church. Those who are outside the church, living presently in the darkness of ignorance, pass on to the darkness of eternal condemnation in the life to come. Whoever has no portion in the church militant will have no portion in the church triumphant, for these are intimately joined: God, the word, faith, Christ, church, and eternal life.

The holy church of God is a mother, a virgin, and a bride. She is a mother because she gives birth to spiritual sons daily. She is a virgin because she keeps herself pure from connections with the Devil and the world. She is a bride because Christ promised to bind himself to her eternally and gave her the pledge of the Spirit. The church is the ship that carried Christ and his disciples (Matt 8:23), and finally us, to the port of eternal blessedness. The church sails a favorable course through the sea of this world equipped with faith as a rudder. It has God as navigator, the angels as rowers, and carries the choir of all the saints. Erected in its midst as the mast is the cross of salvation, and on it are suspended the sails of the evangelical faith by which, when filled by the Holy Spirit, it is brought to the security of eternal rest. The church is that vine that God planted in the field of this world (Matt 21:33), watered with his blood, surrounded with a hedge of angelic protection, in which he constructed the press of his passion, and from which he removed stones and all offensive things (Isa 5:2). The church is that woman clothed with the sun because she is covered with the righteousness of Christ (Rev 12:1). She tramples the moon under her feet because she looks down upon earthly things that are subject to many changes.

Consider, O devout soul, the great dignity of the church and give the thanks you owe to God. Great indeed are the benefits in the church of God, but these are not accessible to everyone. It is an enclosed garden and a sealed fountain (Song 4:12). None will see the beauty of an enclosed garden unless he is in it. So, none knows these great benefits in the church unless he is in it. This bride of Christ is black on the exterior but beautiful on the inside (Song 1:5). For all the glory of the king's daughter is on the inside. This ship is shaken by the tempest of various persecutions (Matt 8:24). This vine is straightened by being bound and grows by being cut back (John 15:2). The hellish dragon lies in wait for this woman in various ways (Rev 12:7). The church is a beautiful lily but nevertheless among thorns (Song 2:1). The church is a most beautiful garden, but when the north wind of tribulation blows through it, only then do its aromas flow forth. The church is the daughter of God but is quite hated by the world. She awaits a heavenly inheritance and therefore thinks of herself as a pilgrim in this world. She is oppressed during her pilgrimage and keeps silent in oppression. She is strong in her silence and conquers by her courage. The church is a spiritual mother but thinks of herself as standing under a cross, just as Mary, from whom Christ was born into this world, also stood under a cross (John 19:25). The church is a palm tree because it grows all the more under the weight of tribulation and temptation.

Consider, O devout soul, the dignity of the church and beware lest you do anything unworthy of her. She is a mother. Therefore, you should always cling to her breasts. The breasts of the church are the word and the sacraments. The church is a virgin, so if you are a true son of her, abstain from close connections with the world. You are a member of the virginal church. See that you do not expose any virginal members to dishonor and have perverse associations with the Devil through sins. The church is the bride of Christ and all devout souls should therefore take care lest they cling to Satan. You are the bride of Christ; see that you do not lose the pledge given to you by the Holy Spirit. You are the bride of Christ; pray with ceaseless prayers so that the bridegroom will make haste and lead you to the heavenly marriage feast (Matt 25:6). The bridegroom will surely come in the security of night, so be vigilant lest the bridegroom come and find you sleeping and shut the door of eternal salvation in front of you. Light the lamp of your faith lest you find yourself looking for it in vain when the bridegroom comes.

You are sailing in this ship; see to it that you do not fall into the sea of this world before you arrive at the port. You are sailing in this ship; pray that you are not swallowed by the tempest of affliction and the waves of temptation. You are called into the vineyard of the Lord; see that you labor strenuously. Consideration of the denarii you will be paid should lessen the labor of the day (Matt 20:8–10). You are a vine of the Lord; throw away useless branches, the infertile works of the flesh, and consider the whole time of life to be a time for pruning (John 15:1). You are a branch in the true vine, which is Christ. See that you remain in him and bear much fruit, because the heavenly husbandman will destroy the branches that do not bear fruit and will purge those that are fruitful so that they might bear more copiously. You have put on Christ through faith and you are clothed with this sun of righteousness (Gal 3:27; Mal 4:2). See to it that you trample underfoot the moon, that is to say, all earthly things (Rev 12:1), and that you care little for all such things as compared to eternal goods.

O good Jesus, who led us into the church militant, also lead us some day to the church triumphant.

Meditation Twenty-Four

Meditation on Predestination

Election was made in Christ.

As often, O devout soul, as you want to think about your predestination, look at Christ hanging upon the cross, dying for the sins of the whole world and rising for the sake of our justification (Rom 4:25). Begin with Christ lying in the manger and proceed only then, in right order, to your disputation concerning predestination.

God chose us before laying the foundation of the world (Eph 1:4), but that election was nevertheless made in Christ. If, then, you are in Christ by faith, you should not doubt that election pertains to you also. If you firmly cling to Christ with confidence in your heart, you should not have doubts about being among the number of the elect. If you want to investigate the depths of predestination, from the start, beyond the limits of the word, it is truly to be feared that you might fall into profound despair. God, apart from Christ, is a consuming fire (Deut 4:24). Be careful, therefore, not to get too near this fire, lest it consume you. Apart from the satisfaction of Christ, God accuses all with the voice of his Law and condemns all. Be careful, therefore, that you do not derive the mystery of predestination from the Law.

You should not inquire about all the reasons for divine counsels, lest your thoughts seduce you too much. God dwells in inaccessible light (1 Tim 6:16). You should not try to advance thoughtlessly toward him. Nevertheless, God revealed himself to us in the light of the gospel. You can safely inquire there about the knowledge of this secret. In this light you will see the true light (Ps 36:9). Let go of the profundity of this decree, made from eternity, and turn to the clarity of the manifestations made in time. Justification made in time is the mirror of the election made beyond time. Learn from the Law about the wrath of God due to sin. Learn from the gospel about the mercy of God due to the merits of Christ and apply that to yourself through faith. Learn the nature of faith and show it through godly conversation. Learn from the cross about the Father's chastening and support yourself through patience. Only then should you begin to deal with the doctrine of predestination. The Apostle displays this method, so the true disciple of the Apostle should follow this method.

Three things should always be observed concerning this mystery: the mercy of a loving God, the merits of a suffering Christ, and the grace of the Holy Spirit, calling us through the gospel. The mercy of God is universal because he loved the whole world. The earth is full of the mercy of the Lord (Ps 33:5); indeed, it is greater than heaven and earth. It is as great as God himself because God is love (1 John 4:16). It is testified in his word that he wishes the death of no one (Ezek 33:11). As if this were not enough, he also confirmed it with an oath. If you cannot believe it when God promises, then at least believe it when he makes an oath regarding your salvation. He is called the Father of mercy (2 Cor 1:3) because it is his nature to be merciful and forbearing. The cause and origin of this mercy derive from his own nature, but his judging or punishing seem to derive more from something foreign, for it seems that his compassion proceeds differently from his heart than his reproach. The merit of Christ is also universal because he suffered for the sins of the whole world (1 John 2:2). Therefore, what proves the mercy of God more than that he loved us when we still had no being, because it was out of love that we were created? He loved us, moreover, when we were enemies, because it is out of love that he gave us redemption through his Son. To the sinner condemned to eternal torment and not having a way to be redeemed, God the Father says: "Receive my only-begotten Son, given for you." The Son himself says: "Accept me, and redeem yourself." Christ is a flower of the field (Song 2:1), not of a garden, because the fragrance of grace is not enclosed for some but rather open for all. And, lest you doubt the universality of this merit, Christ patiently prayed for those crucifying him and poured out his blood for the very ones who poured out his blood (Luke 23:34). The promises of the gospel are universal because Christ says to all: "Come to me all who labor" (Matt 11:28). What was shown to all is also offered to all. As much as you step in faith toward the benefits you have been offered, so much also will you attain. God denies his grace to no one unless that person, feeling unworthy, refuses it.

Therefore, consider, O faithful soul, these three pillars of predestination and lean on them firmly with the confidence of your heart. Consider the benefits of divine mercy that have been offered in the past and you will not doubt your perseverance to the end. When you were nothing, God created you. When you were condemned through the fall of Adam, he redeemed you. When you lived outside the church in the world, he called you. When you were ignorant, he instructed you. When you went astray, he redirected you. When you sinned, he corrected you. When you stood up, he upheld you. When you fell, he raised you up. When you went forth, he led you. When you came to him, he received you. He showed his forbearance in waiting and readiness in pardoning. The mercy of God precedes you, so hope firmly that it will also follow you. The mercy of God came before you so that you would be healed, and it will also follow you so that you will be glorified. It came before you so that you might live piously and will also follow you that you might live with him in eternity. Why, when you fall, are you not destroyed? Who places a hand under you? Who, if not God? Therefore, also trust in the mercy of God in the future, and hope firmly for the end of your faith, eternal salvation (1 Pet 1:9). For in whose hands might the matter of your salvation more securely rest than in the ones that formed heaven and earth, that are never too short to save (Isa 59:1), the ones from which mercy pours forth, which do not lack openings through which mercy may flow?

Consider, therefore, O devout soul, that we are chosen by God so that we might be holy and blameless. Therefore, the benefit of election does not pertain to those in whom there is no zeal for a holy life. We are chosen in Christ (Eph 1:4). We are in Christ through faith. Faith expresses itself through love (Gal 5:6). Therefore, where there is no love, there is no faith. Where there is no faith, there is no Christ. Where there is no Christ, there is no election. The foundation of God truly stands firm, having this seal. The Lord knows who are his own (2 Tim 2:19). But, whoever calls upon the name of the Lord should turn away from wickedness. No one will tear the sheep of Christ away from his hands, but the sheep of Christ also hear his voice (John 10:27). We are the house of the Lord (Hos 3:6), but we must retain a firm faith and the glory of hope until the end.

O Lord, who has given me the ability to will, give me also the ability to finish.

Meditation Twenty-Five

The Salutary Efficacy of Prayer

Sighs penetrate heaven.

It is a great favor of God that he wishes for the friendly address of prayers from the godly. He gives us the desire to pray and also makes prayer effective. There is great power in prayer that is poured forth on earth but does its work in heaven. The prayer of the righteous is the key to heaven. Prayer ascends, and God's liberation descends. Prayer is a salutary shield by which all the arrows of the adversary are repelled (Eph 6:16). When Moses extended his hands, Israel prevailed against the Amalekites (Exod 17:11). If you extend your hands to heaven, Satan will not prevail against you. Just as a defensive wall is put in place against an enemy, so the wrath of God is broken by the prayers of the saints.

Our Savior himself prayed, not because of some necessity of his own, but in order that he might commend to us the dignity of prayer.

Prayer is a register of our subjection because God admonishes us to offer prayer or some kind of spiritual tribute to him daily. It is the ladder of our ascent because prayer is certainly nothing other than a pilgrimage of the mind to God. It is the shield of our defense because the soul of a living person is protected continually in prayer from the assault of demons. It is the faithful messenger of a legion because prayer ascends to the throne of God and summons him to send help. This messenger is never frustrated in his purpose, because God always hears us, if not according to our will, then to our advantage and salvation. We can surely hope for one of two things: he will give either what we seek or that which he knows to be more useful. God gave his Son, that most excellent gift, though it was unrequested. What will he do then with what is requested? We cannot have doubts about the Father's hearing or the intercession of his Son. In any case, you may enter the tabernacle with Moses to seek counsel from the Lord and quickly you will hear the divine response.

When Christ prayed, he was transfigured (Luke 9:29), so great changes take place in the soul through prayer because prayer is the light of the soul. Often, the one it finds despairing leaves rejoicing. How can you gaze upon the sun unless you first worship the one who sent this most sweet light to your eyes? In what way can you find pleasure at the table unless you have first worshiped the one who bestows and supplies such goods? In what hope will you surrender yourself to nighttime unless you fortify yourself with praying? What fruit can you hope for from your labors if you have not first worshiped him without whom all labor is useless? If, therefore, you desire spiritual and corporeal gifts, ask and you will receive (Matt 7:7). If you desire Christ, seek through prayer and you will find. If you desire to open the door of divine grace and salvation, knock through prayer and it will be opened for you. If, in the desert of this world, the thirst of temptation and scarcity of spiritual goods afflicts you, come to the spiritual rock, which is Christ (1 Cor 10:4) and, through devotion, strike him with the rod of prayer. You will find that the streams of divine grace will extinguish your thirst and your need. You want to offer a sacrifice pleasing to God? Offer prayer. God will find the fragrance sweet and will suppress his wrath (Gen 8:21). Do you want to be engaged with God continuously? Love prayers, which are a spiritual conversation between God and the devout soul. Do you want to taste how sweet the Lord is (Ps 34:9)? Invite the Lord by prayers into the dwelling of your heart.

Prayer is pleasing to God, but only when offered in the right manner. Whoever, therefore, desires to be clearly heard should pray wisely, ardently, humbly, faithfully, and confidently. One should pray wisely, in other words, one should pray for those things that serve the glory of God and the salvation of neighbors. God is omnipotent. Therefore, you should not fix limits on him in your prayers. He is most wise. Therefore, you should not prescribe an order to him. Prayers should not burst forth without thought, but they should follow from foregoing faith. Faith, moreover, is mindful of the Word. What God promises absolutely in the Word, you may pray for absolutely. What he promises conditionally, such as temporal things, you may pray for conditionally. What he has not in any way promised, you should not pray for in any way. God often gives when angry what he denies when well-disposed. Therefore, follow Christ who fully resigns his will to God (Matt 26:39, 44).

You should pray ardently, for how can you require God to hear you when you cannot hear yourself? You want God to be mindful of you when you are not mindful of yourself? When you want to pray, enter into your chamber and close the door (Matt 6:6). This chamber is your heart. You ought to enter into it if you want to pray in the right manner. You ought to close the door, lest thoughts of mundane matters disturb you. Voices do not come to the ears of God unless there is a rightful disposition of the soul. The mind should be so moved by the ardor of meditation that it will far exceed what the tongue expresses. This is the worship in spirit and truth, as the Lord requires (John 4:23). Christ prayed on the mountain (Luke 6:12) and raised his eyes to heaven (John 17:1). So, we ought to turn our eyes from all creatures toward God. You injure God if you pray to him so that he might attend to you but you truly do not attend to yourself. We can pray without ceasing (1 Thess 5:17) if we pray in spirit such that our minds are clearly attentive to God with holy desires. It is not always necessary that we pray loudly, because God also hears the sighs of our heart if he lives in the hearts of the godly. It is not always necessary that we pray with many words, because our thoughts are important. One sigh now and then, excited by the Holy Spirit and offered in the Spirit of God, is more welcome to God than the recitation of long prayers where the tongue speaks but the heart is clearly mute.

Pray humbly so that you trust in the grace of God rather than your own merit. If our prayers rely on our own worthiness, they are condemned. Even if the heart sweats blood in consequence of devotion no one is pleasing to God except in Christ. Therefore, no one also prays rightly except through Christ and on account of Christ. Sacrifices were not pleasing to God if they were not offered on the one altar in the tabernacle (Deut 12:5). So, no prayer pleases God that is not offered on that one altar, Christ. It was promised to the Israelites that their prayers would be heard if they prayed facing Jerusalem (1 Kgs 8:44). So, we should turn ourselves in prayer toward Christ, who is the temple of divinity (John 2:21). When Christ was going to pray in his passion, he threw himself on the ground (Mark 14:35). See how this most holy soul humbled himself in the presence of divine majesty?

You should pray faithfully, so that you are prepared to be destitute of all joy and patient with all punishments. The sooner one prays, the better; the more frequently one prays, the more profitable it will be; the more fervently one prays, the more accepting God will be. You should pray with perseverance, because when the Lord responds more slowly, he is commending the gifts, not denying them. Those things that are desired longer are sweeter when obtained. You should pray confidently so that you are truly asking in faith, and not hesitating.

O most merciful God, who has ordered us to pray, give grace that we might pray rightly.

Meditation Twenty-Six

The Guardianship of Angels

The sacred angels stand by the saints.

Consider, O devout soul, how great that divine grace is that consists of the guardianship of the angels over you. The heavenly Father sends his Son for our liberation; the Son of God is incarnated for our salvation; the Holy Spirit is sent for our sanctification; and the angels are sent for our protection. So, therefore, the whole court of heaven serves us, so to speak, and passes on its benefits to us. I am amazed no longer that all inferior creatures are created for humanity when the angels themselves, which are far more worthy, do not deny their ministries to us. Is it amazing that heaven supplies light to us in the daytime so that we might work and darkness at nighttime so that we might rest when the inhabitants of the kingdom of heaven minister to us? Is it amazing that the air offers us the breath of life and all sorts of birds for our indulgence when the heavenly spirits are busy preserving our life? Is it amazing that water is given to drink, to remove dirt, to moisten the dry land, and to offer us many kinds of fish when the angels are present so that they might revive us from the heat of calamities and temptations? Is it amazing that the earth bears us, nourishes us with bread and wine, fills up our tables with all kinds of fruits and animals when the angels are required to watch over us in all ways, to carry us in their hands lest our foot dash against a stone (Ps 91:12)?

The holy angels were solicitous toward Christ because the angels announced his conception (Matt 4:11). Angels made known his nativity (Luke 2:9–11). Angels commanded the flight to Egypt (Matt 4:11). Angels served him in the desert. Angels ministered to him during his whole ministry of preaching. Angels were with him in the agony of death (Luke 22:43). Angels appeared at his resurrection (Matt 28:2, 5). Angels were present at the ascension. Angels will be present at his future return for judgment. Therefore, just as angels served Christ in the days of his flesh, so also they are solicitous toward all those who are incorporated into Christ through faith. In whatever way they serve the head, so also they serve the members. They gladly serve those on earth whom they will have as associates in heaven. They do not refuse ministry to those with whom they hope to share sweet fellowship.

A band of angels appears to Jacob on his way to his homeland (Gen 32:1). So, the guardianship of angels is applied in this life to the godly who are on the way to their heavenly homeland. Angels protect Daniel in the midst of lions (Dan 6:22). So, they offer safety from the snares of infernal lions to all the godly. Angels deliver Lot from the fire of Sodom (Gen 19:15, 16). So, they often rescue us from infernal flames with protections from diabolical temptations. Angels carry the soul of Lazarus to the bosom of Abraham (Luke 16:22). So, they will carry the souls of all the elect to the palace of the heavenly kingdom. An angel led Peter out of prison (Acts 12:7). So, they often snatch the godly from imminent dangers.

The powers of our adversary, the Devil, are indeed great, but the guardianship of angels encourages us. You should not doubt that these helpers are present with you in all dangers because scripture depicts them as winged, in the form of cherubim and seraphim, so that you might be convinced that they will be present, bringing help with incredible swiftness. You should not doubt that these protectors will be present with you in all places because they are most subtle spirits for whom no body gets in the way. All visible things give way to them and equally so all bodies. However solid or dense things may be, they are penetrable and permeable to them. You should have no doubts about whether these spirits know about dangers and afflictions, because they see the face of the heavenly Father and are ready to carry out all his ministries most promptly (Matt 18:10).

Consider also, O devout soul, that these angels are holy. Therefore, eagerly seek sanctity if you want to have fellowship with them. Similarity of character especially brings about friendship. Become accustomed to holy actions if you wish for the guardianship of angels. Show reverence to your angel in all places and in every corner. You should not do anything in an angel's presence that would make you ashamed in the sight of another person. These spirits are pure, therefore they are driven off by unclean actions. Smoke drives away bees and a bad smell repels doves. So, lamentable and grievous sin drives away the angels, the guardians of life. If these protectors have been given up through sins, how will you be safe from the snares of the Devil? Destitute of the protection of angels, how will you be safe from the assault of various dangers? If your soul lacks the angelic wall of defense, the Devil will easily subdue it by his deceitful and distorted eloquence.

The angels are sent from God to minister to the saints (Heb 1:14). Therefore, you should first be reconciled to God through faith if you want to have an angel as your guardian. Where the grace of God is absent, so also is the protection of angels. We should consider the angels to be, as it were, the salutary hands of God that are not set in motion to do any work unless they are directed by him. There is joy in heaven among the angels over the repentance of one sinner (Luke 15:10). The penitential tears of sinners are like wine to the angels. The impenitent heart, however, puts the guardian angels to flight. Therefore, we should repent so that we might arouse joy among the angels. Angels have a heavenly and spiritual nature. Therefore, let us think about heavenly and spiritual things so that it might be agreeable to them to be with us. Angels are humble and inner pride is exceedingly detestable to them because they are also not ashamed to be submissive to little children. Therefore, can we who are dust and ashes be proud if a heavenly spirit humbles itself so much?

At the time of death the craftiness of the Devil should be feared the most, because it is written that the serpent attacks the heel (Gen 3:15). The heel is the farthest extremity of the body so it signifies the extremity of your life. The guardianship of angels is most necessary in the final agony of death because they liberate from the fiery arrows of the Devil (Eph 6:16) and carry the soul leaving its bodily home to heavenly paradise. When Zacharias was performing his duties in the sacred temple, an angel of God came to him (Luke 1:11). So also, if you take delight in the use of the word and prayer, you will also be able to take delight in the patronage of angels.

O most merciful God, who leads us by holy angels through the wilderness of this life, grant that we may be led by them to the heavenly kingdom.

Meditation Twenty-Seven

The Snares of the Devil

Who knows the cunning of the Devil!

Consider, O devout soul, in what danger you constantly live because the Devil, your adversary, is always threatening you. This enemy is most resolute in audacity, most robust in powers, most skillful in arts, most well-equipped in stratagems, most unrelenting in his zeal for struggle, and so able to assume various forms. He entices us to commit various sins, and after he has seduced us, he accuses us before the tribunal of God. He makes accusations about

God in the presence of humans, about humans in the presence of God, and about humans in turn among each other. First he looks precisely for the particular inclination of each person and then sets up the snare of an appropriate temptation. Whenever attackers attempt a siege, they do not target the strongest and most fortified parts but estimate where the walls are weak, the trenches shallower, and the towers unguarded. So, the Devil, who is perpetually attacking a person's soul, first assaults whatever he judges to be soft and weak in the soul. Once he has conquered, he does not completely withdraw but rather steps up his efforts and tempts more boldly so that he might conquer, in times of weariness and negligence, those whom he could not conquer by his ferocious power. Is such a one likely to hold back from tricking anyone if he even dared to approach the Lord of majesty with his cunning deceits (Matt 4:3)? Is he likely to spare any Christian if he tried to sift the apostles of Christ like wheat (Luke 22:31)? If he deceived Adam when he was still in his natural state (Gen 3:1–5), whom among those whose nature has fallen can he not deceive? If he deceived Judas in the school of the Savior, whom can he not deceive in the world, the school of error?

In all circumstances the snares of the Devil should be absolutely feared. In prosperity he tempts us to exalt ourselves. In adversity he tempts us to despair. If he sees someone attracted to parsimony, he delights in binding him with the fetters of insatiable desires. If someone is animated by a heroic spirit, he stirs him up with stings of anger. If he sees someone inclined to gladness, he stimulates an obsession with foolish desires. When he sees those who are fervent in religion, he tries to entrap them with vain superstitions. When he sees those who are in positions of authority, he strikes them with flames of ambition. When he impels us to sin, he amplifies a sense of the mercy of God. After he has cast us down in our sins, he amplifies a sense of the justice of God. First he wants to induce us to sin presumptuously and then he tries to lead us to despair. Sometimes he attacks us externally with persecutions, while at other times he attacks us internally with fierce temptations. Sometimes he assails us openly and violently, while at other times, secretly and deceptively. He inspires gluttony when we eat, intemperance in our intimate relations, laziness in our daily activities, avarice when we govern, anger when we discipline, and pride when we gain positions of authority. He inspires evil thoughts in our hearts, false words in our mouths, and rebellious movements in our bodies. When we are awake, he moves us to commit evil deeds, and when we sleep, he instigates foul dreams. Therefore, the wiles of the Devil are to be feared everywhere and at all times: We sleep, and he watches. We are secure, and he prowls around like a lion (1 Pet 5:8). If you caught sight of an enraged lion attacking you, how you would shudder in fear, and yet, when you hear that this infernal lion lurks to ambush you, you still sleep securely?

Consider, then, O faithful soul, the wiles of this most powerful enemy and seek the aid of spiritual weapons. Let your loins be gird with truth and put on the breastplate of righteousness (Eph 6:14). Put on the perfect righteousness of Christ, and you will be safe from the temptations of the Devil. Hide in the cleft of Christ's wounds (Song 2:14) whenever you are terrified by the darts of this malicious serpent. Whoever truly believes is in Christ, and since Satan has no authority over Christ (John 14:30), so he also has no authority over the true believer. Let your feet be shod with the preparation of the gospel of peace (Eph 6:15). Let the confession of Christ sound perpetually in our ears, and then the temptation of the Devil can in no way hurt us. The words of an enchanter do not drive off a serpent as well as a constant confession of Christ puts to flight this spiritual serpent. Take up the shield of faith (Eph 6:16) so that we might extinguish the fiery darts of this most wicked enemy. Faith moves mountains, mountains, that is, of doubt, persecution, and temptation. The Israelites, whose doorposts were marked by the blood of the paschal lamb, were not killed by the avenging angel (Exod 12:13). Those whose hearts are sprinkled by faith with the blood of Christ will not be harmed by this avenger. Faith rests in the promises of God, and Satan cannot overthrow these promises. Therefore, he will also not be able to prevail against our faith. Faith is the light of the soul. Therefore, the temptations of this evil spirit are plainly apparent in this light. Through faith, our sins are thrown into the deep sea of divine mercy (Mic 7:19), in which the fiery darts of the Devil are quickly extinguished. We should take up the helmet of salvation (Eph 6:17), which is holy hope. Bear temptation, being mindful of the end of this temptation. For, God is the controller of the conflict and has the crown of victory. If there were no enemy, there would be no battle. If there were no battle, there would be no victory. If there were no victory, there would be no crown. A battle that brings us closer to God is better than a peace that separates us from God. We should also take up the sword of the spirit, which is the word of God (Eph 6:17)

Let the consolation of the scriptures be of more worth to you than the contradictions of the Devil. Christ conquered all the temptations of Satan by the word. So also, Christians conquer all the temptations of Satan by the Word (Matt 4:4). Finally, you have the greatest support against temptations in prayers. As often as the little ship of the soul is being overwhelmed by waves of temptation, arouse Christ by prayers (Matt 8:24). We conquer our visible foes by striking them; we conquer invisible foes by pouring out prayers.

Fight, O Christ, for us and in us, so that we may also conquer through you.

Meditation Twenty-Eight

General Rules for a Godly Life

Piety is the perfection of wisdom.

Every day you are drawing nearer to death, to judgment, and to eternity. Consider, therefore, every day, how you will face death, withstand the severe test of the judgment, and live for all eternity. You should take great care respecting all your thoughts, words, and actions, because one day you must give a precise accounting of all your thoughts, words, and actions (Matt 12:36). At evening time, consider that death could be at hand this very night; and in the morning, keep in mind that death might approach you during the day. Do not put off conversion and the practice of good works until tomorrow, because it is not certain that there will be a tomorrow for you. It is certain, however, that death is impending. Nothing is more adverse to piety than procrastination (Sir 18:22). If you continue to disparage the inward call of the Holy Spirit, you will never be truly converted. Do not put off conversion and good works until old age; instead, offer to God the flower of your youth. Old age is not certain to come to the young, but it is certain that destruction is prepared for impenitent young people.

No time of life is more suitable for the service of God than the days of your youth when you have a vigorous body and a lively mind. You should never commit an evil deed to gain the favor of any person, for God, not that person, will one day judge your life. Therefore, never set up the favor of any person in preference to the grace of God.

We are either advancing or retreating in the way of the Lord; therefore, examine your life every single day to see whether you are going forward or backward in your zeal for piety. To stand still in the way of the Lord is really to regress; therefore, do not choose to stand still in the journey of piety but strive earnestly always to walk forward in the way of the Lord. In your conversation be pleasant to all, harsh to none, and familiar with few. Live dutifully toward God, upright with regard to yourself, and justly toward your neighbor. Act graciously toward your friends, patiently with your enemies, benevolently toward everyone, and also generously, as far as you are able. While you live, die daily to yourself and to your vices, so that when you die, you may live unto God.

Show mercy always in the disposition of your mind, kindness in your countenance, humility in your manner, modesty in your dealings with others, and patience in tribulation. Always reflect on three things about the past: the evil you have committed, the good you have omitted, and the time you have let slip away. Always consider three things about the present: the brevity of your present life, the difficulty of salvation, and the small number of those who will be saved. Always ponder these three future things: death, than which nothing is more horrible; the judgment, than which nothing is more terrible; and the punishments of hell, than which nothing can be more intolerable. Let your evening prayers emend the sins of the day that has gone by; let the last day of the week rectify the faults of the preceding days. Every evening, think about how many have fallen headlong into hell this day, and give thanks that God has granted you more time for repentance.

There are three things above you of which you should never lose sight: the all-seeing eye of God, the all-hearing ear of God, and the books of judgment in which all things are recorded. God has totally shared himself with you, so give yourself totally to your neighbor. The best life on earth is that which is completely devoted to serving others. Show reverence and obedience toward your superiors, give counsel and aid to those who are your equals, watch over and discipline your inferiors. Let your body be subject to your mind, and your mind subject to God. Weep over your past misdeeds, give little weight to your present welfare, and with the total desire of your whole heart crave future blessings. Remember your sins, so that you may grieve over them; be mindful of death, so you may avoid sin; keep divine justice in mind, so you may fear to sin; yet remember the mercy of your God, so you do not give in to despair.

Pull yourself away from the world as much as you can and devote yourself totally to the service of the Lord. Always bear in mind that your purity is endangered by the allurements of the world, your humility by its riches, and your piety by its business affairs. Seek to please no one but Christ; do not be afraid to displease anyone but Christ. Always pray to God that he might order for you what he wants and give you what he orders; that he might cover what you have done and might control what will unfold for you in the future. Let what you truly are correspond to what you want to appear to be, for God judges not according to appearance but according to truth. In speech, beware of talkativeness, for at the judgment you must supply a reason for every idle word (Matt 12:36). Your works, whatever they are, do not pass away but are scattered abroad, as it were, like seeds sown for eternity. For if you sow to your flesh, you will reap corruption from your flesh; but if you sow in the Spirit, you will reap the reward of eternal life from the Spirit (Gal 6:8). The honors of this world will not follow you after death, neither will all your accumulated riches nor the pleasures and vanities of the world; but all the works that you have done will follow you after the end of this life (Rev 14:13). Therefore, you should appear in God's sight today as you want to appear at the judgment.

Do not calculate the worth of what you are now but estimate more how you fall short of what you ought to be; instead of feeling pride about what has been given to you, humble yourself because of what you have been denied. Learn to live rightly while you are still permitted to live. Eternal life is either won or lost in this life; after death, the time for working is past and the time for weighing what you have done begins. Let holy meditation produce knowledge within you and from this knowledge a conviction of sin. May this conviction of sin lead to devotion, and this devotion to prayer.

Silence of the mouth is a great good for peace of heart. The more you are separated from the world, the more pleasing you will be to God. Whatever you desire to have, seek it from God; whatever you have already, credit it to God. You are not worthy of receiving more if you are not grateful for what you have already been given. Grace ceases to descend upon you when you cease to return gratitude to God. Convert whatever happens to you to good account: as often as favorable times come your way, consider what a reason they provide for blessing and praising God; if hard times overtake you, consider these as warnings to repent and convert. Display your physical powers in helping others, your wisdom in instructing others, and the quantity of your wealth in beneficence. Do not let adversity crush you, or prosperity lift you up. Let Christ be the aim of your life, the one whom you will follow in this world so that you might reach the heavenly fatherland. In all things let your greatest care be to display profound humility and ardent love. Elevate your heart to God in love so you may cling to him; plant humility deep in your heart lest you become proud. See God as Father in his clemency, and as Lord in his discipline; as your Father when his power is manifested gently, as your Lord when it is displayed severely; love him reverently as a Father; fear him, of necessity, as a lord and master. Love him because he desires to be merciful; fear him because he takes no delight in sin. Fear the Lord, and put your trust in him (Ps 37:5); acknowledge your own wretchedness and proclaim his grace.

O God, who has enabled us to seek to do your will, give us also the power to do it (Phil 2:13).

Meditation Twenty-Nine

Shaking Off Security

To live securely is death.

Think, devout soul, about the difficulty of being saved and you will easily shake off all security. No time and no place is secure, neither in heaven nor in paradise, much less in this world. An angel fell from the presence of God; Adam fell in a place of delight. Adam was created in the image of God (Gen 1:27); nonetheless, he was deceived by the wiles of the Devil. Solomon was the wisest of all men (1 Kgs 3:12); nonetheless, he was turned away from God by his wives (1 Kgs 11:3). Judas was in the school of the Savior and daily took in the saving words of that greatest of teachers (Luke 22:3); nonetheless, he was not safe from the snare of the great seducer. He was thrown into the pit of avarice and out of avarice into the pit of eternal sadness. David was a man after God's own heart (1 Sam 13:14) and was the dearest Son of Jehovah, but through murder and adultery he was made a son of death (2 Sam 12:5). Where, then, is there security in this life? Cling with firm faith of the heart to the promises of God, and you will be safe from the assaults of the Devil. There is no security in this life apart from the infallible promise of God offered to those who believe and walk in the way of the Lord. If we attain our future blessing, then we will finally have full security.

In this life fear and religion are connected, and one should not be without the other. Do not be secure in adversity, but think of all misfortune that befalls you as a punishment for your sins. Often God punishes secret faults through evident affliction. Consider the stain of your grave sins and fear the just punisher of sins. Do not be secure in prosperity, for God is angry at anyone who is not chastened in this life. What are the afflictions of the pious? Bitter arrows sent by the sweet hand of God. God considers many to be undeserving of punishment in this present life whom he will, nevertheless, cast away for eternity. Uninterrupted human felicity now is often an indication of eternal damnation. Nothing is more unfortunate than the good fortune of sinners. No one is more wretched than one who does not recognize wretchedness. Wherever you turn your eyes, you find causes for sadness and observe remedies against security. Consider God above, whom you offend, hell below, which we deserve, sins behind us, which we have committed, judgment before us, which we fear, conscience within us, which we defile, and the world outside of us, which we love. See whence you came and blush, where you are and cry, where you are going and tremble. Narrow is the gate of salvation, but narrower still is the way of salvation.

God gave you the treasure of faith, but you carry this treasure in earthen vessels (2 Cor 4:7). God gave angels to guard you (Ps 91:11), but the Devil is not far away to seduce you. God has renewed the spirit of your mind (Eph 4:23), but you still have many vestiges of the flesh. You have been established in the grace of God, but you are not yet established in eternal glory. A mansion has been prepared in heaven for you, but before then the assault of the world afflicts you. God has promised pardon for the penitent but has not promised to give the will to repent to the willfully delinquent. The consolations of eternal life await you, but you must enter through many tribulations (Acts 14:22). A crown of eternal reward has been promised to you, but first you must pass through a hard battle. God's promise is unchangeable, but you must not change your zeal for a holy life. If the servant does not do what has been ordered, God will do what has been threatened.

Therefore, laying aside security, you should continually sigh and grieve over your sins, lest, by a just and secret judgment of God, you be deserted and turned over to the power of the Devil to be destroyed. As long you stand in the grace of God, rejoice in it, yet you should not think that you possess this gift of God by hereditary right and become secure, as if you could never lose it, lest, by chance, when God suddenly takes away the gift and draws back his hand, you lose heart and become sadder than you ought to be. Happy are you, indeed, if you take all care to avoid carelessness, the parent of all evils. God will not forsake you, but take care that you do not forsake God. God gives grace. Pray that he also gives you perseverance. God ordains that you might be certain of salvation but does not approve of your being secure.

You should fight strongly so that you might find sweet victory (2 Tim 4:7). Your flesh within you fights against you, an enemy that is all the more formidable because it is nearer. The world around you fights against you, an enemy that is all the more formidable because it is so abundant. The Devil above you fights against you, an enemy all the more formidable because it is more powerful. By the strength of God, do not fear to contend with these enemies, for, with the strength of God, you will be able to attain victory. However, you will not conquer such enemies by security, but by fighting assiduously. The time of life is the time of battle. The time you are most under attack is when you don't know you are being attacked. They are gathering their strength at the very time when they seem to submit to a truce. They are vigilant and you are sleeping. They are preparing themselves for doing harm and you are not preparing yourself to resist. Many fall along the way before a place is given to them in the fatherland just as many Israelites died in the desert, none of whom reached the Promised Land (Deut 1:35). How many spiritual children of Abraham perish in the desert of this life before they attain the promised inheritance of the kingdom of heaven? Nothing is more effective for getting rid of security than thinking about the small number of those who persevere. Therefore, let there be a desire in us for the glory of heaven and a longing to attain it; sadness that we have not yet attained it; fear lest we not attain it, so that we feel no joy except in that which either helps or provides the hope of attaining it. What use is it to delight in the moment, if you will be compelled to mourn for eternity? What pleasure can there be in this life if what delights you passes away and what torments us will never pass away?

We live securely as if we have passed by the hour of death and judgment. Christ said that we will come to judgment in the hour when we least expect it (Matt 24:44, 50). The Truth says this and others repeat this in a similar manner. Hear and fear. If the Lord will come in the hour when we least expect it, then we ought to fear greatly lest we come to judgment unprepared. If we come unprepared, how will we be able to endure the severe verdict of this judgment? Nevertheless, what is lost in this single moment will not be able to be recovered in all eternity. In one moment it will quickly be determined how it will be for us forever. In this one moment life and death, damnation and salvation, punishment and eternal glory will be awarded to each person.

O Lord, who has given us grace for good, give, in addition, perseverance in what is good.

Meditation Thirty

Imitation of the Holy Life of Christ

Let Christ be the rule of your life.

The holy life of Christ is the most perfect model of virtue; indeed, every action of Christ is for our instruction. Many wish to attain to Christ but draw back from following him; they want to enjoy

Christ but not to imitate him. "Learn from me, for I am gentle and humble in heart," says our Savior (Matt 6:29). Unless you are willing to be a disciple of Christ, you will never be a true Christian. May the passion of Christ be your merit, but also the actions of Christ a model for your own life. Your beloved is dazzling white and ruddy (Song 5:10), and so may you too be ruddy by the sprinkling of the blood of Christ, and dazzling white by the imitation of Christ's life.

How do you truly love Christ, if you do not love his holy life? "If you love me," says the Savior, "keep my commandments" (John 14:15, 23). Therefore, he who does not keep his commandments also does not love him. The holy life of Christ is a perfect rule of conduct for our lives. The unique rule of the life of Christ should be preferred to all the rules of Saint Francis and Saint Benedict. If you want to be an adopted son of God, observe whatever is associated with the only-begotten Son of God. If you want be a co-heir with Christ, you should also be an imitator of Christ. He who chooses to live a vice-filled life has given himself up to the service of the Devil. Indeed, how can one who wants to be with the Devil also be in any way with Christ? To love vice is to love the Devil, because all sins are of the Devil (1 John 3:8). And how can one be a true lover of Christ who is a lover of the Devil? To love God is to love a holy life, because every holy life is from God; how then can one be a lover of God who is not a lover of a holy life? The proof of love is in the exhibition of works; it is characteristic of true love to obey the loved one, to think and will the same as the loved one. Therefore, if you truly love Christ, you will obey his commands, you will love a holy life with him, and, renewed in the spirit of your mind, you will meditate upon heavenly things (Eph 4:23). Life eternal consists in knowing Christ (John 17:3), for he who does not love Christ does not even know him; he who does not love humility, purity, gentleness, temperance, charity, also does not love Christ, for the life of Christ is nothing other than humility, purity, gentleness, temperance, and love.

Christ says that he does not know those who do not do the will of his Father (Matt 7:21); therefore, those who do not do the will of the heavenly Father have no knowledge of Christ. What, in fact, is the will of the Father? "Our sanctification" (1 Thess 4:3), says the Apostle. Whoever does not have the Spirit of Christ does not belong to Christ (Rom 8:9), but where the Holy Spirit is, there his gifts and fruits will also appear. What are fruits of the Spirit? Love, joy, peace, mildness, kindness, goodness, faith, gentleness, temperance (Gal 5:22). Just as the Holy Spirit rested upon Christ (Isa 11:2), so he rests also upon all those who are in Christ by true faith, for the bride of Christ hastens toward the sweet smell of the ointments of Christ (Song 1:3). Whoever is joined to the Lord is one spirit with him (1 Cor 6:17). Just as the union of the flesh of a man and wife joined makes one flesh out of two (Matt 19:6), so the spiritual union of Christ and the faithful soul makes them one spirit. Truly, where there is one spirit, there is the same will; and where there is the same will, there are also the same actions. Therefore, if one's life does not conform to the life of Christ, it is proven that the person neither clings to Christ nor has the Spirit of Christ.

Is it not right that all of our life should be conformed to Christ's, since he, out of love for us, has totally conformed himself to our life? God manifesting himself in the flesh (1 Tim 3:16) has displayed for us a perfect example of a holy life, so that no one who departs from a holy life to the flesh can take refuge in an excuse. No life can be more pleasing and tranquil than the life of Christ, because Christ was true God, and what can be more pleasing and tranquil than the true God, the highest good? Life in this world bestows short-lived joys that carry eternal sorrow in their train. To whomever you conform yourself in this life you will also be conformed in the resurrection. If you begin to conform yourself to the life of Christ here, then in the resurrection you will be more fully conformed to him, but if you join yourself to the Devil through shameful acts, then in the resurrection you will join him in torment. "If you wish to follow me, deny yourself and daily take up your cross," says our Savior (Matt 16:24). If in this life you deny yourself, then in the judgment Christ will acknowledge you as his own. If, for Christ's sake, you renounce your own honor, your own love, your own will in this life, then Christ will graciously make you share his own honor, his own love, his own will in the future life. If you join him in bearing the cross in this life, you will join him in his eternal light in the life to come. If you are a partner in tribulation with him now, you will share in his consolation in the future. If you suffer persecution with him in this life, you will partake of a plentiful recompense in the future life. "Whoever acknowledges me in this generation," says Christ, "I will also acknowledge in the presence of my heavenly Father" (Matt 10:32). Now indeed we ought to confess Christ not only by a profession of doctrine, but also by conformation of our lives to his; and so at last, he will recognize us as his own on the Day of Judgment. Whoever will deny me before men, I will also deny before my heavenly Father (Matt 10:33). Christ is not only denied by words but also much more by ungodly living. Therefore, whoever denies Christ by actions in this world, Christ will also deny by his actions at the judgment. He is not a Christian who does not have true faith in Christ; moreover, true faith in Christ grafts us as branches into his spiritual vine (John 15:4). Every branch in Christ that does not bear, the celestial Farmer destroys, but whoever abides in Christ and in whom Christ dwells by faith bears much fruit (Eph 3:17). That branch that does not draw its sap from the vine is not really in the vine; the soul that does not draw the spiritual sap of love from Christ through faith is not really united to Christ through faith.

Make us more conformed to your life in this world, O gracious Jesus, so that we may be fully conformed to you in the life to come!

Meditation Thirty-One

Self-Denial

To not deny oneself is to deny Christ.

If any want to follow me, let them deny themselves, says the Savior (Matt 16:24). To deny yourself is to renounce love of self; self-love hinders love of God. If you want to be a disciple of Christ, it is necessary for the root of self-love within you to die completely. No one loves Christ without hatred of oneself. Unless a grain of wheat falls into the ground and dies, it bears no fruit (John 12:24). So also, you will not be able to perceive the fruits of the Holy Spirit unless the self-love in your heart dies. The Lord said to Abraham, "Go forth from your land, and your kindred, and your father's house to a land that I will show you" (Gen 12:1). Abraham would not have been able to be so great a prophet if he had not gone forth from his land. You will not be a true disciple of Christ and a truly spiritual person before you separate yourself from self-love. Jacob became lame in one foot through contact with an angel, while the other remained well and unimpaired (Gen 32:25). Through these two feet two loves are to be understood: love of self and love of God. Now, a person will become a partaker of a divine blessing when the foot of self-love becomes lame, while, at the same time, the other foot, symbolizing love of God, remains well and unimpaired. It is not possible for you to look with one eye at both heaven and earth. So, it is not possible, with the same will, to love both yourself inordinately and God.

Love is the greatest good of the soul. Therefore, this highest good of the soul should be ascribed to the highest good, which is God. Your love is your God. In other words, whatever you love the most you put in the place of God. Now, God is truly the greatest being. Therefore, to love yourself is to judge yourself to be God and put yourself in the place of God, which is certainly the greatest idolatry of all. What you love the most you esteem as the end or goal of all things and judge to be the final fulfillment of your desires. Now, God is the only beginning and end of all creatures, the first and the last (Isa 41:4). God alone fills all the desires of your heart, and nothing that has been created can satisfy your desire. Therefore, you ought to prefer the love of God to self-love. God is the beginning and the end (Rev 1:8). Therefore, our love ought to begin in him and ought also to end in him. The essence of God is far beyond all creatures, since he has been God in himself from all eternity. Therefore, you should withdraw your love from all creatures.

However your love is, so also will your works be. If your works proceed from true faith and love of God, they are pleasing to God and great in his eyes, even though they seem small in the eyes of other people. If they proceed from self-love, they are never able to please God. Self-love contaminates the most excellent works. When Christ was in the home of Simon, a certain woman broke a bottle of precious ointment and anointed the head of Christ (Matt 26:6). This work appeared small, but it was pleasing to Christ because it proceeded from true faith, pure love, and sincere contrition. The sacrifice was a work pleasing to God in the Old Testament, but it was not pleasing to God when Saul set aside the plunder taken from the Amalekites to offer as a sacrifice to God (1 Sam 15:19). Why? Because this did not proceed from love of God. If he had truly loved

God, he would not have disparaged the command of God that all the plunder be destroyed. He loved himself and his devotion. Love is a kind of fire, and so the church prays: "Come Holy Spirit and ignite this flame of your love in the faithful." Fire does not remain fixed in a certain place but always tends upward. So your love ought not to rest within you but should raise itself upward to God.

To deny yourself is, moreover, to renounce your own honor. The greatest honor ought to be only for the greatest good, and God is the greatest good. Whoever seeks glory cannot seek the glory of God, as the Savior said to the Pharisees: "How can you believe if you accept glory from each other?" (John 5:44). Look to the example of Christ and follow it. He testified often of himself that he did not seek his own glory, that he did not accept honor from other people, that he was humble in heart. You receive everything as a gift from God. Therefore, you ought to ascribe everything, in turn, to God. The streams of all good gifts go forth from this fountain of divine goodness. Therefore, all good things should be referred, in turn, back to this sea of grace. The plant that is called the sunflower always turns itself toward the sun from which it derives life and strength. So, turn yourself with all your gifts and honors to God and attribute nothing whatsoever to yourself. If you had anything from yourself, you could seek your own honor and ascribe your gifts to yourself, but because you have nothing from yourself, you ought to ascribe all to God and seek the honor of God rather than yourself. According honor to oneself turns a person from God. Nebuchadnezzar is an example of this; he said, "This is that Babylon, which I built as my royal home by my mighty power and for my glorious majesty" (Dan 4:30). But, what follows: "While the word was in the mouth of the king, a voice declared from heaven, 'Nebuchadnezzar, to you it is said, your kingdom has departed from you, you will be rejected by people and your dwelling shall be with the beasts of the fields'" (Dan 4:31–32). So, if you, out of self-honor and pride, regard the edifice of your good works, your spiritual Babylon, in this way, and ascribe the glory of it all to yourself, and not to God alone, you will be cast away from the presence of God.

Finally, to deny yourself is to renounce your own will. We should always obey the will that is best. Now, the will of God is always the best, so we ought to obey the will of the one from whom we have everything, and all things come down to us from God. We ought to obey the will of the one who always leads us to life and goodness, and it is God who always leads us to life and goodness. Delight in the Lord, and he will give you the desires of your heart (Ps 37:4). Your own will leads you to death and damnation. What caused our first parent to fall from the grace of God and from the state of salvation into eternal damnation? Setting aside the will of God, he followed his own will. He neglected the precepts of the Lord and listened to the advice of the Devil. By contrast, the true disciple of Christ renounces self-will and seeks to follow the divine will. Consider how Christ offered his own will as a most gracious sacrifice to God in the agony of his passion and offer your own will to God (Matt 26:39). And so you will accomplish what Christ requires, the denial of yourself.

O Lord, may your holy will be done on earth as it is in heaven.

Meditation Thirty-Two

True Rest of the Soul

The mind that leans upon the Lord is at rest.

The soul often seeks rest in transitory and worldly things but does not find it. Why? Because the soul is nobler than all other creatures; it cannot find rest and peace in such ignoble things. All worldly things are fleeting and transitory, while the soul is immortal. Therefore, how will you find true rest in them? All these things are earthly, while the origin of our soul is heavenly. Therefore, how is it possible to fulfill its desires with them? In Christ, it finds rest (Matt 11:29). He is able to satisfy and fulfill its desires. Facing the wrath of God, it finds rest in the wounds of Christ. Facing the accusations of Satan, it rests in the power of Christ. Facing the terror of the law, it rests in the preaching of Christ. Facing accusing sins, it rests in the blood of Christ, which is more able to speak before God than the blood of Abel (Heb 12:24). Facing the terror of death, it finds rest and full confidence in Christ's sitting at the right hand of the Father.

And so our faith finds rest in Christ, but our love finds rest there too. Whoever clings to earthly things with love will not have true rest, because these earthly things do not have it. They are not able fully to satisfy the desires of the soul because they are finite, while our souls, made in the image of God, seek that infinite good in which all good things are found. Therefore, just as our faith ought to lean on nothing in all creation except the merit of Christ alone, so our love ought to cling to no creature, not even ourselves. Indeed, love of self impedes love of God, so we ought to prefer love of God to all things. Our soul is the bride of Christ; therefore, it ought to cling to him alone (2 Cor 11:2). Our soul is the temple of God; therefore it ought to give a place only to him (1 Cor 3:16).

Many seek rest in riches, but outside of Christ there is no rest for the soul. Where Christ is, there is poverty, if not externally, then internally. The Lord did not have a place in heaven or earth to lay his head, and so he wanted to commend and entrust poverty to us (Matt 8:20). Riches are outside of us, but what gives rest to the soul ought to be within it. Truly, to what will the soul cling in death when it must relinquish everything in the world? Either riches desert us or we them, often in this life but always in death. Therefore, where will the soul find peace and rest at that time?

Many seek rest in pleasure, which is able to give some kind of rest and delight to the body, but not to the soul. In the end, pain and sorrow follow as its companions. Pleasures are sought in this life, but the soul was not created for the sake of this life. Because it is forced to leave pleasures behind through death, how can the soul find rest in them? Outside of Christ, there is no rest for the soul, but what was the life of Christ? It was full of sorrow from the time of his birth until his death. So, that true appraiser of things wanted to teach us what we should feel about pleasure.

Many seek rest in honors. Truly, they are miserable because they are deprived of rest by every change in the wind of popular opinion. Honor is an external and fleeting good, while what gives rest to the soul ought to be within it. What more will you say of human praise and honor than has been said of that painting by Apelles?*

Consider the little corner in which you are hidden. What is its proportion in comparison to the whole province, to Europe, to the

---

*An innovative Greek artist who made a famous painting of Alexander the Great. There is a story about his work being criticized by a shoemaker. Gerhard takes this illustration from Juan Vives, *Introduction to True Wisdom.*

whole inhabitable world? That, indeed, is true honor, which is obtained some day by the elect from God. The rest for anything is found in its end, nor does anything rest naturally until after it has attained its end and place. The end of the created soul is God, since it has been made according to the image of God. Therefore, it cannot be at rest and peace except in its end, which is God. Just as the soul is the life of the body, so God is the life of the soul. Therefore, just as a soul truly lives in which God lives spiritually by grace, so a soul is dead if God does not inhabit it. Indeed, how can there be rest in a dead soul? That first death in sin necessarily is followed by the second death of damnation (Rev 20:6).

Consequently, the soul that clings firmly by love to God and enjoys divine consolation internally cannot have its rest disturbed by external evils. In times of sadness it is joyful, in poverty it is rich, in times of tribulation it is secure, in the midst of worldly disturbances it is calm, in the midst of human rebukes and insults it is peaceful, in death itself it lives. It does not care about the threats of tyrants because it feels the riches of divine consolation within itself. In adversity it is not sad, because the Holy Spirit effectively consoles it within. It is not distressed in poverty, because it is rich in the goodness of God. It is not disturbed by human abuse, because it enjoys the delights of divine honor. It does not care for the desires of the flesh, because the sweetness of the Spirit is a greater grace. It does not seek worldly friendship, because it experiences the delight of God as its friend and propitiator. It does not marvel at earthly treasures, because it has the greatest treasure hidden in heaven. It does not fear death, because it always lives in God. It does not greatly desire worldly wisdom, because the Holy Spirit teaches it within. What is perfect removes what is imperfect (1 Cor 13:10). It does not fear lightning storms, tempests, fires and floods, distressing configurations of the planets, or the darkening of celestial lights because it rests by faith in Christ, carried upward above nature. It is not distracted by the seductions of the world, because it hears the sweeter voice of Christ within itself. It does not fear the power of the Devil, because it experiences divine compassion. The one who lives within it is stronger than the Devil who attempts, in vain, to conquer it. It does not follow the temptations of the flesh, because it experiences the richness of living in the Spirit. The vivification of the Spirit mortifies and crucifies the flesh (Gal 5:24). It does not fear the accusations of the Devil, because it knows Christ to be its intercessor.

May the only author and granter of this true rest, our Lord, blessed God forever grant it to our souls.

Meditation Thirty-Three

Purity of Conscience

A mind conscious of integrity is life.

In all your activities, have the greatest care for your conscience. If the Devil incites you to commit some sin, trust the internal judgment of conscience. If you fear to sin in the presence of other people, your conscience should hold you back from sin even more. This internal testimony is more effective that any external one. Indeed, however much your sins evade the accusations of all people, you can never escape the internal testimony of conscience. Conscience will be among the books that the Book of Revelation reports will be opened on the future Judgment Day (Rev 20:12). The first book is divine omniscience, which will shed light on all the deeds, words, and thoughts of all people. The second book is Christ, who is the book of life in which are written the names of all those who, through faith, will be led by angels into the heavenly assembly (Rev 13:8). The third book is scripture, which sets standards by which our faith and works will be judged. "The word that I have spoken," says the Savior, "will judge them on the last day" (John 12:48). The fourth book consists of the external testimony of the poor, who will receive us on the Day of Judgment into our eternal habitation (Luke 16:9). The fifth book consists of the internal testimony of conscience, because conscience is the book in which all sins are inscribed. Conscience is a huge volume in which they all are written with the pen of truth. The condemned will not be able to deny their sins at the judgment because they will be convicted by the testimony of their own conscience. They will not be able to flee from the accusation of their sins because the tribunal of conscience is internal and in the very household of their hearts.

A pure conscience is a clear mirror of the soul, in which one sees both the self and God. Clouded vision cannot see the splendor of the true light. Therefore, the Savior says, "Blessed are the pure in heart, for they shall see God" (Matt 5:8). Just as the beautiful and pure face of a person is a pleasure to view, so a pure and clean conscience is acceptable in the eyes of God, but a rotten conscience produces worms that do not die. Therefore, we should be aware of and snuff out the worm of conscience in this life so that it is not kept alive forever.

All other books are devised to improve this one, but what use is great knowledge if the conscience is impure? Not from a book of knowledge but from the book of conscience will you be judged some day before the throne of God. If you want to write this book correctly, write it according to the example of the book of life. The book of life is Christ. Let your profession of faith be conformed to the standard of Christ's teaching. Let your life be led in conformity with the standard of Christ's life. The conscience will be good if there is purity in your heart, truth in your mouth, and honesty in your actions. Use conscience as a lantern for all your actions, for it will undoubtedly show you which actions in life are good and which are bad.

Avoid the judgment of conscience, which is at the same time defendant and accuser, witness and judge, torturer and prison, punisher, prosecutor, and hangman. What kind of an evasion can there be if the witness accuses and it is not possible for anything to be hid from the one who judges? What use is it if all praise you and conscience accuses you? What harm can there be if all disparage you and conscience alone defends you? This judge alone suffices to accuse, judge, and condemn. This judge is incorruptible and cannot be swayed by petitions or bribed by gifts. Wherever you go, wherever you are, conscience is always with you, carrying with it whatever you have placed in it, whether good or evil. Whatever it has received, it keeps while you are alive and returns the deposit when you are dead. Since the enemies of a person will truly be of his own household, so you have accusers, observers, and torturers in your own house and from your own family (Matt 10:36).

What good is it to live with all sorts of wealth and abundance and to be flogged by the lash of conscience? The fount of human happiness and misery is in the same soul. What good is it to be lying on a golden bed while burning up with a fever? What good is it to rejoice in the accumulation of external happiness when you are agitated by the flame of conscience? You care for your eternal salvation as much as you also care for your conscience. For, if a good conscience is lost, faith is lost, and if faith is lost, the grace of God is lost, and if the grace of God is lost, how can you hope for eternal life? Whatever kind of testimony your conscience gives, you can also expect from the judgment of Christ. No one will accuse sinners or bring a charge against them, for they will be their own accusers. Just as a drunk who has imbibed much wine does not feel impaired by the wine but, later, feels the harm done by drunkenness when roused from sleep, so sins, while being committed, darken the mind and obscure the clarity of true judgment with a dense cloud, but conscience later rises up and gnaws at us more severely than any other accuser. There are three judgments: the judgment of the world, the judgment by yourself, and the judgment of God. Just as you cannot escape the judgment of God, so also you cannot escape judgment by yourself, although it may be permitted to you, sometimes, to escape the judgment of the world. There are no walls in the way that can lessen the degree to which your actions are seen by this witness.

Tranquility of the conscience is the beginning of eternal life. You will rejoice more truly and agreeably from a good conscience amid difficulties than from an evil one amid fleeting pleasures. Against all disparagements by evil people, you can confidently appeal to the acquittal of conscience. Interrogate yourself, because you know yourself better than any other person knows you. In the Last Judgment what good are the false praises of others and what harm is there in the false disparagements of others? You stand or fall by the judgment of God and yourself, not by the testimony of others. Conscience never ends in the same way that the soul never ends. As long as infernal punishments suppress the damned, so long will the accusations of conscience endure. No external fire can afflict the body as severely as the internal flame, which scorches the soul. The soul burns eternally, and so does the fire of conscience. No exterior lashing of the body can cause such great discomfort as the internal scourging of the soul by the conscience. Therefore, flee the guilt of sin so that you might escape the torment of the conscience. Blot out sins from the book of conscience by true repentance lest they be read in judgment and you hear the pronouncement of the divine sentence fearfully. Extinguish the worm of conscience through fervent devotion lest its horrible bite remain eternally. Extinguish this internal fire through tears so that you might attain the delights of heavenly refreshment.

O Lord, grant that we might fight the good fight, retaining faith and good conscience, so that, at last, we might be saved and safely reach our heavenly fatherland (2 Tim 4:7).

Meditation Thirty-Four

The Nurturing of True Humility

What is a person? What is a bubble? They are nothing.

Consider, O faithful soul, the miserable condition of humanity and you will easily flee from all temptation to feel pride. A person is so meager upon entrance into life, so miserable during its progress, and so pathetic at its end (Sir 10:9). A person is assaulted by devils, exasperated by temptations, enticed by worldly delights, cast down by tribulations, enveloped by accusations, stripped of virtues, and ensnared by bad habits. Therefore, how can you be proud, being but dust and ashes? What were you before birth? A musty seed. What are you in life? A sack of dung. What are you after you die? Food for worms. Whatever good is in you is not from you but from God. Nothing is yours but sin. Therefore, you can claim nothing of those things, which are in you as your own, except for your sin. It is a foolish and faithful servant that wants to take pride in the good things that come from the Lord.

See the example of Christ. All the glory of heaven served him. Indeed, he alone is true glory, but he rejected all worldly glory. He even proclaims: "Learn of me, because I am gentle and humble in heart" (Matt 11:29). The true lover of Christ is also an imitator of Christ and whoever cares for Christ also cares for his humility. Let the proud servant blush and be confounded by how humble the Lord of heaven is. Our Savior calls himself the lily of the valley (Song 2:1) because it is the noblest flower, but it does not originate and sustain itself in the mountains, in other words, in pride and a haughty heart, but in the valley of humility, that is to say, in contrition and the humility of a pious mind. Truly, the humble soul is the seat and beloved resting place of Christ, as a certain holy one has said. True grace does not exalt but, rather, humbles. Therefore, you are not yet a participant in true grace unless you walk in humility of heart.

The streams of divine grace flow downward not upward. Just as water, by nature, does not seek a high place, so divine grace does not flow except into a humble heart. The Psalmist says: "The Lord dwells on high, and looks down at the humble things in heaven and earth" (Ps 113:5, 6). Truly, this is amazing, that we may not approach the greatest and most high God except in humility. If you see yourself as insignificant, you will be great in God's sight. If you are displeased with yourself, you will be pleasing to God. God made the heavens and the earth from nothing. Just as it was in creation so it was also in the restoration of humanity. God creates from nothing and regenerates from nothing. Therefore, if you wish to partake of regeneration and renewal, be nothing in your own eyes, that is to say, attribute nothing to yourself, do not exalt yourself. We are all weak and frail, so consider no one to be frailer than yourself. There is no harm in judging yourself to be inferior to all others and subordinating yourself to all others through humility, but there is much harm in wanting to subordinate another person to yourself. The twenty-four elders, that is to say, the whole church triumphant, throw down their crowns before the throne, attributing all righteousness and glory to God (Rev 4:10). Therefore, what will you, a mere sinner, do? The seraphim, the holy angels, cover their faces in the presence of divine majesty (Isa 6:2). What, then, should you, such a meager creature who is so ungrateful to the creator, do? Christ, the true and only-begotten Son of God, descended from heaven in such surprising humility and received our frail nature onto himself, lowering himself in the flesh to death and the cross (Phil 2:8). What will you, having strayed so far from God, do?

See, O faithful soul, how amazingly Christ healed our pride by his humility, and, yet, you still seek to elevate yourself? Christ entered into glory through humility and the way of his passion, and you have decided that you will be able to reach the glory of heaven by advancing on the way of pride (Luke 24:26)? The Devil was expelled from the kingdom of heaven on account of pride, and you, who have not yet been in the glory of heaven, strive to get there by the way of pride? Adam was ejected from paradise on account of pride, and you seek to find the way to heavenly paradise by the way of pride (Gen 3:24)? We would do better to serve and wash the feet of others with Christ than to seek the place of dignity with the Devil. Let us humble ourselves in this life, so we might be exalted in the future.

Always consider, O faithful soul, not what you have but what you lack. You should be saddened more by the virtues you don't have than exalted by the virtues you do have. Conceal your virtues and reveal your sins. To be sure, you should fear lest, if you reveal your treasure of good works to get recognition, the Devil plunders them through pride. A fire is best preserved when it is covered with ashes. So the fire of love is never more securely guarded than when it is buried with the ashes of humility. Pride is the seed of all sins. Therefore, guard against exalting yourself, lest it turn out that you are thrown into the abyss of sin. Pride is the pleasure bed of the Devil. Therefore, guard against exalting yourself, lest your wretched soul becomes subjugated to the Devil. Pride is a wind that scorches and dries up the fountain of divine grace. Therefore, guard against exalting yourself, lest it turns out that you are separated from divine grace.

Heal, O Christ, the tumor of our pride. May your holy humility merit eternal life for us and may your life also be our example. May our faith be firmly enfolded by your humility and our life constantly patterned after yours.

Meditation Thirty-Five

Fleeing Avarice

Who is truly poor? The avaricious person.

As we love the salvation of the soul, so should we hate the sin of avarice. The avaricious person is the poorest of all, because what he has is as inadequate as what he does not have. The avaricious person is the most afflicted of all, because he is good to no one and the most harmful to himself. The beginning of all sin is pride. The root of all evil is avarice (1 Tim 6:10). The one sins through turning from

God, the other through turning toward creatures. The acquiring of riches demands sweat, the possessing of them creates fear, the loss of them causes sadness. What is worse, the efforts of an avaricious person will not only be impermanent but also very destructive. Either riches will forsake you, or you them. Therefore, if you put your hope in riches, what will you have at the hour of death? How will you entrust your soul to God, if you do not entrust your body to his care? You are cared for by God who is omnipotent, so why do you doubt if he can sustain you? You are cared for by God who is most wise, so why do you doubt how he will sustain you? You are cared for by God who is most bountiful, so why do you doubt that he wants to preserve you?

You have the promise of Christ, Lord of everything in heaven and earth, that nothing needed will be lacking for those who seek the kingdom of God (Matt 6:33). Trust this promise of Christ, which will not disappoint you because he is truth. Avarice is the height of idolatry, because it puts the creature in the place of God (Col 3:5). Avarice transfers the faith owed to God to creatures. Whatever is loved more than God is preferred to God. Whatever is preferred to God is put in the place of God. Esau sold his birthright for something to eat (Gen 25:33). So, many relinquish the inheritance of the kingdom of heaven offered by Christ in order to acquire temporal goods. Judas betrayed Christ for thirty pieces of silver (Matt 26:15). The avaricious put the grace of Christ up for sale, for the sake of temporal riches. How is it possible to aspire to the kingdom of heaven while daily filling yourself with the husks fed to swine (Luke 15:16)? How is it possible to seek God by the elevation of the heart if you try to find peace of soul through riches? The True One says that riches are thorns (Matt 13:22). Therefore, whoever loves riches truly loves thorns. O thorns, how you suffocate many souls! Thorns impede the growth of seeds. Likewise, concern for riches impedes the spiritual fruit of the Word. Thorns prick the body. Likewise, riches torment the soul with cares. You will perish if you only gather perishable treasures. Those who gather treasures on earth are like those who store their crops in a deep and damp place, not keeping in mind that they will decay there more quickly.

How foolish they are who make riches the object of their desires. How can corporeal things satisfy the soul, which is of the

Spirit, when a spiritual nature includes more by its very nature than corporeal matters in that it cannot be filled by any quantity? Since the soul is created for eternity, you will do harm to it if you make temporary and momentary things the object of its desires. The more the soul is raised up to God, the more it is withdrawn from love of riches. The more things are closer to heaven, the less they desire and associate with lower things. Just as the birds of the air neither sow or reap, so it is a great indication that the soul thinks about heaven if it accords little value to earthly goods and even disparages them (Matt 6:26). Mice and reptiles gather together in holes, for there are of a lower order and are less noble in nature than birds. It is a great indication that the soul has turned from God and fixed itself upon earthy things if it clings to riches with an inordinate love. God gave you your soul, but you cannot commit the care of your body to him? God feeds the birds of the air, but you doubt whether he wants to sustain you though you are created in his image? God clothes the lilies of the fields, but you doubt whether he will provide you with clothes (Matt 6:28)? It is shameful that faith and reason in humanity are not able to effect what an instinct of nature effects in birds. The birds do not sow or reap, but they commit their bodies to the care of God.

Avaricious people will not put their faith in the Word of God until they see for themselves how they will be sustained. Avaricious people are the most unreasonable. Why? Because they have brought nothing with them into the world yet are anxious about worldly goods as if they wished to bring absolutely everything with them out of the world (1 Tim 6:7). Avaricious people are the most ungrateful. Why? Because they enjoy many good things from God and never direct the trust of their hearts to God, the giver of these goods. Avaricious people are the most foolish. Why? Because they give up the true good, without which nothing is truly good, and cling to that which is not good without the grace of God. Whoever is bound by love of worldly things does not possess them but is possessed by them. Avarice is not extinguished by either abundance or scarcity. It is not diminished by scarcity because the desire to have grows when it does not attain what is desired for a long time. Abundance does not diminish it because the more avarice acquires, the more it seeks. As soon as what has been desired is acquired by avarice, new things to be desired are supplied, just as it is the character of fire to grow when it is given wood to consume. Avarice is like a torrential stream. It is small at its origin but grows immense afterward. Therefore, affix a limit to the desire for riches lest cupidity drag you to eternal destruction. Many devour in this life what they must digest afterward in hell. Many, when they thirst for wealth, run toward immediate ruin.

Think about this, O devout soul, and, as much as you can, avoid avarice. You can carry none of these goods with you to judgment except what you give to the poor. Do not withhold your perishable goods from the poor for whom Christ did not refuse to give his life. Give to the poor so that you might give to yourself. Whatever you will not give to the poor, another will have. Much too avaricious is the person for whom the Lord does not suffice. A person who greatly values worldly goods has no hope for heaven. How can a person go so far as to lay down his life for a brother if even temporal goods are withheld from a brother who asks for them (1 John 3:16)? The hand of a poor person is the treasure of heaven. What the poor receive is placed in heaven, lest it perish on earth. Do you want to offer a service pleasing to Christ? Show kindness to the poor, for what good is done to a member of the body is received by the head as if it were done for him (Matt 25:40). Christ says to you: "Give to me from that which I gave. Do good from the good you have so that you might acquire good for yourself. Give lavishly of earthly things so that you might retain them, because if you keep too much you will lose it." Hear the warning of Christ, so that you will not be forced to hear him say to you at the judgment: "Depart from me, you accursed, into eternal fire, because you did not feed me when I was hungry" (Matt 25:41, 42). Alms are like holy seed. If you sow sparingly or bountifully, you will reap sparingly or bountifully. If you want to be among the sheep, show the kindness of the sheep. Be frightened by the goats who are standing on the left side, not because they stole, but because they did not offer food.

Incline our hearts, O God, to your testimony and not to avarice (Ps 119:36).

Meditation Thirty-Six

The Characteristics of True Love

Love marks the saints.

True and sincere love is a constant characteristic of pious people. No Christian is without faith, and no faith is without love. Where the brightness of love is lacking, there is also no fervor of faith. Removing love from faith would be like removing light from the sun. Love is the exterior expression of the interior life of a Christian. Just as the body is dead without respiration, so faith is dead without love (Jas 2:26). No one is a Christian who lacks the Spirit of Christ (Rom 8:9). Whoever does not exercise the gift of love does not have the Spirit of Christ because the fruit of the Spirit is love (Gal 5:22). A good tree is not recognized unless it is seen to produce good fruit (Matt 7:16). Love is the bond of Christian perfection. Just as members of the body are conjoined through the soul, so the true members of the mystical body are united through the Holy Spirit with the bond of love (Col 3:14). Just as in the temple of Solomon everything within and without was covered with gold, so in the spiritual temple of God love adorns everything within and without (1 Kgs 6:21).

Love moves the heart to compassion. Love moves the hand to give freely. Compassion is not sufficient if it does not lead to outward giving, nor does outward giving suffice if internal compassion is not added to it. Faith receives everything from God, and love, in turn, gives everything to the neighbor. Through faith, we are made partakers of the divine nature, but God is love (2 Pet 1:4). Therefore, where love is not revealed outwardly, no one will believe that faith is present inwardly. No one believes in Christ who does not love Christ (1 John 4:16). No one loves Christ unless one's neighbor is also loved. A person does not yet grasp the benefits of Christ by faith in the heart if the service owed to one's neighbor is refused. No work is truly good that does not proceed from faith (Rom 14:23). Neither is any work truly good if it does not proceed from love, for love is the seed of all virtues. A fruit is not good is it does not arise from the root of love.

Love is the spiritual savor of the soul, for it alone gives flavor to everything good, arduous, adverse, or laborious. The taste of love also makes death most sweet, because love is stronger than death (Song 8:6). Indeed, it is stronger than death because love led Christ to his death. Love also truly stirs up the pious such that they do not hesitate to die for Christ. All the works of God proceed from love, and also all chastisements. So also, all the works of a Christian person proceed from love. In all creatures God has placed a mirror of his love for us. Sun and moon do not shine for their own sake, but rather for ours. Herbs are not fragrant for their own sake, but for ours. Air, water, animals, and all other creatures are submissive to humanity. So, you should likewise minister to your neighbor.

Speaking in tongues is useless without love, because, apart from love, this gift of tongues puffs up, whereas love edifies (1 Cor 13:1; 8:1). The knowledge of mysteries is useless without love, because mysteries are also known by the Devil, whereas love is characteristic only of the truly pious. The faith to move mountains is also useless without love, because such faith is only miraculous and not salutary (1 Cor 13:2). Love is superior to the gift of working miracles because the former is the indubitable mark of true Christians while the latter is occasionally granted to the impious. It is useless to distribute all your resources to the poor if love is absent, because without inward love that external action is hypocritical (1 Cor 13:3). Rivers of benevolence are useless if they do not arise from the source of love. Love is patient, because no one who truly loves is easily angered. Love is kind, for whoever has given the heart, the greatest good of the soul, is likely to withhold lesser, external goods. Love is not envious, because it considers the welfare of others as equal to its own (1 Cor 13:4). Love does not act falsely, because no one easily harms another who is truly loved from the soul. Love is not puffed up, because through love we are all made members of one body [and] one member does not place itself before another. Love does not behave indecently, because it is of the nature of an angry person to behave indecently while love restrains anger (1 Cor 13:5). Love does not seek what is its own, because it favors the one it loves more than itself and seeks that person's interest more than its own. Love is not irritated, because all anger comes from pride, while love humbles itself before all others. Love contemplates no evil, because to plot evil against another proves that you do not love that person. Love does not take delight in injustice, because love makes another person's misery its own (1 Cor 13:6). Love bears all things, believes all things, hopes all things, endures all things, for what love wishes for itself, it will not refuse to wish for others (1 Cor 13:7). Tongues will cease, prophecy will disappear, knowledge will perish, but love will not cease (1 Cor 13:8). In the future life its imperfection will be eliminated and its perfection will be increased.

God ordered two altars to be placed in the tabernacle. Fire was transferred from the outer one to the inner one. God also assembled a twofold church: the church militant and the church triumphant. The fire of love will someday be transferred from the church militant to the church triumphant. Knowing this, apply yourself to holy love, O devout soul. Whoever your neighbor is, Christ was willing to die for that person. Therefore, will you refuse love to your neighbor when Christ did not hesitate to offer his life for that person? If you truly love God, you ought also to love the image of God. We are all one spiritual body (Eph 4:4). Therefore, all of us ought to be one spiritual soul. It is not right that we should be at odds on earth when someday we will all live as one in heaven. When minds agree in Christ, wills should also be united together. We are servants of one God, so it is not right to be at odds with one another. A member of the body is dead if it does not feel the pain of another. You should not consider yourself a member of the mystical body of Christ if you do not sympathize with the suffering of another. God is the one Father of us all, whom we are instructed by Christ to call upon daily as "Our Father" (Eph 4:6; Matt 6:9). How will he recognize you as a son if you do not recognize his sons as brothers? Love anyone commended to you by God. Love the worthy because they are worthy. If, however, any are unworthy, love them all the same, because God whom you obey is worthy. Through loving the person who is your enemy, you show yourself to be a friend to God (Matt 5:44, 45). Do not consider what a person may do to you, but consider what you have done to God. Do not consider the injury that your enemy inflicts, but consider the benefit God, who has commanded you to love your enemy, has conferred on you. We are neighbors here on earth by birth and brothers by hope of our heavenly inheritance. Therefore we ought to love one another.

Ignite in us, O God, the fire of love through your Spirit.

Meditation Thirty-Seven

Admonition to Chastity

The chaste mind is the marriage bed of Christ.

Whoever wants to be a true disciple of Christ ought to be earnest about holy chastity. Our most generous God is a chaste and pure mind whom we ought to invoke with chaste prayers. A certain wise person said that chastity of the body and purity of the soul are the two keys of religion and happiness. If the body is not kept pure and unspotted by fornication, it is scarcely possible for the soul to be ardent in prayer. Our body is the temple of the Holy Spirit (1 Cor 6:19). It should be protected with the greatest zeal lest we pollute this holy dwelling of the Holy Spirit. The members of our body are members of Christ's body. They should be protected lest we take away the members of Christ and make them members of a whore's body. Let us cling to the Lord through faith and chastity so that we might be one with him in spirit (1 Cor 6:17). Let us not cling to whores lest we be made of one body with them. The Sodomites, burning with lust, were struck with blindness by the Lord, both bodily and spiritually (Gen 19:11). The impure may expect this same punishment today. The lust of the Sodomites was punished by brimstone and fire falling from heaven (Gen 19:24). So, God will enflame the passion of depraved lust in these fornicators with eternal fire. This fire will not be extinguished, but the smoke of their torment will ascend forever (Rev 14:11). Outside of the heavenly Jerusalem there are dogs, that is to say, impure and lustful people (Rev 22:15). Christ washed us with his precious blood in baptism. So, we should guard against being contaminated by impure desires.

A kind of natural shame makes the impure blush to commit certain acts in the sight of other people, but they do not blush to commit them in the sight of God and the angels. There are no walls obstructing the eyes of God, which are brighter than the sun, nor are there any corners that shut out the presence of the holy angels. No retreats separate us from the internal testimony of conscience. It is amazing that the ardor of lasciviousness ascends, as it were, to heaven, while its stench descends to hell. Brief pleasure will produce eternal sadness. The attraction is momentary, but the torment will be eternal. The pleasure of fornication is brief, but the pain of the fornicator will be perpetual. May remembrance of the crucified one crucify your flesh within you. May the thought of hell extinguish the fever of lust within you. May tears of repentance extinguish the heat of desire within you. May divine fear paralyze your flesh lest you be misled by carnal love. Consider that the craving of lust is full of anxiety and foolishness. The act is abominable and ignominious; the outcome is regret and shame. Do not look at the pleasing face of the Devil inciting you to lust, but rather at the stinging tail as you flee. Do not consider the brevity of delight but more the endlessness of damnation. Love knowledge of the scriptures and you will not love the vices of the flesh. Always keep yourself busy with some kind of work so that when the tempter comes, he will always find you occupied. He deceived David in a time of idleness; he was not able to mislead Joseph during his official duties (1 Sam 11:2; Gen 39:8).

Consider that the instant of death could be at any hour and you will easily reject all desires of the flesh. Love temperance and you will easily conquer perverse lusts. When the stomach is seething with undiluted wine, it quickly whips up lust. Chastity is endangered by sensual pleasure. If, therefore, you feed the flesh with excessive delights, you will nourish your own enemy. The flesh must be nourished in such a way that it is preserved, but it should be subdued so that it does not become proud. Consider the terror of the Last Judgment and you will easily extinguish the fever of lust. If the hidden things of the heart will be revealed, how much more those deeds done in secret (1 Cor 4:5)? If an explanation must be rendered for every useless word, how much more for every foul word? If an explanation must be rendered for every foul word, how much more for impure deeds (Matt 12:36)? However long your life was, so long will be your indictment. There will be as many accusers as you have sins. Those thoughts that have become contemptible by our frequent use of them will not remain unexamined. Therefore, what use is it for your fornication to be hidden for a while from other people when it must be revealed completely before the eyes of all on the Day of Judgment? What use is it to escape from the tribunal of the earthly judge when you will not be able to escape the tribunal of the supernal judge? You will not be able to corrupt this judge with bribes because this judge is most just. You will not be able to sway him with pleas because he is the strictest judge. You will not be able to flee from his province or jurisdiction because he is the most powerful judge. You will not be able to deceive him with vain excuses because he is the wisest judge. You will not be able to appeal the sentence he has promulgated because he is the supreme judge. Here, there is truth in the investigation, openness in the publication, and severity in the execution of his judgment.

Therefore, O soul devoted to God, always keep the terror of this judge in mind so that the fever of lust does not mislead you. Be like the rose in love, the violet in humility, the lily in chastity. Learn humility from Christ, your Bridegroom. Also learn chastity from him. Great is the dignity of chastity that was consecrated in the body of Christ. Great is the dignity of chastity because it makes us live beyond the flesh while in the flesh. Just as there is nothing more vile than to be conquered by the flesh, so there is nothing more glorious than to conquer the flesh. We should not only flee from external fornications but also flee from impure thoughts, because God is not only the judge of external actions but also of internal thoughts. Often, piety is injured by a look, and chastity is often violated by the eyes. Hear what Truth says: "Whoever looks at a women with lust, has committed fornication with her" (Matt 5:28). How difficult this battle is, but the victory will be glorious. It is difficult to quench the fire of lust. It excites the very young, inflames young people, and exhausts the old and decrepit. It does not scorn hovels or stand in awe of palaces. Although it is difficult to fight it, it will be laudable to prevail. The first attack should be repelled immediately and should not add the fuel of perverse thoughts to this flame. When the Apostle advises us to resist all vices, he says we should not fight lusts but flee from them. He says: "Flee fornication" (1 Cor 6:18). A wandering beggar who comes to take advantage of us by feigning simplicity goes away if we do not admit him, but if we permit him to enter, he becomes a guest, gathers strength, and, in the end, becomes our master, if we let him. So, the stirrings of perverse lusts excite us but will go away if we do not welcome them. If you do not want this enemy to dominate you, do not receive him into the home of your heart.

Preserve, O God, the sanctity of our souls and the chastity of our bodies.

Meditation Thirty-Eight

The Shortness of Our Present Life

What is human life? A rolling stone.

Consider, O devout soul, how miserable and fleeting this life is, so that you might raise your heart to the desire of your heavenly inheritance. While this life increases, it decreases at the same time. While it expands, it diminishes at the same time. Whatever is added to it also subtracts from it at the same time. The life we live is but a point in time, even less than that. In the moment we turn around, immortality is at hand. We are in this life as in a foreign house. Abraham had no base of habitation in the land of Canaan besides his hereditary place of burial (Gen 23:4). So, this present life is only a place of temporary lodging and a sepulcher.

The beginning of this life is, right away, the prelude to death. Our life is like a sailor who is always coming closer to the port as he sails, whether he is standing, sitting, or lying down. So, whether we are asleep or awake, lying down or walking around, doing something willingly or unwillingly, we are always being led through the movement of time to our end. This life is more like death because we are dying every single day. Every single day we use up part of life. This life is full of regret on account of what is past, hardship at the present time, and fear about the future. We enter life weeping, because an infant begins life with tears, as if it can foresee future adversities. We progress feebly because we are afflicted with many diseases and many cares torment us. We leave this life horribly because we go out alone but our works go out with us and through death we go to the severe judgment of God (Rev 14:13). We are conceived in sin, born in misery, live in pain, and die in anguish. We are conceived in filth, kept alive in darkness, and brought forth in pain. Before our birth we burden our poor mothers; at birth we lacerate them like a viper. We are aliens when we are born and sojourners while we live, because we are compelled to move on when we die. In the first part of our life we do not know ourselves, in the middle we are overwhelmed with cares, and in the last part we are depressed by the troubles of old age. The entire time of our life consists of the present, the past, and the future. The present is unstable, the past is nothing, and the future is uncertain. We are putrid at our birth, our whole life is a bubble, and in death we are food for worms. We carry earth around, we tread upon the earth, and we will become earth. We have been subjected to the necessity of birth, the miseries of living, and the difficulty of dying. Our body is an earthly dwelling inhabited by death and sin and is consumed by them every single day.

Our whole life is spiritual warfare. Above us demons watch for our destruction, on the right and the left the world battles us, and below and within us our flesh keeps watch. Human life is warfare because flesh and spirit perpetually struggle within us (Gal 5:17). Therefore, how can there be true joy for a person in this life, when there is no secure happiness in it? What can we lay hold of to love in the present when everything is passing away except what threatens us, when that which is loved is completely ended and we are always approaching closer to the place where pain never ends? What do we gain from a longer life? We do more evil, we see more evil, and we suffer more evil.

What is humanity? A possession of death, a transient traveler, an insubstantial bubble, who lives shorter than a moment, is more vacuous than an image, emptier than a sound, more fragile than glass, more changeable than the wind, more fleeting than a shadow, and more deceptive than a dream. What is this life? A waiting for death, a scene in a farce, a sea of miseries, a measure of blood, which any accident can easily destroy, which any sort of fever can annihilate. The course of life is a labyrinth, which we enter from the womb and leave through the threshold of death. We are nothing but earth, earth is nothing but smoke, but smoke is nothing, so we are nothing. This life is like glass: fragile; like a stream: forever rushing onward; like warfare: miserable. And, nevertheless, it appears to many to be desirable. External life seems like a precious nut but, in truth, if you open up with a knife, you will see that there are nothing but worms and decay inside. Apples grow in the region around Sodom that are attractive because of their exterior beauty, but when they are touched they turn into dust. The happiness of this life delights superficially, but if you touch it for more careful examination, it will appear to be like smoke and ashes.

Therefore, do not devote your highest thoughts to this life, but always aspire with your mind toward your future joy. Compare the briefest moment of time granted to us in this life with the infinite and never-ending age to come, and it will seem foolish to cling to this fleeting life while neglecting eternity. Our life here passes so quickly and, nevertheless, during it we gain or lose eternal life. This life is so miserable, yet during it we gain or lose eternal happiness. This life is full of calamities, yet, during it we gain or lose eternal joy. Therefore, if you aspire to eternal life, long for it with your whole heart during this fleeting life. Make use of this world, but do not let your heart cling to the world. Carry on your business in this life, but do not let your mind be fixed on this life. Outward use of worldly things does not harm you if your inward love does not cling to them. Your homeland is in heaven. This world is only a temporary hostel for you. Do not be charmed by your daily lodging in this world such that you are distracted from a longing for your heavenly homeland.

This life is a sea, eternity is our port. Do not be charmed by the momentary tranquility of the sea such that you do not aspire toward the port of eternal tranquility. This life is inconstant. It does not keep faith with those who love it, seeing that, contrary to expectations, it often flees from them. Therefore, why would you want to put your faith in it? It is dangerous even to promise yourself the security of one hour, because, most often, this fleeting life ends in that very hour. It is safest to expect the end of this present life at every hour. In the gourd that delighted Jonah, God prepared a worm that made it shrivel up (Jon 4:7). So it is with worldly things that many cling to with love. None of them is stable. Worms of corruption grow within them. The world has been so ground up by the destruction of such things that it has lost its seductive appearance. They should be praised and commended who do not think it worthy to be cheerful when the world is flourishing, and likewise, they should be reprimanded and accused who take delight in perishing when it is perishing.

Withdraw, O Christ, our hearts from love of this world and arouse a desire in us for the heavenly kingdom.

Meditation Thirty-Nine

The Vanity of the World

The eternal is better than the perishable.

Soul, do not love what is in the world (1 John 2:15). The world will perish and all that is in it will burn up (2 Pet 3:10). Therefore, where will your love be then? Love what is eternally good so that you may live in eternity. All creatures are subject to vanity (Rom 8:20). Whoever, therefore, clings with love to creatures is also made vain. Love what is truly and permanently good so that your heart might be given stability and rest.

Why do you love worldly honor? If you seek honor from other people, you cannot be honored by God (John 5:44). Whoever seeks worldly honor is forced to be conformed to this world. Whoever pleases the world cannot please God (Gal 1:10). All things are perishable and unstable if what has produced them is perishable and unstable. Hence, worldly honor cannot be stable. The one they raised to heaven yesterday with the greatest glory, they often treat with greatest dishonor the next day. Seek to please God so that you might be honored by God. Divine honor is true and stable. What could be better for a person than being considered great by other people? To be honored in the sight of God. That and nothing more. When they sought to make Christ a king, he fled. When they sought to condemn him and execute him on the shameful cross, he offered himself up voluntarily (John 6:15; 18:4). Therefore, if you wish to conform yourself to Christ, love the reproach of the world more than its honor. How likely is it that someone will give up life for Christ's sake if that person will not refuse worldly honor for him? There is no other path to true glory than through contempt for worldly glory, just as Christ entered into his glory through the inglorious cross.

Therefore, you should love to be disparaged, vilified, and rejected in this world. What we should think about worldly honor Christ has taught us by his life. All the glory of heaven served him, indeed, this true glory was his alone, but he rejected such glory (Luke 24:26). Therefore, to the extent to which one is honored and showered with many bodily consolations, one ought to be more profoundly and intimately saddened, seeing oneself to be all the more devoid of conformity to Christ (Bernard of Clairvaux, *Consideration of Death*). Human praise is vain if a bad conscience accuses us inwardly. What use is it to someone with a fever to be placed on an ivory bed if that person continues to suffer from the heat within? The testimony of your conscience is true honor and true praise. No one is a fairer judge of your deeds than God and your conscience. You should desire to test your actions by this judgment. Is it not sufficient to know yourself, and what is the most important of all, to be known by God?

Why do you have such an appetite for riches? If God is not sufficient for you, you are exceedingly avaricious. This life is a path to an eternal homeland. Therefore, what good is great wealth? It is more of a burden to the pilgrim than a vast cargo is to a ship. To servants of God, riches consist of Christ, the king of heaven. The true treasure ought to be within a person, not outside. The true treasure is what you will be able to take with you to the universal judgment, yet, in truth, all external goods will be taken away from us at death. All these collected things will perish but, what is worse, the collector of them will perish unless that person is rich in God. You come poor into the world, and you pass out of it poor (Job 1:21). Why, then, should the middle be any different from the beginning or the end? Riches ought to be viewed according to their use, and thus, very little will be sufficient. The least gift of grace and virtue is superior to all the riches of this world. Why? Because virtue is pleasing to God and riches only for the sake of virtue. The poverty of Christ ought to be more pleasing to us than the riches of the whole world. Poverty has been sanctified by Christ. He was poor at birth, during his life, and poorer still at death. Shouldn't you hesitate to prefer the riches of the world to poverty when Christ preferred it to the riches of the kingdom of heaven? How will you entrust your soul to God if you will not entrust the care of your body to him? How will you lay down your life for your brother if you will not expend your riches on him? Riches require labor to be acquired, produce fear when possessed and pain when lost, and, what is more lamentable, the labor of the avaricious will not only be to no avail but will also bring them to ruin, according to the teaching of Bernard (Bernard of Clairvaux, *On Conversion*). What you love is your God. Where your treasure is, there is also your heart (Matt 6:21). If you love these material, worldly, perishable riches, it is not possible for you to love spiritual, heavenly, eternal riches. Why is that? Because the former weigh down the heart of a person and drag it downward, while the latter truly lift it up. Love of earthly things is like glue on our spiritual wings, a certain true lover of Christ once said (Augustine, Sermon 112). Lot's wife, who was turned into a pillar of salt, should be a lesson for us not to look back at those things that are worldly but to press forward on the right path to our heavenly homeland (Gen 19:26). The apostles left everything and followed Christ (Matt 4:22). Why is that? Because knowledge of true riches destroyed the false desire for so-called riches.

Having tasted the Spirit, the flesh seems tasteless. The world is bitter to the person who cares for Christ. Why do you desire pleasures so much? May remembrance of the crucifixion crucify all desire for pleasure in you. May thought of the fire of hell extinguish all lustful ardor in you. Compare the pleasures that last the briefest moment with eternal punishments. Fleshly pleasures are brutish and make you like a brute beast. Whoever is filled daily with the husks fed to swine has no taste for the sweetness of the kingdom of heaven (Bernard, Epistola 2). Let us kill our sensual desires and, with Abraham, offer a spiritual sacrifice to God, a beloved son, in other words, the desires of our soul, voluntarily renouncing all pleasures and embracing the bitterness of the cross (Gen 22). The path that leads to the kingdom of heaven is not flat and scattered with roses but is harsh and covered with thorns. The outer person prospers through pleasures but the inner person through crosses and tribulations. As much as the outer increases, the inner diminishes. Pleasures sustain the body, but the truly pious minimize concern for the body and maximize concern for the soul. Pleasures captivate our heart so that it is not free to love God. Not pleasures but contempt for pleasures can be carried with you when you die and can be brought to the judgment. Therefore, let holy fear pierce your flesh so that carnal love does not deceive you. Let remembrance of divine judgment continually be kept in mind so that the perverse judgment of your sensual appetites does not lead you into servitude. Have no regard for the face of the seductive serpent, but be aware of its bitter, stinging tail. Conquer through the grace of Christ so that you might be crowned a victor by Christ.

Meditation Forty

The Value of Temptation

A palm tree grows upward though weighed down.

It is valuable for the faithful soul to be tested and strengthened in this world by temptations. Our Savior himself was willing to wrestle with the Devil in the wilderness so that he might vanquish the adversary for the sake of us and our salvation and be the faithful champion in our battles (Matt 4:4). First, he descended into hell, after which he ascended into heaven. So, the faithful soul descends first into hellish temptation so that it might ascend to heavenly glory. The people of Israel were not able to occupy the promised land of Canaan until they were first conquered by various enemies (Josh 23:1). Likewise, the faithful soul may not promise itself the kingdom of heaven until it has come forth as a victor over the flesh, the world, and the Devil.

Temptation tests, purifies, and illuminates. Temptation tests in the sense that faith is rooted more firmly in the rock of salvation if it is battered by adversity. It spreads itself wider in branches of good works. It is raised higher in hope of liberation. The angel of Jehovah appeared to Abraham, who complied promptly with the divine command after being ordered to sacrifice his son, and said: "Now I know that you fear the Lord, when you would not spare your only son for my sake" (Gen 22:12). So, if you have offered the beloved son of your soul, in other words, your own will, in the midst of temptation, you will be considered a God-fearer and will sense God speaking to you in your heart. Fire tests gold and temptation tests faith. Just as a battle shows how strong a soldier is, so temptation shows how firm our faith is. When the whirling winds and tempestuous waves rushed against Christ's boat, then it became evident how weak the faith of his disciples was (Matt 8:24). When the Lord ordered the Israelites to be led forth to conquer the Midianites, they were first brought down to the water to be tested (Judg 7:4). Likewise, those who will be led into the heavenly homeland after having conquered the enemy are first tested by the waters of tribulation and temptation. Therefore, whatever adversity, whatever temptation the faithful soul encounters should be considered a sign of testing rather than rejection.

Temptation also purifies. Christ, our Doctor, uses many purges to draw out the noxious malady of self-love and love of the world. Tribulation stimulates an examination of conscience and calls to mind the sins of our past life. Indeed, just as medicine protects the body from contagious diseases, such tribulation prevents us from sinning. There is a human proclivity to fall into sin, more in times of good fortune than in times of adversity. To many, riches are thorns (Matt 13:22). Therefore, God pulls out the thorns so that they cannot suffocate the soul. A great variety of worldly affairs gets in the way of divine obedience. Therefore, God lets diseases occur so that they might turn us around, making us die to the world and live to God. For many, it has been beneficial to have fallen from a lofty position of wealth and honor to the quiet of a common lot in life. Worldly honor excites pride in many. Therefore, God sends contempt and extinguishes the spark of pride.

Finally, temptation illuminates. We do not recognize how fragile and vain all the consolations of the world are, except in times of temptation. When Stephen was stoned, he saw the glory of God (Acts 7:55). Likewise, Christ shows himself to the contrite soul in the midst of calamities. There is no true and lasting joy except through the indwelling of God. God resides in those who have a contrite and humble spirit. Afflictions and temptations crush and humiliate the spirit, so there is true and lasting joy in the soul of the afflicted. Temptation is the way that leads to the recognition of God. Thus says the Lord: "I will be with them in trouble, rescue them, and make them see my salvation" (Ps 91:15, 16). Tobias, being blind, saw nothing that was above, below, or in front of him, not even himself, but he was illuminated by the angel Raphael from God so that he was able to perceive what he could not see before, using no other medicine besides the gall of a fish (Tob 2:10; 11:11). This confirmed that our eyes must be smeared with the gall of bitterness and must be illuminated so we may find true knowledge of ourselves and of worldly goods. Why does the Apostle say that what we now know is a riddle

(1 Cor 13:12)? Because we realize through temptation that God gladdens the elect under the semblance of sadness, vivifies them under the semblance of death, heals them under the semblance of disease, enriches them under the semblance of poverty. Therefore, the person who is not ungrateful that Christ was crucified and tempted for us ought to welcome crosses and temptations.

O good Jesus, burn me now, persecute me now so that I might be spared later. O good Jesus, you often spare us by casting us away from yourself. Grant that, by being smitten, we might return to you. Afflict and suppress us externally so that we might grow and become vigorous internally. Fight, O good Jesus, within me against myself. Be my regulator as I struggle and my crown when I am victorious. May whatever adversity I experience in life, strengthen and increase my faith. O good Jesus, hasten to aid my weak faith, as, indeed, you promised before through the holy prophet: As a mother consoles her children, so will I console you (Isa 66:13). As a mother caresses with the greatest care and nourishes her child by nursing, so, good Jesus, encourage and confirm my languishing faith. Grant that your internal consolations may be stronger within me than all opposition from humanity and the Devil, and even the thoughts of my own heart.

O merciful Samaritan, pour bitter wine over my wounds, but also add the oil of divine consolation. Multiply my crosses but also give me the strength to bear them.

Meditation Forty-One

The Foundation of Christian Patience

In the end, patience will be the victor.

Rest, devout soul, and patiently bear the cross imposed on you by God. Consider the passion of Christ, your Bridegroom. He was afflicted for all, by all, and in all ways. He suffered for all, even for those who disparaged his precious suffering and impiously trampled his blood with their feet. He was afflicted by all. He was delivered up by his heavenly Father, stricken, forsaken, and deserted by his beloved disciples (Rom 8:32; Matt 26:56). He was rejected by his own people, the Jews, who preferred the robber Barabbas instead of him, and was crucified by the Gentiles (Matt 27:21). He bore the offenses of each and every person, and thus was afflicted by all of them. He also suffered in every way. His soul was sad even unto death and, feeling crushed by divine judgment, he cried out that he had been deserted by God (Matt 27:46). From all his members he sweated blood, his head was crowned with thorns, his tongue tasted a drink of myrrh, his hands and feet were pierced with nails, his side was wounded, his whole body was whipped, and he hung from the cross (Luke 22:44). He suffered from hunger, thirst, cold, contempt, poverty, rebuke, wounds, death, and the cross.

How unjust it would be for the Lord to suffer while his servants are glad! How unjust it would be for the Savior to be punished so harshly for our sins while we take delight in them! How unjust it would be for the head to be afflicted while the remaining members do not suffer with him! Just as it was fitting for Christ to enter into heavenly glory through his suffering, so also it is fitting for us to enter the kingdom of heaven through many tribulations. Consider the bountiful reward. The sufferings of this time are not worthy to be compared to the future glory (Rom 8:18). However much we may suffer, it is temporary, indeed, sometimes for only a day, but the glory to come is eternal. God accurately takes note of all our adversity and will bring it, someday, into judgment (Eccl 14:11). Therefore, how unpleasant it would be to be seen in that grand assembly of the whole world without the adornments of crosses and sufferings. He will also wipe away all tears from our eyes. O happy tears that will be wiped away by such a Lord (Isa 25:8; Rev 7:17). O blessed cross that will gain such a reward in heaven. David spent ten whole years in exile but ruled for forty (2 Sam 5:4). This prefigures the brevity of our suffering and the eternal glory that will follow it. It is only for a point in time that the saints are bothered by crosses and accumulate the sympathy of this age. Favorable evenings truly follow such difficult mornings.

Consider, moreover, the tribulations of all the saints. Look at Job lying on the dung-heap, John thirsting in the desert, Peter stretched out on a gibbet, James beheaded by the sword of Herod (Job 2:8; Luke 3:2; Acts 12:2). Look at Mary, the blessed mother of our Savior, standing beneath the cross of her Son, who is a pattern for the church as the spiritual mother of the Lord (John 19:25). "You are blessed," Christ says, "if you are persecuted for my name, for the prophets were treated in the same way" (Matt 5:11). O glorious persecution of the prophets and apostles and all the saints, which restores us to conformity with Christ himself. Therefore, let us suffer with the sufferers and be crucified with those who have been crucified so that we might be glorified with those who have been glorified. If we are truly children of God, we should not shy away from the fate of the rest of God's children. If we truly desire an inheritance from God, we should completely accept it. Now, the children of God are not only inheritors of joy and glory in the future life, but also of sadness and suffering in this life, because God chastises all the children whom he receives, punishing their sins so that they might be spared future judgment (Heb 12:6). He multiplies their tribulations now so that reward might be increased later. The more persecution there is now, the greater the reward to come.

Consider the blessed circumstance of the cross. It destroys the root of worldly love within us and plants the seed of divine love in our hearts. The cross produces loathing of whatever is worldly and elevates the soul to whatever is heavenly. If the flesh has been mortified, the Spirit lives, and as the world becomes bitter, Christ becomes sweeter. Great is the mystery of the cross, for through it, God calls us to contrition, true fear, and the exercising of patience. Let us open up when God knocks, and let us hear what the Lord speaks to us. The cross appears contemptible to the world and to carnal eyes, but it is glorious to God and to spiritual eyes. What could appear more vile and abject to the Jews than the suffering of Christ, yet what could appear more worthy and precious in the eyes of God? Indeed, this was the price paid for the sins of the whole world (1 John 2:2). So it was that a just man was afflicted, a just man died and no one cared, but the cross and the death of the saints is precious in the sight of God (Ps 116:15). The church, the bride of Christ, is black on the outside on account of her calamities and persecutions, yet white within on account of divine consolations. The church is an enclosed garden and so is every faithful soul. No one, except for whoever is within it, knows how beautiful it is (Song 4:12). We will never fully and perfectly feel the consolation of the Spirit unless our flesh is outwardly afflicted. If love of the world dwells in us, love of God will not enter it. A full vessel cannot be filled with a new liquid unless it is first emptied. Therefore, empty out love of the world so that it might be filled with the love of God. For this reason God himself destroyed love of the world in us through the cross so that there might be a place for divine love. Furthermore, the cross moves us to pray and is the cause of virtue. When the north wind blows across the garden, its fragrance wafts abroad (Song 4:16). This means that when persecutions beset the church, its virtues increase and give off an aroma that is pleasing to God. The beloved bridegroom of the soul is white and ruddy; the white being innocence and the ruddiness suffering (Song 5:10). This is so that the beloved bride of Christ might become white with virtues and ruddy from sufferings. Just as divine grace can produce oil and honey from the stone of our hardest afflictions, so can it also create, from the root of bitter calamity, the sweetest fruit of eternal glory, which it wishes to convey and introduce to us. Amen.

Meditation Forty-Two

How to Conquer Temptation through Perseverance

Hope, trusting in God, will never leave us troubled.

Holy Lord Jesus, my dearest Bridegroom, how can it be that you bring me to your wedding feast (Rev 19:7)? I am a wanderer, exiled from you, but I believe most firmly, never doubting, that I will appear before long, before you, released from the restraints of my body. Fear and trembling come over me because I carry my treasure in earthen vessels (2 Cor 4:7). My mind is prone to errors, my will is prone to sins, nor can I even say that my spirit is always willing (Matt 26:41). The flesh is always weak, sin leads me captive, and the law of my members fights against the law of my mind (Rom 7:23). Fear and trembling come over me because Satan plots to take my treasure. His cunning is great, his zeal for doing harm is most fervent, and his power is the greatest. He deceived Adam in paradise and Judas in the school of the Savior, so how will I, as wretched as I am, be safe from his treachery (Gen 3:1; John 13:27)? Fear and trembling come over me because I am still in this world, which lies totally engrossed by evil (1 John 5:19). Worldly delights attract me, troubles in the way of the Lord terrify me, and sometimes I let myself take pleasure in worldly enticements. The whole world is full of traps. How will I, as wretched as I am, be able to escape them?

Fear and trembling come over me because God is at work in me, both to will and to do (Phil 2:13). I fear lest my negligence and carelessness cause God to take away what he already gave me: his good will. I make use of the remission of sins so unworthily and thrust aside the first grace that has been given to me. Hence, I fear lest the secret and just judgment of God deservedly takes away what I use so unworthily. I am anxious lest I be deserted by the one whom I often deserted after my first conversion. How harshly I am tormented, knowing that these benefits from God will be followed by a harder and more severe judgment if I have used them unworthily. But, the infinite mercy of God will uphold me so that what he made me will he will also make me do. It is so because he is God and does not change (Mal 3:6). His mercy toward me is unwavering and will not change (Ps 117:2). The foundation of the Lord is firm. It is especially firm because it is from God himself in whom there is no variation. It is especially firm because it is confirmed by the blood of Christ who always intercedes before the throne of God (Heb 12:24). It is especially firm because it is stamped with the sure seal of the sacraments (Rom 4:11).

If I should seek for some measure of salvation in myself, I would surely have reason to doubt that I am saved. But just as all my hope for justification is in Christ, so is all my hope for salvation. If I had grasped Christ by my free will, I would surely have reason to be afraid lest I lose Christ by a change of my free will. But since he was found by one who had not sought him, he will surely not withdraw again, after having been found. He who led me from the shadow of death to participation in the light will not permit me to be thrust into the former darkness (Luke 1:79). The gifts and call of God are immutable according to God's will (Rom 11:29). Would that I were so immutable. That treasure is always present, but the hand grasping it sometimes grows weary. However, I will be able to grasp Christ who has revealed himself in his word and promises and will also benevolently allow me to cling to his word and the promise of faith. I will strengthen my faith by the use of prayer as a support and aid, and I will not let the Lord leave the chamber of my heart until he has granted me salvation (Gen 32:26). Through the power of the Lord I will be able to preserve my salvation (1 Pet 1:5). The power of the Lord encourages and comforts me, but my infirmity depresses me and makes me sad. And yet, the power of the Lord is perfected in my infirmity (2 Cor 12:9). He from whom all the power of faith comes will strengthen me. Divine grace uplifts me, but my unworthiness makes me afraid. And yet, if I were worthy it would not be grace or mercy, since salvation would then be by works and not faith (Rom 11:6). Grace is not grace in any way if it is not gratuitous in every way. Thus, I do not look to my works. Whatever is erroneous, God will correct. Whatever is lacking, God will supply. Whatever is sinful, God will abolish. Whatever God does not want to impute to me is just as if it never were. Therefore, insofar as my salvation is from God, it is firm.

Meditation Forty-Three

Daily Consideration of Death

Meditation on death is life.

O faithful soul, expect death at any hour because it lies in wait for you at every hour. Early in the morning, when you rise, consider that this could be the last day of your life. In the evening, when you go to lie down, consider that this could be your final night on earth. Whatever you do, whatever you undertake, always think beforehand and consider carefully whether you would do such things if this was the hour of your death and coming to the judgment of God. Now, do you suppose that if you do not think about death that it will not come near to you? Do you suppose that you will be summoning death if you think about it? Whether you think about it or not, whether you speak about it or not, it stands at your neck. Life has been loaned to you, not given to you to possess. You will exit it in the same condition that you entered it. You came into the world naked, and you leave it naked. Life is a journey. When you have walked about for a while, you will then come back again. You are like a colonist or a tenant in this world, not a permanent landlord.

Think every hour how you hasten through every moment. We are mistaken if we imagine that we die only after the last breath of our life. Every day, every hour, every single moment we are dying. In the same way that we enter life, we depart from it. Whatever is added to life is also subtracted. We do not fall into death suddenly, but proceed toward it minute by minute. Our life is a path, down which we go part way each day. Death and life seem most distant from each other when, in fact, nothing is nearer to another than death to life. The one is slipping away while the other is drawing nearer. Just as those traveling on a ship often do not feel that they are moving and are not aware that they are near the end of their journey, so whatever we do, whether we eat or drink or sleep, we are always coming nearer to death. Many pass through life seeking the means to support and promote life.

No one accepts the approach of death happily unless it has been grappled with for a long time. If you die to yourself in daily life, you will be able to live with God in death. Before you die, the vices within you should be killed. If the old Adam within you is killed during your life, then Christ will live in you in death. The exterior nature should be destroyed every day during your life so that the interior nature will be renewed in you at the time of death. Death transfers us from time to eternity as we are because wood will remain where it falls (Eccl 11:3). Therefore, how carefully we should consider the hour of death. Time passes by and the infinite period of eternity remains. Therefore, prepare yourself in time for eternity. Whether we will be blessed or wretched for eternity will be decided in one hour, at death. In this one moment eternal happiness will be possessed or lost.

For this reason, O faithful soul, you should prepare yourself for that hour. It will be easy for you to belittle everything worldly, if you know that you are dying. Consider how your eyes will become darkened in death, and you will easily be able to turn them away from vain things. Consider how your ears will become deaf in death, and you will easily be able to block out all impious and obscene words. Consider how your tongue will become stiff in death, and you will take greater care with your manner of speaking. If you ponder the sweat and anxiety of the dying, it will be easy for you to depreciate worldly delights. See yourself leaving this life naked, and poverty in this life will be no hardship for you. Consider how the body stiffens in death, and it will be easy for you to devalue the splendor of this world. See the wailing of the soul when it is being forced out of its dwelling place in the body, and it will be easy for you to avoid all sin. Consider the decay following your death, and it will be easy for you to humble your proud flesh. Consider how you will be empty and stripped, how you will relinquish all other creatures in death, and you will easily avert your love away from them and turn it toward the Creator. Consider how anxiously death searches you to be sure you carry nothing with you from this life, and you will easily be able to despise all the riches of the world. Whoever dies daily in this life through vices, passes from death to eternal punishment. No one passes to eternal life unless that person begins to live in Christ in this life. In order to live in death, you must implant yourself through faith in Christ.

Let death always be on your mind because it is always waiting for you. We always carry death around with us, because we always carry sins around in us. Moreover, the wages of sin is death (Rom 6:23). If you truly desire to avoid the bitterness of death, hold on to the words of Christ. Faith joins and unites us with Christ. Therefore, whoever is in Christ will not die, for Christ is that person's life (John 8:51). Whoever clings to God through faith is one spirit with God (1 Cor 6:17). Consequently, the faithful do not die in eternity because Christ is their life. The people of Israel crossed the Red Sea to the Promised Land, but Pharaoh and his troops perished in it (Exod 14:28, 29). So, death is the beginning of true life for the pious and the gate to paradise. Death for the godless is not the end of evil for them but the cord connecting what went before to what follows. They pass from the first death to the second death (Rev 20:14). So close is the union of Christ and the faithful that it cannot be dissolved by death. The torch of divine grace shines into the densest shadow of death. For that dangerous passage into death, Christ provides his beloved with the protection of angels. The bodies of the saints are the temples of the Holy Spirit (1 Cor 6:19). This Holy Spirit will not allow this temple to be destroyed through death. The Word of God is an incorruptible seed, which is not destroyed by death but is hidden in the hearts of the pious and will vivify them at the appointed time (1 Pet 1:23).

Meditation Forty-Four

Consolation in the Death of Friends

In dying we gain life.

Consider, devout soul, that Christ is your Savior, and you will not fear the terror of death. If you are saddened by the ferocity of death, be encouraged again by the power of Christ. The Israelites were not able to drink the waters at Mara because of their bitterness, but Jehovah showed a piece of wood to Moses, which, when he threw it into the waters, made them sweet (Exod 15:25). If you are frightened by the bitterness of death, God shows the piece of wood to you that converts it into sweetness: the shoot, of course, springing from the root of Jesse. This shoot is Christ. Whoever keeps his word will not see death in eternity (John 8:51). Life is full of burdens. Therefore, it is good to be relieved of them. It is the Christian's misery that dies, not the Christian. This going forth we think of as death is not an exit but a transition. We do not lose our loved ones; we send them ahead. They do not die; they rise again. They precede us; they do not recede or secede from us. It is not a demise but more of a departure from us. The relocation of the pious is a beginning again of life. The exit of the pious is a profit for them. When our loved ones die, this means they cease sinning, they cease being troubled, they cease being miserable. When they die in faith, this means they separate from the shadow of life so that they might pass to true life, from shadow to light, from human company to the company of God.

Life is like a sea voyage, and death is the most secure port. Therefore, we should not be sad that our loved ones are dead, but, rather, we should rejoice with them that they have made it through the turbulence of the sea to the port. This life is a prison of the soul. Death, then, is liberation. When Simeon is dying, he exclaims: "Now let your servant depart, Lord" (Luke 2:29). He wishes to depart, as if he were confined in a bodily prison. Therefore, we should rejoice with our loved ones when they aspire to be released from this prison into true liberty. In the same way, the Apostle asks to be released as if being bound to an earthly body were like a miserable servitude (Phil 1:23). Now then, shall we be sad that our loved ones have struggled out of these chains and are now truly free? Shall we put on black garments when they put on white clothing? It is written that the elect will be given white vestments on account of their innocence and will have palms in their hands on account of their victory (Rev 7:9). Shall we be troubled with tears and sighs on account of them when God will wipe all the tears from their eyes (Rev 7:17)? Shall we mourn for them and create more sadness for ourselves in our labors when they are in a place where there is neither sorrow nor pain, where cries are not heard and they are at rest from their labors? Shall we be exhausted by immoderate sadness on account of their deaths when they are in fellowship with the angels and enjoy real happiness? Shall we raise our voices in lamentation on account of them when they sing new songs in the company of angels with harps and golden bowls (Rev 5:8, 9)? Shall we be sad that they have departed from this earth when they themselves are giving thanks that they have departed?

Christ shows how good it is to go out from this world. When his disciples are sad at his remark that he will be going away from them, he responds: "If you loved me, you would rejoice" (John 14:28). If you were sailing through a wild and tempestuous storm and the waves rose up from the force of the wind, foretelling an impending shipwreck, would you not seek a port as quickly as possible? See how the world totters and is about to fall. It gives evidence of its decline, not only due to old age but also because all things come to an end, and you will not give thanks to God? Will you not be happy for your loved ones who have been snatched away by an earlier departure, and have thus been removed from ruin, shipwrecks, and other imminent misfortune? In whose hands can your salvation be more secure than in the hands of Christ? Where can your soul dwell more securely than in the kingdom of paradise? Hear what the Apostle says about death. Death is a gain (Phil 1:21). It is a gain to have evaded the spread of sin. It is a gain to have escaped from what is deteriorating. It is a gain to have been transported to a better place. If those who have been lost through death were very dear to you, God should be dearer because he wished to take them to himself. Do not be angry with God, who took away nothing but what he previously gave (Job 1:21). He has received what is his, not taken what is yours. Do not be angry that the Lord has claimed back what he only loaned out. The Lord alone sees the evils that are coming. Therefore, he wanted to take care of your loved ones lest they be entangled in coming misfortunes. Those who have died in the Lord rest sweetly in their graves, while those who survive are severely tortured in the palaces of their kingdom (Rev 14:13).

If you have lost dear ones through death, believe that they will be dearer to you when you regain them in the future. A brief time separates you from them, but a blessed and secure eternity joins you with them again. We put our hope in the most true promise that we will pass from this life, from which we have sent some of our loved ones in advance, and will come to that life where they will be better known and thus dearer to us and there will be no fear of any dissension in our friendship. However many souls there will be after us and however many there have been before us, they will be received gladly into the great assembly. It will be permitted for us to recognize the faces of the people we know and to converse with one another. Brother will go with sister and children with parents. Night will not end the celebrations of any day.

Therefore, do not look back at the time of abandonment, when they left you in death, but be mindful of the time of restitution, when they will be restored to you in the resurrection. Where our faith in the resurrection is firm, there is no semblance of death but more of rest. The whole world is a mirror of resurrection. The sun sets daily and shines again the next day. Plants that died off in winter truly revive. The phoenix reproduces itself in death. When a season ends, a new one begins. Fruits ripen and come back again. Seeds do not spring up and become fertile unless they first decay and die. All things are maintained by first perishing. Therefore, should we suppose that God places such patterns in nature for no reason? Is nature more powerful than God, who has promised the resurrection of our bodies? The one who gave life to dead and putrid seeds, through which you live in this age, will more certainly resurrect you and your loved ones so that you might live with them for eternity. God called your loved ones to his chamber so you should not want to begrudge them their secure rest. The time of resurrection draws near.

Before they died, perhaps you hoped that your loved ones would be useful members of the church militant, but it pleased God to make them members of the church triumphant. This pleased God, so it should also please you. Before they died, perhaps you hoped they would acquire knowledge of many things, but it pleased God to have them learn true wisdom in the heavenly academy. This pleased God, so it should also please you. Before they died, perhaps you hoped they would be raised out of the dust to converse with princes, but it pleased God to have them associate with heavenly princes, the holy angels (Ps 113:8). This pleased God, so it should also please you. Before they died, perhaps you hoped they would search for many riches, but it pleased God to have them gather riches in the heavenly kingdom. This pleased God, so it should also please you.

Holy God, what you have given you have taken away. Blessed be your name forever (Job 1:21).

Meditation Forty-Five

The Last Judgment

Respect the tribunal of Christ.

The Father does not judge anyone but has given all judgment to the Son (John 5:22). I know, Lord Jesus, that when you come as judge of all, you will bring to light the hidden deeds, words, and thoughts of all people (1 Cor 4:5). Above me will be a severe judge; below me, wide-open hell; within me, a gnawing conscience, outside of me, a burning fire; to the right of me, accusing sins, and to the left of me, terrifying devils. Good angels will appear to drive me away from heaven and evil angels to drag me to hell.

Lord Jesus, to whom shall I flee for refuge in such a predicament as I am in? I am ashamed of all my deeds, knowing that you do not spare any offenders. I will be placed between time and eternity. Time is passing away, and the infinite expanse of eternity still remains. Evil spirits will ask for their works, and will bring all the evil deeds they persuaded me to do to that severest judgment, so that they might drag my soul with them to the gathering of the tormented. All the host of heaven shall crumble into nothing and the heavens shall be rolled up like a scroll. All the host of them shall drop off like the leaves of a vine or fig tree (Isa 34:4). The sun shall blush with shame, and the moon shall be confounded (Isa 24:23). If these works of your hands, which have never committed any evil, shall flee from your view, how shall I, a miserable sinner, be able to appear before your face? If the heavens are not clean in his sight, what about me, a miserable sinner who drinks iniquity like water (Job 15:15)? If the righteous will scarcely be saved, how will sinners get ready (1 Pet 4:18)? To whom, then, shall I flee, to whom shall I turn if not to you, Lord? You will be the judge of my sins, you who died for my sins. For, the Father judges no one but hands all judgment over to the Son (John 5:22). The Father hands judgment over to the Son, but the Son was handed over to judgment, in turn, on account of our sins (Rom 4:25). For God so loved the world that he gave his only-begotten Son, not to judge the world but to save the world through him (John 3:16). Therefore, how will you judge me, Lord Jesus, when you are sent from the Father so that I might be saved through you? You accomplished the will of your Father in all respects; therefore, will you not accomplish it by saving me? It is not the will of your Father that one of the little ones should perish (Matt 18:14). I am one of the little ones in your sight. I am also a little one in my own sight, for what am I but dust and ashes (Gen 18:27)? I am not only dust and ashes but am also little and insignificant in my growth in piety. Therefore, carry out in me, a little one, the will of your Father.

You came, O Jesus, to save what was lost (Matt 18:11). My sins will accuse me and demand a strict sentence from the judge, but you transferred my sins to yourself. You took away the sins of the world, so how could you not also take away mine? How will you, who died for my sins, condemn me because of them? You died for the sins of the whole world. Did you not also die for mine (John 1:29)? Lord Jesus, if you wanted to judge me strictly, why did you force yourself to descend from heaven to become incarnate and die on the cross? The demons will accuse me and will require from my soul the deeds they persuaded me to do. But the prince of this world was condemned and has no power over you (John 16:11). If he has no power over you, then he also has no power over me, for I believe in you, Lord. For that reason you remain in me and I in you (John 6:56). If he accuses me, he will be accusing your friend. If he accuses me, he will be accusing your brother. If he accuses me, he will be accusing the most beloved Son of the eternal Father. Therefore, how will you be able to judge your friend, your brother, your son, severely? Moses will accuse me at that judgment and will curse me for not having kept all of the commandments that were written in his book of laws (Deut 27:26). Truly, you, Christ, were made a curse for me so that you might free me from the curse of the law (Gal 3:13). I will be cursed by Moses but blessed by you, for I long to hear your voice saying: "Come, blessed ones, and take possession of the kingdom of my Father" (Matthew 25:34). Moses will accuse me, but you will truly not accuse me before the Father but will, rather, intercede on my behalf (Rom 8:34). Therefore, I do not fear the curse of Moses because you erased the very record against me (Col 2:14).

The damned will accuse me and will proclaim that I share their guilt. I confess, O Lord Jesus, that I am united with them in guilt, but separated from them by my acknowledgment of guilt and my knowledge of your salvation. Whoever hears your word and believes that it was sent by you will have eternal life and will not come to judgment (John 5:24). I hear your word, Lord, and I believe in you by a feeble faith, but it is still faith. I believe, Lord, but help my unbelief (Mark 9:24). I believe, Lord, but increase my faith (Luke 17:5). Although I am not free from the sins of all the damned, you alone will free me, Lord, from the one sin of unbelief. All my accusers terrify me but you, as judge, raise me up. The Father hands all judgment over to you (Matt 11:27). He placed all judgment in your hands but also handed you over for the sake of all of us (Rom 8:32). You handed yourself over for the sake of the church so that you might sanctify it and cleanse it with washing by your word (Eph 5:26). How will you judge by a severe judgment those for whom you were handed over to death, even the death of the cross (Phil 2:8)? You will not hate your own flesh, and we are members of your body, from your flesh and your bones.

Meditation Forty-Six

The Desire for Eternal Life

Always look upward.

Devout soul, you should not love this life, which is fleeting, but rather the life that is permanent. Ascend by desire to where there is youth without age, life without death, joy without sadness, a kingdom without change. If beauty attracts you, know that the righteous will shine like the sun (Matt 13:43). If swiftness or strength attracts you, know that the elect will be like the angels of God (Matt 22:30). If a long and healthy life attracts you, there you will find a healthy eternity and eternal health. If abundance attracts you, know that the elect will be satisfied when the glory of the Lord appears (Ps 15:17). If melody attracts you, there you will find choirs of angels singing without end. If pure pleasures attract you, know that God will make them drink from the rivers of delight (Ps 36:8). If wisdom attracts you, know that the wisdom of God will show itself to them. If friendship attracts you, know that they will love God more than themselves, they will love each other mutually, and God will love them more than they love themselves. If concord attracts you, know that all will be of one will. If power attracts you, know that everything will be easy for the elect. They will desire nothing that they cannot have and they will desire nothing but what God wills and desires them to have. If honor and riches attract you, know that God will put his faithful servants in charge of many things (Matt 25:23). If true security attracts you, know that just as it will be certain that they will by no means and in no way lack these good things, God will never take these things away from them against their will, and there is no power greater than God that will separate them from God. Whatever the elect are able to desire, they will find there, because they will see, face to face, he who is all (1 Cor 13:12).

The good things of that life are so great that they cannot be measured, so great that they cannot be numbered, so precious that they cannot be estimated. There will be eternal health for the body, the greatest purity for the soul, the richness of divine glory and pleasure, the perpetual friendship of the angels and the saints, and astounding clarity of the body. The elect will rejoice because of the loveliness of the place where they will dwell, because of the pleasing society in which they will rule, because of the glorification of the bodies they will have, because they will have cast off the world and avoided hell. The least crown of eternal life will be superior to a thousand in this world because it is infinite while all the others are finite. It should not be feared that there will be jealousy due to disparity in glory, because a unity of love will reign in all. On account of that great love, whatever is granted to one of the elect will arouse great joy in the rest, as if it had been granted to them. Nothing in heaven and earth is a greater good than God. Thus, there also cannot be a greater and more perfect joy than to see God and dwell with God. To see God for one moment surpasses all other joys, for we will see God in himself, God in us and ourselves in God (1 Cor 13:12).

We have Christ with us during this life but covered by a veil in the word and the sacraments. In the future life we will know him directly. We will see him present when he distributes the bread that is eternally satisfying to us, in the same way that the disciples recognized Christ, not along the way, but at last at the inn when he broke bread with them (Luke 14:31). The heavenly Jerusalem does not have a temple made by hands, nor a sun, nor a moon, because its temple for all eternity is God, who is also its light and its lamp (Rev 21:23). Faith will be followed by sight, hope by apprehension, love by perfect fulfillment. In the building of the temple of Solomon no sound of an axe or a hammer was heard (1 Kgs 6:7). So, in the heavenly Jerusalem neither pain nor suffering will be felt, because the materials of this temple, that is to say, the spiritual stones, were prepared beforehand through tribulations in this world (1 Pet 2:5). The queen coming to Solomon is comparable to the soul being led to Christ in the great company of the holy angels with gold and precious stones, which are various virtues (1 Kgs 10:2). It will be amazed by the wisdom of Christ the King and his ministers, that is to say, the ranks of angels and saints; by the table of food, or in other words, the fullness of eternal refreshment; by the precious vestments, that is to say, the glorification of their bodies; by the beautiful house, or in other words, the magnitude of the heavenly palace; by the sacrifices, which are the many praises of God. Overwhelmed, the soul will acknowledge that what it now sees with its own eyes would have been beyond belief.

Therefore, the faithful soul should rise up and consider the good things prepared for it, and the spirit should be directed toward where it will one day go. While in time, it should strive toward where it will remain for eternity. No one will enter into the glory of the Lord who does not desire to enter. If you hope sometime to appear before the face of God, strive for holiness, because he himself is holy (Lev 11:45). If you long for the heavenly fellowship of angels, see to it that you do not deter their assistance through sin. If you hope for eternity, why then desire temporal things so much? If you seek the future city, why do you desire a permanent place here (Heb 13:14)? If you desire to come to Christ, why then do you fear death? The one who fears death is the one who does not want to go to Christ. If you desire to enter the heavenly Jerusalem, why then do you contaminate yourself with this and that sin when it is written that nothing that contaminates it will enter (Rev 21:27)? If you desire to enjoy the tree of life, you should first apprehend Christ, the true tree of life, in this life through true faith, because it is written: "Blessed are those who wash their robes in the blood of the Lamb so that they might be able to come to the tree of life and enter the city through the gates" (Rev 22:14). Outside are dogs and sorcerers, so beware of impurity. Outside are murderers, so beware of anger. Outside are worshipers of idols, so beware of avarice. Outside are liars, so beware of all the evils of sin (Rev 22:15). If you desire to enter the marriage feast of the Lamb, long for the coming of the bridegroom. The Spirit and the bridegroom say, "Come" (Rev 22:17). If you do not have the dowry of the Spirit through which you might call the Lord to come, the bridegroom will not lead you into the heavenly wedding (Eph 1:14). You are not the bride if you do not long for the coming of the bridegroom. If you want to have a place in the new heaven and new earth, why do you cling to old things (Rev 21:1)? If you want to be a partaker of the divine nature, why then do you cling to creatures? If you await the building of God, the house not made with hands, eternal in the heavens, why then do you not want to be freed from this earthly house of our habitation (2 Cor 5:1)? If you desire to be clothed, why then do you not make provisions so that you are not found naked (2 Cor 5:3–5)? If the holy Trinity does not inhabit your heart in this life through faith, it will not inhabit you in the future through glory. If you do not taste the beginning of eternal happiness in this life, you will never partake of its perfect fulfillment.

Meditation Forty-Seven

The Most Blessed Vision of God in Heaven

Heaven in the homeland of the saints.

In my Father's house are many mansions (John 14:1). These are the words of our Savior. I long to see that place, Lord, where you have prepared an eternal mansion for me. For I am a foreigner and a pilgrim here, just as all my fathers were (Ps 39:12). My days of pilgrimage have been few and hard (Gen 47:9). Therefore, in this world of exile, I long for my heavenly homeland. My *politeuma* (citizenship) is in heaven (Phil 3:20). I long to see the goodness of the Lord in the land of the living (Ps 27:13). Life here passes by like an imagined thing, my days are numbered, and my substance is as nothing in your sight (Ps 39:5, 6). What, then, do I wait for, if not the Lord? Lord Jesus, when will it be that I come to you? When will I appear before your face? As a deer longs for a fountain of water, so my soul longs for you, God (Ps 42:1). O true and perfect and complete joy! O joy beyond all joy, surpassing all joy, without which there is no joy. When I enter into you, I will see my God who dwells in you. You will fill me with gladness by your presence, Lord (Ps 16:11). In your right hand are pleasures forevermore. I will be inebriated by the richness of your house, and I will drink from the river of your delights. Near you is the fountain of life (Ps 36:9, 10).

O longed-for life! O blessed happiness in which the most holy Trinity will be the fulfillment of our desires—seen without end, loved without surfeit, and praised without ceasing. To see God will surpass all other joys. To see Christ, to live with Christ, to hear Christ will surpass all the desires of our hearts. O Jesus Christ, most sweet bridegroom of my soul, when will you lead your bride into the palace of your kingdom? What could be lacking there? What more could be desired or expected where God will be all in all (1 Cor 15:28)? That will be like seeing beauty, tasting honey, hearing the harp, smelling balsam, touching a flower. God will be all and distribute good things to each person according to the heart's desire. Whether you desire life, or health, or peace, or honor, there God will be all in all. Mysteries that are now concealed from the greatest doctors of the church will then be obvious to the littlest children. The blessed humanity of Christ will be present to us, and he will proclaim the mysteries of our salvation with his sweet voice. His voice is sweet, and his face is lovely (Song 2:14). Grace covers his lips, and he is crowned with honor and glory.

If God will be all in all, there will also be fullness of light for the mind, great peace for the will, and unbroken eternity for the memory. The Son will fill the mind with complete knowledge, the Holy Spirit will fill the will with sweetest love, and the Father will fill the memory with secure recollection of both. You, O God, will be the light by which we will see the light (Ps 36:9). That light is the splendor of your face, when we will see you face to face. We will not only see you but also live with you. We will not only live with you but also praise you. We will not only praise you but also share in your joy. We will not only rejoice with you but will also be like the angels (Matt 22:30). We will not only be like the angels but also like God himself, who is blessed forever (1 John 3:2).

You should marvel at this, faithful soul, and pray for the mercy of your Savior. He not only receives us, his enemies, into his grace, but also remits our sins, gives righteousness, leads us to our heavenly inheritance, and makes us like the angels and even like himself. O most blessed city! O heavenly Jerusalem! O seat of the most holy Trinity, when will I enter your temple? The temple of the heavenly Jerusalem is the Lamb (Rev 21:22)—the Lamb, namely, who takes away the sin of the world and was slain for us from the beginning of the world (John 1:29). When will it be that I can worship my God in that temple, or in other words, worship God in God? When will that sun, which illumines the holy city, rise in me (Rev 21:23)? I am still exiled from my homeland, but an ample inheritance has been put aside for me. To those who believe, Christ has given the power to become children of God (John 1:12). If we are children of God, are we not also heirs, heirs of God and co-heirs with Christ (Rom 8:17)?

Rise up, my soul, and seek your inheritance. The Lord is my portion and my very great reward (Ps 16:5; Gen 15:1). What beyond this could the kindness of the most merciful God give us? He gives us life. He gives us his Son. He gives us himself. If he knew anything greater in heaven and earth, he would give it to us. We live in God; we are the temple of God; we possess God, now in spirit and mystery, then in truth (1 Cor 3:16). There, our hope will become reality. There we will not only lodge but also dwell as inhabitants for eternity.

Meditation Forty-Eight

The Most Pleasant Fellowship of Angels in Heaven

Heaven is our court.

In the resurrection of the dead, they neither marry nor are given in marriage, but are like the angels of God in heaven (Matt 22:30). Is there anyone who can adequately celebrate with praises this status of the blessed? Whose heart can fathom the glory of these blessed (1 Cor 2:9)? The elect, renewed by the glory of the resurrection, with no fear of death and no stain of corruption, will enjoy the saving vision of God. "I have seen God face to face and my soul has been saved," the patriarch exclaims (Gen 32:30). If a momentary vision of God was able to bring so much joy, what will the eternal vision of him be able to do? If seeing God, as he appeared in human form, brought salvation and life to the soul, surely seeing God face to face will offer eternal life and happiness. Therefore, what more can be added to this felicity? What more can the elect desire than the vision of God? Blessed and sweet fellowship with the angels will be no less enjoyable. The elect will not only enjoy companionship with them but will also be like them, that is to say, in the agility, clarity, and immortality of their bodies. We will be clothed as they are, in white robes, and, standing near the throne of the Lamb, we will sing eternal hymns to the Lord (Rev 7:9). We will shine with crowns like theirs and will rejoice with them in the privilege of immortality. "We saw the angel of the Lord, so we shall die," exclaims Manoah (Judg 13:22). Yet, we will see thousands of thousands and ten thousands times a hundred thousand angels and we will live for eternity (Dan 7:10).

If we will be *isaggeloi* (like angels), we will no longer fear that we will be separated from them by the dissimilarity of our sins. We will put off the tattered rags of our sinful nature, cover our nakedness with the garments of salvation, and clothe ourselves with a bright robe of innocence (Isa 61:10). There, no one is hurt, no one is angry, no one feels envy. No one is burned up by greed, and no one feels any ambition for honor or power. We will neither be weighed down by the burden of sins nor will we be forced to weep over the stains of our sins with penitential tears. We need to fear no longer that sin will mortally wound the soul because the lion of the tribe of Judah has been victorious, and we conquer all by his strength (Rev 5:5). If we are *isaggeloi* (like angels), we will have no desire for food or drink. God will be our food, and we will be satisfied by his love (Rev 7:16, 17). The blessed will not eat or drink, and the sun or heat will not strike them, because the one who has mercy will guide them to drink at the fountain of water from which a river of living water flows (John 7:38). A meal of fat marrow will be prepared for them there, a meal of wine strained clear (Isa 25:6). They will feast and be glad and shout for joy from their hearts. Lord Jesus, all this will be perfected in spirit and truth. We will drink of the fruit of the vine in the kingdom of your Father, but in spirit and truth, for the words that you spoke to us are spirit and life and, with these words of this age, you declare the joy of the future life (John 6:63).

If we will be *isaggeloi* (like the angels), fear of death will be taken away, and death will be swallowed up in victory (1 Cor 15:55). Death will be cast down forever, and God will wipe away all tears from the eyes of his people (Isa 25:8). Therefore, there will be joy without pain, life without labor, and light without darkness. Love will never grow cold, joy will never diminish, no groans will be heard or any grief felt. Nothing will seem sad, and there will always be joy. There, they will have the greatest and most certain security, secure tranquility, tranquil delight, delightful happiness, happy eternal blessedness, the blessed Trinity, the unity of the Trinity and Deity of unity, and the blessed vision of the Deity.

Arise, my soul, and ponder more carefully the honor conferred by Christ on us. We will enter into fellowship with angels and archangels, thrones and dominions, principalities and powers. We will not only be in fellowship with them, but we will also be like them. There, we will know the angel who was formerly our guardian in life. We will not be in need of the angel's ministry, but we will be glad to have its sweet presence. We will no longer desire its protection, but we will rejoice to have its sweet companionship. We will gaze at its clarity with clear eyes.

If we will be *isaggeloi* (like the angels), our fragile, feeble, mortal bodies will be changed and will become spiritual, agile, and immortal (1 Cor 15:43, 44). They will be light because of their nearness to God, who dwells in inaccessible light and is clothed in light (1 Tim 6:16). They will be incorruptible because they are like angels, or rather, because of their conformity with the glorified body of Christ (Phil 3:21). They are sown here in corruptibility but will rise again incorruptible. There are sown in obscurity but will rise again in glory. They are sown in infirmity but will rise again in strength. It is sown as an animal body but will rise as a spiritual body that will shine like the splendor of the firmament forever (Dan 12:3).

Come, Lord Jesus, and make us participants in your glory.

Meditation Forty-Nine

The Severity of Hell's Torments

Always think about hell.

Consider, devout soul, the severity of the pains of hell, and you will easily overcome every dissolute inclination to sin. All evil will be present there and all good will be absent. What evil could be missing for those who are being punished for the greatest evil, which is sin? What good could be present for those who are separated from the greatest good, which is God? There will be the heat of fire and the numbness of cold. There will be perpetual darkness, smoke, and unending tears. There will be the terrifying sight of demons and ceaseless wailing. There will be dryness, thirst, the stench of sulphur, the worm of conscience, fear, pain, shame, and the confusion of sins made manifest to all, envy, hate, sadness, exclusion from the vision of God, and the abandonment of all hope. The light of the fire will be separated by God's power from its ability to burn. Its light will bring joy to the saints but its ability to burn will cause the torment of the damned. It will not shine to bring consolation to the wretched such that they will see and rejoice but, rather, will increase their misery because they will see and sorrow all the more. They will be deprived of any sight of the sun, the moon, and all stars, and also of any vision of Christ and all the saints. They will undergo punishment with wailing, smoke, and the sight of demons and all of the damned. Their ears will hear the crying of the damned, continual blasphemies, and the horrible roaring of demons. Their sense of taste will be afflicted by thirst and hunger, and they will be deprived of all enjoyment of food and drink. Their sense of smell will be tormented by the stench of sulphur, and their sense of touch will feel the burning of fire externally and internally, penetrating even to the marrow of their bones. The bodies of the damned will be deformed, dark, slow, and heavy.

Their memories will be tortured by recollection of their sins, and they will be sad, not because they sinned, but because they lost their pleasures. A spark of the fire of hell will cause more pain for sinners than being in labor and giving birth for a thousand years. They will weep from pain and gnash their teeth in their frenzy (Matt 22:13). They will be crucified in their flesh by the worm of conscience (Isa 66:24). There will be no vice without some torture appropriate to it. Just as there will be nothing desired in the kingdom of God that will not be attained, in hell, nothing will be attained that is desired. There, it will be of no use to the damned that they enjoyed various delights in this life, but, rather, they will be tormented more severely by the remembrance of this. It will be of no use to the damned that they lived in perpetual satiation and inebriation in this life when, in their next life, they will be unable to obtain even a tiny drop of water (Luke 16:24). It will be of no use to the damned that they had access to splendid garments, when they will be clothed with confusion and their bodies will be covered with shame. It will be of no use that they were accorded honors in this life, because there will be no honor in hell but only endless groaning and pain. It will be of no use that they accumulated riches in this life, because, there, all alike will be poor.

They will be separated from the vision of God. To not see God will surpass all the other punishments of hell. If the damned, locked up in the prison of hell, could see the face of God, they would feel no pain, no sadness, and no sorrow. But, they will experience the wrath of God and never gaze at the blessed face of God. They will feel punishment from his face without ever viewing his face for all eternity. The wrath of God will perpetually kindle the fire of eternal damnation like a river of sulphur. They will not only be removed from contemplation of God but will also be miserably tormented by the sight of demons. They will feel the whips of those whose teachings they followed in this life. If the sight of a specter in this life almost takes the breath out of a person, how will it be possible to endure the horrible sight of demons for eternity? The damned will not only perpetually associate with demons, but they will also feel themselves tormented by them for eternity. If, in this life, the Devil severely afflicts the saints with God's permission, how much more severely will he torture the damned, who have been handed over to his power for eternity? The damned will be tormented eternally not only externally by demons, but also internally by the worm of conscience. Absolutely all the sins that they have ever committed will be continuously cast before their eyes.

The torment will be even more severe because the benefit of repentance is no longer available to them. When the virgins who were ready will enter with the bridegroom, the door will suddenly be shut, the door, that is to say, of pardon, the door of mercy, the door of consolation, the door of hope, the door of grace, the door of holy conversion (Matt 25:10). The damned will cry out and say to the mountains and the rocks, "Fall down on us and hide us from the wrath of the Lamb" (Rev 6:16). However, this cry will be to no avail, because heaven and earth will flee from his wrath, as it is written: "Every island fled and no mountains were found" (Rev 16:20).

Whatever increase is given to the glory of the elect will add to the pain of the damned. There will, indeed, be degrees of punishment, but whoever feels the least torment will find no consolation in that fact. Whoever is racked by the greatest tortures will envy those who are afflicted the least. The damned will feel no consolation in knowing that some of their friends have been received into heavenly palaces, and none of the elect will experience any sorrow from knowing that some of their kindred have been thrown into hell for eternity. The pain and torment of the damned will be such that they will not be able to direct their minds to anything else besides what causes their pain. The damned will hate all God's creatures. They will hate the holy angels, the elect, and even God himself, not because of his nature, however, but because of the effects of his justice.

All the evils of this life come one at a time. One person is burdened by poverty, another suffers from a serious disease, one is oppressed by hard servitude, while another is burdened by a massive abuse. But there, in hell, they will be suffering from all evils at the same time. They will feel pain all over in all their senses and members. In this life all annoyances are mitigated by the hope that they will be lifted, but there, all hope of relief will be abandoned. The pain of hell is not only eternal but also never interrupted for a moment. If all people ever born, from Adam to the present day, and, in addition, all who will ever be born until the last day were to suffer equally from the punishment that a soul in hell is forced to suffer for one sin, every small part of that punishment of one person would be greater than all the torments that all robbers and evildoers ever perpetrated.

O Lord, cause us to think about hell so that we do not fall into hell.

Meditation Fifty

Eternal Torment in Hell

Punishments for sins are eternal.

Consider, devout soul, the fact that punishments in hell are eternal, and you will understand more rightly how severe they are. The fire in hell rages and burns endlessly. The life of the damned is like endless dying. Their death is to live in eternal punishment. The one who torments never grows tired, and the one who is tormented never dies. The fire, there, consumes in such a way that its might remains forever. The torments, there, increase so that they might be renewed forever. The damned will die so that they might always live, and live so that they might always die. For someone to be tormented without any end whatsoever will truly, in the end, produce despair. For, what can be harder than always to want what will never be and to not want what will always be? In eternity, the damned will not attain what they want, and what they do not want they will be forced to suffer for eternity.

When the wrath of God ceases, the punishment of the damned will also cease, but this wrath is eternal, so the punishment will be eternal. When the damned truly repent, they will be freed from their sins, but the time for repentance has passed, so no hope for pardon remains. When the devils cease tormenting, the damned will cease being tormented, but the devils will never cease from raging, so the torment of those who are damned will never cease. When the justice of God changes the punishments of the damned will change, but the justice of God is unchanging, so the punishments of the damned will be eternal. Based on strict justice, the appropriate verdict for those who never stopped sinning in this life is to never be without punishment. It is fair that there should be no end to vengeance for those who, while they were able, never wanted to put an end to misdeeds. If the damned sinned in their eternity, in other words, while they lived, it is just that they should be punished in God's eternity. Their delinquency came to an end because their lives came to an end. They would not have wanted to end their delinquency if they had been able to live without end and sin without end.

The fuel of the eternal fire of hell is eternal, that is to say, the stain of sin. Therefore, punishment is also deservedly eternal. The foulness of the sins of the damned is never removed from the eyes of God, so how could the magnitude of the punishments set for sin ever be diminished? Furthermore, sin is an infinite evil because it is committed against an infinite good, and Christ paid an infinite price for it. Therefore, those who died in sin deserve infinite punishment. The eternal good within human nature has been destroyed, and so, by the just judgment of God, humanity experiences an eternal evil. In the beginning, God created humanity in his image, so that humanity might live with him forever. After the fall into sin, God reformed humanity in his image, through Christ. He prepared the means of eternal salvation for all and offered the gifts of eternal life to all. Therefore, it is just that those who wanted to reject these gifts should be subjected to eternal punishments. The will toward evil will never be taken away from the damned, so the punishment of that evil will never be taken away. The damned chose momentary pleasures and the finite goods of the world above God, the infinite good. They longed more for the fleeting and brief delights of this life than for the riches of eternal life. Therefore, it is fair that they should undergo eternal punishments.

O interminable eternity, O eternity immeasurable by any length of time. O eternity that no human intellect can grasp. You increase the punishments of the damned by your extent! After countless thousands of years they will always be forced to acknowledge that this is only the beginning of their torments. How difficult it is for someone to lie immobile for thirty years in a soft bed. What will it be like to burn for thirty thousand times a thousand years in that sulfurous lake? O eternity, eternity, you alone, more than anything else, enhance the punishments of the damned. The pain of the damned is severe because of the bitterness of the punishments. It is more severe because of the diversity of punishments. It is most severe because the punishments are everlasting. It will be death without death, end without end, failing without failing, because death always lives, the end always begins, the failing never fails. The damned seek life and do not find it; they seek death and death flees from them. After a hundred thousand thousands times a thousand years, the torments will return, renewed, without end. The very thought of the continuation of the pain will make them suffer more that the external sensation of torment. What could be more miserable than to die in such a way that you are always living, and to live in such a way that you are always dying? Such a life will be deadly and an immortal death. If you are life, why do you die? If you are death, how will you always endure?

What eternity is like we will never perfectly understand. Without a doubt, because it will not be marked off by any measure of time; it cannot be comprehended by any created mind. If you want to estimate the scope of eternity, you should think about the time before the world was created. If you can find the beginning of God, you will also be able to find out when the punishment of the damned will come to an end. Picture a very high mountain that surpasses the distance from heaven to earth in magnitude. Picture also a bird that repeatedly carries away from the mountain the smallest grain of sand for however many thousands of years. It is to be expected that after many thousands of years there would cease to be any height to that mountain. But, it cannot be anticipated that the fire of hell would ever go out. The rewards of the elect will never come to an end, nor will the punishments of the damned, because just as the mercy of God is infinite toward the elect, the justice of God is infinite toward the reprobates. Fix in your mind that there are as many different kinds of torments for the damned as there are drops in the sea. Picture a small bird flying down every thousand years and drinking a tiny drop from the sea. It is to be expected that eventually the whole sea would be drained, but it cannot be anticipated that the punishment of the damned will ever come to an end.

O devout soul, you should always take note that the punishment of the damned is eternal. If you think about hell, you will keep yourself from ending up in hell. Take care that you repent while there is still time for pardon. What will that fire consume besides your sins? The more you accumulate sins, the more fuel you lay up for burning.

O Lord Jesus, who made satisfaction for our sins by your passion, protect us from eternal damnation. Amen.

Meditation Fifty-One

The Spiritual Resurrection of the Pious

To rise with Christ is life.

The resurrection of Christ is of no benefit unless Christ also rises within you. Just as Christ ought to be conceived and born in you and ought to live in you, so he should also arise within you. Death precedes every resurrection because nothing can rise up that has not fallen. So it also is with the spiritual resurrection. Christ does not arise within you unless Adam first dies within you. The inner nature does not arise unless the outer nature is first buried. The newness of the Spirit will not come forth unless the oldness of the flesh is put away. It is not sufficient for Christ to arise within you once, because the old Adam cannot be extinguished in one moment. The old Adam wants to revive within you each day. You must extinguish it each day so that Christ might begin to live within you each day. Christ did not ascend to heaven or enter into his glory until after he rose from the dead (Luke 24:26, 46). Likewise, you will not be able to enter glory unless Christ first rises within you and lives in you. There is no part of the mystical body of Christ in which Christ does not live, nor will any part be led by Christ to the church triumphant who has not been part of this body in the church militant. Betrothal precedes marriage. No soul will be led to the heavenly marriage of the Lamb unless it is espoused to Christ in this life through faith and sealed with the pledge of the Holy Spirit (Rev 19:7). Therefore, Christ arises and lives within you so that you might live eternally with him. This is the first resurrection. Blessed and holy are those who partake of the first resurrection, in whom the second death has no power (Rev 20:6). If you want the body to go forth to life in the resurrection, Christ ought to arise within you daily in this life.

When Christ arose, the sun was rising (Mark 16:2). Thus, if Christ arises within you spiritually, the light of the saving knowledge of God will arise in your soul. How can the light of the saving knowledge of God be there where the darkness of grave sin is still located? The fear of the Lord is the beginning of wisdom (Ps 111:10). Therefore, how can the wisdom of heaven be there where the fear of the Lord has no place? How can anyone who does not have the light of divine knowledge in this life partake of eternal light in the life to come? Only the children of light cross over to the eternal light. The children of darkness cross over to eternal darkness. Christ, in rising, triumphed over death, and so the person in whom Christ rises spiritually crosses over from death to life because one in whom the victor over death lives cannot be conquered by death (John 5:24). Christ, in rising, brought perfect righteousness with him, for he died on account of our sins and was raised for our righteousness (Rom 4:25). So, the person in whom Christ rises spiritually is justified from sin because how can sin be there where the perfect righteousness of Christ lives and flourishes? Now this righteousness of Christ is applied to us through faith. Christ, in rising, claimed victory back from Satan because, by descending into hell, Christ destroyed his kingdom, plundered his palace, and shattered his weapons (Luke 11:22). Thus, Satan cannot prevail over the person in whom Christ rises spiritually, for one in whom the victor over Satan lives cannot be conquered by Satan.

When Christ arose, there was a great earthquake (Matt 28:2). Spiritual resurrection with Christ cannot take place without severe commotion and heartfelt contrition. The old Adam cannot be extinguished without wrestling and struggling. Therefore, Christ cannot arise in you spiritually without a great commotion. No resurrection with Christ takes place without the abolition of sin. No abolition of sin takes place unless there is prior acknowledgment of sin. True acknowledgment of sin has not yet happened if serious contrition is absent from the heart. Therefore, the spiritual resurrection of Christ does not take place unless it is preceded by inner heartfelt contrition. Holy Hezekiah said: "Like a lion, he has pulverized all my bones" (Isa 38:13). See the great commotion. But, he immediately adds: "Lord, by these things people live and in all these is the life of my spirit. Take hold of me and I shall live" (Isa 38:16–17). You have cast all my sins behind your back. See here a spiritual resurrection from sin.

When Christ arose, the angel of the Lord, descending from heaven, sat upon the sepulcher (Matt 28:2). Thus, if Christ lives spiritually within you, you will be able to rejoice in the fellowship of angels. Now, the old Adam lives and reigns here where the Devil is pleased to make his resting place. But the angels are pleased to dwell there where Christ truly lives and reigns. It is written that there will be rejoicing in heaven over the repentance of one who has sinned (Luke 15:7). Now, true repentance is there where Christ also spiritually rises. Christ has not yet risen spiritually there where the grace of God is not yet found. Where the grace of God is not yet found, there is no guardianship of the angels. There Christ is not yet spiritually resurrected, there the old Adam still reigns. Where the old Adam still reigns, there sin still reigns. Where sin reigns, there the Devil reigns. Now, how can there be fellowship of angels with the Devil?

When Christ arose, he appeared to his disciples and showed himself to be alive (Luke 24:15). So, if you are made a partaker of spiritual resurrection through faith, show yourself to be a living member of Christ through love. No one is judged to be living who does not outwardly manifest the actions of a living person. Where Christ is, there is also the Holy Spirit. Where the Holy Spirit is, the soul is moved to do good works toward everyone, because those who are prompted by the Holy Spirit are children of God (Rom 8:14). Therefore, if we live in the Spirit, we will also walk in the Spirit (Gal 5:25). The light of the sun scatters the splendor of its rays everywhere. The light of faith diffuses the fervor of love everywhere. If you could take light away from the sun, you would be able to separate love from true faith. Sins are dead works (Heb 9:14). If you walk around in dead works, how are you living in Christ, and how is Christ living in you? Sin belongs to the old Adam. If the old Adam still reigns within you, how can you be resurrected spiritually with

Christ? Sin belongs to the old flesh. If you walk around in the old flesh, how can the new humanity be alive?

Raise us, O good Jesus, from the death of sins so that we might walk in newness of life. Let your death extinguish the old Adam in us. Let your resurrection call our inner humanity to life. Let your blood wash us from our sins. Let your resurrection clothe us with the garments of righteousness. We who have been dead in our sins yearn for you, O true life. We who were turned away from you in our sins, yearn for you, O true righteousness. We who were damned on account of our sins yearn for you, O true salvation. Make us alive, make us righteous, make us holy. Amen.

Johann Gerhard
School of Piety or the Practice of Godliness (1622)

Book Two

Chapter Five: Holy Devout Meditation Promotes Piety

By holy devout meditation we mean to say that a true lover of piety should set aside a certain time each day in which he pulls himself away from all outward earthly and worldly matters, goes into his own heart, and brings up heavenly spiritual things for consideration. Such holy devout meditation is useful for piety for the following reasons:

Ex Dei mandato [from the command of God]: because God the Lord commands such holy meditation of us. God the Lord said to Abraham: "Look at the heavens and count the stars if you are able to count the stars. So shall your descendants be" (Gen 15:5–6). God the Lord presented the innumerably great quantity of stars for consideration as an image and sign that his spiritual offspring would be an innumerable quantity. Job says in his book: "Ask the beasts and they will teach you; the birds of the air and they will tell you. Or the plants of the earth speak to you and will teach you and the fish of the sea will declare to you" (Job 12:7–8). Such teachings and questions are nothing other than a holy zealous meditation by which one considers these creations by God and the creator's wisdom, goodness and power. "Take notice of this and consider the wondrous works of God" (Job 37:14). "Commune with your heart on your bed" (Ps 4:4). "Consider the work of God who can make straight what he has made crooked" (Eccl 7:13). Christ says, "Consider the birds of the air"; "Consider the lilies of the fields" (Matt 6:26, 28). "Consider the ravens" (Luke 12:24). In this way Christ presents the birds of the air, the plants of the earth, so that we should look at and consider them in order to know of God's wonderful, fatherly care and governance.

Ex Sanctorum Exemplo (from the example of the saints): because the saints of God engage in such meditation: See how Isaac went out to meditate in a field in the evening and how the holy scriptures say that he wanted to meditate on the wonders of God in the work of creation and in the promises revealed in his word (Gen 24:63). David says, *in matutinis meditabor,* "I will meditate on you in the morning; when I lie on my bed I will think of you; when I awake I will speak of you" (Ps 63:6). Asaph says, "I commune with my heart in the night as I play music; I meditate and search my spirit" (Ps 77:6). "I meditate on all your works and think about your wonders of old" (Ps 77:12). "I meditate on your precepts and fix my eyes on your ways" (Ps 119:15). "When I consider how you have directed the world, I will be comforted" (Ps 119:52). "I remember your name in the night and keep your law" (Ps 119:55). "When I think of your ways I turn my feet to your testimonies" (Ps 119:59). "I awake early so that I might mediate on your words" (Ps 119:148). "My tongue will sing of your word, for all your commandments are right" (Ps 119:172). The secure and the wicked are punished because "they do not regard the deeds of the Lord or see the works of his hand" (Isa 5:12).

Ex meditationis fructu [from the profit of meditation]: because such meditation is very useful, wholesome, and edifying, bringing us to awareness of God and ourselves, turning our hearts from the earthly to the heavenly, preparing and warning our hearts so that we are afterward more fervent in prayer, defending us against security and wickedness so that we are not without understanding like a dumb animal. David speaks of this: "Blessed is the man who delights in the law and meditates on it day and night" (Ps 1:2). He also uses such a word in the scriptures when he says, "May the words of my mouth and the meditations of my heart be acceptable" (Ps 19:14). "The invisible nature of God, that is his eternal power and deity, has been seen in the things he has made, namely, the creation of the world" (Rom 1:20). It is through inward, heartfelt meditation that one discerns such things.

Ex typo [from typology]: God has ordained in his law that the only animal to be considered pure is the one that chews its cud (Lev 11:3). This shows that it is characteristic of a righteous Christian and someone pleasing to God to ruminate on God's word and works or to meditate on them attentively. The word of God is a holy seed (Luke 8:11). In order for the seed to bear fruit it must be received by good soil where it will be held, kept warm, and moistened. Likewise, if the spiritual seed of the divine word is to be fruitful for piety or godliness, it must be kept warm and protected through meditation in the heart. The word of God is the true bread of life [manna], by which God the Lord feeds our soul (Deut 8:3). In order for the physical bread to be nourishing to the body it must be chewed and digested. Likewise, if spiritual bread, the Word of God, is to feed and fill our souls it must also be chewed and digested through meditation so that it is distributed after that throughout the body.

Chapter Seven

Now that we have dealt with the value of meditation and *de meditationis modo* [the method of meditation], the way in which to engage in it, we must further handle *de meditationis objecto* [the object of meditation], or toward what the meditation should be directed so that it might be useful to piety.

The first type of meditation [The Creator and creation]

In the first book of this treatise we have proved that a person can be moved toward holiness both through consideration of the creator and also the creation or creatures. Concerning God the creator, first to be considered is his unending goodness and mercy, second, his inestimable righteousness, and third, his majesty and divine glory. His many blessings beyond measure testify to his goodness, for he has shown humans, above all other creatures, his certain unfailing promise that he will show still more good things to his beloved children beyond such blessings.

Divine blessings are of three particular classes or types, some of which belong to the article of creation, some to the article of salvation, and some to the article of sanctification. The work of the grace of sanctification embraces the eternal election of grace, which took place before the world was formed, and then also the distribution and communicating of spiritual goods, which take place during this life. To the spiritual goods and blessings that are distributed to us in the fullness of time belong above all else three blessings: first, the divine call to Christ's kingdom, and then his justifying and sanctifying of us, which consists of the forgiveness of sins and the reckoning of Christ's righteousness to us, and then renewal and the sending of the Holy Spirit. The call to Christ's kingdom takes place through the word and through the holy sacraments, which in the New Testament are two, that is baptism and the Lord's Supper.

In addition to these blessings, which are common either to all of humanity or to all believers and true Christians, there are also some special blessings that God has shown to one or the other of us, the consideration of which should urge us toward holiness no less than the former. Divine justification will be understood to include, on the one hand, the internal, essential characteristic that God is innately righteous in his unchanging will, by which the rational creature should be regulated according to the norm and measure of righteousness that God has prescribed in his law. The outward expression of divine righteousness consists of the righteousness that God the Lord shows toward rational creatures, in that he judges all of them according to their works, rewarding the good and punishing the evil.

The creatures or creation of God are of two types or sorts. Some are rational and others irrational. The rational creatures are of two groups, namely, angels and humans. The angels are either good or bad angels. Under humans are both we ourselves and other humans who are commonly comprehended under the name of neighbor. These other humans are either pious and believing or godless and unbelieving, as well as those who are inside or outside of the visible church, some of whom have died already before us and have gone either to the joy of heaven or to the pain of hell, and some who are still living around and near us here on earth. The irrational creatures are either alive or lifeless and earthly or heavenly creatures. How the form of these creatures can awaken either general or specific meditations and urge us toward godliness has been expressly shown in the first book. It will not be unserviceable to a true lover of godliness, after such instruction, to consider God the creator and the creatures in order to practice piety.

The second type of meditation [God, self, and neighbor]

The holy apostle Paul denotes three parts of true piety when he says, "We should scorn ungodly being and worldly lusts and live in a disciplined, upright and godly manner in this world" (Titus 2:12). Be pious toward God the Lord, just toward our neighbor, and disciplined with regard to ourselves. According to this division, three *objecta* [objects] can be set toward which holy meditations could be directed, that is, God the Lord, we ourselves, and our neighbor. Regarding God the Lord, one has to consider the manifold blessings that have been received from him. Concerning yourself, consider simply your manifold sins, then the many needs you have for the sustaining of your body and soul, as well as your longing for eternal life. Regarding the neighbor, you have to consider the many needs of the same, which you have expressed to God in prayer.

There are especially four matters that every true Christian and lover of piety should consider each day: first, his sins and forgiveness of them by God, which he should seek through Christ. The consideration of sin entails two matters: the recognition of the heavy burden of original sin as well as actual violations. Actual sins are committed by thoughts, words, and deeds, when one either does evil or lets opportunities to do good go by. We sin against God, our neighbor, and ourselves when in the sins of our youth and in daily transgressions our flesh and blood entice us to sin. Many times we let them overcome us. We participate often in outward sins and fail in many ways. Indeed, all creatures accuse us on account of our sins, and especially in the suffering and death of Christ we see the earnest, burning wrath of God against sins, as in a mirror.

Second, consider God's blessings, for which we should thank him from the ground of our hearts. For the true lover of holiness, consideration of God's blessings is like walking in the beautiful garden of nature and the Christian church, collecting many rich flowers of divine gifts, delighting in the Spirit through the lovely fragrance, and bringing the offering of his lips as a sweet fragrance to God the Lord.

Every true Christian has God to thank that he has created, saved, and sanctified us, that he has showered us with rich benefits in this life and, even greater, has promised us eternal life in the future. He has made us rich in soul, body, and outward benefits and has protected us from many kinds of harm in this life, for truly the misfortunes that God protects us from out of grace are greater than the goods that he gives us. In summary, true Christians will find by these meditations that we cannot reach the number or worth of divine blessings either with words or with thoughts, for which we will eternally praise and thank him with all the elect.

Third, the lover of holiness has to meditate daily on his many needs, when he asks for the maintenance and increase of the gifts of the Spirit, and also victory and the conquering of all temptations. For the inner consideration of our neediness teaches us that we have nothing in the least of earthly, heavenly, bodily, or spiritual blessings from ourselves and therefore reminds us to give up all trust in our own worth and powers and take our refuge only in the gracious help of divine mercy, which is promised to us in Christ. Then, through this meditation on our manifold neediness, our hearts are directed to God and express our longing for the killing of the old man and the renewal of the new man that is necessary for all rebirth. Such renewal consists in the sustaining and increasing of faith, hope, love, humility, obedience, gentleness, chastity, and other virtues that are sought and acquired from God with earnest prayer. Our flesh, the world, and Satan war daily against us. To be sure, because our flesh wants to move us toward love of what is earthly, and the world with its hate and Satan with his poison seek victory over us, we must concern ourselves with scorn for what is earthly, with self-denial, and with victory over the world. With assiduous prayer we should seek the soul's rest and refreshment, victory over temptation, and gracious protection against the Devil's poison from the Lord of hosts. Also, because we especially have need of grace and help from God in the hour of death and at the Day of Judgment, we should humbly seek and petition God the Lord when we take a holy leave from this life and enter eternal life.

Fourth and last, a true Christian has to consider each day the needs of the neighbor, and request that the neighbor might have all that is needed in this and the future life. Through such meditation on the needs of the neighbor a Christian sees the common need of the church and the civil order and empathetically takes upon himself the needs of the neighbor as if they were his own. This is a fruit of the true honest love that binds us together as members of one body, the head of which is Christ, and makes us heartily accept the general needs of the church and all its members. For this reason we pray daily for the upholding of God's word, for teachers and listeners, for authorities and subjects, and for families, since these are the three main estates that God himself has established for the maintenance of this life and the spread of the Christian church. The Christian prays for his relatives and benefactors to whom he is obligated by the bond of natural law, for his enemies and persecutors whose conversion and salvation he seeks from his heart, and for all who suffer need and are troubled, whose misfortunes he takes to heart, being moved by Christian sympathy. We have expressly handled this type of divine, holy meditation in a special little book, the title of which is *Daily Practice of Piety*. This prayer book deals with confession of sin, thanksgiving, prayer, and petition. It was originally published in the princely press in Coburg and after that in Jena.

The third type of meditation [The books of nature and scripture]

Holy King David teaches us in the nineteenth psalm that there are two books we can study for knowledge of God. The first is *liber naturae*, the book of nature, of which he says, "The heavens tell the glory of God and the firmament announces his handiwork, etc." (Ps 19:1). The same book Paul also speaks of in Romans: "God's invisible nature, that is his eternal power and godhead, are clearly seen in the works he has made, namely the creation of the world" (Rom 1:20). The other book is *liber scripturae*, that is, the book of the holy scriptures, of which David speaks when he says: "The law of the Lord is without change and quickens the soul. The testimony of the Lord is certain and makes the wise foolish" (Ps 19:7). Augustine in *Enarrationes Psalm 34* says: *Due sunt, quae in cognitionem Dei ducunt, Creatura & Scriptura* (there are two things that lead to knowledge of God, creatures and scripture). Now we can study both books for knowledge of God, to a certain measure, and can also use both books for the promotion of piety.

In the book of holy scripture we find both law and gospel. When we consider God's law we find on the one side 1. *Divina praecepta*, often repeated commandments in which God the Lord admonishes us to holiness. 2. *Divina promissa*, divine promises in which he promises temporal and eternal blessings to those who are obedient to him. 3. *Praemiorum exempla*, many examples that God richly awards such blessings to the godly according to his promises. On the other side we find 1. *Divinas prohibitiones*, divine prohibitions that we should not depart from the way of godliness. 2. *Divinas comminationes*, divine threats, in which God the Lord earnestly threatens to punish the godless and disobedient both temporally and eternally. 3. *Poenarum irrogationes*, many examples of how God the Lord punishes the godless and disobedient for their stubbornness. A true lover of piety can hold these matters daily in his heart and zealously mark the words of divine scripture, taking to heart every matter that can promote and be of service to godliness.

To the gospel belong the promises of the Old Testament concerning Christ, the words of consolation that speak of the benefits of Christ, the gracious promises of forgiveness of sins, and the grace of God through Christ. The consideration of the same words altogether can be very beneficial to a Christian for the promotion of piety, as the first book extensively proved.

A meditation on the book of holy scripture can also attend to how God the Lord speaks with a faithful soul, namely, how God the Lord admonishes us and we obediently answer him, how God the Lord makes gracious promises and we answer him in faith, how we call to God in prayer and God the Lord graciously answers us, how we cry out the anguish of our heart to God and God the Lord powerfully consoles us. We have expressly also dealt with this in a little handbook, the title of which is *Two Small Consoling Tracts*, which on the one hand concerns the spiritual speaking of God and the Lord and a faithful soul, and on the other hand deals with divine consolation, especially directed to twelve types of needs. This was first published in Coburg and afterward in Jena.

We can fruitfully study what is presented in the book of nature, if we consider either ourselves or other creatures that God has created. Concerning ourselves we find the inner book of conscience, which steadily admonishes us to commit ourselves zealously to godliness. If we could only hear this preaching within, we would be admonished to all good. Concerning the creatures we find the outer book, which we can steadily read, study, and meditate. So many creatures present themselves to us in the heavens, the air, the earth, the water, and under the earth. So many teachers of godliness are presented before us as we showed at the end of the first book of this treatise.

The fourth type of meditation [Seven days of the week]

Because God the Lord completed all that he created within six distinct days and rested on the seventh day, as Moses teaches us in the first and second chapter of his first book, so meditation on the creatures can be conveniently employed according to each day's works, and can be divided according to the days of the week. In the first day God created the first heaven and earth, that is, a great watery clump of earth as the material from which he thereafter created heaven and earth, as also Moses himself explains in Genesis 1:2. "And the earth was without form and void and there was darkness over the deep." Concerning this day, consider the almighty power of the creator that he could form such a beautiful structure of the heavens and earth out of nothing: He made all that one sees out of nothing (Rom 4:17). Consider also the creator's wisdom that he made it all orderly and completed it all in less than a moment (Heb 1:3). So he also deals with us in our conversion and renewal, which is like a second creation. He forms and improves us daily until we finally become perfect in eternal life. We should truly fear such a powerful Lord who created all from nothing and can make all again become nothing.

Second, on the first day God created the light (Gen 1:3), a noble creature without which we would not be able to see the other creatures. Concerning this day's work, consider that the Lord God is an exceedingly beautiful light (1 John 1:5), in whom there is not darkness or any changing of darkness and light (Jas 1:17). He dwells in a light to which no one can come (1 Tim 6:16). He testified of the eternity of his Son, from his own substance and essence, who is light from light, the true light that enlightens all men who come into the world (John 1:4, 8). He, through the light of his Word and through the Holy Spirit, illumines our heart, which has been naturally darkened, and kindles the light of divine knowledge in us (2 Cor 4:6). God, who called the light out of darkness, has given a bright light to our hearts so that he might kindle the illumination of the knowledge of the clarity of God in the face of Jesus Christ, and so that he might make us children of light (Luke 16:8; 1 Thess 5:5). Therefore it is proper that we act as children of light because we are a light in the Lord (Eph 5:8), that we shun the works of darkness and put on the weapons of light (Rom 13:12), that he has prepared for us also an inexpressible, incomprehensible light in eternal life according to which we see ourselves and toward which we should strive through faith in all piety.

Third, the foremost church teachers hold that God the Lord created the holy angels on the first day, which are heavenly lights and morning stars (John 38:7). Consider concerning this day's work the benefits of God, how he ordained noble servants for humanity who acknowledge with high thanks this responsible service toward God, and especially recognize the steadfast obedience of the holy angels, whose example we should truly follow. One could especially devote the first day of the week or, as we say, Sunday, to this meditation.

On the second day God created the firmament of the heavens, the foundation, which he spread out like a carpet (Ps 104:2). He has stretched it out like a thin coat and spread it out as a tent in which man dwells (Isa 40:22; 42:5). He has, through the same, separated the waters under the foundation from the waters above. Consider concerning this day's work how orderly God the Lord has made the heavens (Ps 136:5), that it has a certain course and never fails. Therefore, we should all the more truly obey the certain unfailing order of God the Lord. Consider that because the visible temporal heaven is so beautiful and full of light that the invisible eternal heaven, which he has prepared for the faithful and godly as a dwelling of his beloved children, must be much more beautiful and light. Consider how the heavens tell of the glory of God and the firmament announces his handiwork (Ps 19:2), and how the waters above the heavens praise God (Ps 148:4). Therefore, as rational creatures we should much more declare praises to God. One could especially devote the second day of the week, which we call Monday, to this meditation.

On the third day God created the earth and the sea, that is, through his divine might he made the water under the firmament, which goes around the earth, gather in a certain place so that one sees the wetness and the dry earth and names the gathering of the water, the sea. Consider, concerning this day's work, the great majesty and might of God the creator and let it move you to inner fear of God, for God the Lord makes himself known to you when he speaks of this day's work in his word: "Who closed the sea with doors when it burst forth from the womb, when I clothed it with clouds and wrapped it in darkness as in swaddling clothes, when I prescribed bounds for it and set a rule and door to it, and said, 'You shall come until here and no further; here should your proud waves stop'?" (Job 38:8–11). "He holds the water together in the sea as in a bottle and lays its depth in darkness. Let all the world fear the Lord and take fright before him who dwells on the earth" (Ps 33:7–8). "You establish the riches of the earth on its foundation such that it remains forever and eternally" (Ps 104:5). "You cover it with darkness as with a cloak and waters stand above the mountains. They fly from your rebuke; at the sound of your thunder they take flight. The mountains rise up and the breadth sets itself in the place where you have grounded it. You have set your limits over which they do not pass and they must not cover the earth again" (Ps 104:4, 7–9). "'Will you not fear me,' says the Lord, 'and will you not be frightened before me? I who set the sand as a shore to the sea where it should remain for all time, over which it must not go and if its waves rage so must they still not travel over it'" (Jer 5:22).

Even on the same day God the Lord also let grass, plants, and fruitful trees grow on the earth. Consider by this day's work that you also are a fruitful tree (Ps 1:3) planted in the house of the Lord (Ps 92:14), as a tree of righteousness, a plant of the Lord to prize (Isa 61:3). You should bring forth good fruit pleasing to the Lord and useful to the neighbor and be fruitful in good works (Titus 3:14). One can refresh the spirit on the third day of the week, or as we say on Tuesday, with this meditation.

On the fourth day God the Lord created both great lights in the firmament of the heavens, the sun and the moon and also the stars. Consider by this day's work that your Lord and Savior Christ Jesus is the true Sun of Righteousness (Mal 4:2). The dawn from on high (Luke 1:78), whose visage shines like the bright sun (Matt 17:2; Rev 1:16), who illumines your heart so that you receive the light of life from him just as the moon receives its light from the sun; so that you should forever more let your light shine before men, by which they see your good work (Matt 5:16), that you should shine in the midst of crooked and perverse people as a light of the world (Phil 2:15). Consider that Christ is the beautiful clear morning star (Rev 22:16), who also makes the morning star of divine knowledge rise in your heart (2 Pet 1:19), who holds you as a beautiful little star in his hand (Rev 1:15). Therefore, you must also let the light of good works shine before you, for what kind of star would that be that did not illumine? Light is the nature and essence of a star. With this meditation one can refresh oneself especially on the fourth day of the week, or as we say, Wednesday.

On the fifth day God the Lord created the fish of the sea and the birds that fly over the earth under the firmament of the heavens. Consider by this day's work the wisdom of God in the many types of fish and birds as well as his goodness that he created the same to be good and useful to men: "Lord, how great and many are your works that you have so wisely ordered, and the earth is full of your benefits, the sea that is so great and wide which teems with animals both great and small without number. There go the ships and there the whales, which you have made for your sport" (Ps 104:24–26). With this meditation one can refresh oneself especially on the fifth day of the week or, as we say, on Thursday.

On the sixth day God created cattle, creeping things, and animals that go upon the earth, each according to its kind. Consider once again the wisdom of God in the many kinds of animals and the blessings of God that he created all of these for the benefit of humanity (Gen 1:26). Some animals were created for humans as food, some for clothing, some for service and work, some for enjoyment, but altogether for their use and for the best. Consider also the *simulachra virtutum*, the mirror of virtues that God holds up in front of you in the animals, for example. the zeal of the ant: "Go to the ant, you sluggard, see its ways and learn from them. Although it has no chief or officer or ruler, it prepares its bread in the summer and gathers its food in the harvest time" (Prov 6:6–8). Examples of thankfulness are the ox and the ass: "An ox knows its master and an ass the crib of its master, but Israel does not know and my people do not understand" (Isa 1:3). Examples of prudence are the stork and crane: "A stork in the heavens knows her times; a turtledove, crane and swallow mark the time of their coming, but my people know not the true ordinances of the Lord" (Jer 8:7). And so forth with the other animals.

On the same day the Lord created humans in his own image and thereby also concluded the work of creation. Consider by this day's work that our first father was formed from a clump of dirt so that we should be led to humility. *Adverte homo, quia limus es, et non sis superbus*, says Bernard [of Clairvaux] in *Sermon 3 on the day of the Lord's birth* (Turn, man, because you are slime, and do not be proud). "I have taken it upon myself to speak to the Lord although I am earth and ashes, says Abraham" (Gen 18:27). Consider how marvelously the vessels, the bones, and all the members of your body fit together and know from that how you are obligated to serve your creator with all the members of your body. Consider the great benefits of the Lord that he gave you a rational soul and know from that how you are obligated to serve your creator with all the powers of your soul. With this meditation one can especially take delight on the sixth day or, as we say, Friday.

"On the seventh day God rested from all the works that he made" (Gen 2:2). Consider therefore how God also wants your soul to rest: "So says the high and lofty One who inhabits eternity, whose name is Holy: I dwell in the high and holy place and also with him who is of a contrite and humble spirit, and thereby I quicken the soul of the humble and the heart of the contrite" (Isa 57:15). "Thus says the Lord: 'Heaven is my throne and the earth is my footstool. What is the house you would build for me or what is the place where I might rest?' My hands have made all that is, says the Lord, but I look upon the one who has a lowly and broken spirit and who trembles at my word" (Isa 66:1–2). So he wants to say: I will dwell and rest in such a heart. Consider also that you should, in turn, rest in God and keep a spiritual Sabbath in which you rest from all the work of your sinful flesh and let God work in you: Blessed is the man who does this and the son of man who holds it fast, that is, holds the Sabbath, not profaning it and keeps his hand from doing any wrong (Isa 56:2). "If you refrain from trampling on the Sabbath, from pursuing your own pleasure on my holy day, if you will call it the Sabbath a delight, if you honor the Lord and praise him, if you do not go your own way then you will find what pleases you. Then you shall take delight in the Lord" (Isa 58:13–14). "Whoever comes to rest rests also from his work as God from his" (Heb 4:10). Consider that God the Lord prepares eternal rest and peace in heaven if you will keep a spiritual Sabbath here and let God rest in you: One Sabbath will come after another. Come worship before me, says the Lord (Isa 66:23). "It is still prepared that some should come to the same rest." "Therefore, a rest is still prepared for God's people." "So let us now strive to enter that rest so that no one may fall by the same example of disbelief" (Heb 4:6, 9, 11). With this meditation, one can find delight especially on the seventh day or, as we say, on Sunday, and consider the shape of the work of God as if it is written down on a tablet.

The fifth type of meditation [Red, white, and black]

One of the old church fathers says that he reads daily in a book that has three pages: one red, one white, and one black. On the red page he reads and considers the blood-red suffering of Christ. On the white page he reads and meditates on the eternal joy of the elect. The color white signifies in the holy scriptures the honor and joy of the elect who appear in white garments before the throne of God (Rev 4:4; 7:7) and the holy angels also allow themselves to be seen in white clothing (Mark 16:6; Acts 1:10). In the transfiguration of Christ, which was a foreshadowing or type of heavenly joy and clarity, his clothing was as white as a light (Matt 17:2), so white that no color on earth could be made so white (Mark 9:3). On the black page he reads and meditates on the eternal torment and pain of the damned as they are singed coal black and burned in the hellfire.

Such is the shape of the daily meditation of a lover of God directed on these three points that he considered: 1. *Christi passionem*, the bitter suffering of our Lord Jesus Christ, 2. *Piorum glorificationem*, the joy and glory of the blessed elect, 3. *Impiorum damnationem*, the pain and eternal heart-suffering of the damned.

The meditation on the suffering of Christ can be undertaken 1. *Historice* [historically], or by considering the story in an orderly manner as the Lord underwent his suffering. Such historical description can be shaped in many ways. First, it can be divided into seven different *Actus* [acts] as one considers 1. *Hortum* (in the garden), what happened to Christ in the garden as he sweated blood, was seized and bound, and also then abandoned by all his disciples. 2. *Pontifices* (before the priests) or what happened to Christ when he went before the court of the high priests Annas and Caiaphas, how false witness was born against him, how he was shamefully struck on the face, interrogated, and condemned to death although he was innocent.

3. *Pilatum praesidem* (before Pilate), what happened to Christ before the governor, Pilate, how he was falsely charged as a rebel. 4. *Herodem* (before Herod), what happened to him in the palace of Herod as he was ridiculed and mocked like a carnival king clothed in a white garment. 5. *Crucem* (on the cross), how he was flogged, crowned with thorns, ridiculed, beaten, condemned to death on the cross, led out to the place of the skull and shamefully and painfully crucified. 6. *Sepulchrum* (in the sepulcher), what took place after his death and how he was laid in a grave. For this type of meditation, consider these old verses:

Hortus, Pontifices, Praeses, Crux atque Sepulchrum.

After that, one can divide the meditation on the suffering of Christ according to time. The suffering of Christ began on the evening of Maundy Thursday and ended before the evening of Good Friday and was accomplished all in one Jewish day, for the Jews reckon the day from an evening to the next. A meditation of this form on the history of the sufferings of Christ can be divided into two parts, considering 1. What he underwent from the evening of Maundy Thursday until the morning of Good Friday. 2. What happened to him from the morning of Good Friday until the evening of the same day.

Concerning the first part it should be observed that the Jews divide the night into four parts or night watches as can be noted from Mark 13:34. The first watch began with the going down of the sun and continued until the ninth hour, as reckoned by the hands of our clocks. The same is called evening in some places, *ratione termini a quo* (with reference to the starting point). The second night watch began at the ninth hour and continued until midnight or until the twelfth hour, as reckoned by our clocks. The same, concerning Christ, is called midnight, *ratione termine ad quem* (with reference to the end point). The third night watch began at midnight and stretched until the third hour, as reckoned by our clocks. The same, concerning Christ, is called the cock's crow because at the same time the cock's cry was heard. The fourth night watch began early around the third hour and stretched until the rising of the sun or until the sixth hour. The same Christ calls the morning because it reached until morning.

In the first night watch Christ ate the Paschal lamb with his disciples in Jerusalem, thereby instituting the holy Lord's Supper, the sacrament of the new covenant, washed the feet of his disciples, spoke in a friendly manner with his disciples, and offered his heartfelt prayer to his heavenly Father, which is written in John 17. Soon after he went out of the city of Jerusalem, over the brook on the way to Kidron, to the Mount of Olives, and preached on the way to his disciples about his impending suffering. As he came to the garden with his disciples he made his inward prayer to God and asked for the averting of the cup. Then his inward difficult suffering began, which pressed on him so hard that he sweat bloody sweat and had to be consoled by an angel. As he underwent such inward suffering, his enemies came toward him but fell to the ground when he spoke one word. He was betrayed with a kiss by Judas, abandoned by his disciples, bound, and taken prisoner by his enemies.

In the second night watch he was also bound and taken captive through the Sheep's Gate into the city of Jerusalem, first to the high priest Annas, then afterward to Caiaphas, accused of false teaching and rebellion, shamefully struck in the face, denied by his own disciple Peter. False witness was born against him, and he was condemned to death as a blasphemer by the entire spiritual council.

In the third and fourth night watch, namely, from midnight until morning, he was ridiculed by the servants of the high priest who kept him, spat upon, and struck with fists. His face was covered and beaten and he was required with derisive words to prophesy or guess which one of them had hit him.

The Jews, likewise, divided the day into four parts. The first part had its beginning in the morning around the sixth hour and stretched to the ninth hour, as reckoned by our clocks. The second part began at the ninth hour and stretched to midday, or the twelfth hour. The third part began at midday, or the twelfth hour, and stretched until the third hour. The fourth part began at the third hour and stretched until evening, or until the sixth hour according to our clocks.

The first part of the day, early in the morning, Christ was condemned by the high priest and the spiritual council in Jerusalem and was led out of the palace of the high priest to the courthouse, condemned as a heretic and rebel, and interrogated by the governor, Pilate. In the second part of the day he was led to Herod, ridiculed by the same, clothed with a white robe to ridicule and scorn him, and sent again to Pilate, where he was presented along with the evil murderer Barabbas, then shackled, crowned with thorns instead of a kingly crown, a reed was put in his hand instead of a kingly scepter, he was clothed with an old purple mantle instead of kingly clothing, and, to ridicule and scorn him, he was called a king. Afterward he was condemned to death by Pilate and led to the place of the skull, together with two murderers. He himself carried the heavy wooden cross on which he would be nailed, drank vinegar in which bitter myrrh and gall were mixed, was stripped naked, crucified between murderers, nailed in hands and feet, while the soldiers divided his clothes among themselves, casting lots over his cloak. He was cursed by the thief, the soldiers, the high priests, and the common people. In the third part of the day he prayed for his crucifiers while hanging on the cross, promised paradise to the converted thief, recommended the care of his mother to John, proclaimed himself forsaken by God, cried out about his thirst, and, as he testified that all was fulfilled and commended his spirit into the hands of his heavenly Father, he died on the cross at the same time as the offering was made in the temple, as the true sacrifice of reconciliation. In the fourth part of the day he was taken from the cross and laid in a grave.

Third, this type of historical meditation is almost identical to the seven-hour meditation used by the ancients, as is written in the old hymn "Patris Sapientia It, Domine Jesu Christe" (Wisdom of the Father, Lord Jesus Christ), which was later translated into the German song "Christ Who Makes Us Holy."

Christ who makes us holy, who caused no evil, was led away as a thief for us in the night, falsely judged before godless people, ridiculed, derided, and spit upon, as the scripture says. In the first hour of the day he was presumptuously presented to Pilate the heathen as a murderer, who found him innocent without reason to die but sent him to King Herod. Around three, the Son of God was smitten with a scourge, his head was ripped with a crown of thorns, and he was dressed up to be derided and scorned. He was badly beaten and had to bear the cross himself to his death. Around six, naked and bare, he was nailed on the cross, his blood gushed forth, he prayed with lamenting cries, was derided by his onlookers and also those who hung with him until the sun withheld its shine from such things. Jesus cried out at the ninth hour, declaring himself forsaken. Soon afterward gall with vinegar was put in his mouth. When he gave up his spirit, the earth shook, the curtain in the temple was ripped, and many mountains shook. When the thieves' legs were broken at the vesper hour, Jesus was pierced in the side with a spear, and blood and water ran out, to fulfill the scriptures, as John showed. When the day came to an end, and evening came, Jesus was taken from the cross by Joseph, laid honorably in a grave according to the Jewish way, and was watched over by guards, as Matthew testifies.

Fourth, this historical meditation on the suffering of Christ can focus on the members of Christ, what he suffered in them, namely, how his head was crowned with thorns, his face was covered with spit, he was struck with a rod, his eyes teared up and were darkened in death, his cheeks were beaten, his mouth tasted myrrh and gall, his hands and feet were nailed to the cross, his side was opened with a spear, his entire body was beaten with a scourge and wounded.

This historical meditation on the sufferings of Christ should go further so that they are considered *mystice et practice* [mystically and practically], that is to say, meditated on in a spiritual way and seen first as a mirror of wrath [*Zornspiegel*], because sin is such a horror before God the Lord that the same could be expiated in no other way than through the death of Christ. So is it sufficient to take from this that God the Lord is heartily a foe of sin. Peter says, in Acts 4:28, that in and by the suffering of Christ, Herod and Pontius Pilate had done what the hand of God and God's counsel had previously determined should happen. Therefore we must see all that Christ endured in his suffering as God deferring payment. He was bound, scourged, and crucified, not because God was his enemy, but because he took upon himself the sin of the whole world to pay for the same. Therefore, God dealt with him as with a great sinner. For this reason Christ felt great anguish, sweated bloody sweat because of the burden of our sins and the wrath of God that we had merited with our sins. Weighed down, he cried out that he was forsaken by God, because God the Lord in wrath demanded of him the judgment due to our sins.

Second, it is also a mirror of love [*Liebesspiegel*]: "God proved his love toward us in that while we were still sinners Christ died for us" (Rom 5:8). "God so loved the world that he gave his only Son in the shameful death on the cross" (John 3:16). Therefore, the suffering of Christ is a public, evident witness of the immeasurable love of God that God the Lord has not spared his Son but has given him for us all: "No one has greater love than the one who lays down his life for his friend" (Rom 8:32). Christ has loved me and given himself for me (Gal 2:20). How can there be a greater love than that Christ gave himself for us in the shameful death on the cross? He bowed his head on the cross to kiss us with love, his arms were stretched out to embrace us with love, he opened his mouth to offer love for his crucifiers, he let his side be opened that one might see his love-rich heart. He let himself through the fire of love as a true Lamb of God be roasted on the wood of the cross, and out of love he thirsted for our salvation.

Third, as a mirror of virtue [*Tugendspiegel*] Christ suffered for us. Saint Peter says, "He gave us an example that we should follow in his footsteps" (1 Pet 2:21). For in his suffering Christ presented us with an example of willing obedience, that he was obedient to his Father, even on to death, even death on a cross (Phil 2:8, 9); of burning love because he suffered all out of love for us; of hearty humility and patience because he did not open his mouth when he was struck and tortured but showed himself to be a patient lamb when led to the slaughter (Isa 53:7); of meekness and friendliness because he did not scold when he was scolded and did not threaten when he suffered (1 Pet 2:23). See from this how one can profitably, helpfully, and wholesomely consider the suffering of Christ. How we might meditate on the joy of election and the pain of the damned is already addressed sufficiently in the first book, second part, chapters 14 and 18.

The sixth type of meditation [Past, present, and future]

Another of the old church teachers prescribed this rule: that we should daily consider three things that are past, that are present, and are in the future. Concerning past things we have to consider 1. *malum commissum*, the evil we have done, or in other words, our many sins, how we inwardly and outwardly, against the first and second tables of the Ten Commandments of God, consciously and unconsciously, secretly and openly have sinned often. 2. *Bonum omissum*, the good that we neglected, namely, how we could have performed many things with the powers of our soul and body but have neglected them. 3. *Tempus amissum*, the time that has passed or, namely, how already ten, twenty, thirty, forty, fifty, sixty years of our lives have flowed past, of which we cannot call or gain back again a single hour.

Concerning present things we have to consider 1. *vitae hujus brevitatem*, the short time of our lives here on earth, namely, how our time goes by so quickly as a year, a month, a day, an hour, one after another fly by, and we come ever nearer to the goal if we do not take it into consideration. 2. *Salvanti difficultatem*, how difficult it is for a person to hold on to salvation against the Devil, the world, and the temptations of the flesh; how one must then struggle so that one can enter through the narrow door (Luke 13:24), how one must work out one's salvation with fear and trembling (Phil 2:12). 3. *Salvatorum paucitatem*, how few people will be saved, for the gate is wide and the way is broad that leads to damnation, and there are many that travel on it. And the door is narrow and the way is small that leads to life, and how few there are that find it (Matt 7:13, 14).

Concerning future things we have to consider 1. *Mortem qua nihil horribilius* (nothing is more horrible than death), how sometime all must die and travel from the inn of this world and how anxiously and painfully this happens. 2. *Judicium quo nihil terribilius* (nothing is more dreadful than the judgment), how suddenly we must be presented altogether before the judgment seat of Christ, because it is appointed to man once to die and then the judgment (Heb 9:27). 3. *Poenam inferni qua nihil intolerabilius* (nothing is more unbearable that the infernal punishment), how many innumerable thousands of people will be plunged into hell and what an unspeakable and incomprehensible torment it is.

The seventh type of meditation
[What is above, in, near, and under us]

One may also make a holy devout meditation in which one considers 1. *Ea quae supra nos* (what is above us). The old Hebrews say there are three things above us, the eye [of God] that sees us, the ear [of God] that hears us, and the book in which all is written. 2. *Ea quae intra nos* (what is in us), how we find goodness and badness. The goodness we have received from God but for which we have not always been thankful from our hearts, though we have truly used it. The badness we have in part inherited from our ancestors, and in part we have committed ourselves. For this reason we find within us a gnawing, accusing conscience, we bear still within us our cursed sinful flesh, and we bear death around with us in our bosoms. 3. *Ea quae circa nos* (what is near to us), how we find the holy angels, which gladly serve us if we are godly, and the evil angels, which entice us to sin in many ways. The world besets us to the right and to the left, the neighbor, which we are obligated to serve through love, and the other creatures, which accuse us before God if we willfully sin. 4. *Ea quae infra nos* (what is under us), where we find the grave in which we must be buried after death, hell, which spews out its smoke and snaps after us if we live in sin. Note that if we are only aware we find instruction here for a holy and good meditation.

The eighth type of meditation [Twelve hours of the day]

Finally, we have a meditation divided according to hours and a spiritual clock presented to a lover of godliness. If it strikes one we have to remember that there is only one God (Deut 6:4) whom we should honor and alone serve, from whom all things come, and to whom all things hasten. That there is one mediator between God and humanity, namely, the man Christ Jesus (1 Tim 2:5), on whom we should depend through faith and love. There is also one spirit, which binds all spiritual members together into the body of Christ and moves them on to all good things (Eph 4:4). There is one heart, one faith, one baptism, and one God and Father of us all (Eph 4:6). Therefore, we should be zealous to hold the unity of the spirit through the bond of peace (Eph 4:3). God the Lord gave only one soul to each of us, of which we should take better notice. Eternity hangs on a moment. That one should remind us so that we sigh with David (Ps 86:11) and meditate on the word of Christ. Jesus says: “Martha, Martha, you have so many cares and troubles but only one is needed” (Luke 10:41).

When it strikes two, we have to remember that God the Lord gave us two special gifts of grace, namely, his Son and the Holy Spirit, so that we should love him. Likewise, there are two main parts of the whole heavenly teachings, namely, the law and the gospel, which both lead us to holiness, and God the Lord himself inscribed his law on two stone tablets, which we should inscribe on our hearts through steady meditation. Furthermore, the two greatest and foremost commandments are the law to love God and love the neighbor (Matt 22:37, 38), which above all else we should make an effort to observe. God set the two essential parts or pieces of human nature together, namely, the body and the soul (Gen 2:7), and with both of them we should serve God. In the New Testament, God the Lord instituted two sacraments, namely, holy baptism and the holy Lord's Supper, both of which lead us to holiness. Likewise, our inner person has two eyes, with one of which we should see God's mercy and the other of which God's judgment. There are two parts of true repentance: the remembrance of sins and the true faith in Christ, which we should cultivate at all times. There are two breasts that the holy mother, the Christian church, holds in front of us so that we might suck on the milk of heavenly wisdom (Song 1:2), namely, the scriptures of the Old and New Testaments. There are also two parts of true Christianity: a good conscience before God and a good name among the godly.

When it strikes three, we have to remember that there are three different persons in the divine essence—God the Father, the Son, and the Holy Spirit—that we should serve in holiness and righteousness. Likewise, in the first table of the Ten Commandments there are three commandments. One issues from our heart, that we should rightly acknowledge God, fear, love, and trust him. The second goes forth from our mouth, that we should not use his name in vain. The third proceeds from the whole person, that we should keep the Sabbath holy with all the powers of our soul and all the members of our body. In the book of nature there are also three great pages: the heaven, the earth, and the sea, which we read daily and from which we should study the knowledge of God the creator. The three parts of our meditation should be directed, first, to what we were, the second to what we are, and the third to what we will become, or in other words, what we are by nature, what we are by grace, and what we will become in glory so that we might heartily lament our past sins, be aware of the present benefits of this world, and consider the future eternal glory with our whole hearts. Similarly we should always consider the bitterness of death, the severity of the Last Judgment, and the unspeakable suffering of the damned. Furthermore, we should think about our sins and lament them, consider the mercy of God so that we do not despair, and also death so that we might resist in the time of sin. We give honor and obedience to those above us, counsel and help to our neighbors and discipline and admonishment to those below us. We also relate to God in three ways: honoring him as our creator, loving him as our savior, and fearing him as our judge. Likewise we relate to our neighbor in three ways: offering honor to our superiors, unity to our fellow Christians, and good will to our associates or members. We also relate to our selves in three ways: maintaining purity in the heart, caution in the mouth, and discipline or moderation in all our members. We should look for three things in all our works, first, whether it is permitted to us to act; second, whether it is fitting for us to act; and third, whether it is useful for us to act. There are also three chief virtues that we should be zealous for in our whole lives: faith, love, and hope. There are three chief enemies that always strive against us: the Devil, the world, and our sinful flesh.

When it strikes four, we should remember that the day is divided into four parts, that there are also four night watches, and that we should expect the return of our Lord in every night watch (Mark 14:3). Sin begins in our hearts in four ways: through provocation, consideration, consent, and defense. There are also four aspects of sin: first, evil thoughts in the heart; second, taking pleasure in such thoughts; third, carrying them out in outward works; and fourth, defending such works instead of abstaining from them through repentance. Lazarus was four days in the grave and began to stink (John 11:39). The seed of the word fell on four types of ground: the first fell on the way, where it was gobbled up by the birds; the second fell on stony ground and dried up; some more fell among thorns and was choked; and finally some fell on good land and brought forth fruit (Matt 13:4ff.). Therefore, we should see what kind of soil we are and how we hear the word. There are four last acts: death, the Last Judgment, hell, and eternal life. Finally, everyone has four things to consider at all times: one's death, Christ's death, the deceitfulness of the world, and the election to eternal joy. *Mors tua, mors Christi, fraus terrae, gloria coeli. Quatuor haec semper sunt meditanda tibi* (you should always meditate on these four). At every striking of the bell four things should be remembered: the lordship of God, our own duty, our death, and eternal life. *Numinis, officii, mortis, vitaeque futurae. Nos moneat praesens quae rapit hora diem* (may the hour at hand, which hastens away, remind us of these).

When it strikes five, we have to remember the five wounds of Christ, on his hands, his feet, and his side, so that we should hide ourselves through true faith thereby from the wrath of God. God has given five outward senses: sight, hearing, taste, smell, and feeling, which we should use according to God's will and command, so that we will not be punished in hell through all our outward senses. We should direct our meditation in five ways, for we have to consider ourselves, the world, the judgment, hell, and heaven. There are also five enemies that struggle against us as spiritual children of Abraham: the Devil, sin, the world, death, and hell (Gen 14:9). Christ as the heavenly Joshua has overcome these five enemies and crushed their heads (Josh 10:22). Consider also the five wise and five foolish virgins in the parable the Lord presented to us so that we should take care that we are found to be among the wise (Matt 25:1).

When the sixth hour strikes, we have to remember that God the Lord created all that was in heaven and on the earth in six days, for which great benefits and blessings we should be thankful and lead us to obligatory obedience (Gen 1:1; Exod 20:11). The span of our life is divided into six parts, namely, childhood, youth, the time of work, the time of slowing down, old age, and the time when we no longer have the ability to spend all parts of our lives in the service of God. Spiritual circumcision should happen to six parts of our lives: to our hearts so we strive against evil desires, the tongue so we do not blaspheme God or abuse our neighbor, the eyes so that we do not see vain or forbidden things, our ears so that we do not hear shameful words or stop them up from the cries of the poor, the hands so that we do not take what is our neighbor's as our own or close them when we should give, and finally, the feet so that we do not go to forbidden places. Six weapons and defenses are useful against the hellish enemy: the helmet of salvation, which is Christ Jesus; the breastplate of righteousness; the girdle of truth, which is a good conscience; the boot of the gospel, which drives up to do our calling; the shield of faith, with which we can quench all the flaming darts of the evil one; and the sword of the Spirit, which is the word of God and faithful prayer (Eph 6:14ff.). There were six types of sacrifices in the Old Testament through which the spiritual sacrifices of the New Testament were signified: the burnt offering signifying a broken and contrite heart (Ps 51:19); the sin offering signifying the atonement through Christ on the cross, which we make our own through true faith (Eph 5:2); the daily offering, signifying that we should present our bodies daily as an offering that is living, holy, and acceptable to God, which is our reasonable service (Rom 12:1); the food offering signifying good actions toward the poor (Heb 1:16); the incense offering signifying a faithful and devout prayer (Ps 141:2, Rev 8:2); and the thank offering signifying thanksgiving for the blessings of God. We must bring these spiritual offerings daily to God if we want to be a different sort of spiritual priest (Rev 1:6).

When the seventh hour strikes, we have to remember that God the Lord rested on the seventh day and sanctified it (Gen 2:2) to remind us that we also should rest in him. As God rested on the seventh day after he created all in six days, so also after the completion of six thousand years of the world the eternal Sabbath and rest day will take place, for which we should be prepared through repentance and godliness. There are seven commandments in the second table of the divine law to which we should always apply ourselves. There are seven days in each week, which we should devote to the service and honor of God. There are seven gifts of the Spirit (Rev 4:5), which we should seek through prayer. The Lord's Prayer has seven petitions in which are contained all that is necessary for this and the future life. We should recite them hourly in true faith. Christ fed his hearers through seven loaves of bread (Matt 15:36), as he will also feed us spiritually in eternal life with seven loaves: with utmost security, secure rest, restful love, loving joy, joyful eternity, eternal blessing, and blessed vision of the Trinity for which we should be longing.

When the eighth hour strikes, we have to remember that Christ was circumcised on the eighth day and received the blessed name Jesus so that he might acquire for us the spiritual circumcision and eternal salvation for which we should be heartily thankful. There are eight sorts of people that Christ praised as blessed. "Blessed," he says, "are the poor in spirit for theirs is the kingdom of heaven. Blessed are they who suffer for they shall be comforted. Blessed are the meek for they shall inherit the earth. Blessed are they who hunger and thirst after righteousness for they shall be filled. Blessed are the merciful for they shall obtain mercy. Blessed are the pure in heart for they shall see God. Blessed are the peace-makers for they shall be called the children of God. Blessed are they who persecuted for righteousness' sake for theirs is the kingdom of heaven. Blessed are those who are persecuted and scorned by men and against whom all kinds of evil are spoken" (Matt 5:3–11). We have these promises of blessing from Christ to cheer and console us in facing all needs and temptation. On the eighth day Christ was transfigured (Luke 9:28). On the eighth day, after the completion of temporal life, which is divided through weeks, blessed eternity and eternal blessing follow, and we will be transfigured in body and soul.

When it strikes nine, we have to remember that Christ died at the ninth hour (Matt 26:46) and through that death saved us from sin and eternal death so that we should henceforth live and serve him (2 Cor 5:15). There is more joy in heaven over one sinner who repents than for the ninety-nine who did not need to repent (Luke 15:7), which should awaken and admonish us to repentance. Among the lepers whom Christ made whole, nine were ungrateful and one was thankful (Luke 17:17), which should keep us from ingratitude.

When it strikes ten, we have to remember that God wrote his holy law in Ten Commandments (Deut 4:13), which we should learn and do for our whole lives. God the Lord demanded a tithe, a tenth to sustain the worship of God and the priesthood, by which we remember that we should give to him and his servants from all that is given to us by grace. The true godly are so pleasing to God the Lord that he was willing to spare an entire city for the sake of ten righteous (Gen 18:32).

When it strikes eleven, we have to remember that Jesus gave his eleven disciples the keys to the kingdom of heaven and the Holy Spirit (John 20:23), for which blessing we should thank him and use to our own consolation. However, if we want to use the key that opens fruitfully we must truly repent, since forgiveness of sins does not take place without repentance (Luke 24:47). If we want to receive the gifts of the Holy Spirit, we must repent (Acts 2:38) and live in true holiness, because the Holy Spirit flees from deceivers (Wis 1:5).

When it strikes twelve, we have to remember that when Jesus was twelve years old he illumined others with the rays of his divine wisdom when he sat in the middle of the learned in Jerusalem (Luke 2:41), thereby sanctifying the work of teachers and learners. He chose twelve disciples, who are signified in the Old Testament through the twelve sons of Jacob (Gen 35:22). He signified the church of the New Testament in a spiritual way through the twelve streams that the Israelites found in the desert (Exod 15:22), and he pointed to the lovely streams of gospel teaching that went into all the world through the twelve gems on the breastplate of the coat of the high priest (Exod 28:21). Furthermore, just as the gems signify the illumination of their teaching and life, so also do the twelve stones from which the altar was built (Exod 24:4). The church is grounded on their teachings as signified by the twelve show-breads that lay daily in the temple before the Lord (Lev 24:5). Their feeding of the hungry with the heavenly bread of the gospel is signified through the twelve oxen on which the sea rested in the temple of Solomon (1 Kgs 7:44). Their bearing the sea of the holy scriptures into the world is signified through the twelve stars in the crown of the bride of Christ (Rev 12:1). That their teachings illumined the church of God is signified through the twelve foundations of the heavenly Jerusalem (Rev 21:14). Their teachings are the first foundation of the church (Eph 2:20). We must maintain and follow these teachings of the Apostles, living according to them so that someday in the heavenly paradise we might eat of the tree of life, which bears twelve kinds of fruit in all twelve months (Rev 22:2). These fruits will be health without weakness, youth without age, sufficiency without revulsion, freedom without servitude, beauty without ugliness, consolation without pain, abundance without lack, peace without strife, security without fear, knowledge without uncertainty, honor without shame, and joy without sorrow. We long for such blessedness and meditate on it in all godliness.

Heinrich Müller Spiritual Hours of Refreshment (1664)

26. Weak Faith

A Spark Is Also Fire

Seek only to lay on coal and blow on it if there is no fire. A weak faith is still faith. Faith is not always a burning torch but often only a flickering candle. The candle lights as well as the torch, though not as brightly. Faith is the eye with which we look at Jesus. A weak eye is also an eye, a weeping eye is also an eye. You sit in tears and cry, how worried I am that I cannot believe. Oh, but you still can believe! My dearest heart, one also believes who heartily weeps over supposed unbelief, for such tears witness to the longing for faith. To want to believe is equal to believing in God. God effects in us the will as well as the achievement. Therefore he can hardly despise this longing.

Faith is the hand by which we grasp Jesus. A trembling hand is still a hand. You also believe if your heart trembles in the body when you reach out and try to grasp Jesus. You often say: "Oh, how can I console myself with the wounds of Jesus? I shudder when I think about my great sins. Am I worthy of such consolation?" Grasping Jesus with trembling hands is still believing. Faith is the tongue by which we taste how friendly the Lord is. A tongue that tastes weakly is still a tongue. Thus, we also believe when we taste no drop of consolation. For, our faith is not grounded in our feelings but in the promise of God. Faith is the foot that bears us toward Jesus. An injured foot is still a foot. Whoever comes slowly still comes. A Christian in his faith must not focus on how but on what. What holds your faith? Jesus. How does he hold you? Weakly. Attach no importance to that as long as you only hold to Jesus. God has not placed salvation in your grasp but in the one grasped, who is Christ.

It is a double hand that helps me to heaven. My faith-hand grasps Jesus and holds on to his merit. Jesus' grace-hand grasps me and comes to help my weakness. My grasp and hold easily loosen again, but his grasp and hold are all the stronger. Thus, I am at the same time weak in myself and strong in my Jesus.

31. Spiritual Drunkenness

"The Wine Speaks through Me"

That is what the drunk says. That is not good. You laugh, but I am shocked. The wine speaks through you; the Devil speaks through the wine; the Devil speaks through you. If the Devil controls your tongue, he also possesses your heart. Nature has connected the heart and tongue closely together through a little vein. The heart is the well within which the Evil One brews his poison; the tongue is the gutter through which it pours out. "How can the Devil come into the wine?" you ask. My dear one, how did he come into the snake? He knows how to coil himself nimbly into the creature and slink through the same into the heart. Truly, I have nothing to do with you. If he could deceive Eve through the snake, why not you or me?

But let that be. You boast that the wine speaks through you, I myself can also boast. The wine speaks through me perhaps more often than through you. Do you not notice, when I preach, how the fullness of the Spirit often flows out of my mouth? Many times my heart stands in a thousand springs and each spring goes up to heaven. I become so courageous that I want to force my way with my Jesus through spear and sword, through fire and flame, through trouble and death. I don't know myself how I have this courage and, as it were, am captivated by the Spirit. The carnal man does not understand, but whoever has tasted the powers of heaven perceives that I am (spiritually) intoxicated. Hear then what I say. When my Jesus has bitterly afflicted me and wants to make it up to me, he leads me into his wine cellar (Song 2:4) and lets me drink with delight as from a river (Ps 36:8). Then I become full of the Spirit, and when the heart is full, the mouth overflows. I sing and say of my Jesus, how sweet he is. I shout for joy and invite the souls that are bound in the

Spirit with me: "Oh, come then, taste and see how friendly the Lord is. Blessed is he who trust in him" (Ps 34:8). Then, I am not speaking; the fullness of the Spirit, the heavenly joy-wine speaks through me. It is as Paul says: "Be filled with the Spirit and speak among each other with psalms and hymns and spiritual songs, sing and make melody to the Lord in your heart" (Eph 5:19). See, then, the wine does not speak only through you but also through me.

O Jesus, let me taste your sweetness in my heart and thirst instead after you.

40. The Nature of Faith and Love

Always Restful, Never Restful

So it is with mother and daughter. That one is faith; this one is love. Faith is the child of God's bosom, which rests calmly in God as a child in the bosom of its mother. It is Mary, who kept still at the feet of Jesus and took pleasure in his words, or the disciple, who rested on Jesus' breast and eagerly drank the milk of his sweet consolation (Luke 10:39). Like the dove in the cleft of the rock, the wild animal in its hole, the chick under the feathers of the hen, so faith takes its rest in the wounds of Jesus where sin, death, and the Devil must leave it undisturbed. What can trouble the one whom Jesus loves?

After the mother, it is customary to name the daughter. But here, it is otherwise. Love is never restful. She is the busy Martha, who has both hands full (Luke 10:40). Her love is to serve the neighbor with goods and blood, with body and life. She does not wait until you request her service but presses in everywhere and takes the initiative, is sad when one scorns her with her good heart, and never has enough to do. She laughs and is happy when many knock at the same time at her door. She is never tired, is ready day and night, helps gladly, and still thinks that one needs her help. As her God acts, so she acts in turn toward her neighbor. Indeed, you might even say that love is a God on earth. Mother and child are so unalike. The mother is poor and always receives. The mother is so lofty that God and the angels must answer her. The daughter is so humble that the very least cast her underfoot. The mother seeks only rest and security. The daughter runs around restlessly, endangering her body and life. The mother must finally die; the daughter lives eternally. Love never fails (1 Cor 13:8). But, if you would have the daughter, hold onto the mother, because faith is active through love. My Jesus, you kindle the light through your Spirit so it will burn.

71. The Likeness of All People

I am earth, are you anything more than that? Why do you put on airs? You are as good as I, and I as good as you. Keep to the earth because you are earth, like to like. But you walk around in velvet and silk, while I walk around in only a smock. Earth is earth, whether you wear purple or cheap linen. Still, you sit above while I sit below. Earth is earth, whether one lies on the table or under the bench. Though you dress yourself elegantly and expensively, I make do very simply. Earth is earth whether one quenches thirst with water or wine. Earth is earth. What do I see then, when one throws so few gold and silver coins in the community chest but such a large number of copper ones. Think what gold is? Gold earth. What is silver? White earth. What is copper? Red earth. Why do you consider a gold or silver penny better than a copper one? Perhaps because it is heavier? What wonder is it then that your heart is heavy? Light penny, light heart. Heavy penny, heavy heart. Heavy penny, heavy care. Or maybe it is because of the color? Color is color, earth is earth. White and red make up gold. Or because they are worth more? That is a fantasy. Why is a copper coin not worth as much as a gold one? Because you can't imagine it? Still, it seems to be so. Gold is better than copper. The best belongs to God. Give him what he has given you. You have more gold than copper from him. Give God what is his. Everything is his, gold as much as copper.

76. Signs of a True Christian

You consider yourself a good Christian. I don't trust you. Prove it. How, you ask? The proof is in the testing. Are you tested in the oven of misfortune? It is no achievement to be pious when all is going well. A Christian is known in the midst of crosses. Anyone can be a helmsman in good wind and still weather. It is especially in bad weather that you see what a sailor knows how to do. Good gold stands up to a fire. Tell me, then, how do you fare in the time of testing? If you have lost your possessions, do you think that you have a better treasure in heaven that no one can take away? Can you say with Job: "The Lord gives, the Lord takes away; blessed be the name of the Lord" (Job 1:21). You are tormented by sickness. Do you complain about your pain? Do you also believe that the inner man is gaining much when the outer man is wasting away (2 Cor 4:16)? You are put to flight. Is your mind still joyful? Do you realize that you are still on your way to your home? If death approaches, are you frightened or do you say with Paul: "Christ is my life, death is my gain" (Phil 1:21)? In a word, whoever accepts crosses willingly is good, whoever bears them patiently is better, and whoever values crosses and thanks God for them is the best Christian.

Among the heathen, one surely finds brave people who either from an inborn magnanimity or the ambition to make a name for themselves in the world bear loss or pain patiently, but none of them claims to find joy in trouble. Only a Christian does that. What others consider misfortune, a Christian considers good fortune and says with Paul, "We rejoice in suffering, as we know that suffering brings patience and patience produces character, and character produces hope and hope does not disappoint us" (Rom 5:3–5). Have you ever been joyful in your suffering? If not, you are not a good Christian and should ask God to make you what you still are not.

77. The Characteristics of a True Christian

How does it come about that one becomes so weary and negligent in Christianity? One thinks of the end, and the beginning still has not been made. I wish that Paul's little saying were not so well-known and taken for granted. "I have fought the good fight, I have finished the race" (2 Tim 4:7). Many think of the prize and have scarcely begun to run. Many look at the crown and hardly see the obstacles on the way. I wish that our Christians were not so inchoate, standing still as soon as they begin and not going any further. No, the crown comes at the end. It would be better not to begin than to begin and not end. I wish that our Christians did not imagine themselves to have already grasped it. While others still must struggle, they think that they are already perfected and need go no further. All the tragedy in Christianity comes from this, that one does not endeavor to become more perfect.

When an arrow is shot from a bow, it flies very fast at the beginning, but the nearer it gets to its target, the slower it becomes, and it finally falls to the ground. Christians who think that today they will begin to become what they should become are eager and do not let up until they have reached the goal of perfection. Those, however, who imagine that they have to begin today but rather that they have already reached the goal become slow and sullen and entirely lose their zeal. Young people grow daily, but old people degenerate. Those who consider themselves young, growing Christians always try to improve. Those who let themselves think that they are perfect and mature in Christ decline rather than advance. The elderly descend the mountain; they do not ascend it.

Oh, how far we still are from perfection. How short the time is. How many hindrances there are. The Devil, the world, and the flesh are always active. How often will we be struck down as soon as we begin? Should we not form a new intention and make a new beginning so it is possible to bring a good work to the end? You have scarcely spoken the first word of the prayer of our Lord, "Our Father," when you fall into useless thoughts. If you wished to go forward, you would shut out your useless thoughts. How can they be pleasing to him? How can you begin? My advice is this: drive away your useless thoughts and make a new beginning. Believe me, I must often begin twenty times before I can bring a Lord's Prayer to its end with devotion. The Christian life is a steady climb. I have already ninety-nine good thoughts and good works together, but one is still lacking: the entire forgetting of myself. Therefore, I must seek as long as I live to begin again to deny myself.

78. The Growth of a Christian

In nature there is a mean between advance and decline. A boy of twelve is advancing in power, and a man of seventy is declining. Whoever bears forty or fifty years on his back is neither advancing nor declining. It is not so with Christianity. If vice is not declining, it is advancing. Unless you crucify your flesh daily and mortify it, gaining one advance after another, it will become bolder and stronger. As soon as you first sin willingly, it occupies your heart with its sweetness such that the desire to sin rises higher and higher like the tide and always eats away at you like a crab. Sin is like food. When you take one bite after another, the desire to eat often increases. If you do not take precautions against the first bite, sinning becomes sweeter and sweeter, for evil becomes attractive. It is rightly said: the older, the greedier.

On the other hand, where virtue does not advance, it declines. The seed of goodness within us is like a faint spark that is easily extinguished if you do not put wood or coal on it. It is like the wick of a lamp that quickly burns out if you do not pour in oil and nourish the flame. It is like a young plant that suddenly perishes if you do not keep it moist and watered. It is like a dilapidated house that will fall down sometime unless you steadily repair and improve it. It is like a newborn child that languishes unless it receives new strength daily from its mother's breast. Therefore, we must always see to it that we become more perfect. We must, like spiritual trees, always grow higher and become more abundant with fruit as we move from one stage of life to another. We are like spiritual pilgrims who are always going forward and coming nearer to the goal. You should not say: "Who among us is perfect?" Instead, my Christian, admit that you cannot be as perfect as you should be and still strive for perfection. Regardless of whether or not you can be perfect, you should want to be perfect and strive with all your powers toward that end. Much is involved in the growth of a Christian. If your faith and holiness always remain as a spark, you have reason to fear that sometime all will be extinguished in a moment. I always like to remember the words of Bernard [of Clairvaux]: "It is not possible to become pious without desiring to become pious, and where you begin and do not want to become pious, you will not be pious."

85. Little Sins

Little Dogs Often Inflict the Most Injury

The stag does not realize this but becomes aware of it as a result of its injury. When it confronts the large hunting dogs, injures them, and dashes them against a tree, the little dogs run in, hang on it in droves, and rip whole pieces of flesh from its body. It is not aware of the wounds until they get infected and putrid, after which it dies. You only combat the great sins and do not want to be called a murderer, thief, or adulterer, so that you have no shame before the world. Meanwhile, little sins, which you do not observe, put your flesh to the test. You love the company of people, follow the example of their elegant, costly clothing, share with them a friendly joke about this or that thing, thereby being wounded in your heart, though you are not aware of the wounds. Your former zeal for Christianity decays gradually, dies away within you, until finally it happens that you die an eternal death from the wounds. See then how many great calamities arise more from little sins than from great ones. You consider great sins to be sins and avoid them, but you do not consider little sins to be sins and do not give them proper attention. I advise you to consider no sin little. However little they may appear, they offend God, wound your conscience, and become a root for many great sins.

How quickly a fire can grow from a little spark when one does not prevent it. When one throws a stone in an eddy, it makes wavering circles in the water, each one greater than the other. Then, when one is agitated, it agitates another that is greater and then another that is greater. So is also the case with sins. The little one is the beginning of a greater one, and the greater is a new beginning of one still greater. Therefore, Bernard [of Clairvaux] rightly says: "A heart given to God protects itself from little as well as great sins because a beginning is made from the little one, which defiles you with greater ones." There is no sin, however small it may be, which does not deserve death. For the wages of sin is death (Rom 6:23). Whoever keeps the whole law but fails in one point becomes guilty of all of it (James 2:10). Augustine gives us something to ponder when he says: "Do not consider sins unimportant because they are little, but fear them because they are many. O, a grain of sand is so little, but when many of them come into a ship, it sinks under them until it goes aground. And, how little rain drops are, yet they make the flood rise and demolish houses." To avoid and flee from little sins is a sign of an enlightened mind. For, while the slightest speck of dust is seen in the light of the sun, one is not aware of a great clump of filth in the darkness. The more a person is illumined by God, the more the slightest sins are also seen and hated. I will consider everything a sin that is against my God, however slight it may seem to be. No sin is so little that it would not condemn me, if God were not gracious.

123. Great Knowledge

Much Science (*Wissen*), Little Conscience (*Gewissen*)

These two are good friends and commonly dwell together. You pride yourself on your great knowledge. The Devil knows more than you do and must still burn in hell for all eternity. What use is much science if there is no conscience along with it? Do you not know what Christ says: "The fool who knows the will of God and does not do it will receive many lashes" (Luke 12:47)? You have studied the scripture but have you also grasped the inner secret meaning? What use is it to the brain and the tongue if it is not in the heart? Love surpasses knowledge. Love builds up; knowledge puffs up. Just as water lessens the strength of wine, so that it does not make you drunk, so must love restrain knowledge so that it does not puff up (1 Cor 8:1). No knowledge improves without love. Just as food does not nourish the body if it is not digested through natural heat, so no knowledge is useful if it does not have the fire of divine love. Why do you elevate yourself on account of your knowledge? A little sickness can weaken your head, impair your understanding and destroy your thoughts. Why do you boast? However much you know, your knowledge is still only partial and childish (1 Cor 13:11, 12). What remains of your knowledge after death? How soon will it be forgotten?

Whoever is conceited does not know what should be known. To know nothing is the highest knowledge. You know everything? Do you also know yourself? The more you endeavor to know things that are outside you, the more you forget yourself and your inner ground.

You know everything? Do you also know God? Apart from God, all wisdom is foolishness, for it leads you away from true wisdom. Fear God. The fear of the Lord is the beginning of wisdom. See to it that you are united with God through faith so you will now see everything in God and understand. Just as you cannot see the sun without the sun and travel on water without water, so you cannot know God without God. Therefore, ask that he might enlighten you. Let the Creator be the mirror within which you behold God. He is the origin of all things and in him is all good, infinitely better than in all other things. What good you know, practice. Knowledge without action is a cloud without rain, a tree without fruit. I will, therefore, always consider that I know nothing and also seek to know nothing other than Jesus the crucified. So, I know enough even though I know nothing else.

130. The Hereditary Nobility

Foreign Feathers/Borrowed Plumes

You make such a show with them. Are you not a fool? It is much better to be noble [by] yourself than to be born a noble. It is much better to have your own treasures than to beg for the treasures of others. What is noble blood [*Geblüt*] without noble humility [*Demut*] and deeds? When the Jews boast, "Abraham is our father," Jesus says to them, "If you were Abraham's children, you would do what Abraham did" (John 8:39). Works prove the man. Birth does not make one a noble, deeds do. David was a shepherd boy, but his heroic deeds made him noble. The same root bears the rose and the thorn. From one mother often a noble and ignoble child is born. Did not one body bear Cain and Abel, Jacob and Esau? Still, they were not equally noble in their morals. Often, an unfruitful plot of ground yields gold and silver, while a fruitful one yields thorns and thistles. Often, an ignoble child springs from noble blood, while a model of noble virtue springs from an ignoble lineage.

Do not boast of a title of nobility, upper nobility or highest nobility; birth confers no nobility. The nobility that you inherit from your parents is called sin and mortality. Open the grave of your ancestor and you will see your noble lineage before your eyes.

"Decay, I call my father," says Job, "and the worms, my mother and sister" (Job 17:14). There you have your nobility. You are dust, a stink comes from you as well as from a peasant. You worm, will you boast of your nobility? If you could preserve your noble lineage from all human hazard, natural or sinful, it would be worthy of note, but you cannot. You sin as well as the peasant, and more often. Also, trouble and death do not go past your door. I feel sorry for you when I consider the words of Paul: "Not many are powerful, not many are called noble, but God has chosen what is low and despised in the world, even things that are nothing, to bring to nothing things that are" (1 Cor 1:26, 27). Whoever is not a slave of the affections is truly noble. A scandalous life darkens the nobility of a line, just as clouds obscure the brightness of the sun. No one imagines that a black raven is a white swan, and I also do not believe that you are noble when I see no noble morals in you and hear of no noble deeds by you. As little as a slave is noble, so little is a soul noble that serves sin.

The signs of a noble mind are these: it is easily moved. Who is nobler than God? Who is more merciful than God? It forgives readily. The king bee lacks a stinger. It is mild and shares with all. The sun as the noblest creation illuminates all; the most noble gold is drawn the farthest. It does not exalt itself in times of good fortune or fall in times of misfortune, but maintains the same fortitude in all situations. It scorns what is earthly, letting itself be satisfied only with heaven. It loves virtue and respectability. Aspire to the nobility of virtue and you will be noble. A hereditary noble is one only as part of a family; the nobility of virtue is your own. This nobility no one can give you. No one can take it away but yourself. The highest noble is born from God. This nobility is common to all Christians. You are a child of God; I am also. Do not elevate yourself over me, and I will not elevate myself over you. We are both equally highly noble.

138. Union with Christ

Black and White Do Not Mix

The card player knows this. The Devil wants to play with you and your soul. He is black. Are you also? If so, it will be a good match. Black with black, like with like. The Devil and you are joined. Your soul is his; his hell is yours. Sin makes the head hard. I was, indeed, black by nature, but now I have become white by grace. Original sin blackened me; the blood of Jesus made me snow white in baptism. White and red is my Jesus; white and red am I also. His innocence is my innocence; his righteousness is my righteousness. I have washed my clothes and made them bright in the blood of the Lamb, and someday I will stand before him attired in white clothes.

Devil, you can make no pact with me; no white stone bonds with a black one. You want to beat me at your game? You can count on it. You already proved this when you kicked my first ancestors out of paradise, from rest to unrest, from innocence to sin, from life to death. But I know this and will not just stand by. Separated from you and bound with Jesus. He is my color: white with white. You can rage but you cannot strike me, because Jesus is bound to me. The head of faith holds fast. O my Jesus, you are mine and I am yours. Who can separate us? You are my shepherd and I am your lamb. I will find pasture with you. You are my clucking hen, and I am your little chick. You cover me with your wings of grace. You are my bridegroom and I am your bride. You kiss me with the kiss of your mouth. What you are, that you are to me. What is yours, that is all mine. Your blessing is my blessing, your life my life, your blessedness my blessedness. Am I poor? You are my riches. In you alone will I find delight, far above all golden treasure. When I have you, I have what should satisfy me eternally. Will I be attacked? You are my shelter. Am I rejected? You are my refuge. Am I sad? You are my consolation and my friend. What I am, I am to you. Sin, what do you want from me? I belong to Jesus and find healing in his wounds. Devil, leave me in peace, for Jesus is my shield. Your arrows do not strike me, but what will you deliver to him? World, you don't have a chance. Jesus is with me. If you assault me, you are running with your head into an iron wall. Whom do you hurt? Yourself or me? Death, where is your victory? Christ is my life, death is my gain. Jesus, you remain mine, and I remain yours. Your love should be eternal.

152. The Idolatry of the Mouth-Christians

"Divine Worship, Idol Worship"

Oh, whose heart does not break from sorrow and dismay. God is made to adorn idols. How much worship of idols [*Götzendienst*] the mouth-Christians conduct under the appearance of and in the name of worship of God [*Gottesdienst*]. With tears I wrote about this in my *Apostolic Chain of Conclusions* and now, weeping, I write about it once more. Christianity today (I speak here of the hypocritical Christians as the surrounding text sufficiently shows) has four dumb church idols, which it follows: the baptismal font, the pulpit, the confessional seat, and the altar. They console themselves with their outward Christianity, that they are baptized, hear God's word, go to confession, and receive the Lord's Supper, but they scorn the inner power of Christianity. They scorn the power of baptism since they do not live in accordance with the new nature but keep to their old nature, even though baptism is a washing of rebirth and renewal. They scorn the power of the word of God, since they do not live as the word intends, but refute the word with their godless living and make a lie of it. They scorn the power of absolution, since afterward they remain unchanged in their character, living today just as they did yesterday, even though the heart, if it is quickened with the consolation of divine absolution, will no longer love evil and hate the good. They deny the power of holy communion since they do not live in Christ with whom they are united but live according to the lusts of their flesh and pour forth all kinds of sins. "How accord has Christ with Belial?" (2 Cor 6:15). All this is idolatry. For God is a Spirit and desires that we should worship him in spirit and in truth (John 4:24).

How is this? Isn't it like the Anabaptists to call baptism, the word, confession, and the Lord's Supper dumb idols? Friend, is there, then, no difference according to you between baptism and the baptismal font, preaching and the pulpit, confession and the confessional bench, the Lord's Supper and the altar? The Anabaptists abolish the right use of the baptismal font, the pulpit, the confessional seat, and the altar; I endeavor to abolish the invalid reliance of the mouth-Christians who depend on and base themselves on these things. Is there no difference between use and abuse? I say then: It is idolatry if the heart attaches itself to something and trusts in something that is not actually God. Whatever the heart of a mouth-Christian relies on or trusts, other than God, that is its idol. For example, he relies on the altar and pulpit, trusting in them despite the fact that he does not believe in Christ or exercise his faith through love. He expects to become holy because he was carried to the baptismal font in his childhood, although now he does not demonstrate the power of baptism in his life, or because he sees and hears the preacher in the pulpit, although he does not receive the word in faith or bring it into his life, or because he comes quarterly to the confessional seat, even though his heart neither means or feels what his mouth confesses, or because he goes with other communicants to the altar, although there is neither devotion nor faith in his use of the Lord's Supper. Isn't that called idolatry when I base my salvation not on true faith in Christ but on a delusive faith in wood, lime, or stone?

I say it one more time: whoever does not serve God as one should according to his word, in Spirit and in Truth, but merely with outward pretenses and actions, is idolatrous. Semblance without the word of God is as much an idol as a wooden or silver image. Tell me why our theologians call the papist worship service idolatry? Because it does not have the word of God as its measure and rule. I call the service of the mouth-Christians idolatry precisely for this reason: because God in his word expressly rejects the sacrifice without fat, the work without faith (Lev 3:16; Rom 3:28).

Oh, one should not make many disputations about this but muster courage in the Lord to endeavor to struggle with Elijah against the Baalites (1 Kgs 18), to purify the temple of the Lord, and to tear down the self-made idols in the hearts of men. It does not help for one to say: "The Anabaptists can misuse such words and thereby excuse their lies." God put up with the Devil ripping the word from his mouth and speaking falsely against Christ in the wilderness (Matt 4; Luke 4). When Paul consolingly taught that where sin is, there also the grace of God is mighty (Rom 5:20), he approached the insolent heap and concluded: so now we must trust to heap sin with sin that the grace of God can show its power to us. Who has gotten them to draw that conclusion? Not Paul and his well-intended words but the Devil and their perverted thinking. Poison from the rose. Who can be against what I say? Now in the preface of my *Apostolic Chain of Conclusions* I wrote to the Christian reader: "Should a slanderer dare to sharpen his poisonous teeth on this book, I will not fret myself to death because of that; my dear Savior, his apostles, and true servants in the world endured such misfortunes patiently. I have not desired a better fate for myself than my Lord and my brothers in the Lord had before me. Right must remain right and all pious hearts will cling to it. It is a bad habit of the world that it blasphemes the good because it is, itself, evil. What the fleshly man does not understand, he must malign." So it remains. Apply this to yourself, you Pharisee.

157. Moving Sermons

From the Heart into the Heart

That applies to me and to you, when we work in the word and in doctrine. You lament, "What I preach does not reach the hearts of the people." I ask, "Does it go forth from your heart?" What is not from the heart will not go into the heart. How can you be confident that the hearer is certain of your teaching, when you yourself are not assured through your own experience? Don't blame the hearer if your teaching does not come with power, before you have discharged yourself. You speak without understanding like a parrot, preach the word sleepily like a dreamer, and what you say is not demonstrated either through your faith or through some felt assent of your heart. Believe me, you are as guilty of unbelief as your hearer. When Christ says to Nicodemus, "We speak of what we know but you do not receive our testimony" (John 3:11), he says enough to suggest that the Jews had a reason, to some measure, to reject the word, insofar as it was expounded to them without knowledge and self-understanding. Preachers are wet nurses of the congregation, who, in order to give healthy, sweet milk from their breasts, must first taste the food of the divine word, chew it, and practice it in life. Bees must begin with themselves, after which they also make honey for others. Oh, how many are like the channel through which the water flows, watering others but remaining dry themselves. How can the water move a ship that is not moved itself by the wind? A speech that goes forth from a stirred-up heart sinks in deep and works powerfully, even though it is the speech of a slight person. Yes, even the silence of such a person is not without power. Origen, when he read the words of Psalm 50:16, "How can you take my covenant on your lips," in a sermon to the people, could not speak without tears and made the entire congregation cry with him. If the heart could speak the teaching, how powerful would your sermons be. On that account, I preach, not eloquently but movingly, not scratching the ears, but moving the heart. I will make a beginning with myself. How will what has not moved me, move others? I have seen the tears flow frequently during my sermon when tears have flown from me before in my study room.

O my God, let your wind blow, so that, having blown through us, we might blow it powerfully upon others. Then one will smell your fragrance.

204. Godless Preachers and Parishioners

Such as the Dish Is, So Is the Cover

I have often wondered how it has come about that so many old, learned, pious *Studiosi* [students] now and then live as if in the diaspora and are not promoted when so many bad rogues creep around in the preacher's gown. The consistory cannot complain about this evil enough. But, what should I say? *Dignum patella operculum* [Like cover, like cup]. As the shepherd is, so must also the flock be. That greedy, proud parishioners choose a greedy, proud pastor is no wonder. Such as the dish is, so is the cover. Who has a golden cover made for a copper dish? How would a humble priest manage among the proud, a pious one among the godless, or a kindhearted one among the greedy? He is gold; they are copper. He teaches; they do not listen. He leads; they do not follow. He chastises; they get angry. He shows the way to heaven; they take the way to hell. Likes attract. What kind of edification can there be where there is no love between the flock and the shepherd? What kind of love can there be if there is no likeness in either mind or morals? How well you do, child of the world, when you love what you can love and please yourself with what resembles you? If the priest is your type, he does the same as you do. You practice usury, rob, steal, covet, exploit, cheat, and so also does he, even better than you do. You drag the poor out of the saddle; he strikes them to the ground. You sheer the sheep; he skins them. You take milk and wool; he the meat and the hide. You serve your belly; he even serves Baal. You can eat and drink to excess, and he can outdo you. You wound the innocent with your tongue; he even slays them. Because he does as you do, you remain in sin, unpunished. One raven does not eat away the eye of another. How can he accuse you if he is guilty himself? His own conscience would testify against him and his own mouth would condemn him. Is it not a splendid life? Do what you desire and face no objection. Yes, indeed, yes. But what results from this? Your shepherd dies in sin and you also. Your shepherd goes to the Devil and you with him. Similar life, similar reward, similar brother, similar gown. God would be unjust if he separated in eternity those who bound themselves together in time. How well have you cared for your soul? You must praise God's justice. For, as you wish, so will it happen to you.

232. The Duty of the Preacher to Discipline and Console

First Bitter, Then Sweet

Frightful and tender. This is how a servant of Christ should be. First the sting, after that honey. First the rod, then manna. First wine, then oil. First strike down, wound, kill, and then raise up, heal, revive. First preach hell, after that, heaven. Christ calls you a shepherd (John 10). Therefore, you must take both the hard staff and the soft staff to hand. Paul calls you a rower (1 Cor 4:1) and wants you to steer cautiously so that the ship of Christ is brought undamaged between the dangerous rocks of security and despair. On this side, you must row with the firm hand of Moses. On the other side, with the gentle, left hand of Christ. If you always console, you do not row rightly. How many become secure and reckless by your consolation? The old nature must be stopped and blocked, or else it will be unruly and will serve the Devil. If you always scold, you also do not row rightly. How many are driven to despair by such admonitions? The new nature must have consolation and comfort in order to be drawn toward the good. If first you rebuke and then console, you have done rightly. If consolation comes to the heart at the wrong time, it does not feel its own grief.

A doctor heals unsuccessfully if a person does not want to know about any sickness. This is the right method used by every true servant of God. First he gets you to recognize what you lament or should lament, and then consolation is appropriate. Similarly, a good doctor first makes the patient weak with medicine and then treats him again with something to strengthen the heart. Moses must go before and prepare the way for Christ. Christ cannot cover what Moses has not first uncovered. If the law has not accused and condemned, the gospel cannot pardon and make holy. The law consists of stone tablets. If the heart is impenitent, stone hard, and wicked, Moses must thunder and lightning, preach of death and the Devil, until it is crushed and knows, in anguish, that nothing remains. Just as no birth takes place without pain, so there will also be no thorough repentance without terrifying the spirit and frightening the conscience. When there is anxiety, a person seeks Jesus and hastens like a thirsty hart to the consoling fountain of Israel (Ps 42:1). Christ is pleasing to no one more than the one who has broken the law. A Pharisee with a full belly, who swaggers with his imagined righteousness, tramples the honey of the consoling righteousness of Christ. Through the terror of the law, the desire to sin must be suppressed in the heart. Whoever has once tasted what hellish anxiety is in the conscience will not commit a sin lightly. When Moses has done his part, then Jesus must step forward and heal the wounds Moses has made. If Moses has led a person into hell, then Jesus must lead that person out again. Whoever leaves a sorrowing soul forsaken, lets it remain dead, and that is soul murder.

262. Faith and Love

"Up and Out"

The ascent of the angel on the ladder of heaven, which Jacob saw in his dream [Gen 28:10–12], is a lovely image of Christ. He is true God and man, became the mediator between God and man, united in himself God and man, heaven and earth, going down in his incarnation and going up in his ascension. It is also a marvelous image of the Christian. For what is our Christianity other than a steady going up and going out? Up to God, out to our neighbor; to God through faith, to the neighbor through love. Upward, heart! Grasp the bountiful Jesus in the arms of faith and say, "You are mine and that which is yours, is all mine." Oh, how rich you are in your Jesus; you can say *Jesum meum et omnia* [My Jesus, my all]. Let the world step up and display its riches; what does its treasure amount to? A little bit of poor earth. What you can show in comparison to that is more costly than heaven and earth. With a treasure in your sight, will you settle for a mite? Jesus above all and all in all. What the world gives is a bunch of scraps [*Stückwerck*]; what Jesus gives is whole and complete [*Vollwerck*]. The former brings thirst, the latter quenches it; the one agitates, the other gratifies. *Jesum meum et omnia.* Jesus is mine, and in Jesus all is mine. He is my light in the darkness, so I cannot go astray, my righteousness against sins, my blessing against the curse, my life against death, my salvation against damnation, my protection against oppression, my joy in suffering, my fullness in need, my one and only, outside of him I desire nothing, my all, for in him I find all. The Lord is my shepherd, I shall not want (Ps 23:1).

> In him alone is my delight,
> Far more than golden treasure,
> If I have him, then all is right
> My joy is without measure.

Outward, heart! And grasp the poor Jesus in love's arms. Oh! how he goes there hungry, thirsty, sad, naked, and wretched before your eyes. Will you let him hunger, he who gives you daily bread and feeds your soul with the hidden manna (John 6:32; Rev 2:17)? To thirst, who gives you to drink with delight as from a river (Ps 36:8)? To go sad and weeping, who consoled you so bountifully in your need and wiped all tears from your eyes (Rev 21:4)? To go naked, who clothed you with the robe of righteousness and adorned you with the garments of salvation (Isa 61:10)? To wallow in wretchedness, who stepped into your distress so that you might enter into his joy (Matt 25:21)? No! my heart. Embrace him and say: I am yours and what is mine is all yours. Are you hungry, my Jesus, I will feed you. Are you thirsty? I will give you drink. Are you naked? I will cloth you. Do you weep? Here is a cloth of consolation with which I will wipe away your tears. He is entirely content with few and little. A morsel of bread is enough to him for his nourishment; a drop of cold water for his refreshment; an old rag to cover him; have you nothing else, at least give him a comforting word. You are completely accountable for all you have, and he will reward you from grace for all that you do to one of the least of his believers (Matt 25:40).

I want to say to you in a few words what I think. In Christ, that faith is only worth something that is active in love (Gal 5). Faith makes the Christian; love reveals the Christian. The former leads to God; the latter to the neighbor. The one takes; the other gives. The one receives what God has given; the other lets the neighbor receive. The richer the in-flow, the richer the out-flow. Do you want to be a Christian? Then practice outwardly what you receive according to the inner man. I want to be a tree that is rooted in heaven but bears fruit on earth. God will give moisture and growth, so my neighbor may break off and eat the fruit.

293. Faith and Love

Mary and Martha

Do not confuse or separate them. Mary sits and is still; Martha goes about and is busy. Mary is without care; Martha is full of care. Mary lets herself be fed and served; Martha serves and feeds. Mary receives; Martha gives. Mary is a hearer; Martha is a doer. I think faith and love are sisters who should not be separated. They are not of one mind and do not do the same work, so do not mix them up. Faith is Mary, who exalts in meditation and prayer, who is bitter in hatred of self, world, and sin, and also in repentance. She sits in still rest and devotion at the feet of Jesus, in deep humility, and hears him speak; she receives his words and keeps them in her admirable heart (Luke 10). Love is Martha the housekeeper, who receives Jesus with his disciples and gives them lodging, who makes herself busy serving Jesus, bowing before him, honoring him, and tending to his needs. Often, she is so busy that she wishes she had a few hours to sit with faith and rest before Jesus. "Lord," she says, "do you not care that my sister has left it to me to serve alone? Tell her, then, that she should also get to work" (Luke 10:40). Jesus is the arbitrator who sets himself between them. He neither mixes nor separates them, but says: "Martha, Martha, you have much care and trouble. One thing is needful. Mary has chosen the better part, which shall not be taken away from her" (Luke 10:41). Both must remain, faith and love. Mary must let herself be fed by Jesus. Martha must feed him again and again. Mary receives; Martha gives. Mary hears; Martha acts. But Mary must take precedence. First, before you take care of your neighbor, you must be a neighbor to yourself. Where would the fruit be without the tree or the outflow without the inflow? That means, as Paul says, "Walk in love, as Christ loved us" (Eph 5:2). And John: "Let us love him who first loved us" (1 John 4:19).

Our love is like a little light that must be kindled by the fire of divine love. First, the heart must have the love of Jesus pour through it in faith. Then you let the neighbor experience what you have experienced. Jesus has offered food, drink, and clothing to our souls, and we feed and clothe him again in our hungry, thirsty, naked neighbor. Jesus is the magnet who draws Mary with his lovely lips; Martha is the magnet that draws Jesus to herself with loving hands and heart. In a word, there can be no true faith without good works, just as there can be no living body without movement, no tree without fruit. If the love of Jesus is known in faith, then it impels people to love and honor Jesus. Where there is a living seed in a field, it does not remain hidden but emerges and reveals fruit. Likewise, there can be no good works without faith, because the word of God plants faith and out of faith grow good work, which are nothing other than the outcome and fulfillment of the same Word of God that was planted in us through faith. Three things hang together in a chain: word, faith, works. The word is the seed of faith; faith is the seed of works. Yet, faith and works are not the same and do not do the same thing. The one makes right; the other follows from justification and gives evidence of it. The one gives life; the other reveals it. The one has to do with God; the other with the neighbor. Apply yourself to both: to faith, so that you might be saved, and to works, so that you might give testimony of your salvation to yourself and others.

Christian Scriver
Gotthold's Occasional Devotions (1667)

Christian Reader. I here present to you a collection of devout thoughts that suggested themselves to a fellow pilgrim named Gotthold on various occasions, and which I have taken pains to write down.... My purpose is to make all of creation converse with you or expound its secret language in order to show how all kinds of objects, incidents, and events can remind you of your God and promote your comfort and growth in Christianity....

1. The Dew

Early one morning Gotthold went out into a field and joyfully watched the sun rise. This made him think of the Sun of Righteousness for whose rise and appearance at the last Day of Judgment he ardently wished. He said: O blessed last day. O desired day of joy. O blessed day of revelation of the children of God. O holy Sabbath. O beginning of eternal rest, when will you finally dawn? O Jesus, you sun and delight of my heart, why do you delay? How long will Satan and his trusted associates, the godless world, consider your promise a lie and hold your future up to scorn? How long must your elect, with the whole of nature, sigh under their burdens and be troubled like a woman in labor? Now you will come, you will come soon, my heart says to me! Only let it be that we are always found ready.

Moving onward, he was aware that his feet were entirely soaked with dew, and all the blades of grass and little plants were moistened to their tips, as if they had been sprinkled with pearls and drops of silver. "Oh," he said, "I have sought edifying enjoyment in my thoughts about the heavens above, my God, and have not yet rightly acknowledged how you also fill the earth with your goodness. Now I am reminded of what one of your good friends [Johann Arndt] said: "The greatest Good has sprinkled all creatures with drops of his goodness so that all may be blessed." Now I may truthfully say that my steps are washed in butter (Job 29:6) and that your grace is like a cloud of dew (Hos 6:4). Your blessings are as countless as these pearls. May your name be eternally praised, my Lord and my God! Let drops of your sweet grace fall again and again on my poor heart and conscience so that I may be consoled in sadness and refreshed for your service.

8. The Sailors

While walking alongside a river full of ships, Gotthold saw that some sailors were propelling a ship against the current with great effort. They either stepped out onto the shore, harnessed themselves to ropes, and towed the ship behind them, or attached a long rope to a tree or pole and [pulled on it in order to] convey the ship forward.

Here, said he, I have a representation of my own voyage to heaven. The world is the powerful current that pulls many along with it into the sea of perdition. I, with my little ship, must struggle against this current because I have been commanded not to be conformed to the world, nor to love either it or its lusts (Rom 12:2; 1 John 2:15). This requires effort. My sighs and yearnings are my ropes, my resolution my pole, and my strength is in God and his Spirit. I strive and strain forward toward what lies before me (Phil 3:13). Here there must be no pause or relaxation, because just as the ship will disappear downstream and take the sailors along with it if they should cease to struggle against the current, so it happens in our Christian life. If we cease to fight with ourselves and the world, or become lax in our prayer or other holy practices, we will soon become aware of our decline and the harm this causes.

My God! Help me always to strive resolutely and press forward through death and life.

16. The Playing Child

A little child was running around a room entertaining himself with many games and childish fantasies. His money was potsherds, his house some little blocks, his horse a stick, his conveyance an apple, his son a puppet, and so forth. The child's father sat at the table, busy with important matters, which he wrote down and set in order for the future benefit of this little tyke. The child often ran to him, asked many childish questions, and requested many things for the enhancement of its game. The father answered briefly, carried on with his work, and at the same time always kept a watchful eye on the child so that it would not meddle with anything dangerous or suffer any harm.

Gotthold saw this and thought: This is a fine image of the fatherly care of God! We old children run around in the world and often play more foolishly than this child. We gather and scatter, build and break apart, plant and pull up, ride and drive, eat and drink, sing and play, and think we are doing great things that must catch the special attention of God. Meanwhile, our all-knowing God sits and writes our days in his book, ordering and shaping what we do before and after, directing all things to our best interests and our salvation, and thereby steadily keeping a watchful eye on us and our child's play so that we suffer no deadly harm.

My God, such knowledge is too wonderful and too high for me. I cannot grasp it, but I will still praise you for it all the time. My Father, do not let me disregard your care and oversight, especially when I do something foolish, like such a child.

26. The Weed

Gotthold saw a nettle bush in a place where it did not belong and, when he tried to uproot it, he found that much earth came up with it because this weed had attached itself with many roots and fibers. So it goes, he thought, with our conversion. When God wants to pull the weed of vice out of our heart, oh, how strongly it has secured itself! Oh, how it has fastened itself with many roots of evil desires and interwoven itself everywhere. When it cannot be otherwise, a piece of the heart must come out with it, by which I mean to say that the uprooting cannot happen without pain, anguish, and sorrow. But, what does that matter? If only the top is pulled off the weed, it soon sprouts again, but if it is pulled up roots and all, then one can certainly plant something good in its place. Thus, it is vain for us to want to make ourselves pious through inconstant and affected resolution while retaining evil desires in our hearts, which only wait for good weather and the opportunity to sprout again.

Therefore, my God, rip the bitter root out of my heart by whatever means you consider proper. It pains sinful flesh, but it is better to have pain temporarily than eternally.

33. The Open Glass

Gotthold had a bottle filled with strong rose water, which he had gotten out to use and had, negligently, let stand open. When he came back to it a short time later, he found that it had lost its beautiful fragrance and most of its potency. This is, he thought to himself, a fitting representation of a heart that is inclined toward the world and open to all opportunities. What help is it if one takes such a heart to church and fills it with the precious water of the rose of paradise (by which I mean the words of scripture) such that it is moved to considerable devotion, if, after that, the sealing cap is forgotten, that is, the word of God is not preserved in an honest and good heart (Luke 8:15)? What help is it to hear much and retain little and still do even less with it? What help is it to feel devotion and good emotions if the heart is not sealed with further reflection and diligent prayer and held unsullied by the world? If the heart is open to the world, the most noble and best of our devotion evaporates and only a weak froth is left in the heart and mouth.

O my Lord Jesus, let me hold your word, that living water of consolation, fast in my heart! Fill it with your spirit and grace! But seal it also in my soul so that it will remain strong and continually be within me.

39. The Wrongly Stitched Pages

He had a little book in his hand in which some pages were sewn in incorrectly through an oversight by the bookbinder. Now, he said, what is on each page is fine, but because they are not placed in proper order, the book is unsuitable. So it goes, he mused, with the thoughts and ideas that come into our minds, many of which, to be sure, are good enough, but if we do not know how to bring them up at the right time or in a suitable place, they will be more distasteful to hear than this book is to read. This also happens, he went on, with the thoughts that we bring up and pour out to God. Often while a father is in the midst of his prayer something will occur to him that is useful and necessary to perform for his family. Or a ruler, while praying and reading scripture, will think of some solution to a problem, which he has previously wrestled with for a long time. It sometimes comes to pass that a preacher, while speaking to God, gets an idea about how to begin a sermon or how to organize and embellish it. Now, this is not bad in itself, but it does not fit this situation, time, or place and will do great harm to prayerful devotion. When the mind and heart pay attention to these intruding thoughts, the mouth speaks words that do not come from the heart, and God, then, also does not know them. A cabbage is a useful vegetable, but if it is growing among rosemary or tulips and competes with them in a garden, then it is a weed and should rightly be taken out and transplanted in another place. So it is with foreign thoughts, which sneak into the heart during prayer and lead it away from devotion.

Help me, my Lord and God, to worship you in spirit and truth with my whole heart, and when I pray, shut the chamber of my heart by your grace so that nothing may enter it to hinder my eager and godly devotion.

41. The Preyed-upon Bees

Gotthold stood before a beehive and noticed with delight how these little honey birds went off and came back to their home again, usually loaded with their flower plunder. Meanwhile, a large yellow hornet also buzzed around, a real wolf among bees, seeking its coveted prey. As it was now around evening time and the bees had settled rather thickly around the entrance of the hive, undoubtedly trying to create a cool breeze after the overwhelming heat of the day, it was delightful to see that this fierce enemy was unsuccessful against the mass and the unified swarm. Although he came quite close, if he observed that they stuck together near one another, he had to retreat in vain, until, finally, a solitary bee, which had perhaps been delayed by something, came flying in. He grabbed this one, fell with it to the ground, and dealt with it as he wished.

Gotthold thought to himself: what a noble thing intimate harmony is. If this little bee, which perhaps went further away than the others and thus returned later, had been in the united swarm, it would not have fallen to its enemy. How does it come about, then, that we humans always give so little thought to the danger of disunity, since the assaults of the enemy of the soul are never more successful than when he sees us separated by discord and envy? Oh, how fine and pleasing it is when brothers dwell with one another in harmony (Ps 133:1).

Help us, my Lord Jesus, to live in agreement with one another, to have the same love, to be of one mind, of one accord, and to devote ourselves to maintaining the unity of the Spirit through the bond of peace (Phil 2:2; Eph 4:3), so that the God of love and peace will be with us (2 Cor 13:11) and the hellish robber will have no power over us.

93. The Pills

A sick person received some pills by a doctor's prescription but took them in a most peculiar way. First, he rolled them around in his mouth so long that they were ground up, causing a very bitter taste. The doctor said that he should not do this. They were not meant to be chewed and tasted but only swallowed. When the patient finally put his mind around this, the doctor gave him some preserved lemon peel so that the taste of the medicine would not come back into his mouth from his weak stomach and cause him to throw up.

This made Gotthold think: the invectives of a slanderous and hostile person are very bitter pills, and not everyone finds it easy to swallow them without chewing. They are, however, very useful to a pious Christian, for they either remind him of his guilt or test his patience and meekness. They can also show him what he needs to guard against and finally increase his honor and glory before God, for whose sake they are patiently endured. It is not advisable, however, to roll the pills of slander around in your thoughts or regard them in accordance with the attitude of the flesh and the world. For they will only become more bitter and fill the tongue and heart with an equally hostile bitterness. It is best to swallow, pass over in silence, and forget. One should devour one's affliction and say: "I will be silent and not open my mouth. O you, my God, will make it well" (Ps 39:10). Against bitterness one should make use of the consoling words of scripture, not the least of which is: "Blessed are you when people revile you and persecute you and say all manner of evil falsely against you. Rejoice and be glad for your reward is great in heaven" (Matt 5:11–12).

O my God, how hard it is to swallow the pills of humiliation, to bless those who curse me, to do good to those who hate me, and pray for those who wrong me. Lord, as you will have it be, give it so to be, for without you I can do nothing.

96. Senseless Thieves

It is said that mice not only delight in nibbling on what might be food for them but also dare to drag silver knobs and necklaces, little coins, and even gold buckles into their holes, when someone leaves these things lying on the table. It occurred to Gotthold that jackdaws and crows, which are sometimes kept in houses for amusement, do the same. Once, such a bird collected a large number of coins, rings, thimbles, and similar items and thereby aroused much suspicion among the members of a household until it was finally observed doing this and its treasure was taken away. Then, it became very incensed and let it be sufficiently known that it was very unhappy with the loss of such things, although they were useless to it.

Gotthold said about this: Notice here a good likeness of selfish and avaricious people who collect things by right or wrong means until they have brought together a hoard, which is of as much use to them as the treasure is to the mice or jackdaws. And it would still be tolerable that they engage in similar foolishness if the harm done were just as little, but to gain earthly possessions and lose eternal ones, to gather gold and forget God, to produce something so laughable for their surviving heirs and weeping and gnashing of teeth for their own poor souls, that is too much. What is so remarkable about being the keeper of a treasure when a mouse, a crow, and a dog can also do that? Isn't it a complete folly, dear soul, since the wrongly acquired possession will be lost?

Lord, my God, incline my heart to your testimonies and not to avarice (Ps 119:36).

111. The Rowers

Gotthold saw several sailors step into a boat to cross a river. Two took the oars and, as usual, sat with their backs facing the shore toward which they intended to sail. A third remained standing at the helm and kept his eye unaverted on the place where they wished to land, and so they swiftly reached the shore. See here, Gotthold said, to those around him, we have a good reminder of our labor and vocation. Life is a swift and mighty river flowing through all of time into the ocean of eternity and never returning. On this river each of us floats in the little ship of our vocation, which we must urge forward with the oars of our diligent labor. Now we should, like these sailors, turn our backs away from the future and, putting our trust in God who stands at the helm and skillfully steers the vessel toward what is profitable and blessed for us; we should diligently labor, unconcerned about anything else. We would laugh if we saw these men turn around and assert that they cannot row blindly but must see the place where they are going. Similarly, is it not foolishness for us, with our anxieties and thoughts, to insist on apprehending all things happening now and in the future? Let us row, and work, and pray, and leave it to God to steer, and bless, and govern.

My God, stay with me in my little ship and steer it according to your good pleasure. I will turn my face toward you, and in accordance with the ability you give me, I will diligently and faithfully labor, leaving it to you to provide all else.

114. The Rope Maker

He saw a rope maker busy at his work and, after he silently watched him for a while, he said: Holy scripture compares sins with cords (Prov 5:22; Isa 5:18), and this is surely appropriate, for just as a cord is twisted together from many threads and interwoven, so a sin is seldom solitary. Rather, one sin grows out of another and is often committed to excuse or cover up the other one. Wicked, wanton thoughts are the first threads; paying heed to these thoughts the second; sinful intentions provide the third; the execution of the sin twists the cord; but persisting in it then binds the wicked sinner to his ruin.

For example, it sometimes happens that a man will secretly steal something from his neighbor; this is one sin. He is inevitably suspected and, when questioned about it, he lies; this is the second sin. Pressed further, he swears and curses; this is the third. On account of the inquiry, he develops an unappeasable hatred toward his neighbor and disseminates all sorts of evil comments about him; these are fourth and fifth. He also keeps what he has stolen and would rather lose his soul than give it back and be subjected to shame. This is the sixth. Oh, what a strong cord of the Devil this is, and there are few who can disentangle themselves from it! And just as this rope maker is always stepping backward in order to stretch out the cord he is working on, so it is with most people who persevere in their sins. They do not look where they are going and care little about the consequences of what they are doing. In this situation, which endangers the soul, it is best not to be inattentive but, rather, to break the cord of sin immediately, before Satan has the time to expand it. Otherwise, we will face what happens to a hen, which first gets a claw entangled in a cord and then gets both feet ensnared. It easily gets captured and will not be able to free itself without the intervention of a human hand.

My faithful God, hold me in your hand and let me not fall into sin or into such a sin that I do not recognize it as sin. Do not let Satan make a cord out of my thoughts that cannot be broken without the greatest danger to my soul.

127. The Plant in the Cellar

When Gotthold went into a cellar to look for something, he found a turnip, which, having been left there by accident, had grown and sent forth long but weak and slender shoots, which were more pale yellow than green and therefore unfit for use. Here, thought he, I have an exemplification of a human undertaking God has not blessed or allowed to prosper. This plant lacks sunshine and open air and therefore cannot thrive. It grows weakly for a while and then withers. So it is with all our aspirations and endeavors that are not irradiated by the grace of God or nurtured by his blessing. As our Savior also said, "Every plant that my Father has not planted will be uprooted" (Matt 15:13).

After a while it further occurred to him that this plant could also be a very good illustration of an inexperienced and unpracticed man who places himself in some obscure corner and endeavors to teach himself about many things. Based on such learning he considers himself a great person and thinks that he is qualified, with his self-taught wisdom, to govern and make prosperous not only a city and church, but even half of the world. When he sets about a task, however, he cannot find in his whole school sack skill enough to execute with success this or that trifling matter, and he learns that it is one thing to know something by yourself and quite another thing to bring it to bear among other people who also know something.

This can also happen in our Christianity. We may imagine that our faith, love, and patience have grown splendidly, and still we often stand on very weak feet. Experience makes people capable, and bearing the cross produces good Christians. This plant was never shone on by the sun, or moistened by the dew, or watered by the rain, or assailed by the wind, or hardened by the cold; therefore, it is good for nothing. So also, a Christian who has not been tested by both prosperity and adversity, favor and affliction, cannot yet be considered fit or proficient. Therefore, the dear and much-afflicted Apostle says: "Tribulation works patience; and patience, experience; and experience, hope; and hope does not disappoint" (Rom 5:3–5).

129. The Boiling Pot

Gotthold saw a pot, standing over a fire, which was boiling so actively that it finally overflowed and mostly extinguished the flame. See, he said to his household, this pot is an emblem of proud and arrogant people whose riches, pedigree, honors, and power are glowing coals, that cause their hearts to seethe with haughtiness, impudence, disdain for others, and self-conceit, through which their presumptuous happiness is spoiled and brought to naught. One kind of person has great resources, but his heart seethes with sensuality, which gushes forth in pompous display and wastefulness. As a result, his income is reduced and he descends from overabundance into poverty. Another person is of a noble and famous lineage and thinks that nobility includes the freedom to do whatever one desires. As a result, he damages the luster of his ancestors, whom he regards merely as dead coals. Another person enjoys the favor of his prince and cultivates what follows from that—honor, esteem, and power—but because his mind does not know how to endure the heat of such good fortune it spews forth crime, mischievousness, and malice. This is commonly the reason why the favorable disposition of his lord grows cold and all his happiness is extinguished. Don't think, however, that this applies only to other people and not to you. All of our hearts are like this pot and become from good fortune and prosperity full of seething, hot blood and overflowing audacity. It can and will put up with nothing from anyone. It sallies forth with a haughty gait, an insolent bearing, scornful words, presumptuous dress, and arrogant actions. Therefore, ask God to bestow on you no more favor and fortune than you need, in consideration of the fact that nothing is more difficult than to endure good days and great fortune with a humble heart.

My God, I do not trust in myself. Great fortune may be my great misfortune. You often give good fortune in anger and misfortune in grace. You give whatever you wish, so give me a heart to bear it in accordance with your will.

132. Wheat

Gotthold watched as a farmer threshed wheat and noticed how the thresher not only beat it vigorously but also stomped on it with his feet and, finally, through various means, separated the pure kernel from the chaff, dust, and other debris. How does it come about, he thought to himself, that in order for anything to become useful and serviceable in the world it must endure so much and be ready to undergo all sorts of difficulties, but people who make use of all things as they please do not want to suffer and let God deal with them as he pleases? Grain, which is the most noble of all [foods], is beaten and trod underfoot, tossed around, smashed together, thrown about, sifted, shaken and agitated, then ground, kneaded, and baked before it finally arrives on the table of a king or prince. What am I thinking, then, if I am discontented because God does not have me carried over rose petals or conveyed to heaven in a sedan chair? How will the grain become pure if it is not processed, and how will I become pious and holy if I wish to know no crosses or misfortune?

Therefore, my God, do with me as you will and grant that I may will what you will. Beat, thresh, and sift me, my God, so that I might finally become pure and fine bread on your table. I will suffer this the more willingly because I know that your prophet says: Grain is ground so that it might become bread, but it is not destroyed by threshing. So it also is with the Lord of hosts, for his counsel is wonderful and leads to glorious results (Isa 28:28–29).

153. Reluctant Alms

While Gotthold was busy with some important work and his thoughts were fully occupied by it, his little daughter came to him unexpectedly and brought a written message about a poor widow, which specified the causes of her misfortune and requested alms for her. He was rather irritated by this and shouted at the girl with harsh words. Soon thereafter he regained his composure and said to himself: "I am a wretched man! What an inflated view I often have of my own Christian life and how boldly I venture to say: 'Lord Jesus, know all things and know that I love you.' But now, when my Savior comes and seeks meager alms for this poor widow as a true testimony of my love, I allow myself to be offended because he causes a small but worthy interruption in my insignificant thoughts. Go, now, and caress yourself with your faith and godliness! 'God loves a cheerful giver'" (2 Cor 9:7). Reluctant alms are like a rose discolored and damaged by sulfuric fumes, like flour mixed with sand and stones, like an over-salted and tasteless food course. Whoever does a good deed with an unwilling heart or harsh words is like a cow that gives milk but then overturns the pail with her foot. A good deed toward the poor should be like oil, which, when it flows from one vessel into another, makes no noise but falls gently and smoothly.

My God, you invite me to come to you whenever I so desire and my need drives me to you. It is never an unwelcome or inopportune time for you when I come. You rule the whole world, and yet you are not angry when I rush in to you, morning, noon, and night, and beg alms from your mercy. What am I thinking, then, when I am inclined to consider my work and thoughts to be more important than the pleas and sighs of a fellow Christian? Now I know that insensitive rashness is a sin and have reason henceforth to receive my Lord Jesus in his members with more friendliness so that he will also not turn away from me when I have need of him.

171. Target Practice

In a certain place some young people had been allowed to set up a target, for their pleasure and amusement, at which they shot, and all of them tried to do their best. Gotthold, when he went near the place, heard the shots and came to the following thoughts. These people aim and shoot at the bull's-eye, but there is no doubt that few reach their goal. So it is with our Christian life and our endeavor to perfect it. Since the lamentable Fall, we no longer have a sure hand, to speak in terms of shooting, but we still often shoot into the field outside the target, even though the outline of divine perfection, the law, is set out before us as the goal toward which all our thoughts, words, and actions should be directed. Our perfection is imperfection, so much so that it is considered a kind of perfection if we simply acknowledge our imperfection, regret it, and are devoted to improving it daily through godly practice. We seek our true perfection in the Lord Jesus and his perfect obedience and merits.

This life is a journey in which we forever go forward from faith to faith, love to love, patience to patience, cross to cross. It is not righteousness but being considered righteous. We have not arrived where we should be, but we are all on the path, on the way, some having progressed further than others. God is pleased if he finds us making a resolute effort. If only people were also pleased with one another when one hits the mark but the other scarcely touches the corner of the target. What scorn we show toward one another when one person gets nearer to the goal than the other who is making the same effort. Show me a person who always hits the target and never misses, and I will stand in awe of him as if he were an angel.

My God, keep my Christian life in steady practice! Practice brings improvement and improvement brings perfection—not of the sort that satisfies other people, but of the sort that satisfies you, the merciful and good judge.

179. The Swallow

In the springtime Gotthold took notice how a swallow was occupied building its nest and attaching it to a church window. It collected clay with its bill and also molded it together. Although it could take so little at a time, through untiring persistence and steady work it enclosed and completed its dwelling. Here, he said to himself, I have an agreeable representation of an industrious godly man. Many begin their sustenance as modestly as this bird, which has nothing except what God bestowed upon it and what it can gather with its bill, but nevertheless, if he does not grow tired of prayer, godliness, and zealous work, the gentle Giver of all good offers him a penny today, another one tomorrow, until he has collected a store that makes one marvel. It is entirely for this reason, I think, that the Almighty often lets the children of rich people become poor and the children of poor people become rich, so that the world will come to understand that all depends upon his blessing. But, if, my God, steady work can accomplish so much when facilitated by your gentle blessing, I should also pay attention to this in the gathering of spiritual riches. My capability is slight, my faith is weak, yet I will not doubt that, by trusting in your gracious help, my Christian life will grow daily through steady practice and godly effort and be improved. It is customary for you, when you want to make something great, to begin with modest things, so that only the glory of your boundless power and unmerited grace abides. So, I will also not be discouraged about the favorable increase of my godliness, as slight as it may now be, as long as your good spirit does not fail to work in me and steadily improve me.

Teach me, my God, to act according to your pleasure at all times. Let your good spirit lead me steadily on a level path (Ps 143:10).

189. The Butterfly Catchers

Gotthold saw some boys in a garden, chasing butterflies, and was amused to observe what pains these simple fowlers took to catch the colorful insects. He said to a good friend: Do you know whom these children resemble? They are like those learned and clever scholars who demonstrate not so much their skill and understanding as their curiosity and pride in their excitement over many useless questions. What else are high-flying and useless thoughts and questions but insects such as these; and is the foolishness of these children any greater than that of the learned who imagine that they have hunted down something special when they come up with all sorts of strange, wonderful, and intricate questions and thoughts concerning spiritual and worldly things? Tell me, is any more benefit to be derived from one catch than from the other? And yet, unfortunately, it has almost come about in the world that whoever will not or cannot hunt and catch such flies and motley flying things is looked upon as an inept person. I, for my part, hold that there is a difference in worldly things between a learned and an intelligent person; as also in spiritual things there is a difference between a learned and a godly or pious person. When both are together, it is like the diamond glittering and sparkling in a setting of gold, or like golden apples in dishes of silver. If, however, I could have only one, I would prefer piety and would rather grasp hold of heaven with the unlearned than be damned while possessing great skill and aptitude.

What is science without conscience? What help is it to learn all things and forget the most important? I have seen people who have many books only for the purpose that, if asked, they can say that they have them. I have known artisans who have many good tools, inherited from their elders or bought from others, but who still do not know how to use them. Do you think these serve any purpose? It is the same with learned people who do not use all of their skills as a tool for honor of God or for the improvement of themselves or their neighbors. I might have imagined that many more clever, learned people would get to heaven if the most learned of all the learned had not said that, on that day, he will say to many who prophesied in his name: "I never knew you, go away from me, you evildoers" (Matt 7:22–23). There are two kinds of people who do futile work and suffer in their hearts as a result: those who gather much money and possessions and do not make use of them, and those who learn and know many things but do not regulate their lives by them.

My God, I know that our knowledge is imperfect in this life and that the most noble and highest wisdom consists in the recognition of you and the Lord Jesus. Therefore, I will direct all my diligence toward believing in the crucified Lord Jesus, loving him, and following him in patience; and if I only comprehend a little, I will still not be deceived with the learned of this world.

216. The Vine

When Gotthold wanted to visit a man who was troubled and sorrowful, the family said that he was in the garden. Gotthold went to him and found him at work removing leaves from a vine. After a friendly greeting, he asked the man what he was doing. I find, said the man, that on account of the abundant rain this vine is overgrown with wood and leaves, which prevent the sun from getting to the grapes and ripening them. Therefore, I am pruning some of them so that the vine can produce mature, ripe fruit. Gotthold replied: Do you sense that the vine resists and opposes you when you do this work? If not, then why should you be displeased with a loving God who does to you what you do to the vine? You prune off the unnecessary leaves in order that the vine might bear better fruit, and God takes away your temporal blessings and earthly comforts in order that faith along with its noble fruits, love, humility, patience, hope, and prayer, might become greater, and finer, and sweeter in you. Whatever one might say, when a person has an overabundance of things, and knows nothing of the cross, the Sun of Righteousness, with its rays of grace, can scarcely reach the heart, and the Christian life is not as it should be. It bears only the tart and sour fruits of hypocrisy, pride, ill will, and harshness. Therefore, let God do with you as he wishes; he will not harm you. Now you strip off some leaves and, earlier, in spring, you hoed, made layers of the vines, pruned, and tied up the branches. My dear friend, you are also a branch on the spiritual vine, which is the Lord Jesus. God is the vine-dresser who knows well that without his grace and care he can expect nothing good from you. For this reason he allows contempt to lay you in the earth and trials to prune you. He binds you up through affliction and strips you through poverty, all to the end that his grace may be made sweeter to you and your heart sweeter to him.

O my God! Do not withdraw me from your care, or else I will grow wild and corrupt. Prune, bind, and strip me as you will; through it all, my comfort shall be that you cannot mean it for evil.

219. The Table Decoration

Gotthold was shown a table decoration that was to be put out for an upcoming banquet. The world, he said, sticks to its old ways, seeking its enjoyment in vanity. It knows well that a table decoration is nothing other than a colored picture made from wood, wax, or some other material that has little or no worth, unless much labor and work has been devoted to it. Oftentimes it is the skin of a bird whose feathers have been removed, which has been stuffed with hemp fiber or straw, whose beak and feet have been gilded and colored. One gains nothing from this endeavor except that it serves as an indication of human luxury and idleness. So, a man finds pleasure in that by which he is deceived and considers himself to be honored and especially entertained if such a worthless thing is served up and set out to be viewed for a while.

So it also goes with paintings. I have seen that a painting of a mendicant nun or of an ugly old woman, a tramp with ragged clothes and a begging bowl, was sold for some hundred, even a thousand dollars, though the buyer himself would never have considered uttering a word to such an old mother who was actually alive and would have scarcely given a penny to a real, naked beggar for her sustenance. So it is that the man loves the trickery and not only finds pleasure in it if it is done by a skillful hand, but will also pay much money for such deceptive amusement. What then is human pleasure? It is vanity. "All men are entirely nothing" (Ps 39:6).

My God, the beautiful heaven, the work of your fingers, is my decoration; the crucified Lord Jesus is my painting. In the one I see what your hand has prepared for my salvation, and in the other I see how I can attain such salvation. Away with all vanity! I only wish for a blessed eternity.

230. The Bier

Gotthold saw a bier standing before a house as an announcement that there was a corpse within the place that would soon be buried. Being reminded by this of his own mortality, he said: "Perhaps this will be the bier that will bear you to the grave. Even if it is not, at least the wood has already grown from which one will be built for you. Therefore, be prepared for death and be sure that, when your body is borne to the grave, the angels may bear your soul to heaven."

Continuing, he thought further: Oh, if such a bier were set before all houses where there is a dead person, we would have far too few, because many people are living dead, that is, they are impenitent and live in deliberate sin. God is the soul of our soul and the life of our life. Christ must dwell in our hearts through faith. He must be heart of our heart such that we can say with Saint Paul: "I live, yet not I, but Christ lives in me" (Gal 2:20). Just as the heart is the source of the spirit of life and the workshop of the soul, from which it distributes natural warmth and vital energy to all veins and members, so must the Lord Jesus produce spiritual life in us and disperse his spirit into all our powers, senses, desires, thoughts, and movements. Where it is not, there is no life. The godless person is a living carcass that stinks before God and his holy angels. The worms of sinful desires bore through his conscience, and he is an abomination in God's eyes. Just as ravens and other impure birds rejoice over a carcass and crowd together, so hellish spirits rejoice over the soul that is dead in sin. Where is a house where you will not find this?

O my Lord Jesus, I would rather not live than not live in you! Let me die that I might live! What good is living a long time if I keep on sinning? I will gladly live longer if you live in me, but if it were better for me, I would be willing to die this hour. Be my life or I do not want to live any longer.

270. Tuning a Lute

Gotthold found one of his good friends busy with the tuning of his lute. Since this involved much effort, he said: The Christian may very appropriately be compared to such an instrument. The lute is made of plain and thin wood and has not itself, but the hand of the artisan, to thank for fashioning it into such a beautiful instrument. Similarly, a Christian has no superiority over other people with regard to the weakness and corruptions of human nature, unless the hand of a merciful God has made of him an instrument of his grace. Now, just as a lute must be strung and skillfully tuned and touched, so also must the finger of God fill the heart of the Christian with good thoughts and then tune and adjust them to the honor of his name and for the common good. Although a lute is a beautiful instrument, it very often gets out of tune and therefore needs continual care. So it goes with our Christian life, which is often put out of tune by the Devil, the wicked world, and our own will. It would sound bad unless the gracious hand of the Most High daily regulated and corrected it.

Having noted this, let us also remember our own duties. If we apply such effort to tune a lute so that its sound may not be disagreeable to human ears, why do we not also take the trouble to tune and regulate our thoughts, words, and works so that they may not offend the most holy and keen eyes and ears of God? We hear at once and declare our displeasure if but a single string is out of tune, and yet we often do not perceive or care if there is discord between our lives or conduct and the holy commandments of God. People instantly tell us if a string is out of tune or misplayed. My friend, let us also remind each other when we perceive a flaw or discord in our Christianity. Self-love and false security can often keep us from noticing our own faults, so it is useful if another person feels free to give a good and suitable reminder to a pious and faithful heart. We should consider it good if someone shows us a better way. Friendship that is not grounded in holiness is not worth having and ends up as eternal enmity.

My Lord Jesus! Tune, regulate, and shape my life to make it consonant with your life. It is true that my weak strings cannot be stretched so tight that I might attain your perfection. I console myself, however, with the thought that, as in this lute, there are higher and lower pitches, so you have both strong and the weak Christians and you are satisfied with both, provided only that they are not false.

272. The Violet

One March, when Gotthold was given a bunch of blue violets, he took delight in their lovely fragrance and thanked God for giving so many kinds of refreshment to people. He also seized this occasion to offer the following thoughts. This pretty and fragrant little flower can furnish me with a very nice image of a humble and godly heart, because it spreads out, near to the earth, as it grows yet becomes radiant with heavenly blue flowers and surpasses many other lofty and dazzling flowers, such as the tulip and emperor's crown, with its noble fragrance. Lowly hearts are this way, for they are plain and modest in their own eyes and in the eyes of others but resemble the humble heart of Jesus. They have the true colors of heaven and also are far preferred by God to others who promote their own spiritual or bodily gifts. Just as the apothecary also mixes the sap of this little flower with liquid sugar and prepares a cool and effective tonic from it, so the Most High pours his grace like melted sugar into a humble heart for the consolation and edification of many others. The deepest sources have the most water and the lowliest spirit has the most beautiful and useful gifts. What is better than grain, which gives people bread, the best and most abundant food? Yet, if it is stale and spoiled, it is more like a poison than food. So it also is with the gifts of the body and spirit. As long as they are employed with humility, in the fear of God, in service to the neighbor, they are a sweet food, but if they are infected with pride and self-conceit, they turn out to be a noxious poison to their possessor and others.

My God, let it be my glory to seek not my own but your glory from my heart. I do not wish to be a dazzling flower if I can only be useful to you and my neighbor. Greatness is not to have great gifts but to use your great gifts to the praise of the Most High with a lowly spirit.

280. The Copy Line

Gotthold watched a boy who went to a writing school as he diligently considered the model script and tried to duplicate it with his own writing. He said to those standing nearby, "See how all perfection arises from imperfection and how one learns to make it right through many errors. One does not expect this boy's writing to be entirely similar to the copy line, but rather one is satisfied with his laborious practice so that he will learn always to improve and finally write fluently and elegantly." We also have a copy line that the Lord Jesus has left for us (1 Pet 2:21), namely, the perfection of his holy life. Do not think that he demands more of us that the schoolmaster does of his student. If he finds us carefully duplicating the model and diligently trying and practicing, he is patient with our failings and gives us power through his grace and spirit to improve each day. The school year of a Christian lasts as long as he lives. The best students in the school of Jesus, those who always remain students, are, I would say, surely those who have the example of their schoolmaster before their eyes each day, try to make themselves more and more like him, and are still never happy with themselves and their imitation. Therefore, one should avoid two things, negligence and faintheartedness, for from the first finally arises laziness and security and from the second a despairing sadness. Heaven stands open not only to the perfect and strong but also to the erring and weak, if they only acknowledge their failings with humble repentance and seek what they lack through the grace of Jesus Christ. It is a greater joy to a father if his little child carries a cushion to him than if a stronger lad brings him something more proper. Thus, God looks more at the will than at the ability.

My God, do not scorn my inabilities! I am learning, my father! Let my lifework still please you. My entire undertaking often fails, but should I therefore entirely give up? Far from it! As long as I live, I will always begin again to lay the masterpiece, whenever it pleases you, at your feet in heaven.

291. The Pumpkin

Gotthold found in a room a pumpkin that the master of the house had marked with his name, the date, and some other letters representing his motto. He said: "See how what you have etched or cut into the tender and small pumpkin also grows with it such that one can still now recognize your hand. Beloved, may it also be so with your children while they are still tender and young." Your tongue must be the pen of a good scribe (Ps 45:2), with which you engrave and write the Ten Commandments, love of virtue, and hate for sin on their hearts. Whatever you cut and fix in their heads from infancy you will be able to read and see on them ever after. Many parents are "a letter written with words of lamentation outwardly and inwardly" (Ezek 2:10). I mean to say that they experience and only go through grief with their children, but they have themselves to thank for that because, through angry speech, a bad example, and overindulgence as well as the omission of good discipline, they imprinted wickedness in their youth that has grown more and more until finally is it almost indelible. Oh, when will we Christians begin to be better about attending to the upbringing of our children? The irritable, godless way of living that we painfully observe daily in so many unchristian Christians cannot be prevented sooner or in any other way than through inculcating the youth with humility, gentleness, scrupulous simplicity, and other virtues instead of insolence, voluptuousness in attire, and lukewarmness in the fear of God. As long as we do not train our children to feel more grief about the commission of a sin than the loss of a thousand imperial dollars or even life itself, we will not leave behind us any better Christians.

My Lord Jesus, cut your name deep into the hearts of me and my family so that we never forget you or the duty with which we are bound.

326. The Keys

Gotthold was asked by a wealthy lady for some good thoughts she might associate with a bunch of keys that lay on a table. He thought a little and said: I call to mind that for a learned man the bunch of keys might be a symbol to pointing out that everyone cannot do everything. God distributes his gifts according to his holy will, and no one is granted all of them. Thus, each person always needs other people, and one should be diligent in serving others according to the measure of the gifts that have been given by God. One key cannot close all locks, and a person cannot accomplish everything. This way we may be bound to one another in the bond of peace and can remain ready to help according to our capabilities. Such a bunch of keys can also represent a good household in which the husband is in charge and earns an income, the wife helps and offers advice, the children and the servants work and obey, but all, together, uphold each one another in the fear of God and pray fervently.

These last thoughts remind me, he went on, of what our Savior said to his Apostle: "I will give you the keys of the kingdom" (Matt 16:19). I admit that he is actually speaking of the power to bind and loose sins, as he clarifies elsewhere (John 20:23). Still, one can rightly say that he has consigned the keys of the kingdom to all his faithful, saying: "Truly, truly, I say to you, whatever you ask of the Father in my name will be given to you" (John 16:23). I know that, once, a ten-year-old boy consoled his mother, a grieving widow, in her great sadness, with this meditation, saying: God was a rich lord who had a great storeroom. His pantries were full and his holdings were inexhaustible, but he had given the key for them to his dear son, namely, our devout prayer. Therefore, if we pray joyfully, we will lack nothing we need. To be sure, prayer is the true key to heaven. Oh, if we would only make diligent use of it.

I am also reminded of a precious thought that a blessed martyr in 1555 wrote down during his imprisonment, shortly before his death. "Let us," he said, "go this way gladly, because death cannot so overcome us that it bestows shame or scorn on us. Rather, it is an entrance to glory. Let us confidently embrace death and accept it, because it no longer has an arrow in its hand to wound us with eternal death, but much more a key with which we gain entrance to the kingdom of heaven where we will be able to gaze upon Jesus Christ, our only eternal life."

So informed, the woman, hearing Gotthold speak, sighed and said: That is indeed a good thought about the keys, which I will not easily forget. He replied, "My friend, tell me, in good conscience, whether all these keys are your own and are constantly under your control." She answered, "What makes you doubt this?" He went on, "In many houses, there are many keys to the cellar, attic, pantry, trunks, and chests, but Satan has them under his control." Many wealthy people have many storerooms and holdings, but what help is that to them if the Devil holds the keys and not only their chests but also their hearts are tightly locked, as the holy Apostle says: "If anyone, having worldly goods, sees his brother starving and closes his heart to him, how can the love of God remain in him?" (1 John 3:17).

I will give you another example of how this goes. Stigand, archbishop of Canterbury in England, lived very miserably and considered himself very wretched. When his friends said to him that he should live better, according to his rank, he protested that he did not have the means. After his death a small key to his secret chest was found around his neck. When it was opened, an inventory of great riches was found that he had hidden in a place under the earth. A similar example is reported from our own time of a worldly minded and unspiritual priest who hung the key to his money chest around his neck and demanded that it not be removed from his body before he was completely dead. Hearing this, the wealthy woman said, "Oh, God keep me from being this way." "Yes," Gotthold concluded, "may God keep both you and me from this, for the Lord Jesus' sake."

329. The Suckling Mother

A mother sat and suckled her child, even while a good man came to visit Gotthold. Holy meditations came to mind as he saw this, and he said to his friend: Come, I will show you a miracle! When Gotthold led him into the room and showed him this mother, the friend said: How is that a miracle? You see, Gotthold said, not one miracle but several. For, first, the child itself, which is produced in the mother's body by the hand of God and so wonderfully shaped in obscurity and then drawn out of the mother's body and preserved alive, is a miracle of God's power, wisdom, and goodness. The second miracle is the mother's breasts, which God fills for the well-being of the delicate child with sweet milk, containing within itself the potency of all foods and drinks, from which the child at all times finds both needed nourishment and pleasure. One can rightly say that it is the child's wine cellar and larder and a complete treasure such that the child has no desire for silver or gold or pearls or precious stones. The third miracle is the mother's heart, over which the all-wise Creator has placed and hung the breasts whereby the milk is, as it were, warmed and made sweet and flavored with love. The mother's heart must have an incomparable, inexhaustible love that, like the milk, never falters. Consider what care, hardship, trouble, attentiveness, effort, and work the mother must put up with even before the child reaches the point when it can call her mother! Tell me, is it not a miracle of the love of God that she joyfully represses and disregards all hardship and still fervently loves, caresses, and kisses the child?

If it will not bother you, I will tell you another miracle of the suckling mother. In Lüttich or Luyck in the Böttgergasse a woman named Oda Josay died in childbirth, leaving behind the little son that she had brought into the world. Her mother, a woman over fifty years old, took the misery of the abandoned and whimpering little orphan deep to heart and, as it cried, lay it on her breast, which for eleven years had been dry and had not suckled a child. The child sucked and God created milk in the grandmother's breast in sufficient quantity until the appropriate time for it to be weaned and sustained by other food. In a former time God also took pity on the rejected Ishmael and opened a spring from which he could quench his thirst. God performs many miracles of this sort. If only they would be recognized and noticed by us unthankful people!

Yes, God himself is the universal suckling mother, that is, the creator and sustainer of all things and thus, as some think, among his other names in the Hebrew language, one which originates from the mother's breast, because he upholds and cares for all with the breasts of his blessings and consolations. One of the ancient church fathers (Clement of Alexandria) calls the Lord Jesus the motherly breast of God, because "from his fullness we receive grace upon grace" (John 1:16), and we find consolation for our soul by suckling from his holy wounds.

O my God, let me think about this as often as I see a suckling mother, and, when my soul is in anguish, like a weak child, in the last sufferings of death, let me fall asleep blissfully, full and satisfied by your consolation.

336. The Stork

A godly company of people walking in a field to get some air became aware of a stork seeking food in a beautiful meadow. One of them said: "Let us think of the complaint our benevolent God conveyed by the prophet: 'A stork in the heavens knows its time, a turtledove, a crane, and a swallow mark the time when they should come again, but my people do not want to know the law of the Lord'" (Jer 8:7). Oh, how many people miss the time of grace, and although our long-suffering God opens the door of heaven wide to them, standing with his hands spread out to them, saying, "See, see, here I am" (Isa 58:9), they still pay no attention but rather seek the open door to hell, by which I mean, the opportunity to give themselves further to their sins. May God protect us from security and a hard heart and allow our lives to be ones of continual repentance and return to God.

Gotthold added: I have recently read some wonderful things about these birds, namely, that they love their young so heartily that they are not afraid to die for their sake. It has been observed during the most intense fires that they will repeatedly and earnestly carry water in their throats and bills to rescue their nests on burning houses. In Delft, Holland, they noticed storks, which could not rescue their young, cover them in their nests, spreading their wings over them, and thus dying along with them. This is what you call dying for love and in love.

This also brings to mind our dearest and most worthy friend, Jesus, about whom it has been fairly written when he is portrayed, hanging, on the cross: He died for love and in love. In truth, love caused the death of the Son of God. Death could not kill him, but love drew him down from heaven for us, laid him in a manger, brought him to the cross, and killed him. We are fond of gathering herbs and plants when they are most potent. Likewise, I maintain, our heavenly Father determined that his beloved Son should die at the time when his love had reached its highest degree, and as he died in love, so did he also rise again and ascend to heaven where now, in all eternity, he loves nothing more dearly than the sons of men. He also wishes nothing else for us than that we should live and die in his heartfelt love.

Saint Augustine wished to be a light that burned in the love of Jesus Christ until it was consumed. One can rightly say of the faithful and loving martyrs that they died in and for love. I found out that Catherine, the Christian queen of Georgia, whom Shah Abbas martyred and executed, was stripped naked and both her breasts and the flesh of her arms and legs were ripped off, during which time the frightened martyr often repeated: "O my God, O my Jesus, my Savior, all this is still of little importance for your sake. I cannot count your merits. One owes life for life, blood for blood, for your love."

O Jesus, I wish my departure to be ordered for nothing else than for your sake; still I know that it is granted to me to speak boldly and like a child with you. If I should die, let my sickness and fever be for your love. Let my bed be the remembrance of your cross, on which you died for love. Let desire for you be my thirst and the foretaste of your eternal love, my refreshment and tonic. Let my imaginings be filled with disdain for the world and derision of its vanity, and my departure from my friends be an exhortation to your love. Let my last sigh be "Jesus, I love you," my death an entrance into your heavenly and eternal love, and my epitaph "Gotthold died for love and in the love of Jesus!"

351. Palpitation of the Heart

A group of people were speaking of the steady motion of the heart and marveled at the power and wisdom of the good Creator who had planted such a steadily flowing rich source of the life spirit in the human body and provided it with such a continuous movement that it is able to keep the blood flowing and full of the power of life. One can rightly compare it, a learned man said, to the water pump one finds in many places that distributes water in a continuous movement through hidden pipes to an entire city. Gotthold then said: Let us think about the phrase the Holy Spirit used twice concerning David: "His heart was stricken." This happened once, in 1 Samuel

24:6, when he cut off the corner of Saul's cloak in the cave, without a doubt signifying that David engaged in self-examination and felt a childlike fear that he might have done something sinful that angered God. His heart was stricken again in 2 Samuel 24:10, after he had numbered the people, indicating that his conscience was aroused and he felt anxiety and dread when his sin was placed before his eyes. Let us ask God also to favor us with his grace so that when we propose to do something questionable and dangerous, perhaps out of negligence or weakness, our heart will warn us with palpitations, or if we have done something wrong and have fallen into sin, that our heart will not let us rest but will pressure and force us and make us anxious until we flee to the crucified Lord Jesus in true repentance and find rest in him for our restless heart. I have, not without reason, called this a grace of God, for it is Christ and his Spirit that either warns us or coaxes us to repent through such palpitations of the heart within us. If the heart is still, the body is dead, and whoever no longer feels this heartbeat of the conscience is spiritually dead, though still alive.

While Gotthold spoke, a learned man from the group said that he had recently come across a nice story, which was appropriate to this discussion, and wanted to tell it briefly since it would please those who were present. In Switzerland, 120 years ago, it so happened that a godly peasant was condemned to be burned for his adherence to the truth of the gospel. He had undergone all sorts of tests of his Christian faithfulness and fearlessness in prison, but shortly before his end, he left behind one that was especially remarkable. After they had bound him and were about to throw him into the flames, he asked to speak once more with the judge, who, according to Swiss custom, was present at the execution. Finally, when the judge came to him after a long delay, he said: You have condemned me to death as a heretic today, but now I truly confess that although I am a poor sinner, there is no way that I am a heretic, for I believe and confess with all my heart what is contained in the Apostle's Creed (which he then recited in its entirety). Proceeding further, he said: Now I have one last request to make of you, my lord, that you would step forward to me and place your hand, first on my breast and then on your own, and then, freely and truly declare before all these people which heart beats hardest out of fear and anxiety, yours or mine. I will joyfully and confidently depart to my Jesus, in whom I have believed, and what your state of mind is will be known to you. The judge did not know what he should say to this and ordered the fire to be made ready; still his appearance was such that one could see he was more frightened than the martyr. Gotthold thanked the man on behalf of the group for this beautiful story, which he said he had never found before in any book of martyrs. Let us then, he went on to say, wish from the heart and ask God in the name of Jesus also to graciously give us, in death, such a tranquil, joyful, and fearless heart. If the heart beats strongly while one lives, it will be tranquil when one dies.

379. The Caterpillar Nest

Gotthold saw many caterpillar nests on the trees in his garden and prepared to remove them and to clean them out of the trees. Meanwhile, he said: There is nothing in the world that does not have its adversary, enemies, and opposition, either secretly or openly. There is no pleasure without pain, no joy without suffering. These trees have first of all shed their fruit in abundance and have already set their buds again for the coming year; still, their enemies are also already there, and if the leaves burst forth again and they feel the warm air, if one does not control them, they will spread all over and rob the trees of their covering. So it is with human life. It is a miserable and wretched thing from when we come forth from our mother's body until we are buried again in the earth, which is the mother of us all. There is always grief, fear, hope, and at last death (Sir 40:1–2). A famous teacher (Drelincourt) has said it well: Human life and misery are twins that were born at the same time and die at the same time in the faithful and godly. Man begins his life with tears and ends it with sighs. One holds the first cry as a sign of life, and the last strong groan is a mark of death. You poor man! How miserable your situation is, especially since your friends take delight in your cries and are troubled if you stop groaning. There are pleasures, riches, honor, and joy in the world, but there is also no lack of grief, humiliation, adversity, and suffering. Where you find leaves, flowers, and fruit, you will also find caterpillars and all sorts of vermin that damage and eat them up. Now, it is foolish to want to seek lasting joy in a vale of tears and paradise in the world, especially for a Christian.

Then, another person said: I know what a caterpillar's nest can suitably signify for us, namely, a godless house, a wicked tavern, a school without needed constraint and discipline in which one wicked man leads many others astray and one child of the Devil hatches forth many others. Here godlessness quickly gains the upper hand, and one does not know how to control it or solve the problem. Unfortunately, today, the tree of the church is infested with caterpillar nests that have robbed it of almost all its leaves and fruit! Atheism and epicurean foulness have spread so quickly. May God rescue his poor church and cleanse it from such filth.

Gotthold continued: The slothful gardeners who are given oversight of the trees by God have not thought to destroy the caterpillar nests with unremitting eagerness. Still, if we want to speak further about this at another time, let us now not forget that every person bears a true caterpillar's nest in his own breast, I mean that fleshly minded heart corrupted by sin in which evil desires, hatched from original sin, crawl around one another and, if they are not attended to, creep through the body and soul until they are ruined. A Christian has enough to do, here, to control and destroy them. Therefore, Luther readily asserted that he was more afraid of his own heart than of the pope and all his cardinals. Another godly man once said to me: My own heart makes my life bitter and death appear sweet.

Lord Jesus, help me to pay heed, with all my power, to the control of these caterpillar nests and their depraved brood. Oh, when will you free and rescue me from myself and my own heart?!

Christian Scriver
The Treasure of the Soul
(1675)

Part 3, Chapter 1: The Necessity of a Godly and Holy Life

2 Corinthians 5:14, 15

1. The Roman emperor Hadrian had a marshal named Similis who, because he was tired of court life, requested and received a discharge. He spent the remaining seven years of his life in tranquility on a country estate, and when he finally died, a grave marker was set up, by his own recommendation, that read "Here lies Similis, who, though he was very old, still lived only seven years." The wise courtier saw that it is not a suitable life to live only in servitude to the whims of another person and forget oneself, or to seek satisfaction in the tiresome and base desires of the world, setting aside virtue and the improvement of the mind, as court people must commonly do. Although such a life may be regarded as appealing, it is almost no life at all, because whoever is animated by a foreign soul or ruled by the will, desires, and inclinations of another is like a bird in a cage, which, although it is provided with food and drink, has been robbed of its freedom and must sing whenever its master wishes. It lives like the gnats and flies, which flutter around a light for a while, as if they are in love with it. They want to warm themselves but finally burn their wings. After that, they can no longer fly and must crawl around, or, many times, they are even burned up completely.

2. Such people, who are old but have not lived long, are found not only around the court but everywhere and in all stations of life. Most people do not know what a proper life is or why they live or how they should use their time and abilities such that it can be said of them that they have lived. Some live, not as humans, much less as

Christians, but as animals that are alive but do not know what living is. Some live like the swallows, which spend the whole day flitting here and there in the air, doing nothing except catching gnats, leaving behind a nest made of mud. Some live like the peacocks, which only preen themselves and strut about, putting on a display. Some live like pigs, which seek pleasure in gobbling up food and take delight in mud. Some live like the lions, bears, and wolves, which only ransack, slaughter, and wreak havoc. Some live like spiders, which spin out a fine thread and prepare an artful web but for no other reason than to catch flies and gnats. Some live like moles, which only burrow in the ground, tossing heaps here and there and paying no attention to the sunlight. Some live like horses, oxen, and asses, which let themselves be driven and used for hard labor, caring about nothing as long as they have their fodder, hay, and straw. Some, although they are old, still live like children who spend all their time eating, drinking, playing, and sleeping. It cannot be said of all these that they are living. Scripture calls them the living dead.

3. The Holy Spirit calls such people shams and shadows (Ps 39:6) because they are not truly human and their lives are not real lives but only shadows. Many people forget themselves in the world and consider great what God views as only a shadow. They have no essence because they have alienated themselves from the life that comes from God. Now, test yourself, and see how the matter rests with you and your life. Perhaps you are already old and have little time left to live. Perhaps you have lived an idle and dissolute life, sleeping away half of it, spending part of it eating and drinking and the rest of it in forgettable, useless, and sinful work. The proper life consists of honoring the Creator, serving the neighbor, and steadily applying oneself to spiritual growth and personal improvement. We live properly if Christ Jesus lives in us, if his Holy Spirit rules and directs us, when we die to ourselves and the world and devote ourselves to modest, righteous, and holy living in this world. Consider now, my Christian, how long have you lived? Perhaps you have, after so many years, still not begun to live. Subtract from your years the time you have spent on amusements, idleness, empty chatter, eating, drinking, playing, sleeping, and so forth. Perhaps little or almost no time remains that you have spent in service to your God and neighbor and in the practice of godliness to perfect your soul?

4. An elderly man was asked how old he was and he answered "forty-five." The other said: "You look like a seventy-year-old." "That may well be," he replied, "but you should know that I spent the years of my foolish youth in sinful idleness. Those years cannot rightly be counted in my age because what I then had cannot be truly called a life." Consider yourself, my Christian, how old are you now? How long have you applied yourself to the upright practice of godliness? Perhaps you have scarcely spent the least part of your life that way. Perhaps you are already thirty years old and have scarcely lived thirty days. Suetonius reported that the Roman emperor Titus Vespasian, when he recalled one evening that he had not rendered a good deed to anyone that day, said, "My friend, I have lost this day or I regard this day as lost." Oh, that we might even learn from a heathen to consider a day lost if we have done nothing good to honor God, serve the neighbor, and improve our soul! Oh, that we might occupy ourselves in making up for those lost days again in the future! Oh, that we might begin to live rightly at least for the rest of our years, until the end of our fleeting lives. Oh, that we might still want to consider why we were created. Why did God shower us with so many blessings? Why were we rescued in so costly a manner, called and sanctified through the word and the holy sacraments? Not that we might live for ourselves but for him who created, saved, and sanctified us, as the entire holy scriptures teach in many places. Now let us reflect on the godly and holy life of a faithful soul in more detail. First, we want to demonstrate the necessity and then the possibility. Lord Jesus, grant that this may happen with great profit and fruit, for the sake of your holy wounds. Amen!

Exposition

5. "Who plants a vineyard without eating of its fruit or who tends a flock without drinking some of its milk?" says the Apostle (1 Cor 9:7). From this a general lesson can be taken: whoever takes pains with something is entitled to make use of it, whoever creates or acquires an object also has the right before all others to enjoy it. Now, I think God took trouble with the human soul (if I may speak in a human way) before he brought it to repentance and faith. How hard it was for the Lord to save it, how much sweat, how many tears,

how much blood it cost him before he rescued it from sin and Satan's power. Therefore, it is most fair that he should enjoy our thanks, praise, love, and the other fruits of our faith. Our most merciful and loving Lord aims in the entire work of our salvation and justification to raise up our fallen souls again, restore the lost image of God, and make it an instrument of divine grace and a vessel of his mercy.

After having taken into account the great grace of the Lord, which he has so richly shown toward us, and having taken delight in the blessings and love of God, we should, henceforth, think about the effects of grace in the soul, its inward and outward manifestations, and consider the fruits of faith and justification. Surely, the grace of God is a great, strong, powerful, and active thing, which does not lie in the soul and sleep or let itself be merely worn like colors on a painted board. No, it moves, leads, drives, draws, changes, and accomplishes everything in a person, letting itself be felt and experienced. It is hidden, but its work is not hidden. It shows what it is in work and words, just as the fruit and leaves reveal a tree's type and nature. The grace of God does not lie in the soul like a stone in a field but, like a noble kernel of grain, it soon begins to sprout and bring forth blade and fruit. Wherever Christ, through faith, dwells in the heart, he lives and rules and has his kingdom there. Whoever he justifies, he also makes holy and awakens within them a holy and ardent desire and a hearty zeal to serve God and humanity....

8. Here it is appropriate to bring up, again, what the dear Apostle said: "I live, yet it is not I, but Christ who lives in me...who loved me and gave himself for me" (Gal 2:20). See how Paul unites the life of Christ with his love and says he can and will not any longer live to himself but for the Lord Jesus because his savior loved him even to the point of dying for him. He wants to say: I have given my body and soul with all their powers, my entire heart, life, and being to my Lord Jesus. I am his possession, I have no heart but Christ's heart, I know no other life than the life that Jesus brought about and created within me. It saddens me if I should turn my eye, move my finger, or place my foot toward anything other than what is pleasing to my Savior. It saddens me if a day or even an hour should pass when I did not say, do, or endure something for the sake of my dear Savior's honor and glory or the edification of his people. Why is that? Because he said that he loved me and gave himself for me. I cannot

and will not ever forget this. Surely, I can never pay him back, but I can also never get out of my mind the fact that Jesus, the crucified, took and possessed my heart with his love. I cannot and will not do anything other than love, praise, and honor him all the time, communicating and spreading a recognition of this everywhere. Here, it becomes evident that a holy and godly life is necessary. True faith and real Christianity are living power from God, which renews the heart and gives a person a new spirit and mind. The heart of a reborn Christian is like a living source of fresh water, which wells up and flows forth, like a flower, which always exudes a sweet fragrance, like a fire, which always blazes and flares up, like the human body, which operates steadily, the heart pumping, the vessels pulsating, the blood being driven up and down, as long as the soul lives within it. So it is with a righteous Christian. The grace of God, the love of Jesus Christ, the power of the Holy Spirit that is within are never idle. It is impossible to find a faithful soul lacking holy practices or a heartfelt desire and longing to serve God.

9. The faithful soul must always have something to do. It cannot be still. It must praise or worship God, be zealous for his honor, care for the state of his church, attend to the neighbor's needs, or do good whenever it has the opportunity. Scarcely has it completed a good work before it is thinking of another. Its model is the creature Saint John imagined in the Book of Revelation, which had six wings, was full of eyes, never rested day or night, and praised God without ceasing (Rev 4:8). The wings signify its readiness and willingness to serve God, its eyes its foresight and vigilance. It finds repose in praising and serving God without rest. O holy unrest! It also dreams at night of the love of God, and its bridegroom comes to it while it sleeps. It often thinks that it is surrounded by a choir of angels singing, "Holy, holy, holy is God." Sometimes while it sleeps, it cries out with a loud voice, "Jesus! Jesus!" It is asleep, but its heart is awake. Where does all of this come from? The love of Christ impels it, the Lord Jesus lives within it, the Holy Spirit urges it on. It partakes of the divine nature through rebirth and has the spirit and mind of Christ (2 Pet 1:4; Rom 8:9; 1 Cor 2:16). It teaches itself what the nature of God and the mind of Christ are with these thoughtful words: "My Father works and I also work," which means that although my heavenly Father has rested from the work of creation,

he still works forevermore in the sustaining and ruling of all things. He cares for and nourishes and upholds all things. So also must I always be working, teaching, consoling, helping, healing, doing good, and so forth. His faithful have such a mind, from and through him. They must always have something to do to honor God, serve the neighbor, and improve themselves. They console, help, counsel, serve everyone with all their powers and abilities. Their faith, the soul of their Christianity, and their new nature cannot be still, just like the soul and heart within the body. An idle soul is no soul, and an idle faith is a dead faith. Whoever wants to be a Christian without the practice of godliness and without good works knows nothing of faith. Whoever has not felt the impelling love of Christ and his forceful, powerful Spirit is dead, though he still claims to be alive....

11. This was also Christ's intention in the work of salvation. "Therefore, he died for all so that those who now live through his death might henceforth live not for themselves but for him who died and was raised" (2 Cor 5:15). The death of the Lord Jesus has a double purpose: first, to save us from sin and, through the appropriation of his merits and faith, to make us righteous and holy, but second, also to renew us through his Holy Spirit, to make us holy and lead us to a blessed and holy life. The death of the Lord Jesus saves not only from sin and for eternal life but also protects from sin and gives a new godly life. The death and life, the blood and spirit of the Lord Jesus, salvation and sanctification must not be separated from each other. Whoever lays claim to the death of Christ must also choose the life of Christ as a testimony of thankfulness. It is impossible to have the benefits of the death of Christ in faith and still not partake of his life.

12. This is the meaning and the aim of the entire holy scriptures, from which we now will take a few passages for further clarification in order to fortify the assertion that a holy and godly life is necessary. "Whoever wishes to follow me," says the Lord Jesus (whoever will be my disciple, benefiting from my righteousness now and blessedness for all eternity), "must deny himself" (he must give up his own will, love, honor, and gain and give himself entirely to my service and will) "and take up his cross" (he crucifies his flesh together with its lusts and desires, goes forth daily in holiness and conquers or suppresses the sin within himself through the power of

my cross and death, and also freely and willingly accepts whatever trouble and adversity God sends him as an aid toward holy living and as a sign of God's fatherly care) "and follow me" (he lets me be not only his Savior but also his example and model; he not only claims my death but also follows me in his holy life) (Luke 9:23). Again, Christ explains this, very thoughtfully, through the image of a grapevine and its branches. "I am the vine," he says, "and you are the branches. Whoever abides in me and I in him, bears much fruit, for without me you can do nothing" (John 15:5). "Whoever does not abide in me" (being cut off, he will yield no worthy fruit) "will be cast off as a useless branch and will wither" (grace and the spirit of God depart more and more from him) "and will be gathered up" (as one binds cut branches in a bundle) "and will be thrown into a fire and burned." Observe, O Christian soul, that the Savior roots our earthly and eternal welfare in union and communion with him when he says we must depend on him as the branches do on the vine from which they receive all their sustenance and strength. He also expects fruit from this communion and even threatens us with the fires of hell....

16. If this, now, has convinced our hearts of the necessity of a holy life and affirmed it sufficiently, we still want to repeat briefly the order that God has described in his word, which we have also followed in the first and second part of this work, concerning all that he has intended or set out to do for the soul and particularly for its renewal and its preparation for a holy life. We have examined the lamentable situation of the sinful soul and shown that a person who persistently lives in willful sin is an abomination before God in all of his worship, prayer, actions, and intentions, and is also bound by the Devil. If, now, a person truly converts and is rescued from the Master of Darkness and placed within the kingdom and fellowship of the Lord Jesus, through faith, is it possible that he should voluntarily throw himself back into such misery through reckless sin? How could he have the desire to thrown off the easy yoke of his Savior and chose the slavery of Satan again? The righteous, converted Christian is appalled as often as he thinks about his former state and thanks his God from the depths of his soul that he was rescued through grace from the mouth of hell. As often as he recalls the danger of his soul, he falls in tears at the feet of his Savior and thanks him for seeking and retrieving a wandering lamb, promising anew to hold onto him

and to remain true. Only a madman would ruin himself again so soon after being rescued from such a great danger. Whoever abhors such a situation and is frightened by the power of Satan and hell will necessarily be eager to live a holy and godly life....

18. Here we will also add what we have taught concerning the nature of faith and how it clings to Christ and unites the soul to him. We can supplement the image of the grapevine, winding itself around a pole or a tree, with another one, which perhaps presents this matter more clearly. Ivy or wintergreen, which is a slender and weak plant, clings to a tree or sometimes a wall, and not only hangs on the tree but also drives its rootlets into the bark and draws sap into itself. This, I say, is not a bad analogy to clarify the nature of a faithful soul which not only clings to Christ but also draws his spirit, power, energy, and life into itself, thereby renewing itself and making itself fit for service to God and neighbor. Scripture not only says that we are like the branches of a grapevine and should therefore bring forth much fruit, but also that the Savior is our bread and his blood our drink, since he not only upholds the spiritual life but gives power to strengthen us within through his spirit so that we can better practice true godliness (Eph 3:16–17). The same passage also says that Christ dwells in our hearts. Now, Christ is not a dead idol but a prince of life, an ever-flowing source of love, a steadily burning and shining light, divine power and wisdom. Thus, it is not possible that he should be in our hearts and not also impart to them his life, love, power, light, and spirit. Can I carry a rose or lemon in my hand and not sense the fragrance of it? Likewise, can I have Christ in my heart and not be aware of the power of his life and the urging of his Holy Spirit? Experience teaches that when a piece of lemon is bound to an artery of a patient who lies faint and weak with a hot fever, it imparts its cooling and heart-strengthening power to the blood. How can this contact compare to the inner spiritual union of Christ with a person? How could it be, then, that our souls should not draw spirit and power for a new and holy life from such a close and strong bond?...

20. We add to this the teachings about our adoption by God, the marriage of the soul with Christ, and the indwelling of the Holy Spirit in the converted and faithful heart. Being a child of God, being born of God, is no shadow work or child's play. God will not produce a lifeless and unfit fruit that is worth nothing. Whoever seeks the

glory of adoption through Christ is also given the spirit of adoption and cries, "Abba, Father." A holy child of God always sees its heavenly Father before its eyes and renews its intention not to provoke him on purpose. So also, when the converted soul considers the great dignity it has acquired through marriage with Christ, it regrets any impure thought that might taint its heart. It hastens, out of heartfelt love, to its dear Savior and wishes nothing more than to die soon so that the sin that always adheres to it may be entirely taken away. It wishes to cast aside the soiled coat of its sinful flesh so that the full glow of the righteousness and holiness of Jesus may be displayed. How could it turn again to intentional and reckless sin? How could it offend and afflict with shameful unfaithfulness and ingratitude its Savior, who purchased it with his dear blood?

21. The Holy Spirit, which dwells in the faithful soul, is also not idle. As the soul gives life to the body and works and creates within it without interruption, so the Holy Spirit gives a new life to a person and is within this person like a light in a dark place, like a fire which melts, heats, purifies, and cauterizes, like a wind that always blows. It dwells within the faithful like a father in a house that he is always improving, like a teacher in a school who is always instructing his students and admonishing them to be appropriately diligent, like a gardener in a garden who is always cleaning and watering it, filling it with flowers and other plants. Oh, one can easily think that if God unites himself with people, if he chooses them as children or as his brides, and his dwelling place, then it must not be difficult to know this, because one can easily differentiate between a palace of a great king and a pigsty or a snake hole. Surely, God's dwelling on earth is covered on the outside with a raw goat hide but is glorious and splendid on the inside, with the sweet smell of smoke and the steadily burning flame of the altar of burnt offerings. I want to say that although a converted person is not entirely free of weaknesses and failings, inwardly all is pure, holy, and glorious. Faith is always glowing and burning there, and a contrite heart is being offered as a daily offering with many heartfelt prayers and tears. Without a doubt, there can be no true repentance and conversion, no justifying faith, no adoption by God, no marriage with Christ, no indwelling of the Holy Spirit without a godly and holy life. All who imagine themselves to be a Christian but lack truly godliness must also imagine

that the work of God is idle talk and an empty appearance without power, which certainly cannot be true.

22. To make this doctrine of the necessity of a godly life useful, we will undertake here a defense of the evangelical church against the false claim of the papists that no good works are found among us and that none of us values or demands them, and that we only preach and emphasize faith apart from godliness. This is a harsh and dreadful accusation, and I affirm that if it can truly be made against us, we are not worthy of the name of Christian. But, we can give evidence that it is untrue from our many distinguished writings, and especially from the powerful daily admonitions that go forth from all pulpits. We certainly emphasize faith and in accordance with the holy scriptures say that it alone justifies, but we also say and teach that justifying faith is active through love and that faith without works is dead (Gal 5:6; Jas 2:26). We consistently teach that true faith can never coexist with a profligate nature and willful sinning. We know of no faithful whores, adulterers, sexual abusers, thieves, or greedy drunkards, as the papist church claimed in their assembly at Trent. We teach from God's word that those who know no true contrition and do not intend to separate and hold themselves apart from sin do not have true and sanctifying faith. Love of God and neighbor is a fruit that unfailingly and necessarily follows from faith. If one does not have such love, it can rightly be concluded that this person is not justified, but rather remains in death or that the righteousness of faith has been lost again. We teach that every tree that does not bring forth good fruit will be cut down and thrown in the fire (Matt 7:19).

23. The teachers of our church have long ago concluded that it is necessary in these last times for godly preachers to emphasize the doctrine of good works as well as faith. It is just as important to admonish and direct people toward true godliness so that they show their faith and obligatory thankfulness to God with good works as it is to avoid mixing up good works with the matter of justification, because people can fall into damnation not only through pharisaic trust in their own merits and works but also through epicurean security and false understandings of faith. We do not consider someone a Christian who intentionally remains in sin, contrary to conscience. We do not consider someone worthy of the name of Christian who does not diligently demonstrate faith in Christ with a godly life,

according to the command of Christ, and we say, frankly, that such a person is deprived of eternal life, although others may be deceived by hypocrisy. We ascribe the righteousness that is acceptable to God only to faith, which we have proved already in detail from the holy scriptures, but we cannot [for that reason] be accused of abolishing the necessity of a holy, godly life any more than one who has planted a root or bulb can be accused of not expecting any flowers. We can with all honesty adopt the words of the Apostle: "Have we abolished the law through faith? By no means. We uphold the law" (Rom 3:31). We do not abolish the doctrine of true godliness and good works but show much more the roots of our holiness and how we must reach the point where we can live according to the law of God in childlike, willing obedience. The tree must first be good before it brings forth good fruit, and the source must be purified before a sweet stream can flow from it. I ask all who live in the community of the papist church, who value the truth and blessedness, either to stop troubling the evangelical church with these godless charges or believing others who make them, so that they do not act against their consciences and stain themselves with a damnable sin.

24. Here we want to turn our attention to the people who live in the outward community of the evangelical church but who misuse the doctrine of the righteousness of faith through security and impenitence, who imagine that they have faith, righteousness, forgiveness of sins, and the certainty of eternal life in Christ, although there is no trace of anything Christian in them other than the name and the outward confession. They offer thanks for the merits of Christ and praise his righteousness, wishing to partake of salvation through Christ, but they want to know nothing about a holy and godly life in Christ and for the neighbor. They are content to know some of the passages from scripture about faith along with the three articles of Christian belief, considering this to be justifying and sanctifying faith, although they have not let what they know by the letter to come into their hearts, which remain unbroken, unchanged, and unrenewed. In these last times, thorn bushes want to be grapevines, thistles want to be roses, and wolves want to be lambs. They want to believe in Christ but not to adhere to his commandments or follow him in his life and suffering. They want to make use of Christ for salvation while still satisfying their desires by sinning. They gladly lis-

ten when the grace of God is preached, but when they are instructed that this grace entails renunciation of worldly desires and living chastely and righteously in this world, they do not think that God is serious or consider this a matter that they can easily handle. They want to have Christ while also holding onto themselves and the world with their sinful desires; they want to serve both God and the Devil; they want to make their way to heaven on the broad path of sin. In short, those who are godless, insolent, proud, haughty, quarrelsome, drunk, profane, adulterous, selfish, deceitful, miserly, and unrighteous want to be called faithful Christians and be consoled by the hope of salvation acquired for them by Christ Jesus and his precious blood. They want to keep Christ with his merits as a trump card by which, if they must leave this world against their will, they may acquire salvation, as soon as he surrounds them with the cloak of his righteousness....

27. Test yourself, now, to see whether you are faithful and Christ is within you. Do you think you have faith? Well, then, where is your holy living? Is Christ within you and does he dwell in your heart? Where is his power, his victory over sin, his love, his gentleness, his humility, his patience, his chastity, his majesty, his moderation, his truth? Can there be an eternal light that does not shine, an uncreated wellspring of all good without water, a precious bloom of paradise without a fragrance? Can one also separate Christ's blood and spirit? His blood purifies us from all sin, and his Spirit protects us from all sin. Who does not have Christ's Spirit is not one of his own. Whoever is not moved by the Spirit of God is not a child of God, does not belong to Christ, and has not crucified the flesh with its lusts and desires. You imagine that you have sanctifying faith, but do you know that faith places us in union with Christ, that we are as near to him and he to us as a branch is to the trunk, as a flower is to its roots, as a soul is to the body? Where there is such a union between two living things, communion must also result. When I grasp Christ Jesus in faith and he grasps and encloses me in his love, my soul is united with his soul, my heart with his heart, my power or even more my weakness with his power, my spirit with his Spirit, my life with his life. That means, "I live, yet it is not I, but Christ who lives in me." Judge, then, whether or not there should be evidence of a change in me. I am still who I was, but not according to my old

nature. I have received a new sense, a new heart. I am no longer in command of myself, nor do I desire to be, but rather Christ has my heart and all that is within me. I no longer have anything more to do with sin, but struggle with it daily as with an enemy, and conquer it in the power of Christ. I find in my Jesus and his blessed communion so much sweetness that I do not consider vile worldly desires. His cross is dearer to me than all the treasures of the world, his crown of thorns and nails more valuable than all earthly pleasures and joys. I desire nothing more than to be his servant, to love and praise him until death and even for eternity. What else can I, a poor child, do and what else can I give to him, for the great love with which he loved me?...

35. So, it does not help you much that you call yourself a Christian. You must be a righteous Christian; you must not only have the name of Christ but also his Spirit and mind. Many live in the church who do not belong to the church. Many have the light but walk in darkness. In a famous city and university of our Germany, in the year 1611, a thieving student was publicly hanged. He had a trick that served to hide his villainy. He used to kindle a light, set it on the table in his room, and let it burn so that his neighbors would think that he was home, studying late into the night. What help was this light to this miserable man when he wandered about like a night bird in the darkness, plotting works of darkness? Could the burning and shining light rescue him from the gallows? So it is, also, with many Christians today. They boast of the light of the gospel and that they hear and read the word. It is true that the word is a light, which also shines clearly in our times. It stands in a candlestick and lights all who are at home, but how does the shining of this light help those who love darkness more than light? How does the preaching of the word help those who scorn it and do not walk in the light? What kind of a defense will it provide on that great day before the judge of the living and the dead against the horrible sentence of damnation? "O Lord, I have had your word, the bright light." Will it not be said: "Yes, you certainly had it, but did you pay attention to it? Have you walked in the light? Have you not loved darkness more than light?"

36. It does not help you much that you are baptized as long as you do not live according to your baptismal covenant. Certainly, baptism is a holy means of our rebirth, through which we are incor-

porated into Christ. However, we must not only be incorporated into Christ but also remain in him....

37. It also does not help you that you go to the Lord's Supper if you do so without repentance, faith, and a good intention. The holy Lord's Supper, in which the Lord Jesus feeds us with his body, given for us onto death, and his blood, shed for us on the cross, is a powerful means to obtain and strengthen our union and communion with Christ, but it can also be received onto judgment, by the secure and impenitent, who go to it without faith and devotion, for they are guilty for having crucified and killed him anew....

38. Others say or think: "I believe I lack nothing because I know my catechism, many psalms and hymns, many verses of scripture, and many prayers. I also set my only trust on the merits and blood of Christ Jesus, so salvation cannot be denied me, even though I am still sinful and do not do everything right." I answer: knowledge of spiritual and divine things still does not make for saving faith, otherwise even the hypocrites who have attained much knowledge of Christ could predict, in his name, that they would not be rejected. The holy apostle James undoubtedly alludes to this when he says, "You believe there is one God. You do well but even the Devils believe and tremble" (Jas 2:19)....A cardinal in Rome had a parrot or parakeet that he bought for 100 ducats and that knew how to recite clearly the three articles of Christian faith. You will understand that this did not help the bird, although it made him precious and agreeable to people. So also it does not help the hypocrites and godless that they know something about the scripture and other spiritual things, if they remain earthly minded....

40. Others raise an objection: "We are humans and not angels. Who can live in this world without sin? We still bear sinful flesh and blood." I answer: This is no excuse. You are certainly human but, not only that, you are also a Christian, baptized in the name of Christ, saved by Christ's blood, and sealed by the Holy Spirit, so you have means at hand by which you can be enlivened, exhorted, strengthened, and improved. God does not demand that you be without sin but rather that it not be lord over you. He knows well that you are not an angel, but he will not tolerate that you live like a devil. He knows that you still have flesh and blood, but he has given you his Word and offered you his grace and Spirit each day so that you might con-

strain your flesh and blood and overcome them in the power of Christ. Consider the examples of many holy children of God who were human as you are, who had flesh and blood in which sin dwells, as you do. Still, they have not lived according to the flesh but rather according to the Spirit. They have struggled and conquered and thereby acquired the crown of life. The way also stands open to you. The source of grace that should create such power is still not dried up. The Spirit of Christ, whose urging you should follow, is still within the church of God. We can now say with the Apostle: "I can do all things, through Christ, who strengthens me."...

42. I willingly admit that the saints also have sinned and have reason to seek forgiveness of their sins as often as they ask for their daily bread, yet those who are not serious about godly living and have never pursued it cannot appeal to the saints and the pious. There was an honorable man who slipped and fell in a street that had been made slippery by rainy weather. He got covered with mud, but he stood up and hastened home where he cleaned himself off. A sow, however, goes out in the street and finds a puddle to lie in up to its ears and seeks pleasure and refreshment from this dirty bath. How can the one be compared to the other? So it is with the failings of the saints, when they act rashly against their will. They become upset with themselves and shed many hot tears. They appeal daily to God and seek correction through his grace. Such failings cannot be compared to the intentional sins, which the godless never shun the opportunity to commit. Such people know nothing of sorrow for sin or amendment of life, but rather think only of the pursuit of their godless pleasures. If you wish to be holy and pious, struggle with your sinful desires and aspire to dispose of them more and more....

51. We find no place where God the Lord demands a complete perfection of penitents, but he is pleased with uprightness of heart and a renewed will in grace. Certainly the law demands perfect obedience or else the punishment of eternal death, but the faithful are now under grace and no longer under the law. God deals with his servants as with children. He pays attention to the intention more than the deed and has patience with their failings and weaknesses. Some of his children are like babies who lie on the breast and do nothing while their parents smile at them lovingly and kindly. Some are like those who are beginning to babble, saying "father" and

"mother," and who can walk from stool to bench. Some are like those who walk and speak more skillfully, who go to school to be instructed in praying, reading, and writing. Some are like grownup children who are well-educated and whose good conduct is a joy to their parents. They are, nevertheless, all beloved children, and the least of them, with many weaknesses, is not excluded from fatherly love and care anymore than the best among them, who deserve fatherly love for their good conduct. God has called us all to pray ceaselessly not only for our daily bread, but also for forgiveness of sins. All of us, the high and low, the weak and strong, the beginners and the perfected, live by means of his grace and blessing, and there is no one who can glory except in the love of our merciful God....

52. ...O Lord Jesus, prince of life, live in me! Conquer sin, death, the Devil, and hell within me. See, here is my heart, which I freely offer to you so that you will dwell in it and nurture my spiritual life. What would life be for me if you did not live within me and me in you?

LUTHERAN HYMNS

PHILIPP NICOLAI (1568–1608)
Wachet auf, ruft uns die Stimme
(Wake, awake, for night is flying)

1599 FREUDENSPIEGEL (SEE USE BY BACH BMV 140)

Translation by Catherine Winkworth
Lyra Germanica, Second Series: The Christian Life, *pp. 225–26*
London: Longman, Brown, Green, Longmans, and Roberts, 1858

Wake, awake, for night is flying,
The watchmen on the heights are crying;
Awake, Jerusalem, at last!
Midnight hears the welcome voices,
And at the thrilling cry rejoices:
Come forth, ye virgins, night is past!
The Bridegroom comes, awake,
Your lamps with gladness take;
Hallelujah!
And for His marriage-feast prepare,
For ye must go to meet Him there.

Zion hears the watchmen singing,
And all her heart with joy is springing,
She wakes, she rises from her gloom;
For her Lord comes down all-glorious,
The strong in grace, in truth victorious,
Her Star is ris'n, her Light is come.
"Now come, Thou Blessed One,
Lord Jesus, God's own Son,
Hail! Hosanna!
The joyful call
We answer all
And follow to the nuptial hall."

Now let all the heav'ns adore Thee,
Let men and angels sing before Thee,
With harp and cymbal's clearest tone.

Of one pearl each shining portal,
Where, dwelling with the choir immortal,
We gather round Thy radiant throne.
No vision ever brought,
No ear hath ever caught,
Such great glory;
Therefore will we
Eternally
Sing hymns of praise and joy to Thee.

PHILIPP NICOLAI
Wie schön leuchtet der Morgenstern
(O Morning-Star, how fair and bright)

1599 Freudenspiegel (See use by Bach BMV 1)

Translation by Catherine Winkworth
Christian Singers of Germany, *pp. 160–62*
London: Macmillan and Co., 1869

O Morning-Star, how fair and bright
Thou beamest forth in truth and light!
O Sovereign meek and lowly!
Sweet Root of Jesse, David's Son,
My King and Bridegroom, Thou hast won
My heart to love Thee solely!
Lovely art Thou, fair and glorious,
All victorious,
Rich in blessing,
Rule and might o'er all possessing.

O King high-born, Pearl hardly won,
True Son of God and Mary's Son,
Crown of exceeding glory!
My heart calls Thee a Lily, Lord,
Pure milk and honey is Thy Word,
Thy sweetest Gospel-story.
Rose of Sharon, hail! Hosanna!
Heavenly Manna,

Feed us ever;
Lord, I can forget Thee never!

Clear Jasper, Ruby fervent red,
Deep deep within my heart now shed
The glow of love's pure fire;
Fill me with joy, grant me to be
Thy member closely joined to Thee,
Whom all my thoughts desire;
Toward Thee longing doth possess me,
Turn and bless me,
For Thy gladness
Eye and heart here pine in sadness.

But if Thou look on me in love,
There straightway falls from God above
A ray of purest pleasure;
Thy Word and Spirit, flesh and blood,
Refresh my soul with heavenly food,
Thou art my hidden treasure.
Let Thy grace, Lord, warm and cheer me,
O draw near me;
Thou hast taught us
Thee to seek, since Thou hast sought us.

Lord God, my Father, mighty Shield,
Thou in Thy Son art all revealed
As Thou hast loved and known me;
Thy Son hath me with Him betrothed,
In His own whitest raiment clothed,
He for His bride will own me.
Hallelujah! Life in heaven
Hath He given,
With Him dwelling,
Still shall I His praise be telling.

Then touch the chords of harp and lute,
Let no sweet music now be mute,
But joyously resounding,

Tell of the Marriage-feast, the Bride,
The heavenly Bridegroom at her side,
'Mid love and joy abounding;
Shout for triumph, loudly sing ye,
Praises bring ye,
Fall before Him,
King of kings, let all adore Him!

Here my heart rests, and holds it fast,
The Lord I love is First and Last,
The End as the Beginning;
Here I can die, for I shall rise
Through Him, to His own Paradise
Above all tears and sinning.
Amen! Amen! Come, Lord Jesus,
Soon release us,
With deep yearning,
Lord, we look for Thy returning.

JOSUA STEGMANN (1588–1632)
Ach bleib' mit deiner Gnade
(Abide among us with Thy grace)

1629

Translation by Catherine Winkworth
The Chorale Book for England, *#14*
London: Longman, Green, Longmans, Roberts, and Green, 1865

Abide among us with Thy grace,
Lord Jesus, evermore,
Nor let us e'er to sin give place,
Nor grieve Him we adore.

Abide among us with Thy word,
Redeemer whom we love,
Thy help and mercy here afford,
And life with Thee above.

Abide among us with Thy ray,
O Light that lighten'st all,
And let Thy truth preserve our way,
Nor suffer us to fall.

Abide with us to bless us still,
O bounteous Lord of peace;
With grace and power our souls fulfill,
Our faith and love increase.

Abide among us as our shield,
O Captain of Thy host;
That to the world we may not yield,
Nor e'er forsake our post.

Abide with us in faithful love,
Our God and Saviour be,
Thy help at need, Oh let us prove,
And keep us true to Thee.

JOHANN HEERMANN (1585–1647)
Herzliebster Jesu, was hast Du verbrochen
(Alas, dear Lord, what law then hast Thou broken)

1630 DEVOTI MUSICA CORDIS (SEE USE BY BACH BMV 244, 245)

Translation by Catherine Winkworth
The Chorale Book for England, *#52*
London: Longman, Green, Longmans, Roberts, and Green, 1863

Alas, dear Lord, what law then hast Thou broken,
That such sharp sentence should on Thee be spoken?
Of what great crime hast Thou to make confession—
What dark transgression?

They crown His head with thorns, they smite, they scourge
Him,
With cruel mockings to the cross they urge Him,

They give Him gall to drink, they still decry Him—
They crucify Him.

Whence come these sorrows, whence this mortal anguish
It is my sins for which my Lord must languish;
Yes, all the wrath, the woe He doth inherit,
'Tis I do merit!

What strangest punishment is suffer'd yonder!—
The Shepherd dies for sheep that loved to wander!
The Master pays the debts His servants owe Him,
Who would not know Him.

There was no spot in me by sin untainted,
Sick with its venom all my heart had fainted;
My heavy guilt to hell had well-nigh brought me,
Such woe it wrought me.

O wondrous love! whose depths no heart hath sounded,
That brought Thee here by foes and thieves surrounded;
All worldly pleasures, heedless, I was trying,
While Thou wert dying!

O mighty King! no time can dim Thy glory!
How shall I spread abroad Thy wondrous story?
How shall I find some worthy gift to proffer?
What dare we offer?

For vainly doth our human wisdom ponder—
Thy woes, Thy mercy still transcend our wonder.
Oh how should I do aught that could delight Thee!
Can I requite Thee?

Yet unrequited, Lord, I would not leave Thee,
I can renounce whate'er doth vex or grieve Thee,
And quench with thoughts of Thee and prayers most lowly,
All fires unholy.

But since my strength alone will ne'er suffice me
To crucify desires that still entice me,

To all good deeds, oh let Thy Spirit win me,
And reign within me!

I'll think upon Thy mercy hour by hour,
I'll love Thee so that earth must lose her power;
To do Thy will shall be my sole endeavour
Henceforth for ever.

Whate'er of earthly good this life may grant me
I'll risk for Thee,—no shame, no cross shall daunt me;
I shall not fear what man can do to harm me,
Nor death alarm me.

But worthless is my sacrifice, I own it,
Yet, Lord, for love's sake Thou wilt not disown it;
Thou wilt accept my gift in Thy great meekness,
Nor shame my weakness.

And when, dear Lord, before Thy throne in heaven
To me the crown of joy at last is given,
Where sweetest hymns Thy saints for ever raise Thee,
I too shall praise Thee!

JOHANN HEERMANN
Herr unser Gott, lass nicht zu Schanden werden
(Ah! Lord our God, let them not be confounded)

1630 Devoti musica cordis

Translation by Catherine Winkworth
Christian Singers of Germany, *p. 198*
London: Macmillan and Co., 1869

Ah! Lord our God, let them not be confounded
Who, though by want, and woe, and pain surrounded,
Yet day and night still hope Thy help to see,
And cry to Thee.

But put to shame Thy foes, who breathe defiance,
And make their own vain might their sole reliance,

And turn, oh turn to those who trust Thy Word:
Have pity, Lord!

Against our foes some succour quickly send us;
If Thou but speak the word they shall not end us,
But change to friends, lay down their useless arms,
And cease all harms.

We stand bereft of help, and poor and lonely,
'Twere vain to trust in man,—with Thee, Lord, only
We yet may dare great deeds whoe'er oppose,
And quell our foes.

Thou art our Champion who canst overthrow them,
And save the little flock now crushed below them,
We trust in Thee; Helper, Thy help we claim
In Jesu's name! Amen.

JOHANN HEERMANN
O Gott, du frommer Gott
(O God, Thou faithful God)

1630 DEVOTI MUSICA CORDIS
(See use by Bach BMV 24, 71, 399)

Translation by Catherine Winkworth
The Chorale Book for England, *#132*
London: Longman, Green, Longmans, Roberts, and Green, 1863

O God, Thou faithful God,
Thou Fountain ever flowing,
Without whom nothing is,
All perfect gifts bestowing;
A pure and healthy frame
O give me, and within
A conscience free from blame,
A soul unhurt by sin.

And grant me, Lord, to do,
With ready heart and willing,
Whate'er Thou shalt command,
My calling here fulfilling,
And do it when I ought,
With all my strength, and bless
The work I thus have wrought,
For Thou must give success.

And let me promise nought
But I can keep it truly,
Abstain from idle words,
And guard my lips still duly;
And grant, when in my place
I must and ought to speak,
My words due power and grace,
Nor let me wound the weak.

If dangers gather round,
Still keep me calm and fearless;
Help me to bear the cross
When life is dark and cheerless;
To overcome my foe
With words and actions kind;
When counsel I would know,
Good counsel let me find.

And let me be with all
In peace and friendship living,
As far as Christians may.
And if Thou aught art giving
Of wealth and honours fair,
Oh this refuse me not,
That nought be mingled there
Of goods unjustly got.

And if a longer life
Be here on earth decreed me,
And Thou through many a strife

To age at last wilt lead me,
Thy patience in me shed,
Avert all sin and shame,
And crown my hoary head
With pure untarnish'd fame.

Let nothing that may chance,
Me from my Saviour sever;
And dying with Him, take
My soul to Thee for ever;
And let my body have
A little space to sleep
Beside my fathers' grave,
And friends that o'er it weep.

And when the Day is come,
And all the dead are waking,
Oh reach me down Thy hand,
Thyself my slumbers breaking;
Then let me hear Thy voices
And change this earthly frame,
And bid me aye rejoice
With those who love Thy name.

JOHANN HEERMANN
O Jesu Christe wahres Licht
(Christ, our true and only Light)

1630 DEVOTI MUSICA CORDIS

Translation by Catherine Winkworth
Lyra Germanica, Second Series: The Christian Life, *pp. 21–22*
London: Longman, Brown, Green, Longmans, and Roberts, 1858

Christ, our true and only Light,
Illumine those who sit in night,
Let those afar now hear Thy voice,
And in Thy fold with us rejoice.

Fill with the radiance of Thy grace
The souls now lost in error's maze,
And all whom in their secret minds
Some dark delusion hurts and blinds.

And all who else have stray'd from Thee,
Oh gently seek! Thy healing be
To every wounded conscience given,
And let them also share Thy heaven.

Oh make the deaf to hear Thy word,
And teach the dumb to speak, dear Lord,
Who dare not yet the faith avow,
Though secretly they hold it now.

Shine on the darken'd and the cold,
Recall the wanderers from Thy fold,
Unite those now who walk apart,
Confirm the weak and doubting heart.

So they with us may evermore
Such grace with wondering thanks adore,
And endless praise to Thee be given
By all Thy church in earth and heaven.

JOHANN HEERMANN
Hilf mir, mein Gott
(Oh help me, God, that e'er for Thee)

1630 Devoti musica cordis

Translation © 2009 Matthew Carver.
Used by permission. Available online.

Oh help me, God, that e'er for Thee
My heart be filled with yearning,
That I may seek Thee fervently,
In fright and anguish turning;
Bestow on me a glimpse of Thee,

Thy joy all fears to banish,
Grant will and sense to drive from hence
All sins, and make them vanish.

Upon Thy grace, by pain and smart
Affix my whole ambition,
To cultivate a lowly heart,
To live in true contrition;
To Thee I flee, a piteous plea
For all my sins to offer:
Each hour prepare my heart to bear
The weights of them who suffer.

Suppress the fleshly lust in me,
Defeat it with Thy merit,
Let true delight and love for Thee
Be kindled by Thy Spirit;
Let me confess all in distress
Thy Word till death should take me;
Grant not that ill or selfish will
From all Thy truth may break me.

Restrain me from all wrath and ire,
Let kindness gleam inside me,
Remove from me all proud desire,
To humbler temper guide me.
Whatever sin still lurks within
Let me henceforth be shunning.
Let comfort, peace, and joy not cease,
But keep me in them running.

Confirm my faith, maintain in me
All love, with strength preserving
My hope and trust, for unto Thee
The best is faith unswerving;
My lips beware lest peril e'er
Should by them be awoken.
My flesh constrain, that, free from stain,
Its way be here unbroken.

Give faithfulness and zeal, I pray,
To do what works are fitting,
And never to be led astray
Through pride or lust unwitting;
Of envy, strife and hatred rife
Leave not a drop within me,
My stubborn sense expel from hence,
To honest dealing win me.

Oh help me Thy true counsel heed,
All wayward thoughts betraying,
Assist my arms in every deed,
For friend and foe e'er praying.
To serve each man as best I can,
Upright and sober-hearted,
According to Thy precepts true,
Until from hence I'm parted.

MARTIN RINCKART (1586–1649)
Nun danket alle Gott (Now thank we all our God)

1636 Praxis pietatis melica with 1648 tune by Johann Crüger
(See use by Bach BMV 79, 192, 252, 386)

Translation by Catherine Winkworth
Lyra Germanica, Second Series: The Christian Life, *pp. 145–46*
London: Longman, Brown, Green, Longmans, and Roberts, 1858

Now thank we all our God
With heart and hands and voices,
Who wondrous things hath done,
In whom His world rejoices;
Who from our mother's arms
Hath blessed us on our way
With countless gifts of love,
And still is ours today.

Oh, may this bounteous God
Through all our life be near us,
With ever joyful hearts
And blessed peace to cheer us;
And keep us in His grace
And guide us when perplexed
And free us from all ills
In this world and the next.

All praise and thanks to God
The Father now be given,
The Son, and Him who reigns
With them in highest heaven:
The one eternal God,
Whom earth and heaven adore!
For thus it was, is now,
And shall be evermore.

MARTIN OPITZ (1597–1639)
O Licht geboren aus dem Lichte
(O Light, who out of Light wast born)

1634 ZEHEN PSALMEN DAVIDS

Translation by Catherine Winkworth
Christian Singers of Germany, *pp. 173–74*
London: Macmillan and Co., 1869

MORNING HYMN

O Light, who out of Light wast born,
O glorious Sun of Righteousness,
Thou sendest us anew the morn
With pleasant light and cheerfulness;
Therefore it beseems us well
Now with thankful lips to tell
All we owe to Thee;
Let our hearts to Thee arise,

Open Thou our inner eyes
All Thy love to see.

O let Thy Spirit's clear-eyed day
Break in upon our hearts' deep night,
And with its glowing radiance slay
Our self-trust's cold deluding light;
See, we waver and are weak,
Act and thought alike oft seek
Paths that are not Thine!
That our way may grow more clear,
And our life more steadfast here,
Bid Thy Sun to shine.

Unite, Lord, in the bonds of peace
Our Church's scattered band;
Bid wars and persecutions cease
Through our sad fatherland;
Grant us, Lord, O grant us rest!
That we, not too sore opprest,
May our course fulfill
Through this fleeting Time, till Thou
Bring us where the angels now
Praise Thy goodness still.

PAUL FLEMING (1609–1640)
In allen meinen Thaten
(Where'er I go, whate'er my task)

1633 TEUTSCHE POEMATA (SEE USE BY BACH BMV 367)

Translation by Catherine Winkworth
Lyrica Germanica, Second Series: The Christian Life, *pp. 108–11*
London: Longman, Brown, Green, Longmans, and Roberts, 1858

Where'er I go, whate'er my task,
The counsel of my God I ask,
Who all things hath and can;

Unless he give both thought and deed,
The utmost pains can ne'er succeed,
And vain the wisest plan.

For what can all my toil avail?
My care, my watching all must fail,
Unless my God is there;
Then let him order all for me
As he in wisdom shall decree;
On him I cast my care.

For nought can come, as nought hath been,
But what my Father hath foreseen,
And what shall work my good;
Whate'er he gives me I will take,
Whate'er he chooses I will make
My choice with thankful mood.

I lean upon his mighty arm,
It shields me well from every harm,
All evil shall avert;
If by his precepts still I live,
Whate'er is useful he will give,
And nought shall do me hurt.

But only may he of his grace
The record of my guilt efface,
And wipe out all my debt;
Though I have sinned he will not straight
Pronounce his judgment, he will wait,
Have patience with me yet.

I travel to a distant land
To serve the post wherein I stand,
Which he hath bade me fill;
And he will bless me with his light,
That I may serve his world aright,
And make me know his will.

And though through desert wilds I fare,
Yet Christian friends are with me there,
And Christ himself is near;
In all our dangers he will come,
And he who kept me safe at home,
Can keep me safely here.

Yes, he will speed us on our way,
And point us where to go and stay,
And help us still and lead;
Let us in health and safety live,
And time and wind and weather give,
And whatsoe'er we need.

When late at night my rest I take,
When early in the morn I wake,
Halting or on my way,
In hours of weakness or in bonds,
When vexed with fears my heart desponds,
His promise is my stay.

Since, then, my course is traced by him,
I will not fear that future dim,
But go to meet my doom,
Well knowing nought can wait me there
Too hard for me through him to bear;
I yet shall overcome.

To him myself I wholly give,
At his command I die or live,
I trust his love and power;
Whether tomorrow or today
His summons come, I will obey,
He knows the proper hour.

But if it please that love most kind,
And if this voice within my mind
Is whispering not in vain,
I yet shall praise my God erelong

In many a sweet and joyful song,
In peace at home again.

To those I love will he be near,
With his consoling light appear,
Who is my shield and theirs;
And he will grant beyond our thought
What they and I alike have sought
With many tearful prayers.

Then, O my soul, be ne'er afraid!
On him who thee and all things made
Do thou all calmly rest,
Whate'er may come, where'er we go,
Our Father in the heavens must know
In all things what is best.

JOHANN VON RIST (1607–1667)
Hilf, Herr Jesu, lass gelingen
(Help us, O Lord! Behold, we enter)

1642 HIMLISCHE LIEDER

Translation by Catherine Winkworth
The Chorale Book for England, *#172*
London: Longman, Green, Longmans, Roberts, and Green, 1863

NEW YEAR'S DAY

Help us, O Lord! Behold, we enter
Upon another year today;
In Thee our hopes and thoughts now center,
Renew our courage for the way.
New life, new strength, new happiness,
We ask of Thee—oh, hear and bless!

May every plan and undertaking
This year be all begun with Thee;
When I am sleeping or am waking,
Still let me know Thou art with me.
Abroad do Thou my footsteps guide,
At home be ever at my side.

Be this a time of grace and pardon.
Thy rod I take with willing mind,
But suffer naught my heart to harden;
O, let me then Thy mercy find!
In Thee alone, my God, I live;
Thou only canst my sins forgive.

And may this year to me be holy;
Thy grace so fill my every thought
That all my life be pure and lowly
And truthful, as a Christian's ought.
So make me while yet dwelling here
Pious and blest from year to year.

Jesus, be with me and direct me;
Jesus, my plans and hopes inspire;
Jesus, from tempting thoughts protect me;
Jesus, be all my heart's desire;
Jesus, be in my thoughts all day
Nor suffer me to fall away.

And grant, Lord, when the year is over,
That it for me in peace may close;
In all things care for me and cover
My head in time of fear and woes.
So may I when my years are gone
Appear with joy before Thy throne.

JOHANN VON RIST
Werde Licht du Stadt der Heiden
(All ye Gentile lands awake!)

1655 FEST-ANDACHTEN

Translation by Catherine Winkworth
Lyra Germanica: The Christian Year, *pp. 30–31*
London: Longmans, Green, and Co., 1879

EPIPHANY

All ye Gentile lands awake!
Thou, O Salem, rise and shine!
See the day spring o'er you break,
Heralding a morn divine,
Telling, God hath called to mind
Those who long in darkness pined.

Lo! the shadows flee away,
For our Light is come at length,
Brighter than all earthly day,
Source of being, life, and strength!
Whoso on this Light would gaze
Must forsake all evil ways.

Ah how blindly did we stray
Ere shone forth this glorious Sun,
Seeking each his separate way,
Leaving Heaven, unsought, unwon;
All our looks were earthward bent,
All our strength on earth was spent.

Earthly were our thoughts and low,
In the toils of Folly caught,
Tossed of Satan to and fro,
Counting goodness all for nought!
By the world and flesh deceived,
Heaven's true joys we disbelieved.

Then were hidden from our eyes
All the law and grace of God;
Rich and poor, the fools and wise,
Wanting light to find the road
Leading to the heavenly life,
Wandered lost in care and strife.

But the glory of the Lord
Hath arisen on us today,
We have seen the light outpoured
That must surely drive away
All things that to night belong,
All the sad earth's woe and wrong.

Thy arising, Lord, shall fill
All my thoughts in sorrow's hour;
Thy arising, Lord, shall still
All my dread of Death's dark power:
Through my smiles and through my tears
Still Thy light, O Lord, appears.

Let me, Lord, in peace depart
From this evil world to Thee;
Where Thyself sole Brightness art,
Thou hast kept a place for me:
In the shining city there
Crowns of light Thy saints shall wear.

JOHANN VON RIST
Wie wohl hast du gelabet
(O Living Bread from heaven)

1651 NEUER HIMLISCHER LIEDER

Translation by Catherine Winkworth
The Chorale Book for England, *#94*
London: Longman, Green, Longmans, Roberts, and Green, 1863

Holy Communion

O living Bread from heaven,
How richly hast Thou fed Thy guest!
The gifts Thou now hast given
Have fill'd my heart with joy and rest.
O wondrous food of blessing,
O cup that heals our woes,
My heart this gift possessing
In thankful songs o'erflows;
For while the life and strength in me
Were quicken'd by this food,
My soul hath gaz'd awhile on Thee,
My highest, only Good!

My God, Thou here hast led me
Within Thy temple's holiest place,
And there Thyself hast fed me
With all the treasures of Thy grace;
O boundless is Thy kindness,
And righteous is Thy power,
While I in sinful blindness
Am erring hour by hour;
And yet Thou comest, dost not spurn
A sinner, Lord, like me!
Ah how can I Thy love return,
What gift have I for Thee?

A heart that hath repented,
And mourns for sin with bitter sighs,—
Thou, Lord, art well-contented
With this my only sacrifice.
I know that in my weakness
Thou wilt despise me not,
But grant me in Thy meekness
The favour I have sought!
Yes, Thou wilt deign in grace to heed
The song that now I raise,

For meet and right is it indeed
That I should sing Thy praise.

Grant what I have partaken
May through Thy grace so work in me,
That sin be all forsaken,
And I may cleave alone to Thee,
And all my soul be heedful
How she Thy love may know:
For this alone is needful,
Thy love should in me glow;
Then let no beauty please mine eyes,
No joy allure my heart,
But what in Thee, my Saviour, lies,
What Thou dost here impart.

O well for me that, strengthen'd
With heavenly food and comfort here,
Howe'er my course be lengthen'd,
I now may serve Thee free from fear.
Away then earthly pleasure,
All earthly gifts are vain,
I seek a heavenly treasure,
My home I long to gain,
Where I shall live and praise my God,
And none my peace destroy,
Where all the soul is overflow'd
With pure eternal joy.

JOHANN VON RIST
Gott sei gelobet der allein
(Now God be praised, and God alone!)

1651 Neuer himlischer Lieder

Translation by Catherine Winkworth
Christian Singers of Germany, *pp. 192–94*
London: Macmillan and Co., 1869

Now God be praised, and God alone!
The Source of joy Thou art;
Thy love no stint or bound hath known,
But loves a happy heart,
And sends full many a bright clear day
To cheer us on our mortal way,
Bids many a cloud depart.

Yea, Lord, I thank Thy gracious power
That hath bestowed on me
A mind that lives from hour to hour
From sad foreboding free;
A mouth that Thou hast made so glad,
It smiles when other lips are sad,
And fails the trembling knee.

But Thou so oft hast blessings shed,
So oft bade sorrow cease,
That I with joy can eat my bread,
And lay me down in peace;
In Thy hands only lies my health,
'Tis Thou my honour and my wealth
Canst lessen or increase.

And so with joy I drink my cup,
And all this heart of mine,
O faithful God, to Thee looks up,
And sings when Thou dost shine;
With joy its daily task doth greet,
And doth its utmost, as is meet—
But, Lord, success is Thine.

Then take not, Lord, this joy away,
But let me cleave to Thee
Let pining melancholy stay
For ever far from me,
Nor sadness make me slow to hear
When Thou, O Lord, art drawing near,
And my heart's guest wouldst be.

Thy strength and solace let me prove,
And bid my soul to know
Who loveth Thee with childlike love,
No trial, fear, or woe,
Nor Satan's self can harm, nor death;
A friend of God, a man of faith,
Can conquer every foe.

Mere earthly pleasure cannot please,
It were not to my mind
To live in proud, luxurious ease,
And leave much gold behind;
My highest aim, while here I dwell,
Is to live piously and well,
To Thy will all resigned.

And ever do I take delight,
My Maker, to behold
Thy flowery earth, Thy sun's dear light,
All things Thy hand doth mould,
All living creatures that by field,
Or flood, or air, Thy praises yield,
Who formed them from of old.

So grant me then in weal and woe
Joyful and true to be;
And when life's lamp is burning low
And death at hand I see,
Then let this joy pierce through its pain,
And turn my very death to gain
Of endless joys with Thee

PAUL GERHARDT (1607–1676)
Wie soll ich dich empfangen
(Ah Lord, how shall I meet Thee)

1653 Crüger Praxis pietatis melica
(See use by Bach BMV 248)

Translation by Catherine Winkworth
The Chorale Book for England, *#21*
London: Longman, Green, Longmans, Roberts, and Green, 1863

Advent

O Lord, how shall I meet Thee,
How welcome Thee aright?
Thy people long to greet Thee,
My Hope, my heart's Delight!
O kindle, Lord, most holy,
Thy lamp within my breast
To do in spirit lowly
All that may please Thee best.

Thy Zion strews before Thee
Green boughs and fairest palms,
And I, too, will adore Thee
With joyous songs and psalms.
My heart shall bloom forever
For Thee with praises new
And from Thy name shall never
Withhold the honor due.

I lay in fetters, groaning,
Thou com'st to set me free;
I stood, my shame bemoaning,
Thou com'st to honor me;
A glory Thou dost give me,
A treasure safe on high,

That will not fail or leave me
As earthly riches fly.

Love caused Thy incarnation,
Love brought Thee down to me;
Thy thirst for my salvation
Procured my liberty.
O love beyond all telling,
That led Thee to embrace,
In love all love excelling,
Our lost and fallen race!

Rejoice, then, ye sad hearted,
Who sit in deepest gloom,
Who mourn o'er joys departed
And tremble at your doom.
Despair not, He is near you,
Yea, standing at the door,
Who best can help and cheer you
And bids you weep no more.

Ye need not toil nor languish
Nor ponder day and night
How in the midst of anguish
Ye draw Him by your might.
He comes, He comes all willing,
Moved by His love alone,
Your woes and troubles stilling;
For all to Him are known.

Sin's debt, that fearful burden,
Let not your souls distress;
Your guilt the Lord will pardon
And cover by His grace.
He comes, for men procuring
The peace of sin forgiven,
For all God's sons securing
Their heritage in heaven.

What though the foes be raging,
Heed not their craft and spite;
Your Lord, the battle waging,
Will scatter all their might.
He comes, a King most glorious,
And all His earthly foes
In vain His course victorious
Endeavor to oppose.

He comes to judge the nations,
A terror to His foes,
A Light of consolations
And blessed Hope to those
Who love the Lord's appearing.
O glorious Sun, now come,
Send forth Thy beams so cheering,
And guide us safely home.

PAUL GERHARDT
Frölich soll mein Herze springen
(All my heart this night rejoices)

1653 CRÜGER PRAXIS PIETATIS MELICA

Translation by Catherine Winkworth
The Chorale Book for England, *#31*
London: Longman, Green, Longmans, Roberts, and Green, 1863

CHRISTMAS

All my heart this night rejoices,
As I hear,
Far and near,
Sweetest angel voices;
"Christ is born," their choirs are singing,
Till the air
Ev'rywhere
Now with joy is ringing.

Hark! a voice from yonder manger,
Soft and sweet,
Doth entreat,
"Flee from woe and danger;
Brethren, come, from all doth grieve you,
You are freed,
All you need
I will surely give you."

Come then, let us hasten yonder;
Here let all,
Great and small,
Kneel in awe and wonder,
Love Him who with love is yearning;
Hail the Star
That from far
Bright with hope is burning!

Ye who pine in weary sadness,
Weep no more,
For the door
Now is found of gladness.
Cling to Him, for He will guide you
Where no cross,
Pain or loss
Can again betide you.

Hither come, ye heavy-hearted,
Who for sin
Deep within,
Long and sore have smarted;
For the poison'd wounds you're feeling
Help is near,
One is here
Mighty for their healing!

Hither come, ye poor and wretched!
Know His will
Is to fill

Every hand outstretched;
Here are riches without measure,
Here forget
All regret,
Fill your hearts with treasure.

Thee, dear Lord, with heed I'll cherish,
Live to Thee,
And with Thee
Dying, shall not perish;
But shall dwell with Thee for ever,
Far on high,
In the joy
That can alter never.

PAUL GERHARDT
O Haupt voll Blut und Wunden
(O sacred Head, now wounded)

1656 CRÜGER PRAXIS PIETATIS MELICA
(See use by Bach BMV 155, 244)

Translation by James W. Alexander
Philip Schaff, Christ in Song—Hymns of Immanuel, *Vol. 1, p. 178*
New York: Anson D. F. Randolph and Co., 1895

O sacred Head, now wounded,
with grief and shame weighed down,
Now scornfully surrounded
with thorns, Thine only crown;
How pale Thou art with anguish,
with sore abuse and scorn!
How does that visage languish,
which once was bright as morn!

What Thou, my Lord, hast suffered,
was all for sinners' gain;
Mine, mine was the transgression,
but Thine the deadly pain.

Lo, here I fall, my Savior!
'Tis I deserve Thy place;
Look on me with Thy favor,
vouchsafe to me Thy grace.

Men mock and taunt and jeer Thee,
Thou noble countenance,
Though mighty worlds shall fear Thee
and flee before Thy glance.
How art thou pale with anguish,
with sore abuse and scorn!
How doth Thy visage languish
that once was bright as morn!

Now from Thy cheeks has vanished
their color once so fair;
From Thy red lips is banished
the splendor that was there.
Grim death, with cruel rigor,
hath robbed Thee of Thy life;
Thus Thou hast lost Thy vigor,
Thy strength in this sad strife.

My burden in Thy Passion,
Lord, Thou hast borne for me,
For it was my transgression
which brought this woe on Thee.
I cast me down before Thee,
wrath were my rightful lot;
Have mercy, I implore Thee;
Redeemer, spurn me not!

What language shall I borrow
to thank Thee, dearest friend,
For this Thy dying sorrow,
Thy pity without end?
O make me Thine forever,
and should I fainting be,

Lord, let me never, never
outlive my love to Thee.

My Shepherd, now receive me;
my Guardian, own me Thine.
Great blessings Thou didst give me,
O source of gifts divine.
Thy lips have often fed me
with words of truth and love;
Thy Spirit oft hath led me
to heavenly joys above.

Here I will stand beside Thee,
from Thee I will not part;
O Savior, do not chide me!
When breaks Thy loving heart,
When soul and body languish
in death's cold, cruel grasp,
Then, in Thy deepest anguish,
Thee in mine arms I'll clasp.

The joy can never be spoken,
above all joys beside,
When in Thy body broken
I thus with safety hide.
O Lord of Life, desiring
Thy glory now to see,
Beside Thy cross expiring,
I'd breathe my soul to Thee.

My Savior, be Thou near me
when death is at my door;
Then let Thy presence cheer me,
forsake me nevermore!
When soul and body languish,
oh, leave me not alone,
But take away mine anguish
by virtue of Thine own!

Be Thou my consolation,
my shield when I must die;
Remind me of Thy passion
when my last hour draws nigh.
Mine eyes shall then behold Thee,
upon Thy cross shall dwell,
My heart by faith enfolds Thee.
Who dieth thus dies well.

PAUL GERHARDT
Ein Lämmlein geht und trägt die Schuld
(A Lamb goes uncomplaining forth)

1648 Crüger Praxis pietatis melica

Composite translation in the public domain
Internet Christian Library
Available on the iclnet.org website

A Lamb goes uncomplaining forth,
The guilt of all men bearing;
And laden with the sins of earth,
None else the burden sharing!
Goes patient on, grow weak and faint,
To slaughter led without complaint,
That spotless life to offer;
Bears shame and stripes, and wounds and death,
Anguish and mockery, and saith,
"Willing all this I suffer."

This Lamb is Christ, the soul's great Friend,
The Lamb of God, our Savior;
Him God the Father chose to send
To gain for us His favor.
"Go forth, My Son," the Father saith,
"And free men from the fear of death,
From guilt and condemnation.
The wrath and stripes are hard to bear,

But by Thy Passion men shall share
The fruit of Thy salvation."

"Yea, Father, yea, most willingly
I'll bear what Thou commandest;
My will conforms to Thy decree,
I do what Thou demandest."
O wondrous Love, what hast Thou done!
The Father offers up His Son!
The Son, content, descendeth!
O Love, how strong Thou art to save!
Thou beddest Him within the grave
Whose word the mountains rendeth.

From morn till eve my theme shall be
Thy mercy's wondrous measure;
To sacrifice myself for Thee
Shall be my aim and pleasure.
My stream of life shall ever be
A current flowing ceaselessly,
Thy constant praise outpouring.
I'll treasure in my memory,
O Lord, all Thou hast done for me,
Thy gracious love adoring.

Of death I am no more afraid,
New life from Thee is flowing;
Thy cross affords me cooling shade
When noonday's sun is glowing.
When by my grief I am opprest,
On Thee my weary soul shall rest
Serenely as on pillows.
Thou art my Anchor when by woe
My bark is driven to and fro
On trouble's surging billows.

And when Thy glory I shall see
And taste Thy kingdom's pleasure,
Thy blood my royal robe shall be,

My joy beyond all measure.
When I appear before Thy throne,
Thy righteousness shall be my crown,
With these I need not hide me.
And there, in garments richly wrought
As Thine own bride, I shall be brought
To stand in joy beside Thee.

PAUL GERHARDT
Auf, auf mein Herz mit Freuden
(Awake, my heart, with gladness)

1648 Crüger Praxis pietatis melica
(See use by Bach BMV 441)

Translation by John Kelly
Paul Gerhardt's Spiritual Songs, *#71 alt.*
London: Alexander Strahan, 1867

Easter

Awake, my heart, with gladness,
See what today is done;
How, after gloom and sadness,
Comes forth the glorious Sun.
My Savior there was laid
Where our bed must be made
When to the realms of light
Our spirit wings its flight.

The foe in triumph shouted
When Christ lay in the tomb;
But, lo, he now is routed,
His boast is turned to gloom.
For Christ again is free;
In glorious victory
He Who is strong to save
Has triumphed o'er the grave.

This is a sight that gladdens;
What peace it doth impart!
Now nothing ever saddens
The joy within my heart.
No gloom shall ever shake,
No foe shall ever take,
The hope which God's own Son
In love for me hath won.

Now hell, its prince, the Devil
Of all their powers are shorn;
Now I am safe from evil,
And sin I laugh to scorn.
Grim Death with all his might
Cannot my soul affright;
He is a powerless form,
Howe'er he rave and storm.

The world against me rageth
Its fury I disdain;
Though bitter war it wageth
Its work is all in vain.
My heart from care is free,
No trouble troubles me.
Misfortune now is play
And night is bright as day.

Now I will cling forever
To Christ, my Savior true;
My Lord will leave me never,
Whate'er He passeth through.
He rends Death's iron chain,
He breaks through sin and pain,
He shatters hell's dark thrall,
I follow Him through all.

To halls of heavenly splendor
With Him I penetrate;
And trouble ne'er may hinder

Nor make me hesitate.
Let tempests rage at will,
My Savior shields me still;
He grants abiding peace
And bids all tumult cease.

He brings me to the portal
That leads to bliss untold,
Whereon this rhyme immortal
Is found in script of gold:
"Who there My cross hath shared
Finds here a crown prepared;
Who there with Me hath died
Shall here be glorified."

PAUL GERHARDT
O Jesu Christ, mein schönstes Licht
(Jesus, Thy boundless love to me)

1653 Crüger Praxis pietatis melica

Translation by John Wesley, alt.
Hymns and Sacred Poems
London: William Strahan, 1739

Jesus, Thy boundless love to me
No thought can reach, no tongue declare;
Unite my thankful heart to Thee
And reign without a rival there.
To Thee alone, dear Lord, I live;
Myself to Thee, dear Lord, I give.

Oh, grant that nothing in my soul
May dwell but Thy pure love alone!
O, may Thy love possess me whole,
My Joy, my Treasure, and my Crown!
All coldness from my heart remove;
My every act, word, thought, be love.

O Love, how cheering is Thy ray!
All pain before Thy presence flies;
Care, anguish, sorrow, melt away
Where'er Thy healing beams arise.
O Jesus, nothing may I see,
Nothing desire or seek, but Thee!

This love unwearied I pursue
And dauntlessly to Thee aspire.
O, may Thy love my hope renew,
Burn in my soul like heavenly fire!
And day and night be all my care
To guard this sacred treasure there.

O, draw me, Savior, e'er to Thee;
So shall I run and never tire.
With gracious words still comfort me;
Be Thou my Hope, my sole Desire.
Free me from every guilt and fear;
No sin can harm if Thou art near.

Still let Thy love point out my way;
What wondrous things Thy love hath wrought!
Still lead me lest I go astray;
Direct my work, inspire my thought;
And if I fall, soon may I hear
Thy voice and know that love is near!

In suffering be Thy love my peace,
In weakness be Thy love my power;
And when the storms of life shall cease,
O Jesus, in that final hour,
Be Thou my Rod and Staff and Guide
And draw me safely to Thy side!

PAUL GERHARDT
Sollt' ich meinem Gott nicht singen
(I will sing my Maker's praises)

1653 Crüger Praxis pietatis melica

Composite translation in the public domain
Internet Christian Library
Available on the iclnet.org website

I will sing my Maker's praises
And in Him most joyful be,
For in all things I see traces
Of His tender love to me.
Nothing else than love could move Him
With such sweet and tender care
Evermore to raise and bear
All who try to serve and love Him.
All things else have but their day,
God's great love abides for aye.

Yea, so dear did He esteem me
That His Son He loved so well
He hath given to redeem me
From the quenchless flames of hell.
O Thou Spring of boundless blessing,
How could e'er my feeble mind
Of Thy depth the bottom find
Though my efforts were unceasing?
All things else have but their day,
God's great love abides for aye.

All that for my soul is needful
He with loving care provides,
Nor of that is He unheedful
Which my body needs besides.
When my strength cannot avail me,
When my powers can do no more,
Doth my God His strength outpour;

In my need He doth not fail me.
All things else have but their day,
God's great love abides for aye.

When I sleep, He still is near me,
O'er me rests His guardian eye;
And new gifts and blessings cheer me
When the morning streaks the sky.
Were it not for God's protection,
Had His countenance not been
Here my guide, I had not seen
E'er the end of my affliction.
All things else have but their day,
God's great love abides for aye.

As a father never turneth
Wholly from a wayward child,
For the prodigal still yearneth,
Longing to be reconciled,
So my many sins and errors
Find a tender, pardoning God,
Chastening frailty with His rod,
Not in vengeance, with His terrors.
All things else have but their day,
God's great love abides for aye.

Since, then, neither change nor coldness
In my Father's love can be,
Lo! I lift my hands with boldness,
As Thy child I come to Thee.
Grant me grace, O God, I pray Thee,
That I may with all my might,
All my lifetime, day and night,
Love and trust Thee and obey Thee
And, when this brief life is o'er,
Praise and love Thee evermore.

PAUL GERHARDT
Was Gott gefällt O frommes Kind
(What pleases God, O pious soul)

1653 Crüger Praxis pietatis melica

Translation by Catherine Winkworth
Lyra Germanica, Second Series: The Christian Life, *pp. 193–95*
London: Longman, Brown, Green, Longmans, and Roberts, 1858

What pleases God, O pious soul,
Accept with joy, though thunders roll
And tempests lower on every side,
Thou knowest nought can thee betide
But pleases God.

The best will is our Father's will,
And we may rest there calm and still,
Oh make it hour by hour thine own,
And wish for nought but that alone
Which pleases God.

His thought is aye the wisest thought,
How oft man's wisdom comes to nought,
Mistake or weakness in it lurks,
It brings forth ill, and seldom works
What pleases God.

His mind is aye the gentlest mind,
His will and deeds are ever kind,
He blesses when against us speaks
The evil world, that rarely seeks
What pleases God.

His heart is aye the truest heart,
He bids all grief and harm depart,
Defending, shielding day and night
The man who knows and loves aright
What pleases God.

He governs all things here below,
In Him lie all our weal and woe,
He bears the world within His hand,
And so to us bear sea and land
What pleases God.

And o'er His little flock He yearns,
And when to evil ways it turns,
The Father's rod oft smiteth sore,
Until it learns to do once more
What pleases God.

What most would profit us He knows,
And ne'er denies aught good to those
Who with their utmost strength pursue
The right, and only care to do
What pleases God.

If this be so, then World, from me
Keep if thou wilt, what pleases thee;
But thou, my soul, be well content
With God and all things He hath sent;
As pleases God.

And must thou suffer here and there,
Cling but the firmer to His care,
For all things are beneath His sway,
And must in very truth obey
What pleases God.

True faith will grasp His mercy fast,
And hope bring patience at the last,
Then both within thy heart enshrine,
So shall the heritage be thine
That pleases God.

To thee for ever shall be given
A kingdom and a crown in heaven,
And there shall be fulfill'd in thee,
And thou shalt taste and hear and see
What pleases God.

PAUL GERHARDT
Ist Gott für mich, so trete
(If God Himself be for me)

1656 Crüger Praxis pietatis melica

Translation based on Richard Massie; in the public domain
Internet Christian Library
Available on the iclnet.org website

If God Himself be for me,
I may a host defy;
For when I pray, before me
My foes, confounded, fly.
If Christ, my Head and Master,
Befriend me from above,
What foe or what disaster
Can drive me from His love?

This I believe, yea, rather,
Of this I make my boast,
That God is my dear Father,
The Friend who loves me most,
And that, whate'er betide me,
My Savior is at hand
Through stormy seas to guide me
And bring me safe to land.

I build on this foundation,
That Jesus and His blood
Alone are my salvation,
The true, eternal good.
Without Him all that pleases
Is valueless on earth;
The gifts I owe to Jesus
Alone my love are worth.

My Jesus is my Splendor,
My Sun, my Light, alone;
Were He not my Defender

Before God's awe-full throne,
I never should find favor
And mercy in His sight,
But be destroyed forever
As darkness by the light.

He canceled my offenses,
Delivered me from death;
He is the Lord who cleanses
My soul from sin through faith.
In Him I can be cheerful,
Bold, and undaunted aye;
In Him I am not fearful
Of God's great Judgment Day.

Naught, naught, can now condemn me
Nor set my hope aside;
Now hell no more can claim me,
Its fury I deride.
No sentence e'er reproves me,
No ill destroys my peace;
For Christ, my Savior, loves me
And shields me with His grace.

His Spirit in me dwelleth,
And o'er my mind He reigns.
All sorrow He dispelleth
And soothes away all pains.
He crowns His work with blessing
And helpeth me to cry,
"My Father!" without ceasing,
To Him who dwells on high.

And when my soul is lying
Weak, trembling, and opprest,
He pleads with groans and sighing
That cannot be exprest;
But God's quick eye discerns them,
Although they give no sound,

And into language turns them
E'en in the heart's deep ground.

To mine His Spirit speaketh
Sweet word of holy cheer,
How God to him that seeketh
For rest is always near
And how He hath erected
A city fair and new,
Where what our faith expected
We evermore shall view.

In yonder home doth flourish
My heritage, my lot;
Though here I die and perish,
My heaven shall fail me not.
Though care my life oft saddens
And causeth tears to flow,
The light of Jesus gladdens
And sweetens every woe.

Who clings with resolution
To Him whom Satan hates
Must look for persecution;
For him the burden waits
Of mockery, shame, and losses,
Heaped on his blameless head;
A thousand plagues and crosses
Will be his daily bread.

From me this is not hidden,
Yet I am not afraid;
I leave my cares, as bidden,
To whom my vows were paid.
Though life and limb it cost me
And everything I won,
Unshaken shall I trust Thee
And cleave to Thee alone.

Though earth be rent asunder,
Thou'rt mine eternally;
Not fire nor sword nor thunder
Shall sever me from Thee;
Not hunger, thirst, nor danger,
Not pain nor poverty
Nor mighty princes' anger
Shall ever hinder me.

No angel and no gladness,
No throne, no pomp, no show,
No love, no hate, no sadness,
No pain, no depth of woe,
No scheme of man's contrivance,
However small or great,
Shall draw me from Thy guidance
Nor from Thee separate.

My heart for joy is springing
And can no more be sad,
'Tis full of mirth and singing,
Sees naught but sunshine glad.
The Sun that cheers my spirit
Is Jesus Christ, my King;
That which I shall inherit
Makes me rejoice and sing.

PAUL GERHARDT
Befiehl du deine Wege
(Commit whatever grieves thee)

1656 Crüger Praxis pietatis melica
(See use by Bach BMV 153, 244, 270, 271)

Translation based on John Kelly 1867; in the public domain
Internet Christian Library
Available on the iclnet.org website

Commit whatever grieves thee
Into the gracious hands
Of Him Who never leaves thee,
Who Heav'n and earth commands.
Who points the clouds their courses,
Whom winds and waves obey,
He will direct thy footsteps
And find for thee a way.

On Him place Thy reliance
If thou wouldst be secure;
His work thou must consider
If thine is to endure.
By anxious sighs and grieving
And self tormenting care
God is not moved to giving;
All must be gained by prayer.

Thy truth and grace, O Father,
Most surely see and know
Both what is good and evil
For mortal man below.
According to Thy counsel
Thou wilt Thy work pursue;
And what Thy wisdom chooseth
Thy might will always do.

Thy hand is never shortened,
All things must serve Thy might;
Thine every act is blessing,
Thy path is purest light.
Thy work no man can hinder,
Thy purpose none can stay,
Since Thou to bless Thy children
Wilt always find a way.

Though all the powers of evil
The will of God oppose,

His purpose will not falter,
His pleasure onward goes.
Whate'er God's will resolveth,
Whatever He intends,
Will always be accomplished
True to His aims and ends.

Then hope, my feeble spirit,
And be thou undismayed;
God helps in every trial
And makes thee unafraid.
Await His time with patience,
Then shall thine eyes behold
The sun of joy and gladness
His brightest beams unfold.

Arise, my soul, and banish
Thy anguish and thy care.
Away with thoughts that sadden
And heart and mind ensnare!
Thou art not lord and master
Of thine own destiny;
Enthroned in highest Heaven,
God rules in equity.

Leave all to His direction;
In wisdom He doth reign,
And in a way most wondrous
His course He will maintain.
Soon He, His promise keeping,
With wonder-working skill
Shall put away the sorrows
That now thy spirit fill.

A while His consolation
He may to thee deny,
And seem as though in trial
He far from thee would fly;
A while distress and anguish

May compass thee around,
Nor to thy supplication
An answering voice be found.

But if thou perseverest,
Thou shalt deliverance find.
Behold, all unexpected
He will thy soul unbind
And from the heavy burden
Thy heart will soon set free;
And thou wilt see the blessing
He had in mind for thee.

O faithful child of Heaven,
How blessèd shalt thou be!
With songs of glad thanksgiving
A crown awaiteth thee.
Into thy hand thy Maker
Will give the victor's palm,
And thou to thy Deliverer
Shalt sing a joyous psalm

Give, Lord, this consummation
To all our heart's distress;
Our hands, our feet, e'er strengthen,
In death our spirits bless.
Thy truth and thy protection
Grant evermore, we pray,
And in celestial glory
Shall end our destined way.

PAUL GERHARDT
Jesu, allerliebster Bruder
(Jesus! Thou, my dearest Brother)

BASED ON JOHANN ARNDT'S PARADIESGÄRTLEIN 1, 33, 92
1661 CRÜGER PRAXIS PIETATIS MELICA

Translation by John Kelly
Gerhardt's Spiritual Songs, *pp. 112–17*
London: Alexander Strahan, 1867

Jesus! Thou, my dearest Brother,
Who does well to me intend,
Thou mine Anchor, Mast, and Rudder,
And my truest Bosom-Friend.
To Thee, ere was earth or heaven,
Had the race of man been given;
Thou, e'en me, poor guest of earth,
Chosen hadst before my birth.

Thou art free from guile, Lord! Ever
Innocent of all that's base;
But on this sad earth whenever
I in meditation gaze,
There I find deception living;
Who excelleth in deceiving,
Who the bests dissemble can,
He's the best and wisest man.

Hollow and unfaithful ever
Is the friendship of the earth;
Seemth she a man to favour!
'Tis but for the gold he's worth;
Are we prosp'rous, do we flourish?
She will smile on us, and nourish;
Doth misfortune o'er us low'r?
She forsakes us in that hour.

Drive away from me, and shield me
From such instability;

If I, Father, have defil'd me
(For I also human be)
With this mire, and did I ever
Falsehood love, oh! Now deliver.
All my guilt I own to Thee,
Patience give, and grace to me!

May I ne'er be overtaken
By the evils Thou hast said
Come on those who've truth forsaken,
And with wares deceptive trade;
For Thou sayest Thou disownest,
As abomination shunnest,
Ev'ry hypocrite's false mood,
Who talks, but doth not the good.

May my heart be constant ever,
Faithful still to every friend;
When to grief Thou dost deliver
Them, and 'neath the cross they bend,
May I even then ne'er shun them,
But like unto Thee, Lord, own them,
Who, when we were poor and bare,
Tended'st us with fondest care.

After Thy will, Saviour, give me
One in whom I may confide,
Who will faithful counsel give me
When my heart is sorely tried;
To whom I may freely utter
All I feel, with nought to fetter,
In the measure I may need,
Till my heart from care is freed.

Oh! Let David's bliss betide me,
Give to me a Jonathan
Who will come and stand beside me
Like a rock, though every man
From my company should sever,

Who his heart will give me ever,
Who'll stand firm in every hour,
When sun shines or tempests low'r.

Out of all the men who're living,
Choose me a believing friend,
Who to Thee is firmly cleaving,
On Thine arm doth aye depend;
Who may by Thy will relieve me,
Help and comfort ever give me,
Help, from sympathizing heart,
Comfort, when I feel grief's smart.

When 'tis only the mouth loveth,
Then the love is ill bestow'd;
Whose love but to good words moveth
While he keeps a hateful mood,
Whom self-interest rules ever,
Who when honey fails, stays never,
But escapeth speedily,—
Ever far be such from me!

In my weakness and my sinning,
Move my friend to speak to me,
By his words of kindness winning,
Never as an enemy.
Who reproves in love and sadness
Is like him, in days of gladness,
Who pours balsam over me
That by Jordan floweth free.

Riches great were I possessing,
Priceless were my property;
Jesus! Did Thy hand such blessing
Graciously bestow on me,
Were such friend, Lord! ever near me,
By His constancy to cheer me;
Who doth honour Thee, and fear
He hath such a treasure near.

Good friends like to staves are ever,
Whereon men lean as they go,
That the weak one can deliver,
When he slides and lieth low:
Sad his case who such ne'er knoweth,
Who through life all friendless goeth,
Weary is his lonely way,
When he falls, to help who stay?

Gracious Saviour! Let it please Thee,
Be my Friend in every hour,
Be my Friend, till death release me,
Be my faithful Staff of pow'r!
When Thou to Thyself wilt bind me.
Then a heart Thou soon wilt find me,
By Thy Holy Spirit fir'd
With good thoughts to me inspir'd.

PAUL GERHARDT
Auf den Nebel folgt die Sonn'
(Cometh sunshine after rain)

1659 Crüger Praxis pietatis melica

Translation by Catherine Winkworth
The Chorale Book for England, *#4*
London: Longman, Green, Longmans, Roberts, and Green, 1863

Cometh sunshine after rain,
After mourning joy again,
After heavy bitter grief
Dawneth surely sweet relief!
And my soul, who from her height
Sank to realms of woe and night,
Wingeth new to heav'n her flight.

Bitter anguish have I borne,
Keen regret my heart hath torn,
Sorrow dimm'd my weeping eyes,

Satan blinded me with lies;
Yet at last am I set free,
Help, protection, love, to me
Once more true companions be.

None was ever left a prey,
None was ever turn'd away,
Who had given himself to God,
And on Him had cast his load.
Who in God his hope hath placed
Shall not life in pain outwaste,
Fullest joy he yet shall taste.

Though to-day may not fulfil
All thy hopes, have patience still,
For perchance to-morrow's sun
Sees thy happier days begun;
As God willeth march the hours,
Bringing joy at last in showers,
When whate'er we ask'd is ours.

Now as long as here I roam,
On this earth have house and home,
Shall this wondrous gleam from Thee
Shine through all my memory.
To my God I yet will cling,
All my life the praises sing
That from thankful hearts outspring.

Every sorrow, every smart,
That the Eternal Father's heart
Hath appointed me of yore,
Or hath yet for me in store,
As my life flows on, I'll take
Calmly, gladly for His sake,
No more faithless murmurs make.

I will meet distress and pain,
I will greet e'en Death's dark reign,
I will lay me in the grave,

With a heart still glad and brave;
Whom the Strongest doth defend,
Whom the Highest counts His friend,
Cannot perish in the end.

PAUL GERHARDT
Die güldne Sonne (The golden morning)

1666 Johann Ebeling P. Gerhardi Geistliche Andachten
(See use by Bach BMV 451)

Translation by John Kelly
Paul Gerhardt's Spiritual Songs, *pp. 270–76*
London: Alexander Strahan, 1867

The golden morning,
Joy her adorning,
With splendor near us
Draweth, to cheer us
With her heart-refreshing and lovely light.
My head and members
Lay wrapt all in slumbers,
But now awaking,
And sleep from me shaking,
Heaven's bless'd sunshine doth gladden my sight.

Mine eye beholdeth
What God upholdeth,
Made for His glory,
To tell the story
To us of His power and might so great,
And where the Father
The faithful shall gather
In peace, whenever
Earth's ties they shall sever
And leave this mortal and perishing state.

Come ye with singing,
To God be bringing

Goods and each blessing—
All we're possessing—
All be to God as an offering brought.
Hearts with love glowing,
With praises o'erflowing,
Thanksgiving voices,
In these God rejoices,
All other off-rings without them are nought.

To morn and even
His thoughts are given,
Increase He giveth,
Sorrow relieveth,
These are the works that He doeth alone.
When we are sleeping
Watch is He aye keeping,
When we're awaking
Care still of us taking,
He makes the light of His grace to shine down.

My thoughts I've raised
To Thee who'rt praised
For aye in Heaven!
Success be given,
May all my endeavours unhinder'd be!
From ev'ry evil
And work of the Devil,
All malice ever,
Oh do Thou deliver!
In all Thy precepts establish Thou me!

May't pleasure give me,
May no pain grieve me
To see flow over
The cup my brother
Or neighbor hath, with Thy blessings so free.
Covetous burning
And unchristian yearning
For ill possessions,

Blot out such transgressions,
Cast them, O Father! All into the sea!

The life we're living
What is it giving?
Ere any thinketh
To ground it sinketh,
Soon as the breath of the grave on it blow.
All things together
Dread ruin must shiver,
The earth and heaven
They must perish even,
Wrapt in the flames that shall ardently glow!

All—all decayeth,
But God still stayeth
His thoughts they waver
A moment never,
His word and will both eternally 'dure.
His grave and favour
Uninjur'd are ever,
Deadly wounds healing,
The heart with peace filling,
Health here and yonder to us they ensure.

My God for ever
Do Thou deliver!
Shield me, and cover
My debts all over,
In grace, Thine eyes from my sins turn away.
Govern and guide me,
Be ever beside me,
As it is pleasing
To Thee! Am I placing
All in Thy hand and disposal for aye.

Wilt Thou give ever
To me whatever
My life is needing?

May I be heeding
Ever the faithful word spoken by Thee.
God is the highest,
The greatest, the nighest,
Gracious is ever,
Is changeable never,
Of all our treasures the noblest is He.

Wilt Thou then grieve me,
Gall to drink give me?
Must I be passing
Through cares harassing?
Do then as seemeth it good unto Thee.
Whate'er supporteth,
Is useful or hurteth,
Thou knowest ever,
And chastenest never
Too much, in case we o'erburden'd should be.

Trial God sendeth,
Speedily endeth
The storms of ocean,
The wind's commotion
Lightens the sunshine so gladsome and bright.
Fulness of pleasure
And glorious leisure,
Will then be given
To me in yon Heaven
Whither my thoughts aye to turn take delight.

PAUL GERHARDT
Nun ruhen alle Wälder
(Now all the woods are sleeping)

1653 CRÜGER PRAXIS PIETATIS MELICA
(See use by Bach BMV 392)

Translation by Catherine Winkworth
The Chorale Book for England, *#169*
London: Longman, Green, Longmans, Roberts, and Green, 1863

EVENING HYMN

Now all the woods are sleeping,
And night and stillness creeping
O'er city, man, and beast;
But thou, my heart, awake thee,
To pray'r awhile betake thee,
And praise thy Maker ere thou rest.

O Sun, where art thou vanish'd?
The Night thy reign hath banish'd,
Thy ancient foe, the Night.
Farewell, a brighter glory
My Jesus sheddeth o'er me,
All clear within me shines His light.

The last faint beam is going,
The golden stars are glowing
In yonder dark-blue deep;
And such the glory given
When called of God to heaven,
On earth no more we pine and weep.

The body hastes to slumber,
These garments now but cumber,
And as I lay them by
I ponder how the spirit
Puts off the flesh t' inherit
A shining robe with Christ on high.

Now thought and labour ceases,
For Night the tired releases
And bids sweet rest begin:
My heart, there comes a morrow
Shall set thee free from sorrow,
And all the dreary toil of sin.

Ye aching limbs! now rest you,
For toil hath sore oppress'd you,
Lie down, my weary head:
A sleep shall once o'ertake you
From which earth ne'er shall wake you,
Within a narrower, colder bed.

My heavy eyes are closing;
When I lie deep reposing,
Soul, body, where are ye?
To helpless sleep I yield them,
Oh let Thy mercy shield them,
Thou sleepless Eye, their guardian be!

My Jesus, stay Thou by me,
And let no foe come nigh me,
Safe shelter'd by Thy wing;
But would the foe alarm me,
Oh let him never harm me,
But still Thine angels round me sing!

My loved ones, rest securely,
From every peril surely
Our God will guard your heads;
And happy slumbers send you,
And bid His hosts attend you,
And golden-arm'd watch o'er your beds.

GEORG NEUMARK (1621–1681)
Wer nur den lieben Gott lässt walten
(If thou but suffer God to guide thee)

1657 Fortgepflantzter musikalisch-poetischer Lustwald
(See use by Bach BMV 21, 88, 93, 197, 434)

Translation by Catherine Winkworth
The Chorale Book for England, *#134*
London: Longman, Green, Longmans, Roberts, and Green, 1863

If thou but suffer God to guide thee,
And hope in Him through all thy ways,
He'll give thee strength whate'er betide thee,
And bear thee through the evil days.
Who trust in God's unchanging love
Builds on the rock that nought can move.

What can these anxious cares avail thee,
These never-ceasing moans and sighs?
What can it help, if thou bewail thee
O'er each dark moment as it flies?
Our cross and trials do but press
The heavier for our bitterness.

Only be still and wait His leisure
In cheerful hope, with heart content
To take whate'er thy Father's pleasure
And all-deserving love hath sent,
Nor doubt our inmost wants are known
To Him who chose us for His own.

He knows the time for joy, and truly
Will send it when He sees it meet,
When He has tried and purged thee throughly
And finds thee free from all deceit,
He comes to thee all unaware
And makes thee own His loving care.

Nor think amid the heat of trial
That God hath cast thee off unheard,
That he whose hopes meet no denial
Must surely be of God preferred;
Time passes and much change doth bring,
And sets a bound to everything.

All are alike before the Highest.
'Tis easy to our God, we know,
To raise thee up though low thou liest,
To make the rich man poor and low;
True wonders still by Him are wrought
Who setteth up and brings to nought.

Sing, pray, and keep His ways unswerving,
So do thine own part faithfully,
And trust His Word, though undeserving,
Thou yet shalt find it true for thee!
God never yet forsook at need
The soul that trusted Him indeed.

JOHANN FRANCK (1618–1677)
Jesu, meine Freude (Jesu, priceless treasure)

1653 CRÜGER PRAXIS PIETATIS MELICA
(See use by Bach BMV 64, 81, 227, 358)

Translation by Catherine Winkworth
The Chorale Book for England, *#151*
London: Longman, Green, Longmans, Roberts, and Green, 1863

Jesus, priceless treasure,
Source of purest pleasure,
Truest Friend to me;
Ah! how long I've panted,
And my heart hath fainted,
Thirsting, Lord, for Thee!
Thine I am, O spotless Lamb,

I will suffer nought to hide Thee,
Nought I ask beside Thee.

In Thine arm I rest me,
Foes who would molest me
Cannot reach me here;
Though the earth be shaking,
Every heart be quaking,
Jesus calms my fear;
Sin and hell in conflict fell
With their bitter storms assail me,
Jesus will not fail me.

Wealth, I will not heed thee,
For I do not need thee,
Jesus is my choice;
Honours, ye may glisten,
But I will not listen
To your tempting voice;
Pain or loss, nor shame nor cross,
E'er to leave my Lord shall move me,
Since He deigns to love me.

Farewell, thou who choosest
Earth, and heaven refusest,
Thou wilt tempt in vain;
Farewell, sins, nor blind me,
Get ye all behind me,
Come not forth again:
Past your hour, O Pride and Power;
Worldly life, thy bonds I sever,
Farewell now for ever!

Hence, all fears and sadness,
For the Lord of gladness,
Jesus, enters in;
They who love the Father,
Though the storms may gather,
Still have peace within;

Yea, whate'er I here must bear,
Still in Thee lies purest pleasure,
Jesu, priceless treasure!

JOHANN FRANCK
Du o schönes Weltgebäude
(Let who will in thee rejoice)

1653 CRÜGER PRAXIS PIETATIS MELICA

Translation by Catherine Winkworth
Lyra Germanica: The Christian Year, *p. 182*
London: Longman, Green, Longmans, and Roberts, 1863

Let who will in thee rejoice,
O thou fair and wondrous earth!
Ever anguished sorrow's voice
Pierces through thy seeming mirth;
Let thy vain delights be given
Unto them who love not Heaven,
My desire is fixed on Thee,
Jesus, dearest far to me!

Weary souls with toil outworn,
Drooping 'neath the glaring light,
Wish that soon the coming morn
Might be quenched again in night,
That their toils might find a close
In a soft and deep repose;
I but wish to rest in Thee,
Jesus, dearest far to me!

Others dare the treacherous wave,
Hidden rock and shifting wind—
Storm and danger let them brave,
Earthly good or wealth to find;
Faith shall wing my upward flight
Far above yon starry height,

Till I find myself with Thee,
Jesus, dearest Friend to me!

Many a time ere now I said,
Many a time again shall say,
Would to God that I were dead,
Would that in my grave I lay!
Rest were mine, and sweet my lot
Where the body hindereth not,
And the soul can ever be,
Jesus, dearest Lord, with Thee!

Come, O Death, thou twin of Sleep,
Lead me hence,—I pray thee come,
Loose my rudder, through the deep
Guide my vessel safely home.
Thy approach who will may fly,
'Twere a joy to me to die,
Death but opes the gates to Thee,
Jesus, dearest Friend to me!

Would that I today might leave
This my earthly prison here,
And my crown of joy receive
Waiting me in yon bright sphere!
In that home of joy, where dwell
Hosts of angels, would I tell
How the Godhead shines in Thee
Jesus, dearest Lord to me!

But not yet the gates of gold
I may see nor enter in,
Nor the heavenly fields behold,
But must sit and mourning spin
Life's dark thread on earth below;
Let my thoughts then hourly go
Whither I myself would be,
Jesus, dearest Lord, with Thee!

JOHANN FRANCK
Schmücke dich o liebe Seele
(Deck thyself, my soul, with gladness)

1653 Crüger Praxis pietatis melica
(See use by Bach BMV 180)

Translation by Catherine Winkworth
Lyra Germanica, Second Series: The Christian Life, *pp. 94–96*
London: Longman, Green, Longmans, Roberts, and Green, 1858

Deck thyself, my soul, with gladness,
Leave the gloomy haunts of sadness;
Come into the daylight's splendor,
There with joy thy praises render
Unto Christ whose grace unbounded
Hath this wondrous banquet founded.
Higher o'er all the heav'ns He reigneth,
Yet to dwell with thee He deigneth.

Hasten as a bride to meet Him
And with loving reverence greet Him;
For with words of life immortal
Now He knocketh at thy portal.
Haste to ope the gates before Him,
Saying, while thou dost adore Him,
Suffer, Lord, that I receive Thee,
And I nevermore will leave Thee.

He who craves a precious treasure
Neither cost nor pain will measure;
But the priceless gifts of heaven
God to us hath freely given.
Though the wealth of earth were offered,
Naught would buy the gifts here offered:
Christ's true body, for thee riven,
And His blood, for thee once given.

Ah, how hungers all my spirit
For the love I do not merit!

Oft have I, with sighs fast thronging,
Thought upon this food with longing,
In the battle well nigh worsted,
For this cup of life have thirsted,
For the Friend who here invites us
And to God Himself unites us.

In my heart I find ascending
Holy awe, with rapture blending,
As this mystery I ponder,
Filling all my soul with wonder,
Bearing witness at this hour
Of the greatness of God's power;
Far beyond all human telling
Is the power within Him dwelling.

Human reason, though it ponder,
Cannot fathom this great wonder
That Christ's body e'er remaineth
Though it countless souls sustaineth
And that He His blood is giving
With the wine we are receiving.
These great mysteries unsounded
Are by God alone expounded.

Sun, Who all my life dost brighten,
Light, Who dost my soul enlighten;
Joy the best that any knoweth;
Fount, whence all my being floweth;
At Thy feet I cry, my Maker,
Let me be a fit partaker
Of this blessèd food from heaven,
For our good, Thy glory, given.

Lord, by love and mercy driven
Thou hast left Thy throne in heaven
On the cross for me to languish
And to die in bitter anguish,
To forego all joy and gladness

And to shed Thy blood in sadness.
By this blood redeemed and living,
Lord, I praise Thee with thanksgiving.

Jesus, Bread of Life, I pray Thee,
Let me gladly here obey Thee.
By Thy love I am invited,
Be Thy love with love requited;
From this supper let me measure,
Lord, how vast and deep love's treasure.
Through the gifts Thou here dost give me
As Thy guest in heaven receive me.

JOHANN FRANCK
Herr, ich habe mißgehandelt
(Lord, to Thee I make confession)

1653 CRÜGER PRAXIS PIETATIS MELICA

Translation by Catherine Winkworth
The Chorale Book for England, #44
London: Longman, Green, Longmans, Roberts, and Green, 1863

Lord, to Thee I make confession,
I have sinn'd and gone astray,
I have multiplied transgression,
Chosen for myself my way;
Forced at last to see my errors,
Lord, I tremble at Thy terrors.

But from Thee how can I hide me,
Thou, O God, art everywhere;
Refuge from Thee is denied me,
Or by land or sea or air;
Nor death's darkness can enfold me
So that Thou shouldst not behold me.

Yet though conscience' voice appall me,
Father, I will seek Thy face;

Though Thy child I dare not call me,
Yet accept me to Thy grace;
Do not for my sins forsake me,
Let not yet Thy wrath o'ertake me.

For Thy Son hath suffer'd for me,
And the blood He shed for sin,
That can heal me and restore me,
Quench this burning fire within;
'Tis alone His cross can vanquish
These dark fears and soothe this anguish.

Then on Him I cast my burden,
Sink it in the depths below!
Let me feel Thy inner pardon,
Wash me, make me white as snow.
Let Thy Spirit leave me never,
Make me only Thine for ever!

CHRISTIAN SCRIVER
Der lieben Sonne Licht und Pracht
(The lovely sun hath ushered west)

1684 Vollständigen Gesangbuch
(See use by Bach BMV 446)

The lovely sun hath ushered west
The day in pomp and beauty,
The world is settled to its rest;
Now, soul, attend thy duty,
To heaven's gate draw near,
And with thy hymn appear
Thine eyes, and heart, and senses let
On Jesus be devoutly set.

Ye brilliant stars in heaven shine
And cast your beams so brightly,
Ye fill the night with candles fine
That none can number rightly;
Yet in my heart more clear
Shines heaven's Candle dear:
My Jesus, glory of my soul,
My prize, protector, light, and goal.

Now all in slumber's net is caught,
Both man and beast are sleeping;
Yet One there is who sleepeth not,
Who still His watch is keeping,
No rest will Jesus take,
His eye for thee doth wake
So now, my heart, thy Keeper own,
Let not thy Jesus watch alone.

O Jesus, do not scorn my song,
Though poorly I may sing it;
My heart for peace must ever long,
Until to Thee I bring it.
I'll bring it as I may,
Oh, gracious be, I pray,
'Tis meant with love most genuine
O Jesus, dearest friend of mine.

With Thee to sleep I now will go,
My soul to Thee commended,
Thou shalt, my Keeper, watch for woe
And keep me well attended.
No trouble will I fear,
Not even death so drear;
For who to sleep with Jesus lies
Again in gladness will arise.

Ye wraiths of hell, disperse, begone,
Here's naught for your molesting;
This house is home to Jesus' throne,

So leave it safely resting;
The angels' Keeper strong
Protects it from all wrong;
And heaven's host is my defense,
So fly, ye Devils all, from hence!

Now in Thine arms I will be laid
And sleep in Thine affection;
Thy watchfulness shall be my bed,
Thy mercy, my protection,
My pillow be Thy breast,
My dream, that bliss of rest
That from Thy cloven side outflows
Which in my heart Thy Spirit blows.

At night when all my vessels thrill,
I'll hold Thee till I'm tiring;
And when my heart is stirring still
Let this be my desiring,
That I might fill the sky
With this resounding cry:
"Oh! Jesus, Jesus, Thou art mine,
And I am now and ever Thine."

Faint body, take thy sweet repose
May peace and stillness fill it;
Ye drooping lids, now softly close,
For so thy God doth will it.
And with these words resign:
"Lord Jesus, I am Thine!"
So is thine ending made aright!
Oh, Jesus! Jesus, now, good night!

Bibliography

Aston, Trevor, ed. *Crisis in Europe 1560–1660*. Garden City, NY: Doubleday Anchor Books, 1967.

Axmacher, Elke. *Johann Arndt und Paul Gerhardt*. Tübingen: Francke Verlag, 2001.

Bath, Michael. *Speaking Pictures: English Emblem Books and Renaissance Culture*. London: Longman, 1994.

Bauer, Jörg. "Johann Gerhard." In *Orthodoxie und Pietismus*. Gestalten der Kirchengeschichte 7, edited by Martin Greschat, 99–119. Stuttgart: Kohlhammer, 1982.

———. *Luther und seine klassichen Erben*. Tübingen: J.C.B. Mohr/Paul Siebeck, 1993.

Beck, Hermann. *Die religiöse Volksliteratur der evangelischen Kirche Deutschlands*. Gotha: Friedrich Andreas Perthes, 1891.

Blankenburg, Walter. "Der Einfluß des Kirchenliedes des 17. Jahrhunderts auf die Geschichte des evangelischen Gesangbuches und der Kirchenmusik." In *Das protestantische Kirchenlied im 16. Und 17. Jahrhundert*, Wolfenbüttler Forschungen 31, edited by Alfred Durr and Walter Killy, 73–85. Wiesbaden: Harrassowitz, 1986.

Brecht, Martin. "Ein 'Gastmahl' an Predigten. Christian Scrivers Seelenschatz (1675–1692)." *Pietismus und Neuzeit* 28 (2002): 72–117.

———, ed. *Geschichte des Pietismus*. Vol. 1: *Der Pietismus vom siebzehnten bis zum frühen achtzehnten Jahrhundert*. Göttingen: Vandenhoeck and Ruprecht, 1993.

Bunners, Christian. *Paul Gerhardt: Weg-Werk-Wirkung*. 4th ed. Tübingen: Vandenhoeck and Ruprecht, 2006.

Daly, Peter. *Literature in the Light of the Emblem*. 2nd ed. Toronto: University of Toronto Press, 1998.

Dodson, Geran. "Johann Heermann: Silesian Hymn Writer." *The Hymn* 20, no. 3 (1969): 58–60.

Fechner, Jörg-Ulrich. "Paul Gerhardt." In *Orthodoxie und Pietismus.* Gestalten der Kirchengeschichte 7, edited by Martin Greschat. Stuttgart: Verlag W. Kohlhammer, 1982.

Fischer, Albert Friedrich Wilhelm, ed. *Kirchenlieder-Lexikon.* Gotha: Friedrich Andreas Perthes, 1878.

Fischer, Albert, and Wilhelm Tümpel, eds. *Das evangelische Kirchenlied des 17. Jahrhunderts*, 5. Gütersloh: Bertelsmann, 1911.

Foss, Lisbet. *Paul Gerhardt: Eine hymnologisch-komparative Studie.* Copenhagen: University of Copenhagen, 1995.

Gritsch, Eric. *A History of Lutheranism.* Minneapolis: Fortress Press, 2002.

Große, Constantin. *Die alten Tröster. Ein Wegweiser in die Erbauungslitteratur der evangelische-lutherische Kirche des 16. bis 18. Jahrhunderts.* Hermannsburg: In Kommission bei der Missionshandlung, 1900.

Headley, John, Hans Hillerbrand, and Anthony Papalas, eds. *Confessionalization in Europe, 1555–1700: Essays in Honor and Memory of Bodo Nischan.* Aldershot, UK: Ashgate, 2004.

Holl, Karl. "Die Bedeutung der großen Kriege für das religiöse Leben innerhalb des deutschen Protestantismus." In Karl Holl, *Gesammelte Aufsätze zur Kirchengeschichte*, Vol. 3: *Der Westen*, 302–84. Tübingen: J.C.B. Mohr/Paul Siebeck, 1928.

Irwin, Joyce. "Celestial Harmony in Baroque Lutheran Writings." *Lutheran Quarterly* 3 (1989): 281–97.

Johansen, John. "Paul Gerhardt (1607–1676): An Assessment on the 300th Anniversary of His Death." *Lutheran Quarterly* 28 (1976): 21–29.

Julian, John. *A Dictionary of Hymnology.* New York: Charles Scribner's Sons, 1892.

Kantzenbach, Friedrich Wilhelm. *Orthodoxie und Pietismus.* Evangelische Enzyklopädie, edited by H. Thielicke, H. Thimme. Vol. 11/12. Gütersloh: Mohn, 1966.

Kaufmann, Thomas. *Dreißigjähriger Krieg und Westfälischer Friede: Kirchengeschichtliche Studien zur lutherischen Konfessionskultur.* Tübingen: J.C.B. Mohr/Paul Siebeck, 1998.

Kemper, Hans-Georg. "Das lutherische Kirchenlied in der Krisen-Zeit des frühen 17. Jahrhunderts." In *Das protestantische Kirchenlied im 16. und 17. Jahrhundert*, Wolfenbüttler Forschungen 31, edited by Alfred Durr and Walter Killy, 87–108. Wiesbaden: Harrassowitz, 1986.

Klueting, Harm. *Johann Jakob Fabricius (1618/20–1673): Ein Beitrag zu Konfessionaliserung und Sozialdiziplinierung im Luthertum des 17. Jahrhunderts*. Münster: Lit Verlag, 2003.

Koch, Eduard Emil, ed. *Geschichte des Kirchenlieds und Kirchengesangs der christlichen, insbesondere der deutschen evangelische Kirche*. 3rd ed. 9 vols. Stuttgart: C. Belser, 1866–77.

Koch, Ernst. *Das konfessionelle Zeitalter—Katholizismus, Luthertum, Calvinismus (1563–1675)*. Leipzig: Evangelische Verlagsanstalt, 2000.

———. "Therapeutische Theologie. Die Meditationes sacrae von Johann Gerhard (1606)." *Pietismus und Neuzeit* 13 (1987): 25–46.

Kolb, Robert, ed. *Lutheran Ecclesiastical Culture 1550–1675*. Leiden: E. J. Brill, 2008.

Lehmann, Hartmut. "Die Krisen des 17. Jahrhundert als Problem der Forschung." In *Transformationen der Religion in der Neuzeit: Beispiele aus der Geschichte des Protestantismus*, 11–20. Göttingen: Vandenhoeck and Ruprecht, 2007.

———. "The Cultural Importance of the Pious Middle Classes in Seventeenth-Century Protestant Theology." In *Religion and Society in Early Modern Europe 1500–1800*, edited by Kaspar von Greyerz, 33–41. London: George Allen and Unwin, 1984.

———. "Zur Bedeutung von Religion und Religiosität im Barockzeitalter." In *Religion und Religiosität in der Neuzeit*, edited by Manfred Jakubowski-Tiessen and Otto Ulbricht, 19–27. Göttingen: Vandenhoeck and Ruprecht, 1996.

———, and Anne-Charlotte Trepp, eds. *Im Zeiten der Krise: Religiosität im Europa des 17. Jarhunderts*. Göttingen: Vandenhoeck and Ruprecht, 1999.

Leube, Hans. *Die Reformideen in der deutschen lutherischen Kirche zur Zeit der Orthodoxie*. Leipzig: Dörffling and Franke, 1924.

———. "Die Theologen und das Kirchenvolk im Zeitalter der lutherischen Orthodoxie." In *Orthodoxie und Pietismus:*

Gesammelte Studien, edited by Dietrich Blaufuss, 9–35. Bielefeld: Luther Verlag, 1975.

Lohr, Lawrence. "'If Thou but Suffer God to Guide Thee': The Journey of a Lutheran Hymn." *The Hymn* 49, no. 3 (July 1998): 28–30.

Lund, Eric. "The Problem of Religious Complacency in Seventeenth-Century Lutheran Spirituality." In *Modern Christian Spirituality*, edited by Bradley Hanson, 139–59. Atlanta: Scholars Press, 1990.

———. "The Second Age of the Reformation: Lutheran and Reformed Spirituality 1550–1700." In *Christian Spirituality: Post-Reformation and Modern*, edited by Louis Dupré and Don E. Saliers, 213–23. New York: Crossroad, 1989.

———, ed. *Documents from the History of Lutheranism, 1517–1750*. Minneapolis: Fortress Press, 2002.

Lütkemann, Heinrich. *Joachim Lütkemann: Sein Leben und Sein Wirken*. Braunschweig: H. Wollermann, 1902.

Maravall, José Antonio. *Culture of the Baroque: Analysis of a Historical Structure*. Translated by Terry Cochran. Minneapolis: University of Minnesota, 1987.

Merkel, Gottfried. "Deutsche Erbauungsliteratur." *Jahrbuch für Internationale Germanistik* 3, no. 1 (1971): 30–41.

Müller, Holger. *Seelsorge und Tröstung: Christian Scriver (1629–1693) Erbauungsschriftsteller und Seelsorger*. Waltrop: Hartmut Spenner Verlag, 2005.

Oelmann, Doreen. *Kirchenlieder als Spiegel der Geschichte*. Norderstedt: GRIN Verlag, 2004.

Parker, Geoffrey. *Europe in Crisis, 1598–1648*. 2nd ed. Oxford: Blackwells Publishers, 2001.

———. *The Thirty Years' War*. Rev. ed. New York: Military Heritage Press, 1987.

———, and Lesley Smith, eds. *The General Crisis of the Seventeenth Century*. 2nd ed. London: Routledge, 1997.

Preus, Robert. *The Theology of Post-Reformation Lutheranism*. Vol. 1. St. Louis: Concordia Publishing House, 1970.

Rublack, Hans-Christoph, ed. *Die lutherische Konfessionalisierung in Deutschland*. Gütersloh: Gerd Mohn, 1988.

Sattler, Gary. "The All-Sufficient Jesus in Heinrich Müller's Geistliche Erquickstunden (Moments of Spiritual Refreshment)." In *Perspectives on Christology: Essays in Honor of Paul K. Jewett*, edited by Marguerite Shuster and Richard Muller, 127–39. Grand Rapids, MI: Zondervan Publishing House, 1991.

———. *Nobler than the Angels, Lower than a Worm: The Pietist View of the Individual in the Writings of Heinrich Müller and August Hermann Francke*. Lanham, MD: University Press of America, 1989.

Scharlemann, Robert. *Thomas Aquinas and John Gerhard*. New Haven, CT: Yale University Press, 1964.

Schmidt, Martin. "Christian Scrivers 'Seelenschatz': Ein Beispiel vorpietistischer Predigtweise." In Martin Schmidt, *Wiedergeburt und neuer Mensch*, 112–28. Witten-Ruhr: Luther Verlag, 1969.

Simonsson, Axel. "Christian Scriver och hans uppbyggliga skrifters betydelse, huvudsakligen med hänsyn till Sverige." *Kyrkohistorisk Årsskrift* (1971): 142–65.

———. "Christian Scrivers naturskildring och hans relationer till Joseph Hall." *Svensk teologisk kvartalskrift* 48, no. 2 (1972): 69–83.

Sommer, Wolfgang. "Johann Arndt und Joachim Lütkemann—zwei Klassiker der lutherischen Erbauungsliteratur in Niedersachsen." *Jahrbuch der Gesellschaft für Niedersächsische Kirchengeschichte* 84 (1986): 123–44.

———. *Politik, Theologie und Frömmigkeit im Luthertum der frühen Neuzeit*. Göttingen: Vandenhoeck and Ruprecht, 1999.

Steiger, Johann Anselm. "Der Kirchenvater der lutherischen Orthodoxie—Johann Gerhard (1582–1637) und ein Forschungssprojekt." *Kerygma und Dogma* 43 (1997): 58–76.

———. *Johann Gerhard (1582–1637): Studien zu Theologie und Frömmigkeit des Kirchenvaters der lutherischen Orthodoxie*. Doctrina et Pietas 1. Stuttgart: Frommann-Holzboog, 1997.

———. "Pastoral Care according to Johann Gerhard." *Lutheran Quarterly* 10, no. 3 (1996): 319–39.

———. "Seelsorge, Dogmatik und Mystik bei Johann Gerhard: Ein Beitrag zu Theologie und Frommigkeit der lutherischen Orthodoxie." *Zeitschrift fur Kirchengeschichte* 106 (1995): 329–44.

Sträter, Udo. *Meditation und Kirchenreform in der lutherischen Kirche des 17. Jahrhunderts*. Tübingen: J.C.B. Mohr/Paul Siebeck, 1995.

———, ed. *Pietas in der Lutherischen Orthodoxie*. Wittenberg: Edition Hans Lufft, 1998.

Strom, Jonathan. *Orthodoxy and Reform: The Clergy in Seventeenth Century Rostock*. Tübingen: J.C.B. Mohr/Paul Siebeck, 1999.

Tholuck, August. *Lebenszeugen der lutherischen Kirche aus allen Ständen vor and während der Zeit des dreissigjährigen Krieges*. Berlin: Verlag von Wiegandt und Grieben, 1859.

Vaahtoranta, Martti, "Unio und Rechtfertigung bei Johann Gerhard." In *Uniom Gott und Mensch in der nachreformatorischen Theologie*, edited by Matti Repo and Rainar Vinke, 200–248. Helsinki: Luther-Agricola Gesellschaft, 1996.

van Andel, Cornelis Pieter. "Paul Gerhardt, ein Mystiker zur Zeit des Barocks." In *Traditio, Krisis, Renovatio aus theologischer Sicht: Festschrift Winfried Zeller am 65 Geburtstag*, edited by Bernd Jaspert and Rudolf Mohr, 172–83. Marburg: Elwert, 1976.

Veit, Patrice. "Das Gesangbuch als Quelle lutherischer Frömmigkeit." *Archiv für Reformationsgeschichte* 79 (1988): 206–29.

Wackernagel, Philipp. *Das deutsche Kirchenlied von der ältesten Zeit bis zu Anfang des XVII. Jahrhunderts*. Leipzig: B. G. Teubner, 1874.

Wallmann, Johannes. *Der Theologiebegriff bei Johann Gerhard und Georg Calixt*. Tübingen: Vandenhoeck and Ruprecht, 1961.

———. "Lutherische Orthodoxie." In *Religion in Geschichte und Gegenwart*. 4th ed. Vol. 6, 696–702. Tübingen: J.C.B. Mohr/Paul Siebeck, 2003.

Zeller, Winfried. *Der Protestantismus des 17. Jahrhunderts*. Bremen: Carl Schünemann, 1962.

Index

Other Volumes in This Series

Abraham Isaac Kook • THE LIGHTS OF PENITENCE, LIGHTS OF HOLINESS, THE MORAL PRINCIPLES, ESSAYS, LETTERS, AND POEMS
Abraham Miguel Cardozo • SELECTED WRITINGS
Abū al-Ḥasan al-Shushtarī • SONGS OF LOVE AND DEVOTION
Albert and Thomas • SELECTED WRITINGS
Alphonsus de Liguori • SELECTED WRITINGS
Anchoritic Spirituality •ANCRENE WISSE AND ASSOCIATED WORKS
Angela of Foligno • COMPLETE WORKS
Angelic Spirituality • MEDIEVAL PERSPECTIVES ON THE WAYS OF ANGELS
Angelus Silesius • THE CHERUBINIC WANDERER
Anglo-Saxon Spirituality • SELECTED WRITINGS
Apocalyptic Spirituality • TREATISES AND LETTERS OF LACTANTIUS, ADSO OF MONTIER-EN-DER, JOACHIM OF FIORE, THE FRANCISCAN SPIRITUALS, SAVONAROLA
Athanasius • THE LIFE OF ANTONY, AND THE LETTER TO MARCELLINUS
Augustine of Hippo • SELECTED WRITINGS
Bernard of Clairvaux • SELECTED WORKS
Bérulle and the French School • SELECTED WRITINGS
Birgitta of Sweden • LIFE AND SELECTED REVELATIONS
Bonaventure • THE SOUL'S JOURNEY INTO GOD, THE TREE OF LIFE, THE LIFE OF ST. FRANCIS
Cambridge Platonist Spirituality •
Carthusian Spirituality • THE WRITINGS OF HUGH OF BALMA AND GUIGO DE PONTE
Catherine of Genoa • PURGATION AND PURGATORY, THE SPIRITUAL DIALOGUE
Catherine of Siena • THE DIALOGUE
Celtic Spirituality •
Classic Midrash, The • TANNAITIC COMMENTARIES ON THE BIBLE
Cloud of Unknowing, The •
Devotio Moderna • BASIC WRITINGS
Dominican Penitent Women •
Early Anabaptist Spirituality • SELECTED WRITINGS
Early Dominicans • SELECTED WRITINGS
Early Islamic Mysticism • SUFI, QUR'AN, MI'RAJ, POETIC AND THEOLOGICAL WRITINGS
Early Kabbalah, The •
Early Protestant Spirituality •
Elijah Benamozegh • ISRAEL AND HUMANITY
Elisabeth Leseur • SELECTED WRITINGS

Other Volumes in This Series

Elisabeth of Schönau • THE COMPLETE WORKS
Emanuel Swedenborg • THE UNIVERSAL HUMAN AND SOUL-BODY INTERACTION
Ephrem the Syrian • HYMNS
Fakhruddin 'Iraqi • DIVINE FLASHES
Farid ad-Din 'Attār's Memorial of God's Friends • LIVES AND SAYINGS OF SUFIS
Fénelon • SELECTED WRITINGS
Francis and Clare • THE COMPLETE WORKS
Francis de Sales, Jane de Chantal • LETTERS OF SPIRITUAL DIRECTION
Francisco de Osuna • THE THIRD SPIRITUAL ALPHABET
George Herbert • THE COUNTRY PARSON, THE TEMPLE
Gertrude of Helfta • THE HERALD OF DIVINE LOVE
Gregory of Nyssa • THE LIFE OF MOSES
Gregory Palamas • THE TRIADS
Hadewijch • THE COMPLETE WORKS
Henry Suso • THE EXEMPLAR, WITH TWO GERMAN SERMONS
Hildegard of Bingen • SCIVIAS
Ibn 'Abbād of Ronda • LETTERS ON THE ṢŪFĪ PATH
Ibn Al'-Arabī • THE BEZELS OF WISDOM
Ibn 'Ata' Illah • THE BOOK OF WISDOM AND KWAJA ABDULLAH ANSARI: INTIMATE CONVERSATIONS
Ignatius of Loyola • SPIRITUAL EXERCISES AND SELECTED WORKS
Isaiah Horowitz • THE GENERATIONS OF ADAM
Jacob Boehme • THE WAY TO CHRIST
Jacopone da Todi • THE LAUDS
Jean Gerson • EARLY WORKS
Jeremy Taylor • SELECTED WORKS
Jewish Mystical Autobiographies • BOOK OF VISIONS AND BOOK OF SECRETS
Johann Arndt • TRUE CHRISTIANITY
Johannes Tauler • SERMONS
John Baptist de La Salle • THE SPIRITUALITY OF CHRISTIAN EDUCATION
John Calvin • WRITINGS ON PASTORAL PIETY
John Cassian • CONFERENCES
John and Charles Wesley • SELECTED WRITINGS AND HYMNS
John Climacus • THE LADDER OF DIVINE ASCENT
John Comenius • THE LABYRINTH OF THE WORLD AND THE PARADISE OF THE HEART
John of Avila • AUDI, FILIA—LISTEN, O DAUGHTER
John of the Cross • SELECTED WRITINGS

Other Volumes in This Series

John Donne • SELECTIONS FROM DIVINE POEMS, SERMONS, DEVOTIONS AND PRAYERS
John Henry Newman • SELECTED SERMONS
John Ruusbroec • THE SPIRITUAL ESPOUSALS AND OTHER WORKS
Julian of Norwich • SHOWINGS
Knowledge of God in Classical Sufism • FOUNDATIONS OF ISLAMIC MYSTICAL THEOLOGY
Late Medieval Mysticism of the Low Countries •
Luis de León • THE NAMES OF CHRIST
Luther's Spirituality •
Margaret Ebner • MAJOR WORKS
Marguerite Porete • THE MIRROR OF SIMPLE SOULS
Maria Maddalena de' Pazzi • SELECTED REVELATIONS
Martin Luther • THEOLOGIA GERMANICA
Maximus Confessor • SELECTED WRITINGS
Mechthild of Magdeburg • THE FLOWING LIGHT OF THE GODHEAD
Meister Eckhart • THE ESSENTIAL SERMONS, COMMENTARIES, TREATISES AND DEFENSE
Meister Eckhart • TEACHER AND PREACHER
Menahem Nahum of Chernobyl • UPRIGHT PRACTICES, THE LIGHT OF THE EYES
Miguel de Molinos • THE SPIRITUAL GUIDE
Nahman of Bratslav • THE TALES
Native Mesoamerican Spirituality • ANCIENT MYTHS, DISCOURSES, STORIES, DOCTRINES, HYMNS, POEMS FROM THE AZTEC, YUCATEC, QUICHE-MAYA AND OTHER SACRED TRADITIONS
Native North American Spirituality of the Eastern Woodlands • SACRED MYTHS, DREAMS, VISIONS, SPEECHES, HEALING FORMULAS, RITUALS AND CEREMONIALS
Nicholas of Cusa • SELECTED SPIRITUAL WRITINGS
Nicodemos of the Holy Mountain • A HANDBOOK OF SPIRITUAL COUNSEL
Nil Sorsky • THE COMPLETE WRITINGS
Nizam ad-din Awliya • MORALS FOR THE HEART
Norbert and Early Norbertine Spirituality •
Origen • AN EXHORTATION TO MARTYRDOM, PRAYER AND SELECTED WORKS
Philo of Alexandria • THE CONTEMPLATIVE LIFE, THE GIANTS, AND SELECTIONS
Pietists • SELECTED WRITINGS
Pilgrim's Tale, The •

Other Volumes in This Series